FINDING TIME

FINDING TIME

The Economics of Work-Life Conflict

HEATHER BOUSHEY

Harvard University Press

Cambridge, Massachusetts
London, England
2016

First printing

Library of Congress Cataloging-in-Publication Data

Names: Boushey, Heather, 1970- author.
Title: Finding time : the economics of work-life conflict / Heather Boushey.
Description: Cambridge, Massachusetts : Harvard University Press, 2016. |
    Includes bibliographical references and index.
Identifiers: LCCN 2015043606 | ISBN 9780674660168 (alk. paper)
Subjects: LCSH: Work-life balance—United States. | Work and family—United States. |
    Flexible work arrangements—United States. | Quality of life—United States. |
    United States—Social policy—21st century.
Classification: LCC HD4904.25 .B68 2016 | DDC 650.1/1—dc23 LC record available at
    http://lccn.loc.gov/2015043606

To all those too busy to read this book, in the hope that it reaches those with the power to find and return our lost time.

CONTENTS

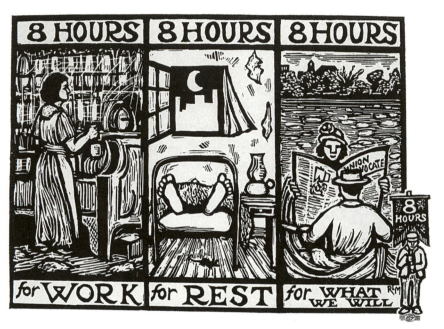

Slogan from the late-1800s campaign for a forty-hour workweek. Courtesy of Ricardo Levins Morales.

PREFACE

I have a poster of a woodcut triptych on my office wall (at left). The three panels, labeled "8 hours for work," "8 hours for rest," and "8 hours for what we will," make up the slogan from a late-1800s campaign for a forty-hour workweek. I like it because the engraving under "what we will" is a couple seemingly enjoying a leisurely afternoon on a rowboat.

As I wrote this book, I found myself mulling over the ideas conveyed in this triptych. A century ago, workers' movements knew what they wanted: an eight-hour day. Today, however, the boundary between time for work and time for "what we will" is less clear. In 2016, I can edit a memo on my laptop over the weekend or check email on my phone at a dinner party. If I had any woodcutting talent, how would I carve a vision for today's workers and families? Sadly, my guess is that the happy couple on the little boat would both be checking their phones with furrowed brows.

The triptych also confuses me. I don't see where all the cooking, cleaning, and care work fit into the picture. If I work eight hours, then I sleep eight hours, I'll need to spend a good chunk of the eight hours for "what we will" doing laundry, grocery shopping, and taking care of my family. I won't have eight hours to lounge around on a little boat. Where, exactly, did the woodcutter think household chores and care work fit into the picture? Maybe he was planning a tetraptych but quit at three panels when he realized there were no hours left in the day. Or maybe he was anticipating the "house elves" from J. K. Rowling's Harry Potter books—magical creatures that do all the housework for wizarding families. Or maybe he didn't actually think about it at all. Maybe for him, someone else was at home taking care of all those chores.

The idea of having a house elf is certainly a nice fantasy. While American families once typically had a real-live person who stayed at home as a full-time caregiver to tend to the family's daily needs, this is no longer the case for most families. The stress this causes is often discussed in women's magazines and in the lifestyle section of the newspaper. This fundamental issue of time, which was so central to the workers' rights movement of the late 1800s, is now often framed as just a woman's problem.

I disagree. This book is about time and how our differences blind us to a common experience of losing time. I wrote it because I think accounting for the missing panel in the woodcutter's triptych is a profoundly important economic issue. My conclusion from looking at the evidence is that this issue belongs at the top of the news and in the business section. The hidden work of what I call in the pages that follow America's "Silent Partner"—the traditional American Wife—and how it has disappeared for families up and down the income ladder is part and parcel of the economic anxieties facing families and affecting the well-being of the economy overall.

I'm certainly not the first person to discover that families have lost time. Many scholars before me have written of the changes inside families and what they mean. Judith Warner showed us the *Perfect Madness* of a world where work and life always seem to be in conflict; Arlie Russell Hochschild and Anne Machung documented how *The Second Shift* that women and, increasingly, men put in at home after a long day at the office or factory leaves us what Brigid Schulte calls in her new book *Overwhelmed*. Through a large body of scholarship, we learn from experts like Nancy Folbre about the "caring economy" and from Stephanie Coontz about how our vision of the traditional family was always part myth. Jerry Jacobs and Kathleen Gerson documented how what they call the *Time Divide* between work and life is a big piece of what Anne-Marie Slaughter and Eileen Appelbaum and Ruth Milkman call the *Unfinished Business* for policymakers and business leaders alike.[1]

My contribution to this scholarship is to show that family's loss of time to care is as much an economic issue as a challenge for individual households. As such, fixing the problem requires macrolevel thinking—indeed, nothing less than a rethinking of the social contract between governments, firms, and families.

I didn't just stumble into this research project. For the past fifteen years, I've worked in Washington, DC, alongside a dedicated group of thinkers and doers. I've talked to members of Congress, governors and mayors, policy and economics experts, as well as union leaders and workers' advocates. And I've engaged with business leaders who understand the importance of work-life reforms to our economy's performance.

I learned that we need practical solutions, ones that are good for the economy overall. To this end, the solutions in this book aren't just pie-in-the-sky ideas. Every single one of them has already been put into place somewhere in the United States. In the past decade, over two dozen states and localities have passed laws giving workers the right to earn paid sick days; four states have passed laws for paid parental leave; two localities have passed laws that give workers the right to ask their employer for a schedule that works for them and their family; many communities have put in place new programs to address the need for care for children and the elderly; and two states have made it illegal to discriminate against those with care responsibilities. The advantage to pulling together a list of ideas with a solid track record—as I do in the book—is that policymakers can see the likely effects of a reform.

These successes show that Americans are ready—and eager—for change. When I came to Washington, DC, in 2000, I would have had to write a book that looked to other countries for solutions. That is no longer true today, and this is the best evidence that the momentum for change is building.

I have no talent for wood carving. But I hope this book can provide a roadmap for how today's families can regain lost time.

FINDING
TIME

Introduction

It's easy to get depressed listening to the policy debates in Washington. When it comes to issues that affect workers and their families, it's hard to see anything but two partisan camps pointing accusatory fingers at each other. One side portrays the other as bleeding hearts who want taxpayers to support families who can't or won't support themselves—no matter the cost. What these families really need, opponents say, is tough love. The other side replies that "tough love" is just a euphemism for a refusal to spend money—any money—on families facing the challenges of the twenty-first century and for the mistaken belief that dependency is perpetual and will lead to economic ruin. To pass any new laws in Washington we need the support of both sides, so the result is that social needs are addressed (if at all) through cheap solutions that reduce some social inequities but never fully solve the problem. Without consensus on the problem or the solution, there is no viable political path forward—and families suffer the consequences of this inaction.

With this book, I hope to show that there is another way. A set of small changes in a few areas of our social policy can not only address a major source of human suffering but also unleash economic potential. While the political debate may be stuck at opposing poles, the evidence gathered by economists and other social scientists increasingly points in a new direction. Modest measures may not change the world overnight, but they can still make a huge difference, especially if they work in tandem.

The good news is that my proposals will cost taxpayers—and businesses—very little. But they will require a new way of thinking about what business, government, and households owe one another when it comes to work-family policies. These include paid sick days, paid time off to care for a family member, work schedules that fit today's lifestyles, and high-quality child care and elder care. Everyone at some point faces these work-family problems—whether you're a bleeding heart or a proponent of tough love—but we have yet to agree on the right course of action. My aim is to show that when the main roads are blocked, there's more you can do than sit on your horn to complain.

Before going any further, let me get something out of the way. I *hate* the term "work-family policy." To many people it immediately brings to mind working mothers and child care, in contrast to what are considered more masculine areas of policy (I call these so-called masculine policy concerns the Three M's: military, macroeconomics, and manufacturing). Compared with traditional male issues, work-family policy doesn't sound serious. It sounds like something that should take a backseat to real economic matters. As a result, politicians tend to trot out their positions on work-family issues when courting female voters ahead of elections, only to forget them after the victory lap in favor of the Three M's.

The kinds of policy changes I am talking about will absolutely benefit women and children—no question about it—but these reforms are about so much more. They are crucial to our economy's well-being. Researchers studying the kinds of policies that families and households need to make ends meet, and in turn what businesses need from their employees, have some surprising findings to share. Across a range of different social science traditions, methods, and topics, they find that addressing sources of anxiety *inside* the home has a profound impact on what happens *outside* the home, including in the larger economy, and can affect the current and future competitiveness of American firms and workers. That's why I prefer the term *work-life* policies. This phrase reminds us of the intimate connection between the hours we clock for a job and the off-the-job hours that support strong families and a strong economy.

Handouts versus Help-Outs

I grew up in Mukilteo, Washington, in pretty nice circumstances from a child's point of view. My father worked as a crane operator at the Everett Boeing plant, the largest building in the world, which in those days (the 1970s and 1980s) built 747s and now builds 787 Dreamliners. When I was young, my dad, Mike, worked the 3–11 PM shift. He always took overtime when he could get it. Because he was a member of the International Association of Machinists Local 751, his wages and benefits were good. Even so, his paycheck took a hit whenever orders were down, and there were layoffs at times.

About the time I started walking, my mom, Bobbi, took a job as a bank teller and was soon promoted to account manager. Her hours were 9 to 5, but with her commute in the dreadful Seattle-area traffic, they were more like 8 to 6. That meant that my sister, Michelle, and I, like many of the other children in our suburban neighborhood and millions of young people across America, were latchkey kids. We played, did homework and chores, and got dinner ready in time for Mom to get home. We also spent way too much time watching reruns of *The Brady Bunch* and *Leave It to Beaver*, fun shows with families where the parents didn't seem to worry about jobs and money as much as ours did—and only Dad had a paying job.

When I was in high school, I exploited the lack of parental supervision, driving into Seattle whenever I could to see bands, smoke cigarettes, and generally get into as much teenage trouble as my introverted nature would allow. But it was not all a teenage wasteland. I was a precocious kid (some might say annoyingly nerdy) who, when I finished taking all the classes my high school had to offer, enrolled in college courses at the University of Washington. There I took my first political economy course, taught by a bearded graduate student, a compelling teacher enthralled with his course topic. I learned all about the questionable role of U.S. corporations and governments in poor parts of the world. Late at night over a reheated dinner, I would regale my mother with stories about U.S. business leaders' support for the 1970s Chilean dictator Augusto Pinochet and how the United States was behind the coup that installed the Shah of Iran. "That's nice, dear," my exhausted mother would say.

Those classes shaped my early interests. When I went to college, I focused my studies on the economics of developing countries—a left-leaning academic discipline that prompted my Reagan Democrat father to needle me with accusations of coddling Fidel Castro. (This has always amused friends of mine who know how culturally illiterate I am on such matters: I can barely find Cuba on a map and need a Spanish pronunciation guide even at Tex Mex restaurants!) Largely because of a lack of linguistic talents, alongside a desire to look at the economy closer to home, I had decided by senior year to focus on economic and social policy issues in the United States.

One afternoon several years later, when I was a graduate student in economics home for the holidays, I was chatting with my mom in the kitchen when suddenly the stresses of my parents' lives were laid bare. I was telling Mom about a paper I was writing on how we could help women move off welfare by giving them access to subsidized child care. My mother got angry, which was quite unusual for her. She wanted to know why "handouts" should go to folks who "weren't working for a living." She asked me, "Why isn't anyone focusing on making child care affordable for families like *ours*?" Hadn't I noticed that she worked a full-time job when I was a child? Had I ever wondered why Dad took overtime whenever he could get it? Hadn't I noticed that she and Dad were hardly ever relaxed and always stressed about money?

She then shared her concerns about the quality of care at the day-care centers she could afford at the time and her anxieties about leaving us home alone as we got older. In short, she would have benefited from a help-out on child care but was repelled by the notion of a handout that benefited only the poor.

I was dumbstruck. I had been blind to how the economy and policymakers had failed families like mine. I had paid no heed to what had happened to America's middle-class families. My mother was frustrated by a way of life that hadn't met her expectations. She and my dad worked hard but were economically squeezed and never felt they had enough time for family life. Sometime between my mom's childhood and mine, the rules for succeeding in America had changed. She had the right questions. Why wasn't I working to answer them?

That day marked a turning point for me. I shifted my attention to understanding what's happened to America's middle class and how to create broad-based economic security and a strong economy for all. I finished my doctoral dissertation and moved to Washington, DC. As my research progressed, I discovered that my family's experience and my mom's frustrations were not unique. In fact, her concerns were not only widespread but also fundamentally connected to the increasing struggles of the middle class as our nation entered the twenty-first century

Then and Now: America's Silent Partner

American businesses used to have a silent partner. This partner never showed up at a board meeting or made a demand but was integral to profitability. That partner was the American Wife. She made sure the American Worker showed up for work well rested (he didn't have to wake up at 3 AM to feed the baby or comfort a child after a nightmare), in clean clothes (that he neither laundered nor stacked neatly in the closet), with a lunch box packed to the brim with cold-cut sandwiches, coffee, and a home-baked cookie. She took care of all the big and small daily emergencies that might distract the American Worker from focusing 100 percent on his job while he was at work. Little Johnny got in a fight on the playground? The American Wife will be right there to talk to the school. Aunt Bea fell and broke her hip? The American Wife can spend the afternoon bringing her groceries and making her dinner. The boss is coming over for dinner? The American Wife already has the pot roast in the oven. Even if she had a job—and many American wives, like my mom, worked and had to work despite suburban cultural expectations—she was still the primary caregiver when work-life conflicts arose with her family or her employer. The presumption was that she would be the one at home.

This meant that for decades, the American Wife gave American businesses a big fat bonus. Her time at home made possible the American Worker's time at work. This unspoken yet well-understood business contract is now broken. Moreover, it doesn't look like we're going back to it anytime soon. Nor should we. American families look different today. Wives—and women more generally—work outside the home because they need to and because they want to. Families need a new contract with their employers, one that provides stability in today's world where families interact with the economy in new ways.

Today, the American Wife is a family breadwinner and contributor to economic growth. Her economic contribution is no longer silent—it shows up in our nation's gross domestic product. A family with a working woman is not an anomaly, it's the norm—and has been for some time. While some women have always worked outside the house—newly emigrated women and women of color have historically been an integral part of the workforce compared with white or native-born women—it wasn't until the 1960s and 1970s that large numbers of white and middle-class women entered the labor force. Now women bring home at least a quarter of the earnings in more than two-thirds of families with children. In a growing number of households, women bring in half or even more of the earned income. This shift has been good for businesses and the economy. More women in the workforce means more women earning money—adding to overall demand—and using their talents to boost firms' profits. As women have increased their employment, they have ramped up their educational credentials, making them that much more valuable to businesses and the broader economy.

Working outside the home provides women with many exciting social and personal opportunities, yet the picture is not all rosy. Women are not working just to fulfill their dreams and learn new things. Many hold down a job out of sheer economic necessity. Most families would have seen their income drop precipitously over the past few decades if it were not for women going to work. Greater employment of women was a solution to the economic transformations of the past few decades that have left male earnings stagnant for nearly forty years.

While the change in employment patterns was most pronounced for white, middle-class women, all kinds of families have been transformed. Families have become more complex. People marry later—if at all—and the number of children born to unmarried mothers has risen, along with the number of women who never have children (the same is true of men, presumably, though they are not tracked so well). High rates of nonmarriage and divorce mean more blended families, with parents and stepparents, siblings and stepsiblings all under one roof or spread out across different households. In addition, the Supreme Court recently ruled that any two people—regardless of sex—have the right to marry.

Not all families have experienced the loss of the American Wife in the same way. Across the income spectrum, most families no longer have a full-time, stay-at-home caregiver. But low-income and middle-class families are more likely than those at the top to have only a single earner. Nearly 40 percent of today's families with children have a sole female breadwinner. Those families, disproportionately low-income, don't have a wife, let alone someone who can fulfill the role of the traditional American Wife. Families in the middle and at the top more often than not have two breadwinners. While there may be a wife (or two same-sex partners), she certainly isn't at home fulfilling the role of the traditional American Wife (see Figure I.1, which looks at the living arrangements of children aged 14 and under).

What is common across families is the fact that the shift from American Wife to Family (co-)Breadwinner has left a gap at home. Who's caring for the children and teaching them all they need to know? Who's tending to an aging family member who needs some extra care? Today's families report feeling insecure and pressed for time, whether they're high-achieving dual-career couples, low-income

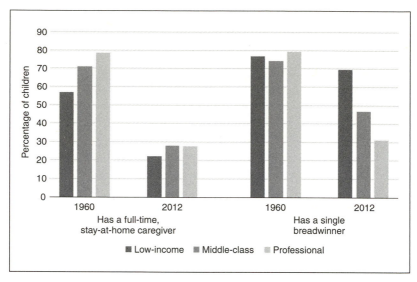

Fig. I.1 Living arrangements of children aged 14 and under by income group, 1960 and 2012. In 1960, most children lived in a family with a single breadwinner, but children living in professional families were more likely than others to have a full-time, stay-at-home caregiver. By 2012, fewer than a third of children lived in a family with a stay-at-home caregiver, and only lower-income families relied on one, as opposed to two, breadwinners. *Note:* Data on cohabitating available only for 2012.

single mothers, or the middle-class families in between. For all kinds of families across the income spectrum, the dual demands of home and out-of-home work cause significant stress. The aging of our society adds a layer of people who need care, but few families have someone at home to provide it. The world of work and the needs of families always seem to be in conflict—and it's been this way for decades.

Our political process approaches this issue as a private matter or as a values issue rather than as a serious economic issue. When my mother shared her frustrations with me that day in our kitchen, she gave me an insight into just how long families have been struggling. Ironically, a solution was almost enacted when my family could have used it. In 1971, both the U.S. House of Representatives and the U.S. Senate passed a bill that would have established a network of nationally funded, locally administered, comprehensive child-care centers to provide high-quality education, nutrition, and medical services. The program had a budget five times the size of today's Head Start program, which provides preschool for very low-income children. Had the bill become the law of the land, in all likelihood I would not have had the conversation with my mom that inspired this book.

A political argument about the proper role of women in society rather than serious policymaking prevented the enactment of this child-care program. At the outset, all signs were that President Richard Nixon would sign the bill into law. In his autobiography, *The Good Fight: A Life in Liberal Politics*, Walter Mondale, who was at the time a senator from Minnesota leading the fight in the Senate for the bill, talked of how Nixon's secretary of health, education, and welfare, Elliot Richardson, had "conducted several quiet meetings with [Mondale's] staff and Representative John Brademas of Indiana, the lead sponsor in the House, to find common ground." Richardson went so far as to send Mondale a letter "outlining the administration's general support to consolidate and coordinate federal child care programs" and to have Ed Zigler, from the Office of Child Development, testify in support of the legislation in 1969 hearings in front of the Subcommittee on Children and Youth. Nixon himself had come out in favor of child care, saying, "so crucial is the matter of early growth that we must make a national commitment to providing all American children an opportunity for healthful and stimulating development during the first five years of life."[1]

Washington insiders were shocked when, on December 9, 1971, Nixon not only vetoed the bill but scathingly repudiated its aims. He said: "We cannot and will not ignore the challenge to do more for America's children in their all-important early years. But our response to this challenge must be a measured, evolutionary, painstakingly considered one, *consciously designed to cement the family in its rightful position as the keystone of our civilization*" (emphasis added). Nixon went on to say that the proposed law would be "a long leap into the dark for the United States Government and the American people."[2]

How did Nixon and his team come to believe that a policy that would have helped tens of millions of families would do the very opposite? Nixon's speechwriter, Pat Buchanan, proudly takes credit for pushing for the veto and, specifically, for encouraging the president to include the statements portraying a federal child-care program as antifamily. Buchanan saw an active policy of providing government support for child care as the federal government's effectively encouraging women to be workers rather than supposedly traditional stay-at-home moms. (I say "supposedly" because the idealized American Wife was never a reality for many families.) In his view, the poorest mothers deserved a handout—an act of charity—because they couldn't afford to purchase child care in the market. For other families, child care wasn't so critical to their well-being that the government should step in to help.[3]

This political setback established child care as a values issue. But left out of this cultural argument is any economic analysis. The real problem (then as now) was how to help families struggling to cope with the new economic reality that even though both Mom and Dad work—or there's just one parent—children (and the sick and the aged) still need care. It was as though the millions of families like mine where no one was at home full-time to address daily conflicts between work and family life were invisible.

Worse, it sounds like an insult. My parents certainly weren't antifamily. Even many families who wish Mom could stay at home have a hard time making that work for their bottom line. My parents needed the same thing today's families need: a set of policies to allow them to be both caregivers and breadwinners. This includes child care and, increasingly, elder care, but it is by no means limited to just those areas, as we'll learn in the chapters that follow.

The 1970s are now history, but the kind of thinking that torpedoed a promising child-care program remains, locking our society in a no-win debate. During a presidential debate in 2012 between President Barack Obama and Governor Mitt Romney, Romney answered a question about equal pay by saying, "I recognized that *if you're going to have women in the workforce* that sometimes you need to be more flexible" (emphasis added). While this gaffe got less attention than his remark that when he put his cabinet together, women's groups "brought [him and his staff] whole binders full of women" who could serve, it illustrates an ongoing tension in American politics. Too often, we are still debating "whether" or "if" women work outside the home, rather than acknowledging that most already do. The question now is how this change in the way women spend their days affects families, firms, and the economy more generally. The time has come to focus on the economic reality of this transformational shift for families and firms.[4]

In this book, I focus on the core economic question underlying partisan debates: if we sought to alleviate family economic insecurity today, what would our agenda look like? Would our efforts be good or bad for the economy overall? The current, tired debate gets stuck on the question of who deserves a handout—a values question—when really we need to be thinking about how keeping people gainfully employed while they care for their families benefits the economy overall. By looking at these questions through the lens of hard-nosed economics, we can chart a new path.

I start with a brief history of how we got here. The two poles of the debate between supporters and opponents of government action began within the context of whether to provide charity to those without land or employment. Chapter 1 delves into the history of the debate and lays out how U.S. policymakers—led by President Franklin D. Roosevelt and his secretary of labor, Frances Perkins—charted a new course in the 1930s. The New Deal's social contract put in place a new role for government. The reforms introduced were not about handouts; they were about helping families cope with the realities of the industrial economy. In this way, the debate moved beyond partisan arguments. Policymakers realized that families instead needed a "help-out" that would support their ability to engage in the economy as workers and consumers.

The New Deal's social contract demarcated what our society thought families needed to become economically secure. But this social contract is no longer enough for today's families. In the 1930s, policymakers had the advantage of being reasonably certain what a family looked like and how it engaged with the economy. Most families—not all, but most—had a single breadwinner. That bread-winner deserved to earn a "family wage," a paycheck that would provide for *him* and *his* family. Policymakers could see that as fair. This idea was so entrenched that women and children earned less not because they were less productive but because the assumption was that they didn't need to support a family.

Today, of course, families neither look the same nor interact with the economy in the same way they did in the 1930s. One person's earnings may support an entire family or be combined with another breadwinner's. This new reality means we must ask the question, does this social contract still meet the needs of today's working families? At the very least, we cannot define economic security through the concept of a single family wage. If one breadwinner doesn't nec-essarily support a family and if families come in all shapes and sizes, then how should we think about economic security? This is a core question of this book. Although I don't have all the answers, I hope to convince you that this question and the changes in how we an-swer it provide the foundation for our labor and social policy.[5]

To understand both what the new agenda should be and its eco-nomic implications, we need to start by looking at what's happened inside today's families. One of the most important developments affecting families is the rise in inequality. In the 1950s and early 1960s, when the New Deal's macroeconomic benefits became patently clear, our economy was far less unequal than today. Since then, there has been a sharp and sustained rise in inequality across all measurable economic indicators, including wages, incomes, job quality, and wealth. Fewer people feel they're in the middle class, and there's growing anxiety about being able to pass on a middle-class lifestyle—and economic security—to the next generation. Workers in the middle class are increasingly squeezed by rising costs and stag-nant wages. Jobs for low-wage workers are more precarious and often have unpredictable schedules and hours. For those on or near the top of the ladder, the payoffs are sky-high salaries and big homes in communities with excellent schools and services, but they come with long hours of work. In order to understand how to support today's workers, we need to see how economic shifts have played out within and across income groups.

At the same time, families across the income spectrum have become more diverse. Greater economic inequality overlaps with greater family complexity in specific ways. In 1960, two-thirds of children lived in a family where their parents were married and only their father worked outside the home. This kind of family was common across all income levels. That's no longer the case. The closer we get to the top of the income ladder, the more likely it is that the family has two earners and that the children live with two parents. The closer we get to the bottom, the more likely we are to see more complex families and those with only a single earner.

Chapters 2, 3, and 4 trace the trends in family economics for families in the middle, the bottom, and the top of the economy and society. This helps us understand the intersection of economic inequality and family complexity. We learn that families face different kinds of economic challenges depending on the quality of their jobs and their financial resources. We learn that significant economic transformations—the demise of manufacturing and the rise of a service economy—have coincided with shifts in family forms, leaving breadwinners coping by trying (and not always succeeding) to work more. We see how families in different financial situations struggle daily with very real conflicts between work and family life.[6]

I focus on family income because most of us live in a family and that's how we interact with the economy. This is not to say that many of us don't live on our own, but most of us will spend a good deal of our lives within some kind of family—defined by birth or by choice. While we have jobs and pursue a variety of activities as individuals, we pool our earnings within a family. The big economic decisions—whether to rent or buy, how much to set aside for retirement or college, or even where to go on vacation—are decisions that we tend to make together, as a family. This is not the traditional way economists look at the economy. Economists—and mythmakers—

tend to tell stories in which individuals, the heroes, drive the action. But if we start with the individual, not the family, we won't see how the changes in the divide between time for work and time for life have affected family economic security.

One conclusion from these three chapters is that while their economic and home circumstances differ, families across the income spectrum share a common concern: they have lost time. They must address conflicts between bringing in a paycheck and caring for family members without an American Wife. This shared experience gives policymakers an opportunity to craft a new agenda that would benefit all kinds of families. This agenda, like the New Deal, could form the basis of a strong and stable political coalition.[7]

Throughout these three chapters—and the remainder of the book—I look across families using precise definitions for low-income, middle-class, and professional families. I define low-income families as those in the bottom third of families by income. Professional families are those families both in the top 20 percent by income and in which at least one member of the family holds at least a college degree. Middle-class families are everyone else, a little over half of all families in 2012. (See the Appendix for more information on data and methods for defining income groups across the earnings spectrum.)[8]

Throughout the book, however, I also draw on a wide range of research from across academic disciplines. To understand the economy, we must do more than consult economic models; we need to see how the economy is embedded within a society. For this reason I often cite research that uses a definition of low-income, middle-class, and professional families that is different from my own. In doing so I lose some precision, but it allows me to draw from a wider array of research. I note throughout where the definitions differ from mine.

In any conversation about family and income, we must consider the growing importance of diversity by race and ethnicity in our society. By the mid-2040s, most Americans will be nonwhite. Understanding the role of changes in family patterns across low-income, middle-class, and professional families as they engage with the broader economy also requires knowledge of our country's racial and ethnic differences as we move toward becoming a majority-minority society. These differences certainly matter in the work-life analyses and proposed reforms presented in this book, and I highlight them throughout.

In Chapter 5, I focus on the core economic question: if we addressed the economic security needs of today's families, as the New Deal did for families in the 1930s, would this be good or bad for the economy overall? What can we learn from economic theory and empirical evidence? Chapter 5 lays out the basic theory of how the economy works, taking into account both sides of the system— families *and* firms—and the role of conflicts between work and family life. Economists don't see the economy only from the perspective of firms; they see an economy that includes both firms and families, as well as other actors, like government and international trade. What happens to the family side of the system is just as important for the economy as what happens to the short-term, bottom line of firms. Families house the workers whom firms hire and families buy most of what firms produce. What happens inside families is an economic issue.

Taking an economic approach allows us to see the new challenges facing firms. Changes in families affect all aspects of the economy. When employers could tap into the time and talents of their Silent Partner, the American Wife, they could assume that most of their employees didn't have regular conflicts between family care and work. This doesn't mean that conflicts never happened, but they were the exception, not the rule. Today it's the opposite. To get the most out of their workforce, employers have to find ways to address these issues. The work-life reforms I explore in this book could help businesses and families become more cost-effective than they are today.

Armed with a view that explains the full economy, not just one slice of it, I then turn to the solutions and the real-world evidence showing that they work. There are four areas where we need new solutions to the everyday economic problems facing middle-income, lower-income, and professional workers. For shorthand, I call them Here (at home), There (at work), Care, and Fair.

The first area addresses a worker's occasional need to be at home. There are days when a worker cannot be at work because he's sick, his child's sick, or he needs to care for an ailing family member. This doesn't mean that he can't hold down a job and be productive most of the time. But there will be days when he needs a little time away from work. Or maybe he needs a week to care for his mom when she breaks her hip or a few weeks to spend with his new baby. Without the security of knowing he will have a job to go back to, he either risks his paycheck or risks not meeting crucial off-the-job needs. The need to be Here (at home) cannot always come second to the need to be There (at work).

Especially for those on the middle and bottom rungs of the income ladder, these kinds of justifiable absences from work must be paid. Otherwise, it's a nice idea but not one that is affordable. Two ideas whose time has come are to allow workers to earn *paid sick days*, short-term leave for the occasional illness of a worker or their children, and *paid family and medical leave* for at least twelve weeks for the good times, when the family welcomes a new child, and the not-so-good times, when a seriously ill family member needs care. Only about two-thirds of workers have paid sick days, and the overwhelming majority do not have paid family and medical leave. Some employers and some states and cities have taken steps to change this, but we need national coverage that includes all workers, not just some of us—and everyone needs to know that they can use this leave without fear of retribution. Like our nation's longstanding rules on the minimum wage and workplace safety, paid sick days and paid family leave should be required for all employees and employers, no exceptions.

The second set of ideas covers what happens when we're at work. Work hours need to fit our lives. Some people don't get enough hours and cannot earn enough to pay their bills. Others have to cope with too many hours, or too many hours at the wrong times. Schedules are too often tilted toward the minute-by-minute demands of businesses, with little or no appreciation for the needs of workers. To rebalance this relationship, we must address overwork, underwork, and unpredictable schedules when people are There (at work).

Some employers have taken positive steps, offering their employees *flexible schedules*—be they hours that fit family life, or even telecommuting. The evidence shows that such policies benefit both firms and families, by motivating workers to be at their best at a company that cares about them and their families and by reducing turnover. But it may not be in the short-term interest of some individual firms to adopt such measures, even if doing so is good for the economy overall. That's where policies to promote flexible schedules that work for both employers and employees come in. We also need to strengthen the protections of the New Deal–era Fair Labor Standards Act by *limiting overwork* for a larger swath of workers, and putting in place greater *scheduling predictability* for workers up and down the economic ladder. These steps improve the conditions for employees when they are at work and thus boost the productivity of firms and the overall economy.

Next are solutions to the daily concern of who's caring for those who need it. Families need high-quality, affordable solutions for caring for children, the elderly, and the sick. One of the toughest choices a family makes is finding the right caregiver for a young or ill family member. We need to ensure *affordable, safe, and enriching care for children and elders* for every family who needs it. Our future depends on it. Rethinking the 1971 comprehensive child-care legislation would be a good place to start, as would be building on the work in cities and states today that are offering free or low-cost universal access to pre-kindergarten for all three- and four-year-olds. For elder care, we need better options both for keeping seniors at home and for long-term palliative care. Enabling families to provide the best care for their children and elderly relatives delivers intergenerational benefits to both families and society.

Finally, these work-life systems must be Fair. With both men and women in the workforce, at some point most of us need time off for family. But no one should be discriminated against because they need some flexibility to care for their loved ones. And if only some people have access to work-life policies that help them address conflicts between work and family life—and those who do are afraid to use them—then this isn't a real set of solutions. Solutions must address the challenges up and down the economic spectrum. Some ideas are now being tested in states and localities, such as prohibiting *family responsibilities discrimination*, in conjunction with existing protections such as the Americans with Disabilities Act; Title VII of the Civil Rights Act, which prohibits racial, ethnic, religious, and gender discrimination in the workplace; and the Pregnancy Discrimination Act.

Fairness also means tailoring and adjusting workplace policies to meet the needs of different breadwinners in different professions with different workplace needs. As the first half of the book documents, job quality, incomes, and access to family-friendly workplace options look different depending on where employees work. Work-life policies will not affect everyone the same way. What works for one worker may not work for another. An option to telecommute may not help a working parent whose home office has been turned into a playroom or the receptionists and line workers who must physically be at work. But better scheduling practices may be especially helpful to all these workers. Being Fair to all employees and employers means finding solutions for all families that are uniformly adhered to by everyone.

So we have a set of solutions: Here, There, Care, and Fair. We don't need one magic fix; we need policies in all four areas. And they need to cover everyone, helping all kinds of families. Paid leave, for short-term and long-term needs and when a new child comes into the family. Schedules that work for families, as well as for their employers, that are predictable and don't require too many—or too few—hours each week. High-quality, affordable care for children and the aging. This is what's fair; those who have care responsibilities are not second-class or secondary workers. In the pages that follow, we'll look at how these fixes will affect the economy. We'll learn how the overall economic benefit of addressing these issues is just as important for low-income and middle-class families as for professional families. The United States—one of the richest countries the world has ever seen—can afford to do this; in fact, we cannot afford not to act. I won't just assert this. I'll show you the evidence—evidence that I hope will convince you that we need to try a different path.

The Economics of Work-Life Conflict

Throughout this book, I look at the economy as an economist. In order to understand how policy affects the economy, economists, policymakers, and business owners alike have to examine both demand and supply. The tough-love crowd has a point: there are some added costs for businesses when implementing work-life policies—as there are with implementing any policy. Yet these work-life reforms will enable workers—most of whom also have care responsibilities—to meet the needs of their families and of the firms they work for in better and more productive ways. There are economic benefits to implementing work-life policies.

Once we start thinking like economists, we can see where these benefits outweigh the costs. I will show you how to spot not only the upfront costs but also the benefits, some hiding in plain sight, and others requiring a broader macroeconomic lens to discern. We will look beyond what the policy costs today to find the medium- and long-term benefits. We will then see how policies that address work-life conflicts have many positive economic effects. Because these policies address the ways our economy and society operate today, they not only improve productivity and boost firms' bottom line but also stabilize demand.

Three conclusions emerge from the evidence. First, overall economic performance and stability do not equal the short-term performance of individual businesses. Opponents of reform often point to a single business's bottom line to make their case, but one business's short-term interest is not—by a long shot—the whole story of the economy. If we start thinking about the economy by first considering how an employer will cope with a rise in costs, assuming no capacity to change prices or that the rising cost has no positive effect on productivity, then we miss the full story about how the economy really works. Once we think like an economist and look at both demand and supply, we can see our economic system in full.

What happens inside families is just as important to making the economy hum along as what happens inside firms. We need both, but we must start with families. Work-life policies make it easier for people to find and keep jobs, improving what economists call the "labor supply." This helps to grow and stabilize family income. Work-life reforms are an important factor in the most fundamental of the Three M's, the macroeconomy. Further, work-life policies help families function, which is good for our future economy. Today's children are tomorrow's workforce. They need their parents and their caregivers to help them become the most productive workers they can be when they reach adulthood.

Second, we need public action. We need the collaboration of both the public and the private sectors to make sure that all workers—from low-wage fast-food workers to C-suite executives—have workaday schedules that fit their work and life. I'll present a good deal of evidence that work-life policies are good for the private sector, but even so, not every employer has embraced them. While many businesses are leading the way, too many others are falling behind. That's where public policy must play a role.

Third, we must blaze the trail anew, as policymakers did in the early part of the twentieth century. This will require letting go of the partisan tropes we're so used to falling back on. Too often we're told that advocates of new policies are putting values or fairness above practical concerns, while supporters of laissez-faire are the ones who are serious about the economy. This isn't correct. For today's economy, the question isn't whether we should help families with handouts; it's how to help families so they can thrive as workers and consumers. To boost long-term economic growth, businesses need a highly skilled workforce, ready and able to work. In today's economy, where most workers also have care responsibilities, this means we must find ways to address conflicts between work and life. These conflicts aren't trivial private travails; they're serious economic problems.

The good news is that every idea discussed in this book is being tested right now someplace in America. We can learn a good deal from these experiences about what works—and what does not. One thing is clear: communities around the nation are eager to address the economic and social changes of the past several decades. And some leaders have been listening. A growing number of politicians find these to be winning campaign issues. Once the policies are in place, they find that the economic evidence shows that supporting working families across the income distribution is good for businesses and the economy.

This book is not about nostalgia for a bygone era. Like many, I watched *Mad Men* and cringed at the casual sexism, racism, and homophobia (not to mention being flabbergasted by the quantity of alcohol consumed mid-day). Our economy will not thrive by putting our hopes in yesterday's industries, either. Economic policy must be conducted with an eye to our national interest, and this means maintaining our competitive advantage by having a high-skilled workforce. This will not happen so long as we ignore the economic trends and solutions presented in the pages that follow.

We can, however, look back to learn about what worked and why. Evidence shows that by acknowledging the full economic cycle—families *and* firms—we can grow a stronger, more vibrant national economy. Thinking about the whole economy—not just the firm's supply side—isn't a new idea. But unfortunately, it's not one we've heard much about recently. We've been driving around in the dark, lost. Our goal is to move beyond thinking there is a trade-off between policies that address family economic security and policies that promote economic growth. In the pages that follow, I'll show why we need to consider instead what is good for the economy as a whole. The evidence points to the conclusion that families—and the institutions that support them—matter. Policymakers too often fail to recognize this and instead keep taking the same road not because it's the right way to go but because it's familiar.

When I was in high school, I would drive into Seattle to see bands and sip coffee late into the night, and I always ended up taking the long way home. I'd be a little anxious about stalling my Datsun on one of the hills around the city, so when I saw Denny Way, I always turned onto it, even though it led away from my home to Seattle's Capitol Hill district. From there I navigated winding hills and eventually ended up at home. A quick look at a map would have revealed the freeway that heads straight to my house, but since my circuitous route was familiar, I stuck to it. I should have known better, but I was just a kid. What excuse does the richest nation on earth have for driving around in the dark like an adolescent? Just because our familiar arguments over how best to help families and the economy lead us along well-trod paths doesn't make them the best ones we could be taking.

Our Roots

"Bleeding hearts" and advocates of tough love have been debating what governments, firms, and families owe one another for centuries. The questions at the core of this argument are always about who deserves a helping hand, how generous the handout should be, and whether such help will ultimately lead people to economic ruin. One side argues that the economically insecure need society's help, while the other argues that people must deal with their troubles on their own, for their own sake and for the good of the economy.

This debate hinges on the idea that social policy keeps people out of the job market and reduces economic efficiency. The economist Arthur Okun perhaps most eloquently laid out the economic rationale for this view. In his 1975 book *Equality and Efficiency: The Big Tradeoff,* he argued that while it might be nice to provide supports to those in need—and the public may push leaders toward this path—such action undermines growth. Policymakers can *either* provide transfers to those at the bottom *or* promote economic efficiency; they can't do both. Providing benefits for those at the bottom of the income distribution paid for by taxes on those higher up both reduces employment incentives and inefficiently allocates resources. He used a well-known proverb to frame his fundamental concern, saying, "We can't have our cake of market efficiency and share it equally." While Okun may not have planned it this way, his argument easily morphs into one where any government support is seen to hinder economic growth.[1]

This long-running debate—and Okun's formulation—miss almost entirely the key economic issues facing today's families. A debate starting with the premise that a handout reduces the incentive to work ignores how some help in fact makes it possible for workers to become and remain active in our economy. It focuses us on the poor, when we also need to see the economic challenges facing the middle class and even professional families. In a world where the American Wife is also the American Worker (and the American Worker is also a caregiver), the idea that policies that address family economic security automatically undermine those that promote economic growth no longer makes sense. A helping hand may be exactly what families and firms need to ensure that workers are available to take jobs and that employees are able to get to work and fully participate in the labor force. Yet we continue to be locked into a volley of arguments and counterarguments in this outdated debate.

We can trace this debate back to the dawn of the Industrial Revolution in England. The 1597 and 1601 Poor Laws gave responsibility for the sick, the aged, orphans, and the unemployed to local parish leaders. Parliament implemented this system after King Henry VIII confiscated the property of monasteries and common lands were enclosed, leading to the eviction of tenant farmers. Between 1536 and 1541, Henry VIII closed nearly 900 religious institutions— monasteries, nunneries, friaries, and others—and appropriated the property, leaving tens of thousands of people without a home or a vocation. This affected not only those in the religious orders but also the servants, staff, and others who relied on these institutions for employment and income. Additionally, these religious establishments were the main providers of charity, and their demise left the poor with nowhere to turn for help. The English state's answer was the Poor Laws. These laws made local parishes responsible for providing support to poor people living in their homes and jobs for the able-bodied.[2]

Over the course of the seventeenth and eighteenth centuries, the English economy underwent another profound economic change: the Industrial Revolution. As Adam Smith documented in *The Wealth of Nations*, changes in how goods were produced fundamentally transformed the economy. The invention of the steam engine and other new technologies forever altered the process of production. In the 1700s, for example, families wove cotton fabric at home using a wooden handloom. Edmund Cartwright's invention of the steam-powered loom changed not only the rate of fabric production, but also how and where production occurred. By 1830, a weaver at a power loom could produce forty times as much fabric in a day as he could have in 1800 with more rudimentary tools. Weavers who used to work at home on their own loom now walked over to a factory to work on a power loom they did not own. Investments in big machinery were costly, and only those who had enough money to invest in the new power looms owned factories. This nascent industrialization, preceded by the tumult of the confiscation of the Catholic Church's riches and the closure of the commons, all created the need for a new kind of social policy.[3]

As industrialization proceeded, the debate over what governments, firms, and families owed one another became focused on how to ensure that charity did not get in the way of finding and keeping a job. Getting people to work in the newly emerging industries wasn't always easy. Many were wary of working in what the poet William Blake termed the "satanic mills" spawned by the Industrial Revolution. For England, the 1834 Poor Law Amendment Act settled the debate over who could—and should—work for nearly a century. This act required that the poor be incarcerated in a poorhouse—known more colloquially as the workhouse—where anyone deemed able-bodied was put to work. Conditions were dreadful. Most would do anything to avoid entering the workhouse, as evocatively portrayed in the novels of Charles Dickens.[4]

The English cleric and scholar Thomas Malthus was an ardent advocate for the 1834 reforms. In his famous article "An Essay on the Principle of Population," first published in 1798, Malthus argued that poor relief served only to immiserate the poor because it encouraged them to rely on charity rather than employment. The way to aid the poor was to refuse aid and thereby encourage economic independence: "The love of independence is a sentiment that surely none would wish to be erased from the breast of man, though the parish law of England, it must be confessed, is a system of all others the most calculated gradually to weaken this sentiment, and in the end may eradicate it completely."[5] In this incarnation of the age-old debate over the proper role of government, Malthus argued that government support put a family on the path of dependence on handouts because accepting charity was easier than taking the path toward economic independence by finding work. It was an either/or proposition; there was no role for government to play in encouraging greater employment other than restricting assistance to the poorhouse.

The experience of the United States was similar to that of England, but differed in key ways. Early American settlers were mostly farmers, as in England, but in North America, land was abundant and there was no landed gentry to keep people from working it. What was similar in both countries before the Industrial Revolution was that families produced most of what they consumed. In pre-industrial England and America, women and men worked on the farm side-by-side, along with children and the aged. We can see this even in the English word "economics," which traces back to the Greek word "oikonomikós," a combination of "oîko," house, and "nómos," manager.

By the mid-nineteenth century, industrialization had transformed economic and social life in the United States, leading to new insecurities and new debates over what governments, firms, and families owed one another. These economic changes meant that more goods were produced at a far lower cost. Consumption rose, as did life expectancy as a result of public health programs, better access to health care, and improved sanitation. The nature of work also changed. Most people were no longer self-employed agrarians but wage-earning employees. Industrialization, moreover, shifted to where families lived. In 1840, about one in nine people lived in urban areas, but by 1920, urban-dwellers had grown to more than half of the population. The mass exodus to the city happened alongside changes in the composition of households. Rather than multiple generations living under one roof, families became more likely to consist of parents and their minor children.[6]

The Industrial Revolution transformed the nature of economic insecurity in two specific ways. Instead of the family being its own economic production unit, its survival was now dependent on a firm and the job it gave the family breadwinner. On the farm, a husband's incapacitation created hardship, but other family members could usually step in to help. In the new industrial economy, families tended to interact with the economy through one person earning a family wage (or such was the aspiration, at least). When the family breadwinner could not work—because he was sick or had an on-the-job accident, lost his job because of an increasingly ugly boom-and-bust industrial cycle, died, or abandoned his household—the family often had little to fall back on.

The idea that a single breadwinner could support a family on his earnings alone had become the ideal of trade unionists and other worker advocates by the end of the nineteenth century. The historian Martha May quotes a 1905 issue of the *Shoe Workers' Journal* that stated that a living wage should be "sufficient to maintain life for the worker and those dependent upon him. . . . Everything necessary to the life of a *normal man* must be included in the living wage: the right to marriage, the right to have children, and to educate them."[7] This idea of the family wage served two purposes: it provided a moral (and economic) foundation for wages high enough to support a family, and it reinforced the idea that women did not belong in the workforce.[8]

The crisis of the Great Depression, which pushed the U.S. unemployment rate from 5 percent in 1929 up to more than 20 percent just two years later, underscored the necessity of addressing the economic insecurity of families. The unemployed began to camp in "Hoovervilles," or shantytowns, and mass unemployment led to mass discontent. Radical protests and labor strikes proliferated across America, and marchers descended on Washington. This unrest combined with political pressure from communist revolts abroad pressured U.S. political leaders to take steps to mitigate the crisis. Franklin Delano Roosevelt was elected in 1932 with 57 percent of the popular vote, winning all but six states. With the New Deal, he put in place a set of policies that addressed the specific ways that unemployment could decimate family finances. His administration

laid out the nation's first set of rules aimed at reducing conflicts between work and stable family life.[9]

The New Deal is referred to as if it were a single piece of legislation, but it was actually dozens of separate bills and regulations
covering areas as diverse as manufacturing, agriculture, and banking.
Three pieces of the New Deal puzzle are especially relevant for the
argument of this book, the 1935 Social Security Act, the 1935 National Labor Relations Act, and the 1938 Fair Labor Standards
Act. Together these three laws continue to define what government, firms, and families owe one another in terms of the day-in,
day-out conflicts between work and family life and what happens
when a breadwinner can no longer work or is unemployed. This
policy agenda marked a turning point in economic thinking in the
United States. Instead of viewing social policy primarily as a disin-
centive to getting or keeping a job, the New Deal put in place policies to help out those who worked for a living. It laid out a clear
boundary between time for work and time for families as they looked
in that era.

The United States was not the first country to embark on an am-
bitious program of proemployment welfare-state policies. European
countries had begun to experiment with a similar group of social
policies about half a century before. In the late 1880s, Germany's
first chancellor, Otto von Bismarck, put in place old-age pensions,
accident insurance, and medical care programs, thereby establishing
the first modern welfare system. These programs were modeled on
reforms already established in Prussia and Saxony before he unified
those kingdoms and other German principalities into the nation of
Germany. The United Kingdom undertook similar reforms in the
early 1900s, and, like Germany, set up old-age pensions as well as
unemployment and health-care funds. The purpose of these programs was to address the series of market failures that had emerged
through industrialization, leaving families with new kinds of economic insecurity—even those who wanted to work but sometimes
could not.[10]

The Woman behind the New Deal

The ideas embodied in the New Deal didn't emerge out of thin air. The seeds had been germinating for decades in states and cities around the United States, as well as within the private sector. Progressive reformers in the late 1800s and early 1900s had developed—and tested—a set of ideas to address the new economic insecurities caused by the urban industrial economy. They worked to establish state laws to limit the length of the workday, to prohibit child labor, to provide unemployment insurance, to implement health and safety regulations to prevent deaths by fire and on-the-job accidents, and to ensure that widows and orphans didn't have to turn to begging—or worse, stealing or prostitution—to support themselves. These policies gave Franklin D. Roosevelt a menu of fully formed ideas that would become the New Deal.

In 1932, when Roosevelt won his first presidential election, Frances Perkins was a leader among Progressive-era reformers. She would become the driving force behind the three pillars supporting our nation's employment and family policy—Social Security, fair labor laws, and meaningful labor standards—leading the charge inside the White House to push the legislation through Congress. In her view, the proper role of government was to guide families and firms toward a system that would give families real economic security *and* encourage a strong and competitive economy. Her reforms were grounded in the idea that the recipients of government support would work for a living; these were help-outs, not handouts. Her story sheds light on why the New Deal was successful and provides a number of lessons for how to think about work-life policies today.[11]

Perkins came to policy work after being exposed to the economic challenges facing working families. She grew up in a well-to-do family in Maine and attended Mount Holyoke College in South Hadley, Massachusetts, at a time when very few women (and very few men) graduated from college.[12] In her senior year, she took a course on American economic history where she learned about industrialization in the United States and Britain. She saw firsthand

the economic realities of families of her day when she visited the
mills on the Connecticut River in the neighboring city of Holyoke.
Perkins later said of that experience,

> From the time I was in college I was horrified at the work
> that many women and children had to do in factories.
> There were absolutely no effective laws that regulated
> the number of hours they were permitted to work. There
> were no provisions which guarded their health nor ade-
> quately looked after their compensation in case of injury.
> Those things seemed very wrong. I was young and was
> inspired with the idea of reforming, or at least doing what
> I could, to help change those abuses.[13]

This question of how society must reshape itself to cope with the
newly industrialized economy informed her career.

After graduating, Perkins took a teaching job at Ferry Hall, an
elite school for girls in Lake Forest, Illinois, north of Chicago.
There, she spent her evenings and weekends at Hull House, the
first so-called settlement house. These were places where university-
educated women engaged with the local community and provided
services, such as day care, classes, or help with employment, as well
as where they developed and shared new policy ideas. Jane Addams,
cofounder of the Hull House, described their work as "close cooper-
ation with the neighborhood people, scientific study of the causes of
poverty and dependence, communication of [these] facts to the
public, and persistent pressure for [legislative and social] reform."[14]
It was at Hull House that Perkins became one of an emerging group
of progressive leaders, many of them women.

In 1910, Perkins took a prominent position leading the National
Consumers League in New York City. There, in 1911, she witnessed
the infamous Triangle Shirtwaist Factory Fire, which killed 146
people, 123 of whom were women and girls. The doors of the factory were locked and the only escape route was through ninth-floor
windows, which the fire truck's ladders couldn't reach. Many chose

to jump to their deaths rather than burn alive. After watching this horrific tragedy from across the street, Perkins focused her efforts on policies to improve workplace safety. She became a social worker and the driving force behind the newly established New York State Factory Investigating Commission.[15]

It was also in New York City that Perkins met Franklin Delano Roosevelt. In 1929, when he became governor of New York, Roosevelt appointed her as New York State industrial commissioner. Then, in 1933, a week before his inauguration as president of the United States, Roosevelt called Perkins to his office to invite her to serve as the first secretary of labor and the first woman to hold a cabinet-level position in the United States (and, as such, the first woman in line for the presidency). She was ready with a plan. All along, Perkins had kept notes of what needed to change for workers and their families. She preserved the ideas "on individual slips of paper, storing them in the lower right-hand desk drawer," waiting for the right moment to unfold them. According to the biography by Pulitzer Prize–winning journalist Kirstin Downey, Perkins told Roosevelt that she would take the job on one condition: he must agree to support her work-life reforms.[16]

Perkins presented Roosevelt with a to-do list for the family of the 1930s. This list covered the most common reasons for economic insecurity for working families in her day. It included addressing unemployment through temporary public works, prohibiting child labor, instituting an eight-hour day and a minimum wage, creating workers' compensation for those injured on the job, establishing workers' safety regulations, devising plans for a national system of unemployment insurance, and creating an old-age pension. These reforms became the cornerstones of the New Deal. The benefit programs for the aged and the unemployed were the core elements of the Social Security Act, while the prohibition of child labor, the eight-hour-day, and the minimum wage were combined into the Fair Labor Standards Act. Perkins understood the importance of giving workers a voice, and she was a fierce advocate for the National Labor Relations Act, which gave workers the right to unionize, even when her boss was not always as keen as she was on the idea.[17]

Perkins navigated a new path through the old debate. In the sections that follow, we will see how her proposals were carefully tailored to the needs of her time. A few conclusions jump out. First, this wasn't a welfare agenda; this was an agenda to support working families and reduce economic insecurity. Key pieces of the New Deal elevated what the historian Michael Katz later called the "deserving poor," those who should receive assistance because they were striving to be part of the workforce. These were not handouts to encourage people to disengage from the economy when they could not work. Rather, they were help-outs for those for whom work wasn't possible (the young, the old, the sick) or for whom work wasn't available (the unemployed). They also governed the time spent on work and the ability of workers to bargain over working conditions with their employer.[18]

Second, Perkins's reforms established the roles of government, firms, and families in addressing economic insecurity *in that era*—not for all time, but for that time. The New Deal was grounded in contemporary assumptions about what families looked like and how they interacted with the economy. Specifically, the policies were designed for an economy in which most women married and did not work outside the home, and most men assumed the role of family breadwinner and so needed a family wage. Policymakers did not need to prioritize the issue of how workers split their time between work and care. In Perkins's day, she—a married mother *and* breadwinner—was the exception to the rule. Most women who worked outside the home did so out of necessity because the male breadwinner was incapacitated or no longer around.[19]

The ideal of a stay-at-home mother never applied to the families of African American or immigrant women, many of whom toiled in the homes of upper-class whites. In 1920, married African American women were five times more likely than white married women to work outside the home. Further, many working women were newcomers to the United States. But the family with a male breadwinner was the norm among whites and among the majority of families.[20]

It wasn't just that women were unlikely to work outside the home. Leading Progressive-era feminists actively sought to encourage families to adopt the male breadwinner/female homemaker model in the belief that this was best for children and mothers. Some activists did seek a set of policies that would support working women, but the overriding sentiment at the time was that policymakers should not actively encourage women to take outside employment. There were good reasons for this position. At the time, work was typically arduous, often unsafe, and the hours were long. This was not good for anyone, but working conditions were especially hard for pregnant women and mothers of young children. Seeing women's employment as a choice, however, didn't change the fact that the women who were in the workplace were there out of necessity; they needed the money.[21]

Third, every item on Perkins's list had already been put in place somewhere within the United States. Perkins was able to look to state and local models for inspiration and validation. State and local policy experimentation showed what worked—and what did not—as well as how social policy interacted with the economy. Further, it demonstrated the public's appetite—at least at the local level—for this new and practical set of work-life ideas.

Finally, the New Deal reforms were not always inclusive. Political compromises often meant that some people and families were not covered. The politics of the day drove these choices, as did the capacity of the government to implement and enforce reforms. At the end of the day, to get the votes necessary to pass the legislation into law, many of the New Deal's employment protections and social policies included eligibility rules that categorically excluded African Americans.[22]

The combination of these factors points to a key failing of the New Deal: the needs of workers with caregiving responsibilities were left out, as were the needs of many of those who worked for pay as caregivers, mostly women of color. Perkins successfully pushed for her reforms in the decade just after women had earned the right to vote and during the heyday of Jim Crow in the South. Perkins was the lone woman among the men of Roosevelt's cabinet. To this day, however, the lack of attention to the compromises made at the time limited the economic benefits of the New Deal—a serious flaw that has continued to reverberate in the decades since. Today, families have neither policies to let them stay at home nor policies to support them when they work outside the home. Therein lies the key contradiction still facing families.

The Social Security Act of 1935

The premise of the Social Security Act was that to be economically secure, families needed a system to replace the earnings of a male breadwinner when he was too old to work, couldn't find work, or died. In the inner workings of the legislation, Perkins strove to forge a new path beyond the age-old debate between advocates and opponents of government action. The Social Security Act would help those who could not work and would encourage, not discourage, work. To this end, it created two national social insurance programs: retirement benefits for workers after they reached the age of sixty-five and unemployment compensation administered by the states for workers who had lost their jobs through no fault of their own. The act also created federal grants for states to run means-tested programs for the aged and the blind, as well as for maternal and child health and welfare services, and public health services and vocational rehabilitation services.[23]

The retirement program—what we call Social Security—is paid out of current workers' contributions (a "pay-as-you-go" system), with employers paying an equal amount. Eligibility depends on a worker's—or her or (less likely) his spouse's—history of employment and payment into the system. The contribution side of the system is regressive as the tax applies only to earned income up to a fixed maximum, set at $118,500 for 2015. The distribution side, however, is progressive, repaying more to low earners relative to their contributions. The system was designed to supplement, not supplant, private pensions.[24]

The retirement program built on ideas that were implemented in the decades prior to the New Deal. The sociologist Theda Skocpol argues that the Civil War Pension program, which began in 1862 shortly after the start of the war, laid the groundwork for the retirement program. Originally, the Civil War Pension gave benefits only to Union soldiers disabled in the line of duty. Later, it was expanded to cover both Union and Confederate veterans who became disabled later in life, and eventually veterans in old age. Widows and orphans could also qualify for benefits equal to what would have been available to their veteran husbands and fathers. By 1910, nearly half a century after the war ended, the veterans' pension program covered just under a third (28 percent) of men over age sixty-four and about 300,000 widows, orphans, and other dependents.[25]

We tend to think of Social Security's retirement program as universal, that is, covering everyone, but the original program was quite restricted. Federal and state employees, agricultural workers, and domestic workers were ineligible. As a result, when the act was signed into law in 1935, about 20.1 million employed workers, or about half of all workers, were excluded from retirement benefits. We don't know for sure why policymakers excluded workers in these fields; hearings on the matter included testimony that collecting taxes from them would be very difficult. But, we do know that Roosevelt needed the votes of Southern Democrats concerned that this policy might either reduce labor supply or lead to demands for higher wages among African Americans. We also know that coverage played out along the lines of race: among those working, about two-thirds of African Americans were not covered, compared with only one-third of whites. The law has been expanded over time, and now nearly the entire labor force is covered. Further, it has been extended to cover the disabled who cannot work. In 1956 Social Security was expanded to cover long-term disabilities, and in 1972 it was amended to include those born with disabilities. Still, some people have had to wait a very long time to be included.[26]

The unemployment insurance system provides income support to workers who have lost their jobs through no fault of their own. When workers and their families are dependent on wages to make ends meet, involuntary unemployment has a devastating effect on family well-being. Like Social Security's retirement program, unemployment compensation is similar to insurance: workers' income risks are pooled and payments into the system are made on the basis of expected benefits. However, in this case, the states each set their own eligibility rules and benefit levels. If workers meet their state's requirements (such as a minimum duration of employment, sufficient earnings, and a qualifying reason for losing their job through no fault of their own), they are eligible to receive benefits regardless of wealth or nonwage income. The funds for unemployment insurance typically come from a tax on employers, although some states tax employees as well.

The states provided a model for this program. In 1932, Wisconsin created the first unemployment compensation system, which was quickly followed by similar programs in six other states, including New York, where Perkins helped with the initial planning.[27]

The unemployment insurance system, like the retirement program, categorically excluded a wide variety of workers. Agricultural and domestic workers, professionals, nonprofit employees, and workers in federal, state, and local governments were all left out. Even today after extensions, while the unemployment insurance system imposes payroll taxes for nearly every employee, restrictions related to work histories and hours mean that only about 40 percent of the unemployed actually receive benefits. Because states set the eligibility rules and the benefit levels, coverage and benefits vary widely across the country. The rules often mean that those with a history of intermittent work or part-time employment are less likely to be eligible, which reduces the program's coverage for women and people of color.[28]

The other program for able-bodied adults is what is commonly known as "welfare" for widows and children. Aid to Dependent Children, which later became Aid to Families with Dependent Children, and more recently Temporary Assistance for Needy Families, was originally designed to provide support to the children of widows. This was a charitable program; without husbands, widows would need help from the state. To encourage employment, however, the program gave benefits to dependent children only up until the age of fifteen and did not give assistance to their parents, though they needed to live with a parent or guardian in order to be eligible. Unlike Social Security and unemployment insurance, the welfare program was paid out of general tax revenues.[29]

The program was modeled on the Mothers' Pensions, which by 1931 had been established in forty-six states and what were then the territories of Hawaii and Alaska, as well as the District of Columbia. Mothers' Pensions emerged from an early-twentieth-century movement to give cash payments to families with children without male earnings.[30]

From the start, Aid to Dependent Children excluded certain families from receiving assistance. Up until 1960, states could require that children live in "suitable homes" in order to receive benefits, which most frequently meant denying benefits to never-married mothers, who were more often African American. Today this program has stringent work requirements and is time-limited. However, when changes were made to this legislation in 1996, Congress also increased funding for programs that would help parents be both caregivers and workers, by increasing funding to help pay for child care and health insurance, raising the minimum wage, and expanding the Earned Income Tax Credit.[31]

National Labor Relations Act

To find private-sector solutions that work for both employers and employees, the two sides need a way to hash out their differences of opinion on a level playing field. Progressive-era advocates—Frances Perkins included—understood that there's only so much government can do. The balance of power is on the employers' side, and if they refuse to engage with employees about the boundary between time for work and time for life, how work is done, or what constitutes a fair day's pay, then it can be nearly impossible to find any solution that works for both sides. This is where unions come in. Unions can advocate on behalf of their members so that government doesn't have to step in.

In the early twentieth century, no legal right existed for workers to form a union. They could try, but at the time the laws were such that employers could turn to the courts to thwart them. The National Labor Relations Act, signed into law in 1935, gave workers the right to form unions and bargain on their own behalf without retaliation from employers. The act also established the National Labor Relations Board, which ensures that union elections are fair and that both the union and the employer play by the rules. This act was effective in boosting union coverage. By 1940, union membership had nearly doubled, up to nine million union members.[32]

Here, too, Perkins had models for how to give workers a voice. In 1932, Congress passed the Norris-LaGuardia Act, which gave unions the right to organize and strike by curbing courts' powers to issue injunctions and restraining orders against strikes. That law prohibited federal courts from enforcing "yellow dog" contracts, which barred workers from joining unions or forced them to end existing union membership. This opened the door for the National Labor Relations Act, and importantly, gave evidence that such legislation could be successfully implemented.[33]

All workers need a voice, but unions have a track record of excluding some from their ranks. In the early twentieth century, the craft unions of the American Federation of Labor (AFL) focused on organizing skilled workers, typically white men, to the exclusion of women and African Americans. As documented by the sociologist Ruth Milkman, the AFL "viewed women and other skilled workers as 'unorganizable.'"[34] One implication of the exclusion of women and people of color is that unions focused only on what pertained to their members, not on the kinds of work-life conflicts that result from women's employment, or on the domestic or care workers, who were (and still are) most commonly women of color. In fact, the goal for many unions—like that of some Progressive-era feminists—was for a man to earn a family wage that was enough to support his family without his wife's having to work.

Unions are far more inclusive today. African Americans make up about 14 percent of union members—about the same as their share of the total U.S. population—and women now account for 45 percent of all union members. Unions have also made progress on supporting issues important to workers with care responsibilities, such as paid sick days, paid family leave, and schedules that work for employees. One indication of how far unions have come is that in 1992, the Labor Project for Working Families was formed with the goal of building "alliances between unions, advocacy and community groups to advance and implement family-friendly workplace policies such as family leave, paid sick days and worker-controlled flexibility." The Labor Project highlights best practices in union contracts from around the country so that other people in unions—and those without a union—can share ideas on how to put in place policies that meet the needs of today's families.[35]

The Fair Labor Standards Act

The third pillar of the New Deal is the 1938 Fair Labor Standards Act, which prohibited child labor, established a minimum wage, and defined a regular workweek as forty hours. It was crafted to address the work-life issues of its day and to create limits to how much time employers could demand of their workers and under what conditions. When Congress passed the act into law, its intent was to encourage employers to curtail the long hours of their current employees and to put more people to work. When enacted, it meant a change in the ability of employers to do whatever they wanted. While unions could bargain for higher wages and working conditions on the job, this act set an economy-wide floor for wages and a ceiling for hours.

The Fair Labor Standards Act pulled together the good ideas that had been tested in the states and laid out new national standards. First, it prohibited child labor. In the early twentieth century, children often toiled long hours in factories and coal mines. Working upward of twelve hours a day near dangerous machinery, children regularly suffered serious injuries. They were typically paid less than adults, and employers could hire them instead of adult workers to keep labor costs down. This lowered adult employment rates and earnings. Child labor was also bad for the economy more generally, since child laborers were not in school learning the skills they would need to be productive adults. But children worked in no small part because their parents didn't earn enough.

The act also set a federal minimum wage and rules on overtime, defining the standard workweek at forty hours. The minimum wage was initially set to $0.25. In terms of overtime protections, workers covered by the law must be paid 150 percent of their usual hourly wage for any hours they work beyond forty in a given week. These overtime provisions cover only workers who are paid hourly wages, which today is about six in ten workers, and certain lower-paid salaried workers. The law does not address employee-led flexibility, scheduling issues, predictability of hours, sufficient hours, or part-time parity. Employers can demand unlimited hours of work from "exempt" employees, or those who are not eligible for overtime pay.[36]

The original legislation was passed following decades of state efforts to establish labor standards by restricting child labor, setting a minimum wage, and limiting excessive work hours, primarily for women and children. By 1913, the minimum age for factory work was set at fourteen in thirty-nine out of forty-eight states. In 1897, the Women's Trade Union League adopted the minimum wage as a goal for policy as a way to address the low wages of garment workers in factories, and states began to pass minimum-wage laws for women. In 1913, Massachusetts became the first state to pass such a law; by 1923, minimum-wage laws for women were in place in sixteen states. As early as the mid-nineteenth century, most skilled trade workers had won legislation giving them the right to a ten-hour workday.[37]

Frances Perkins also had a federal model to look to on these issues. In 1933, President Roosevelt established the National Recovery Administration to promote economic recovery and create industry-wide workplace protections, excluding domestic and agricultural workers. Although the administration was dismantled two years later, it demonstrated that it was possible to implement overtime protections and wage requirements that could help workers without damaging the economy.[38]

Like the Social Security Act, the Fair Labor Standards Act did not cover all workers. Its overtime provisions excluded domestic and agricultural workers. These were jobs typically held by African

Americans, especially in the South. As with the Social Security Act, Roosevelt needed the votes of white Southern Democrats to pass the legislation into law. Historians have argued that, as with the Social Security Act, the politics of getting the bill passed included racial bias.[39]

Also like the Social Security Act, the Fair Labor Standards Act has been updated over time. As of January 2015, the federal minimum wage stood at $7.25 an hour, although twenty-nine states and the District of Columbia have set a higher threshold. However, even today, the overtime provisions of the law leave out most salaried employees. Employees who earn more than $455 a week, or about $23,600 a year; who are paid on a salary basis with a "guaranteed minimum"; and who perform exempt job duties within certain jobs; including but not limited to police and other first responders, executives, and administrators, are all excluded. In June 2015, the Department of Labor proposed a new regulation to increase this earnings threshold to $50,440—the first increase in forty years— about what it would be had it had kept pace with inflation. And it was only in January 2015 that home care workers—those who work in people's homes tending to the sick and elderly—finally received overtime and minimum-wage protections.[40]

The Legacy of Perkins and the New Deal

Perkins left us more than an alphabet soup of government programs. She showed that there were effective ways to address family economic security that were both pragmatic and bipartisan. She learned from people who worked for a living, from the successes at the state and local levels, and from the relationships that she actively cultivated with business leaders. Her agenda did not create handouts; it established a set of rules and programs to support work, including putting boundaries on employees' time.

Perkins had found the right path for her era. The policy agenda she helped put into place was good not only for families but also for the economy. The decades that followed the New Deal and the end of World War II have been called the "golden age" of U.S. capitalism. Up until the mid-1970s, the economy grew at a healthy clip and hovered near full employment, while inflation and interest rates remained at reasonable levels. Even if many other factors contributed to the performance of the economy, it's clear that the New Deal social policies discussed here were not harming the economy.

New Deal–era policies and reforms to those programs invested in families, creating economic security and sustained consumer demand, which led to investment and growth while also improving productivity. These policies rewarded work and supported greater adult employment by limiting hours—creating demand for more employees—and removing children from the workforce. By lowering inequality and improving economic security in families, these policies provided a foundation to stabilize and grow consumer demand. Decades of research confirms that in times of high unemployment, unemployment benefits have a strong, positive effect on demand. The minimum wage stabilizes consumption for workers at the low end of the wage ladder, as well as potentially boosting productivity at the very low end of the labor market. Consistent consumption growth signals to business that consumers will be there in the future and promotes business investment.[41]

These economic effects don't fit into the traditional debate between the so-called bleeding hearts and the advocates of a tough-love approach. That debate focuses on the role of government help in reducing individuals' incentives to find work. Perkins, however, focused on how to support workers and their families when a breadwinner could not work. Her program set out rules—such as banning child labor and limiting hours of work—to help ensure that jobs didn't destabilize family life. This view pushes us to think about the economy in a way that includes not just the firm's need for cheap labor but also the full economic effects of work-life stability.

The New Deal helped workers, their families, and the economy, but it wasn't perfect. In order to get the legislation passed, Perkins and her allies had to make compromises, some of which were unsavory. One could argue that compromising was a mistake. Yet it made the difference in corralling enough votes to pass the legislation, and later reformers have been able to undo the most egregious exclusions. And, over time, the Social Security Act and the Fair Labor Standards Act have been amended to extend coverage.

There were other omissions as well. Perkins did not push for paid sick leave or flexible working schedules (policies that I argue are essential today) for a simple reason: she didn't need to. As noted, at the time, most families had a stay-at-home wife. Perkins knew that some women worked. She also knew they needed child care and time off for maternity and sick leave. But in her era, women were not encouraged to work.

In the 1930s, Frances Perkins could usher in her New Deal reforms knowing with great confidence what families looked like and how they interacted with the economy. That's not the case today. There is a greater variety and complexity among U.S. families. Some have one parent, many have combinations of stepsiblings and stepparents, and same-sex couples lead some. But even as we've seen an increase in the variety of family types, one common characteristic is that fewer families have a stay-at-home caregiver. Overall, in 2012, only about a third of children age fourteen and under lived in a family with a full-time, stay-at-home caregiver, compared with nearly three-quarters of children in 1960. For families at the top of the income ladder, this decrease can be attributed to the fact that two parents work, whereas the further we travel down the ladder, the more likely families are to have a single, working parent.[42]

Even in her era, though, Perkins and later policymakers understood that addressing conflicts between work and family life was a serious issue. At times, they took steps to address the problem. During World War II, the nation needed workers for the war effort. The men were off fighting and women were encouraged to do their part and become a "Rosie the Riveter." Yet the lack of access to affordable, high-quality child care hindered women's employment and too often left children, especially those from poor or moderate-income families, in less-than-ideal care. In 1940, Congress passed the Lanham Act, which authorized federal grants and loans to public or private agencies for the maintenance and operation of public works. Policymakers quickly interpreted this act to include child-care facilities for mothers employed in the war effort.[43]

As soon as the war ended, however, the Lanham Act's child-care centers were closed up everywhere except in California.[44] During the hearing over what to do with the child-care centers, a Federal Works Agency official said, "We are not subsidizing an expanded educational program nor a Federal welfare program, but we are making money available to assist local communities in meeting a war need for the care of children while their mothers are engaged in war production."[45] Child care was seen as akin to "welfare"—a handout—rather than as a help-out for parents who needed to be at work.

The archetypal New Deal family headed by a male breadwinner would continue to be the norm in the three decades that followed the enactment of the reforms. This was a time when family incomes at the bottom, middle, and top grew at the same pace and in line with the productivity of the overall economy. By the early 1970s, however, families and family economics were transforming into something new. The 1950s and 1960s brought new opportunities for women—and people of color—to gain access to education and jobs, due in no small part to the passage of the Civil Rights Act and the control over the "if and when" of parenthood brought on by the introduction of the birth control pill.[46]

The added earnings of wives should have alleviated economic insecurity. But it didn't turn out that way. Even though women marched out of the home and into the job market—and families put in more hours at work—the typical family's income grew more slowly in the 1970s and 1980s than it had in the 1950s and 1960s. As we will see, up and down the income ladder, working more but not earning more continues to add to family stress and economic insecurity.

The New Deal was then; this is now. The policies advocated by Perkins made sense in a radically different social environment (even though those reforms still underpin the basic—though now inadequate—protections for today's families). At that time, the industrial workforce needed rules on maximum hours and minimum wages. They still do. But when the New Deal was introduced, families typically engaged with the economy by having one wage earner, and they needed social insurance to cover lost income when the male breadwinner couldn't support the family. They had someone at home with the time to care for those who needed it without jeopardizing their family's earnings.

But families, much like firms and governments, do not stay the same. For many reasons (some economic, some not), families look different today. Our economy has changed as well. American business has lost its Silent Partner. The boundaries between work and life are no longer clear. Having work-life policies solely derived from the 1930s makes about as much sense as giving typewriters to incoming college students. In the next few chapters, we will see how families across the income spectrum have adapted to economic changes. In the final half of the book, we will see how policy can address these changes to benefit families and the economy.

Stalled: Today's Middle Class

The middle class has been on a downhill slide since the enactment of the New Deal and the glory days of the postwar period, when income gains climbed in lockstep with broader economic growth. Beginning in the late 1970s—just as the civil rights laws were finally opening opportunities for women and African Americans to compete for jobs and houses and retirement savings plans—middle-class incomes began to fall far behind productivity gains (a measure of the value of goods and services produced by one unit of labor). The middle-class standard of living was beginning to slip relative to that of wealthier Americans.

How middle-class families coped is the story of this chapter. As we will see, the lack of sorely needed work-life policies has made a bad situation worse—for families and for businesses, too. While the New Deal policies remain important, they are no longer enough to keep families on the path of economic security, which in turn hurts our communities and the economy overall.

Figure 2.1 shows what has happened between 1948 and 2013 to the income of families in the middle of the income distribution, adjusted for inflation. This figure shows the median family across the entire economy so that we can look at the trend going back all the way to 1948. From 1948 until 1979, income rose 118 percent. Since 1979, family income has bounced around, but it has risen just 19 percent. Looking only at the middle class, which I define as families with incomes above the bottom third who are not professionals—that is, families in the top fifth in which at least one earner holds a college degree—average family income was $79,000 in 2012, about the same as it had been in the mid-1990s. The march upward has stalled.[1]

When I think about what's happened to the income of the typical U.S. family, the image that comes to mind is one that was etched

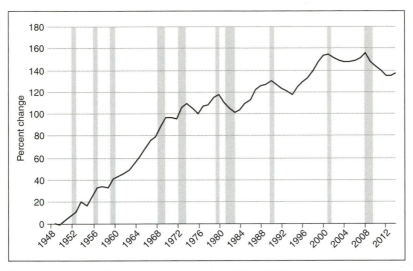

Fig. 2.1 Change in U.S. median family income, 1948 to 2013. Between 1948 and 1979, average median family income grew by 118 percent, or an annual rate of 2.6 percent. However, between 1979 and 2013, it has grown by only 19 percent, which averages out to only 0.3 percent per year. *Note:* Median income across all U.S. families, measured in 2013 dollars and indexed to 1948. Shaded areas indicate recessions as defined by the National Bureau of Economic Research.

into my memory in 1980. The Pacific Northwest, where I grew up, is known for its stunning views. If we were driving on Interstate 5 on a clear day (rare given the region's copious rainfall), my father would unfailingly exhort, "Look, the mountains!" One of the loveliest mountains in the Cascades was Mount St. Helens, which sits about 120 miles south of where I grew up. Its summit was a perfectly shaped cone, earning it the nickname "Fuji-san" after the iconic Mount Fuji of Japan. On May 18, 1980, that all changed. The mountain erupted, killing fifty-seven people. It was the most destructive volcanic eruption in recorded U.S. history. Everyone at my house felt the accompanying earthquake. The International Trade Commission estimated that the eruption caused $1.1 billion in damages to timber, infrastructure, and agriculture. Mount St. Helens no longer has a perfect peak. The eruption blasted the top right off.[2] (See Figure 2.2a and b.)

I look at Figure 2.1 and I see Mount St. Helens. The decades after the New Deal were years when families grew together. The television

Fig. 2.2a and b Mount St. Helens, before and after the 1980 eruption. *Source:* Photos courtesy Harry Glicken, U.S. Geological Survey.

reruns of *The Brady Bunch* and *Leave It to Beaver* that my generation watched after school showed an American middle class characterized by economic stability and traditional family structures. These shows idealized a middle-class life (even though many families did not live such picturesque lifestyles) that for those generations defined economic security. Dad worked outside the home in a job he held for life while Mom cared for the home and the children. The parents were married and stayed married. Something happened around 1980 that changed this picture.

The tectonic shift affected more than just incomes. The typical middle-class family looks different today than it did in the past. The sociologist Philip Cohen analyzed Census Bureau data for children aged fourteen and younger in middle-class families and found that in 1960, 69.5 percent of middle-class children lived in a family with two married parents and in which Dad alone had a job, as shown in Figure 2.3. By 2012, the latest year for which data are available, only 24.2 percent of children lived in such a family. Most middle-class children now grow up in a dual-earner or a single-parent family. Viewed with the data in Figure 2.1, Figure 2.3 shows that even as families aren't seeing the same income gains as previous generations, they also have less time at home to care for loved ones.

This reality forces us to reconsider what is necessary to achieve economic security. In the early twentieth century, a "family wage" was a wage a man needed to support his family, which typically included a stay-at-home wife, along with children and other dependents. Policymakers could provide a menu of supports that fit the typical family and the way it related to the economy. Today, about half of middle-class children live in a family with one earner and half with two. This nullifies the concept of a single family wage and puts a clear limit on the effectiveness of the supports currently in place.

Mount St. Helens will never return to the exact same shape and structure it had before the eruption. Similarly, I am not arguing that the American family can—or should—return to the way it was portrayed on *Leave It to Beaver*. The mid-twentieth-century American

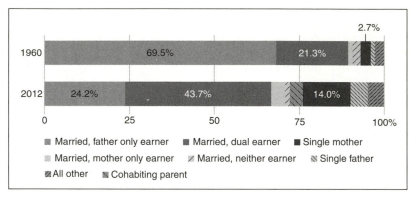

Fig. 2.3 Living arrangements of children aged 14 and under in middle-class families, 1960 and 2012. In 1960, 70 percent of middle-class children lived in a two-parent family where their father was the sole breadwinner, compared with only a quarter in 2012. Compare these changes in family composition between 1960 and 2012 of the middle-class families shown here with the changes in composition of low-income families shown in Fig. 3.2 and professional families in Fig. 4.2. *Note:* Data on cohabiting available only for 2012.

middle class had a number of features we now consider unacceptable. The way of life represented on our television screens kept women off the career path and excluded people of color, particularly African Americans, from economic opportunities. Part of what's changed for the good—albeit often too slowly—is that it's no longer okay to exclude anyone from economic opportunity.

We turn now to the strategies that middle-class families use as they try to cope with the erosion of economic stability and where they could use help. In the two chapters that follow, we'll look at the strategies of low-income and higher-income professional families to see whether they echo those of middle-class families and where and how the help they need differs from that needed by middle-class families.

Economic Changes

Mount St. Helens erupted because tectonic plates far below the earth's surface moved, causing gases to accumulate and, eventually, explode. What changed the trajectory of U.S. family income? This question keeps economists busy. We know that we cannot blame weak family income growth on a slow-growing or unproductive economy. Between 1979 and 2007, just before the housing bubble burst and the Great Recession began, U.S. gross domestic product—that is, the sum total of all the goods and services produced in the United States—rose by 130 percent while U.S. corporate profits (nonfinancial) grew by 162 percent, after accounting for inflation. Over that same time, however, typical family income grew by only 19 percent, as shown in Figure 2.1. America grew richer. American companies grew richer. But the typical U.S. family's income did not grow in tandem.[3]

We can see this in Figure 2.4, which takes Figure 2.1 and adds productivity. There is a clear shift in the trends right around 1980. From the 1950s to the 1970s, family income and productivity grew together. As production rose, incomes increased at about the same rate. That's no longer the case after 1980; since that time we have seen a growing gap between productivity and income. Between 1979 and 2007, productivity increased by 95 percent, that is, the economy produced 95 percent more goods and services per hour, about five times the pace of growth in family incomes. In plain English, even as U.S. workers produced more and more goods and services during each hour, year after year, family incomes did not rise at the same pace with productivity. The growing gap between family income and economic growth represents a growing fault line in the U.S economy—and is a key driver of economic inequality. The close relationship between the two held historically in many countries in the postwar era, but it has broken down in the United States since the 1970s.[4]

Since middle-class families get most of their income from employment, as opposed to capital investments or state support, we have to look at what happened inside the workplace to understand why productivity and income grew apart. Some economists argue that globalization puts U.S. workers in direct competition with workers abroad and explains the decoupling of productivity and workers'

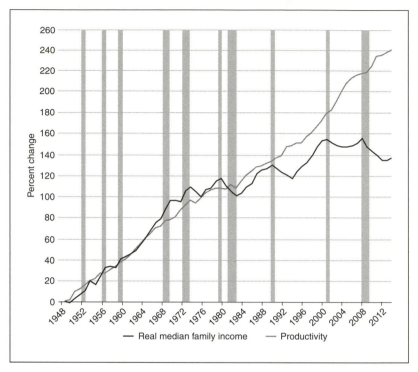

Fig. 2.4 Change in U.S. median family income and productivity, 1948 to 2013. From 1980 onward, median family income growth slowed, dropping from an average annual rate of 2.6 percent between 1948 and 1979 to just 0.3 percent from 1979 to 2013. However, productivity continued to rise at about the same pace since 1948, which means that by 2013, it had outpaced income growth by 104 percent. *Note:* Median income across all U.S. families, measured in 2013 dollars and indexed to 1948. Shaded areas indicate recessions as defined by the National Bureau of Economic Research.

wages, which then drives the trends in family income. As developing countries began to catch up and their manufacturing sector matured, their lower labor costs meant that, to compete, U.S. firms were forced to either close their doors or slash costs by packing up and moving abroad themselves.

Other economists suggest that technological changes have made many middle-class jobs redundant. Because of new technologies, employers no longer need whole categories of employees. This has meant the extinction of many formerly solid middle-class jobs:

ATMs have replaced bank tellers, robots have replaced workers on the shop floor, and voice-recognition software has put typists out of business.

Still others point to the fall in the inflation-adjusted value of minimum wage and the decline in unionization. Without a solid wage floor and, increasingly, without a seat at the bargaining table, working families have lost out.

It is not the purpose of this book to adjudicate among all these possible explanations. But a common thread connecting them is an economic transformation characterized by wages that failed to keep pace with productivity and a shift in the balance of power of U.S. working-class and middle-class workers—and even some professional workers—vis-à-vis employers. This power shift affects how middle-class families interact with the economy and what they can demand from employers to help them. It also signals the need to revisit the twentieth-century understanding of what governments, firms, and families owe one another.

From the perspective of the family, this means a decline in the share of good jobs. A job that can support a middle-class lifestyle includes decent pay, as well as benefits, such as health insurance coverage, paid time off, predictable schedules, and a retirement plan. For today's workers, finding a good, middle-class job is harder than it was a generation or two ago. The economists John Schmitt and Janelle Jones find that since 1979, the U.S. economy has lost about a third of its capacity to produce good jobs, that is, jobs with wages at least at their 1979 level (adjusted for inflation), and employer-provided health insurance and a retirement plan. What is remarkable is that the decline in the share of good jobs has occurred even though U.S. workers are today on average better educated and older than they had been a few decades ago, characteristics that normally signal higher pay.[5]

To understand what has happened to middle-class families, we have to start by focusing on what happened to the jobs of the traditional family breadwinner: men. Family income didn't grow in line with productivity because men's earnings didn't grow in line with productivity. In the 1950s and 1960s, men saw solid gains in pay year after year. In the early 1970s, however, men's earnings hit a plateau. Over the ensuing two decades, into the early 1990s, the typical working man didn't see his paycheck rise at all, after accounting for inflation. By the mid-2000s, most men had been bringing home the same paycheck year after year for nearly two decades. Overall, from 1979 to 2012, average earnings for men in middle-class families fell by 9.5 percent.[6]

Falling earnings were the result of both falling hourly pay and reduced working hours. One of the most striking trends in the U.S. economy has been the long downward trend in male employment. In 1979, a man brought home a paycheck in 84.4 percent of middle-class families. By 2007—just before the Great Recession—that share had fallen to just below three-quarters. The crisis was hard on male employment, and it has not recovered. As of 2012, there was a male earner in 76.3 percent of middle-class families. Among developed countries, this trend is unique to the United States; we have one of the lowest rates of male labor force participation of any advanced economy.[7]

In the 1930s when Frances Perkins put together the New Deal, most families relied on a single breadwinner, typically a man. His job was the core of the family's budget. But in recent decades, his earnings have stalled. American middle-class families have had to find a new route to economic security and a middle-class lifestyle. They have a few choices. They can downsize their expectations of what constitutes a middle-class lifestyle, the women within them can enter the labor force, or they can take on more debt and cross their fingers that happy days will be just around the corner. Middle-class families often do all three.

Strategy 1: Lower Expectations

Stalled incomes for middle-class families wouldn't cause economic insecurity if costs fell at the same time. For some items, this has been the case. Many of us can now afford to carry powerful computers in our back pockets, and the relatively low price of basic electric appliances means that most homes now have a television, washer (and dryer), dishwasher, and cabinets filled with gadgetry. Food costs also continue to fall relative to inflation. But the prices for many of the other big-ticket items that define a middle-class lifestyle have grown faster—in some case, far faster—than typical family income. A home in a neighborhood with good schools, a car or two that work, doctor visits when necessary, and enough money to pay a child's college tuition—none of these come cheap.[8]

Big-ticket expenses are typically fixed costs, which can be near impossible to cut back on in the short run if the family wants—or needs—to trim their budget. It may take months—or years—to sell a home, many are locked into multiyear car leases or loans, and most of us can change our health insurance coverage only during the "open enrollment season" in the fall. Further, with big-ticket items, saving money can actually cost money. Cutting back on the cost of housing may require moving, which might save money in the long run (if the family isn't selling at a rock-bottom price) but entail short-run costs for the boxes, the moving van, the expense of finding a new home and selling the old one—not to mention the emotional costs of transitioning to a new church, synagogue, or mosque. It also may be hard on children to change schools, which may affect their academic performance.[9]

Housing is one of the largest expenses for the typical middle-class family. This expense can eat up a fifth or more of total take-home pay. Many middle-class families stretch—a lot—to afford the right house. As the economist Robert Frank documents, the number of hours that the typical earner must toil each month to afford the median-priced house has almost doubled since 1970. In some cases, a house is just a home and what people are willing to spend isn't anyone else's concern. But housing isn't just about where you live; it's about where your children go to school. The United States is home to one of the most baffling school-financing arrangements in the developed world. We fund primary and secondary school through taxes on local homeowners. This means that wealthier neighborhoods can marshal more resources for their schools, giving children in those communities greater advantages and children in nonrich communities fewer. Research shows that increased per-pupil spending helps boost educational outcomes. So parents feel pressure to buy or rent a home in the districts with the best schools, adding significant expenses to the family budget.[10]

Middle-class families also find it hard to cut back on health care. For decades, U.S. health-care costs have been rising much faster than inflation. Families in the United States spend more per person on health care than their counterparts in any other developed country. As of 2013, the typical person in the United States spent approximately 62 percent more for health care than their neighbor in Canada. Yet we aren't any healthier and we don't live any longer—and, still, not everyone is covered. The rate of health-care cost increases in the United States has slowed down in recent years, but whether the decline has been due to slow growth of the economy in the wake of the Great Recession, changes in the health-care industry, or the Affordable Care Act—perhaps better known as Obamacare—remains up for debate. Regardless of the current trend, the new health law will, with luck, reduce the rate of future increases in health-care costs. It is currently increasing health insurance coverage and improving health outcomes, but we still have a long way to go.[11]

Middle-class families often also have to find ways to help cover the cost of caring for their aging parents. Over the past fifteen years, the number of adults providing care to a parent has increased three-fold. Thanks to Medicare—the federal program that provides health insurance coverage for those over age sixty-five—most families invest more in time spent with elders than in dollars to care for them, but families still have high out-of-pocket costs and find little support for long-term palliative care outside the home. In a 2014 survey of family caregivers by Caring.com, nearly half (46 percent) of respondents spent more than $5,000 annually on caregiving expenses and a third (30 percent) spent more than $10,000 annually. These expenses come later in life when families may have had time to save up. But we've also seen the rise of what the sociologist Dorothy Miller termed "the sandwich generation," those individuals—one of every eight Americans—who now care both for children still at home and for an aging parent, while trying to save for their children' college tuitions and their own retirement.[12]

Investments in the skills necessary to get a middle-class job have also become more expensive because of the rising cost of higher education. When I was getting ready to head off to college and my mother and I sat down to sort through the financial aid forms, she told me that she had worked her way through college. She got a summer job, saved her money, and was able to cover tuition and room and board for the school year. At the time, I was working as a lifeguard, happy to be earning about 50 percent more than the minimum wage. I knew that even working every day all summer, I could never pay for college. I thought she was joking—or that this was one of those "when I was young, we walked ten miles through the snow to get to school" stories parents tell children to make them stop whining. To satisfy my curiosity, I looked up the numbers. When my mom went to college in the late 1960s, a minimum-wage worker would have had to put in just under 800 hours to afford one year of the average in-state tuition, fees, room, and board at a four-year public university. This amounts to 100 working days—more or less the summer vacation. Today, that same student would have to work full-time for a year plus an additional three months to cover the cost of school.[13]

The high cost—and often large debts—for college may be an excellent investment, but not always. In 1979, the earnings of those with a college degree were about 40 percent greater than those with only a high school degree, but by 2013 the college grad's earnings were 80 percent higher. That's a significant increase. In fact, as many economists have shown, in recent decades workers with a college degree have seen faster rising earnings than those without. Still, the high cost of college is a large financial burden, and many students who start don't end up graduating; they just end up in debt. Further, getting a degree doesn't pay off for everyone. About one in five men aged 25 to 34 with a college degree actually earns less than the typical, similarly aged man with a high school diploma.[14]

Finally, middle-class families are faced with the high cost of care for their youngest members. Families—rightfully so—may not want to scrimp on these costs because doing so may mean sacrificing quality. Child-care costs are especially challenging because they come at a time when parents themselves tend to be young and near the low point of both their career earnings and their lifetime savings. According to the Children's Defense Fund, in 2013, the typical cost to keep a four-year-old in full-time day care ranged from $4,800 to $17,304, depending on the state. At the high end of the range, this is just about the same as the total cost of sending an eighteen-year-old to a four-year public university (room, board, tuition, and fees).[15]

Strategy 2: Mom, the New Breadwinner

For many families, achieving economic security meant that the American Wife got a paying job. I was born in 1970, a time when only a third of mothers with children under the age of six worked outside the home and nearly half of all families with children had a breadwinner dad and a stay-at-home mom. That wasn't my family. My mom had a job. While we didn't know it at the time, she was part of a national—and even global—trend. During the 1970s, an additional 14.1 million women entered the workforce, followed by another 11.5 million in the 1980s. The pace and magnitude of the shift from not working outside the home to holding down a paying job were most pronounced within the middle class. Most women working in the 1980s who wouldn't have done so twenty years earlier were either married or college-educated middle-class women.[16]

The added hours of work for women in middle-class families made the difference between family income rising or falling. Figure 2.5 shows that between 1979 and 2012, middle-class families saw their income rise by a total of $7,697 (in 2013 dollars), and of that total the single largest contributor was the rise in women's hours of work, which accounted for $5,057 of the total increase. The second-biggest factor was women's pay, which contributed $4,625 of the total increase. Combined, women's greater hours and higher pay are equal to more than the total rise in middle-class family

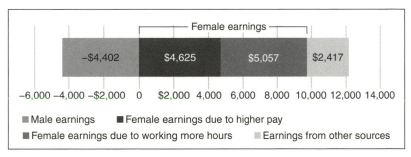

Fig. 2.5 Effect of women's earnings on total income of U.S. middle-class families, 1979 to 2012. Between 1979 and 2012, middle-class families saw their income rise by a total of $7,697 (in 2013 dollars). The single largest contributor to middle-class incomes was the rise in women's hours of work, closely followed by the rise in women's pay. Without women's added hours and pay, middle-class incomes would have fallen. *Note:* Analysis done at the household level. Sample includes households with at least one person aged 16 to 64. Individuals with zero or missing personal income dropped from sample.

income—meaning that without them, family income would have fallen. Changes in men's earnings dragged down family income by $4,402. Today's middle-class men don't bring home the earnings they used to.

The stagnation in middle-class income shown in Figure 2.1, combined with the reality that incomes would have fallen without women's added hours and higher pay, means that we have to take seriously the idea that women took jobs because they and their families needed them to. Whether women and their families liked it or not, the cold, hard truth was that they needed the extra earnings. Often there was not much choice.

This is not the story President Nixon told Americans in 1971 when he vetoed comprehensive child care on the recommendation of Pat Buchanan. He framed the question of whether middle-class women work outside the home as a private choice. In Nixon's reasoning, it was not the role of federal government to take steps to render working outside the home an easy choice for middle-class mothers. With his veto pen, Nixon tried to force reality to bend to his (and his conservative advisers') unrealistic notion that most middle-class families have a real choice over whether mom works or is at home. But for today's families—and even families as far back as the 1970s—the only path to economic security is for both parents to have a paying job.

Nixon's view didn't resonate with my family's experience in the 1970s, nor does it resonate today. In a *New York Times* column, journalist Nicholas Kulish, born four years after Nixon's veto, laid out an argument for why the men of his generation couldn't support a family on their own, pointing out that middle-class families need women's earnings just to make ends meet. As he put it, "These days, Ward Cleaver wouldn't be able to afford a house in the suburbs or Beaver's tuition—unless June went to work, too. No version of the American dream is cheap." He also pushed back on the idea that women's employment is a cultural rather than an economic issue:

> The switch from the single-breadwinner to the dual-income family has less to do with values than with economics. There have been some structural changes in the economy since "Leave It to Beaver" went off the air. . . . Expressions like "choosing to have a career" have misled some women. Not working is no longer a choice for many. It's a luxury—or at a minimum, a serious sacrifice.[17]

This is an anecdote, of course. But even with the best data available, researchers cannot say with 100 percent accuracy whether women work outside the home as a choice, in which case policymakers do not need to intervene, or whether they enter the workforce out of necessity, to make ends meet. The reality is that multiple trends overlap. While male earnings fell, making the dual-earner family an economic necessity, other events opened up new choices and opportunities for women. The factors that pushed some women into the labor market, such as needing to work to pay the rent, were more important for some women while others were pulled in by new opportunities.

There is truth to the idea that women have more choices and economic opportunities than ever before. One advance was the invention of the birth control pill, first made available to the public in 1960. The Pill gave women unprecedented freedom to decide when they would make investments in education and careers and when they would start a family. By the early 1970s, after Supreme Court cases in 1972 and 1974 overturned state laws that prohibited prescribing the Pill to unmarried women, contraception was widely available. It gave women (and men) sexual freedom, but more than that, it meant that for the first time in history, women had effective control over when they had children. This was a fundamental work-life policy.[18]

The 1960s also saw the rise of the civil rights movement, which led to passage of the 1964 Civil Rights Act granting women and people of color far greater access to higher education and career paths, boosting family incomes in the process. In the decades just after World War II, when the United States saw strong growth in family incomes overall, Jim Crow laws meant that discrimination against African Americans was commonplace. Title VII of the law made this kind of long-standing discriminatory practice illegal and made it possible for those previously excluded to find and keep good jobs. As a result, there has been a remarkable increase in the share of African American and Latino families in the middle class. Between 1979 and 2012, the share of African American families in the middle class grew from 7.9 to 11.2 percent and from 4.4 to 14.8 percent for Latinos.[19]

These legal changes also profoundly altered women's economic opportunities and responsibilities. Whereas in 1960 women were routinely fired when they married or became pregnant, by 1978, a series of court decisions and the 1978 Pregnancy Discrimination Act made it clear that this was now illegal. Job advertisements could no longer ask for a "pretty-looking, cheerful gal," and firms had to stop openly discriminating against women in terms of pay and promotions. Whereas in 1960, many universities still refused to accept women students, by the early 1980s, all Ivy League schools had gone coed. Today, women earn six in ten baccalaureate degrees and about one in two law degrees.[20]

It's important to recognize that the addition of "sex" in the Civil Rights Act was meant as a joke. The idea that women should have the same education and career choices as men was not supposed to become law. When Congressman Howard W. Smith of Virginia added "sex" to Title VII of the Civil Rights Act, his supposed intention was not to hasten equality of the sexes but to kill the bill. His critics say he believed that sexual equality was so laughable that there was no way a bill that aimed to make women and men equal could pass the House of Representatives. Of course, President Johnson signed the act into law and equality of the sexes was no longer a joke; it was the law of the land. But dismissive attitudes about the economic importance of women's earnings lingered on.[21]

The civil rights movement boosted incomes. As women of all races and ethnicities entered the labor force and gained education and on-the-job experience, their pay rose. Between 1979 and 2007, the end of the last economic peak, the average working woman saw her wages rise by 26 percent, and, as of 2013 (the latest year for which data are available), the typical woman working full-time all year brings home 78 percent of what a man in a similar position earns. Women of color don't earn as much: in 2013, African American women earned 64 percent and Latinas 56 percent of what white men earned. While this certainly is not parity—and on-the-job segregation and discrimination continue to hamper women's earnings—it is a significant improvement. In 1970, women earned only 59 cents on the male dollar.[22]

Higher pay means that women's earnings are increasingly important to family economic well-being. In 2012, women in middle-class families brought home 37.3 percent of all earnings, up from 24.9 percent in 1979. Over that time, the share of middle-class mothers who were breadwinners (bringing home at least as much as their husbands or as single, working mothers) or co-breadwinners (bringing home at least a quarter of the family's earnings) rose from 41.4 percent to 60.8 percent.[23]

But all this work adds a layer of conflict between work and family life—in ways that no longer neatly map onto the traditional bargain between government, families, and firms. Longer work hours have left families struggling to cope with care issues, for children, the sick, and the elderly, as well as the daily chores that all families have to do. As women have moved out of the home and into the workplace, a caregiving gap and a "time bind" have emerged. Home production—all the work that goes into making sure there is food in the fridge, dinner on the table, clean clothes in the morning, and everything else that keeps a household functioning—is now often outsourced or bickered over by tired and grumpy people when they return from their "day" jobs, which often run well beyond the traditional 9-to-5 time frame. This leaves people "stressed out": According to an October 2014 Gallup poll, 40 percent of all adults experienced "stress a lot yesterday."[24]

Families with children face an especially acute time crunch, and they report more stress than others, in no small part because of the incompatibility of work and home life. Between 1979 and 2012, the rise in earnings and hours of women in middle-class, married-couple families with children accounts for 99 percent of the total growth in income for these families; 32 percent of the total is in the rise of these mothers' hours alone. This helps explain why, according to the Gallup poll cited above, 45 percent of adults with children under age eighteen in the home experienced "stress a lot" yesterday compared with 37 percent of adults without a child in the home— still a high share. According to a 2014 survey by the American Psychological Association, parents are more stressed out than nonparents. Parents—compared with their childless counterparts—are more likely to report that their stress has increased in the past year and that they feel as though they aren't doing a good job managing it.[25]

Maybe families would be less stressed if only the American Wife would go back home. It would help families cut back on child-care and elder-costs cost. Some families choose this path. Having a full-time, stay-at-home caregiver is the right path for some. But many others see both short-term and long-term costs to this strategy. In the

short term, families who choose not to have someone employed outside the home pay a steep economic price that does not compensate
for the expected savings. Over the past four decades, the typical income of married-couple families with a wife who doesn't work outside the home has seen no growth. It's about the same today as it was
in the early 1970s, accounting for inflation.[26]

There are also long-term wage penalties for leaving the labor
force, even for just a few years. The overwhelming majority of women,
including those who are not working now, will work outside the
home at some point in their lives. This adds to the pressure families
feel to keep Mom—and Dad—in the workforce. Even if they can
get by without the earnings today, they'll need that extra income
over a lifetime (and the retirement savings, too!). While the option
of having a stay-at-home caregiver is still on the table, it's increasingly rare—especially within middle-class families, as shown in
Figure 2.3.[27]

This all means that conflicts between work and family life aren't
only women's issues; they're family issues. We see this reflected in
the data. According to the 2008 National Study of the Changing
Workforce, the majority of fathers in dual-earner couples (60 percent)
report that they experience "some or a lot" of work-family conflict,
as do nearly half of mothers (47 percent). This is a remarkable shift
in a short period. In 1977, only 35 percent of fathers and 41 percent
of mothers in dual-earner couples reported work-family conflict.
Men report more conflict between work and family life because
few families have that iconic 1950s American Wife at home, even as
they still need someone with the time to keep family life running
smoothly. Without some support for workers to be caregivers, too,
everyone—not just Mom—is more stressed out. Time is in short
supply.[28]

We all know many people who wrestle with conflicts between the
demands of their job and their family's needs. Like most new parents, my sister, Michelle, and her husband both worked when they
had their first child, and they were struggling to adjust to this new
little person in their life while holding on to their jobs. Michelle

needed her job. She still lives in the Seattle area where we grew up, and the traffic remains abominable. She wanted to adjust her schedule to leave work a half hour early, making up the time during her lunch hour, so she could get home forty-five minutes earlier each evening, in time to see her daughter before bed. Her boss agreed as a special favor to her, but he also reassigned one of her top clients. And because this was a "special perk" just for her, her colleagues were resentful. She felt like an outcast. She was coping, but for her, it felt like a no-win situation.

Strategy 3: Debt

One thing is certain: working more and trying to keep down expenses wasn't enough to prevent the stall in middle-class incomes. We might logically assume that when family income stopped growing, family spending would remain flat as well. That's not what happened. Families maintained their spending by borrowing, much of it against the rising value of their homes. As costs have risen, families have begun borrowing to buy homes, to buy cars, to put their children through school, and for anything else. Up until the 1980s, across all families, total debt was about 60 percent of annual income. Over the following decades, debt rose significantly, until the housing bubble burst in 2008. By then, families' debts were equal to a whopping 130 percent of after-tax income. Even now, six years after the economic crisis, household debt is equal to 102 percent of after-tax income.[29]

In the 1990s and 2000s, families could use debt as a way to maintain spending in no small part because of the rise in home values. Between 1990 and 2008, the price of the typical home increased by more than 250 percent, after accounting for inflation. Families began to realize that lower prevailing interest rates—and a rise in easy-to-get-loans—meant that they could tap into this rising value. They could refinance their mortgage and take out cash or they could add a second mortgage or home equity line. Between the fourth quarters of 1991 and 2008, the share of single-family home refinancing through which homeowners "cashed out" value from their

homes nearly tripled, from 19.8 percent to 53.6 percent. In plain English, people began using their homes like ATMs. This extra money
reverberated throughout the economy.[30]

Yet, the rise in mortgage debt wasn't all about refinancing to take
out cash. Higher mortgages were also a way to ensure that families
were living in neighborhoods with the best schools—or at least not
the worst ones. As home prices skyrocketed during the housing
bubble, many families faced a tough choice: they could either borrow
beyond their means or risk living in a home in a lower-quality school
district, which would potentially lead to implications for their
children's future ability to move up the economic ladder.

Families have tapped into all kinds of debt, not just mortgages.
"Revolving consumer credit," which is mostly credit card debt, hit
an all-time high of $1,021 billion in April 2008. It has since fallen to
$901 billion, but this is still high in historical terms. And year after
year, students and their parents take on ever-higher levels of debt to
pay for college. During the 2010–11 academic year, more than half
(57 percent) of students attending a public four-year college graduated with student debt, with the typical student borrowing $23,800.
Federal student aid has shifted away from grants, which do not need
to be repaid, toward loans. But families still borrow. The scale of the
shift boggles the mind. In the 2000s, loans constituted about half of
a typical student's financial aid package, up from about 20 percent
in the 1970s.[31]

To be sure, not all borrowing by families went to pay for better
houses in better school districts, cars, education, health care, child
care, and elder care. Lots of families used their added borrowing to
go on spending sprees and take vacations they couldn't really afford.
Even so, the actual distribution of spending shows that frivolity was
a minor cause of family debt.

Taking on debt isn't necessarily a bad thing. It can be an excellent short-term solution to a cash-flow problem. So long as you will
have the money to pay back the loan, it can be an ideal strategy. Borrowing for long-term investments or to smooth spending over a lifetime can help families acquire things they need when they're young
and pay them off gradually. A college degree, a home, or a car may

all be necessary for getting a good job or raising a family. It's good that families don't have to save up first—very few of us would ever be able to afford those things when we actually need them.

But too much debt or debt that patches over falling incomes that don't go back up can lead to real problems. When families get into financial trouble, it's more often than not because of an unanticipated health-care crisis. According to an analysis of 2007 data published in the *American Journal of Medicine*, which is consistent with a more recent study by the online financial firm NerdWallet, approximately three in five bankruptcies follow a major health crisis, not a spending binge. And, if we've learned anything from the past decade, it's that an economy built on debt is inherently unstable.[32]

Debt is not a long-term solution for lack of income. As wages failed to keep pace with productivity, families had a few options for how to cope. They could pare back their spending, work more, or borrow more. They did all three but now, especially in the wake of the financial crisis of 2008, the options for borrowing more are increasingly limited. In 2008, the collapse of the housing market and the ensuing economic crisis led to a sharp fall in borrowing as lenders pared back and home prices plummeted. While debt remains high—as of the end of 2014, total household debt in the United States amounted to $11.83 trillion, a mere 6.7 percent below the peak in the third quarter of 2008—the ability of families to use this as a coping strategy may be near its end.[33]

Tough Choices, Time Crunches

Imagine for a moment that I told you only that middle-class women put in more hours at work and we made significant progress closing the gender pay gap. On that evidence alone, you might assume that U.S. families were much richer today than they had been decades ago. You might assume that women's greater employment was a choice that families made because it improved their economic outcomes. Maybe they experience a bit of a time crunch, but logically, with two earners rather than one and more combined hours of work, incomes should have grown much faster. Maybe not twice as fast, but at least as fast as the rise in women's earnings. You probably wouldn't conjure up a picture of posteruption Mount St. Helens as an apt comparison. But as Figure 2.1 showed, the trends don't look good. Even with the added earnings of wives in married households, typical family income grew more slowly between the mid-1970s and today than it had in the three decades following World War II, when families typically had one earner. We've lost lots of family time but not gained a lot of money—certainly, not enough to pay for all we've lost.

Yet, even as women put in more hours at work, families continue to prioritize the work that gets done inside the home. As shown in Figure 2.6, both mothers and fathers still spend just as much—or more—time with their children than was the case before both parents typically worked. Between 1965 and 2012, mothers increased time spent on child care from 10.2 to 11.8 hours per week and reduced their hours of housework from 31.9 to 17.6 hours per week, all while increasing their work hours (on average) from 8.4 to 21.7 hours per week. This is consistent with research indicating that by 2000, working mothers were recording as much time caring for their children as nonworking mothers did in 1975. Figure 2.6 also shows that fathers have more than doubled their time with children, increasing time spent on child care from 2.5 to 7.1 hours per week. They have also doubled their time spent on housework from 4.4 to 8.8 hours per week.[34]

The American Wife is no longer a feature of the typical middle-class household. The rise in the number of working mothers had a big effect on the lives of middle-class families. Family economics no longer presume that men earn a family wage; families combine earnings to establish a family income. But families cannot work much more, especially not without addressing the conflicts between jobs and home life.

Changes in how families interact with the economy are counter to key assumptions of the New Deal–era policy package. The understanding of what governments, firms, and families owe one another that Frances Perkins articulated with the Social Security Act, the

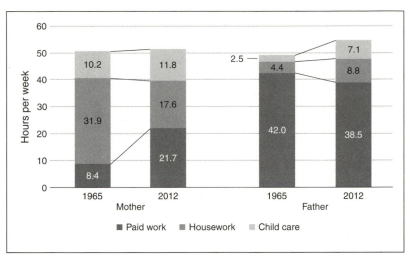

Fig. 2.6 U.S. parents' time use, in hours per week, 1965 and 2012. The difference in how mothers and fathers spend their time has shrunk. Between 1965 and 2012, mothers nearly tripled their hours of paid work and reduced their hours on housework by a third, while fathers have doubled their time on child care and housework.

National Labor Relations Act, and the Fair Labor Standards Act was right for her era. But while this foundation continues to support economic security, it isn't sufficient for today's families. The agreement is off balance, and families are bearing most of the weight. It no longer makes sense to present a set of prowork policies that fail to acknowledge that most families do not have a stay-at-home caregiver.

Everyone has a story to tell. In the end, my sister felt trapped in a job that wasn't working for her and her family. She quit. One might argue that she was forced out. This decision pushed her family down the income ladder and added stress of a different kind. She became one of the one in five families with a full-time stay-at-home mother. Over the next few months, she called me often to talk through ideas for how she and her husband could reduce expenses. We discussed how to cook from scratch—and then there was the call to say that she wouldn't be able to afford to fly out for a planned visit.

My sister has made it work, but at a cost to her career and her family budget. She and her husband worry about paying for college, and things got scary during the Great Recession amid talk of lay-offs at her husband's job. They've been lucky so far. Even so, now that her children are in school and she wants to get back into the workplace, it's been a real struggle. The lack of available jobs certainly hasn't made that transition any easier. In the end, she traded one kind of work-life stress for another.

My sister left her job because of an inflexible workplace. Compare her story to that of a woman I met a few years ago. She was a reporter. She called to thank me for a report I'd just released on work-life issues and to share her story with me. She was working, even though she had a toddler at home. Her family thought she was "crazy" for working since all "her" earnings went to pay for child care. (I put "her" in quotes because she also expressed frustration that no one talked about child care when her husband got a job.) She had been trying to explain that she couldn't afford to quit. She felt that if she dropped out of the workforce, she might not be able to get back into journalism. Besides, her toddler would soon be old enough for kindergarten, cutting their child-care costs. So she stayed at work because she liked and needed her job and feared not being able to get back later on.

The reporter's and my sister's financial situations were about the same in the short run—my sister didn't have an income, but she didn't have child-care expenses; the journalist had an income, but her salary was about equal to child-care expenses. Neither family had good options. They had tough choices, but at least they both had a choice. If child care were cheaper or if work were more flexible, both would have had even better options. As we'll learn in the next chapter, many low-income families have also lost time, but they have even fewer coping mechanisms than the middle class.

Stuck: Today's Low-Income Families

In the last chapter, we learned how the upward trajectory of America's middle class has stalled. Families have coped by working more, but these added hours haven't delivered much economic security. If financial stability has become more elusive for today's middle-class families, what does this mean for those with incomes just below those of the middle class?

In the post–World War II Golden era decades, even families within the bottom third of the income distribution could be economically secure. It seemed most everyone considered themselves middle class. When I was young, I would go with my grandmother to her Episcopal church on Lopez Island. One Wednesday evening the church's study group was discussing economic issues. The deacon leading the conversation asked who thought they were middle class. Everyone from rich pensioners with second homes to unemployed lumberjacks raised their hands. This evokes radio host Garrison Keillor's famous sign-off, "Well, that's the news from Lake Wobegon, where all the women are strong, all the men are good looking, and all the children are above average." The same logic Keillor is poking fun at is true for the idea of a "middle" class: in defiance of statistical reality, people with radically different incomes considered themselves in the middle rather than at the ends of the income distribution. The fact that so many people used to think of themselves as middle class said something about our values and the general feeling of economic security at the time I was growing up.

This identification with the middle class has changed in recent years. People don't just feel as though they've stalled temporarily; they report feeling stuck, unable to reach the economic security associated with the middle class. Surveys now show that people are more likely to consider themselves lower or working class than middle class. According to a 2012 *USA Today*/Gallup poll, just under half of the American public (42 percent) considered themselves middle class, down from 48 percent in 2000. At the same time, 41 percent saw themselves as lower or working class, up from a third in 2000.[1]

When Mount St. Helens erupted, we all felt the earth's quake. But my family's life wasn't upended. Many other lives, livelihoods, and neighborhoods were lost, however. When the blast occurred, it caused the largest known debris avalanche in recorded history. A fast-moving current of hot gas and rock poured down the mountainside in a massive mudflow that flattened everything in its course over a 230-square-mile area. More than 200 homes were destroyed, as were more than 4 billion board feet of saleable timber. Ultimately, more than 65 million cubic yards of sediment were deposited in the lower Cowlitz and Columbia Rivers. The eruption of Mount St. Helens left parts of my home state literally stuck in the mud.[2]

That's what life looks like for many self-identified lower- and working-class families today. They're stuck. All families have had to cope with the marked changes in our economy, but while truly middle-class families experienced an income stall—with earnings growing much slower than in the decades just after World War II— low-income families have found themselves not moving up the income ladder at all. Figure 3.1 shows the change in average income (in inflation-adjusted dollars) between 1979 and 2012 for low-income families compared with middle-class families. Unlike middle-class families, low-income families, which I define as those in the bottom third of the income distribution, have seen their income fall. Between 1979 and 2012, income fell by 2.4 percent, compared with a rise of 10.9 percent for middle-class families. In 2012, among low-income families, average annual income was $23,000 per year. That's nearly $600 *less* than in 1979. For those at the bottom, there's been no growth in family income since 1979. None. Nada. Zilch.

No growth for low-income families, combined with stalling middle-class incomes, means that it's harder for those at the bottom

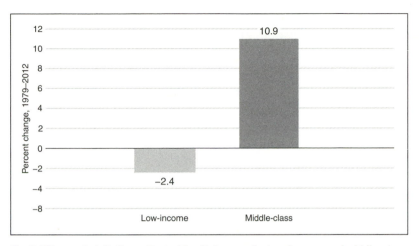

Fig. 3.1 Change in inflation-adjusted family income for low-income and middle-class families, 1979 to 2012. Between 1979 and 2012, middle-class families saw their average income rise by 10.9 percent, while low-income families saw theirs fall by 2.4 percent. *Note:* Analysis done at the household level. Sample includes households with at least one person aged 25 to 64. Individuals with zero or missing personal income dropped from sample.

to move up. It's not just that low-income families have seen no income growth; it's that they now need to jump higher to move into the middle class. Economists call this jump "economic mobility," whether and how families move from one income class to another. Contrary to myth, we're a nation of little upward economic mobility, and we lag behind other developed economies, among them our neighbor Canada. People become stuck at both ends of the income ladder, with few at the bottom moving up and few at the top moving down. Two-thirds of sons and half of daughters who grow up in low-income families never earn much more than their fathers did. One reason for this is that, as the economist Raj Chetty and his coauthors put it, the "rungs of the ladder have grown further apart." As incomes in the middle grew just a little faster than those in the bottom, movement up to the next rung became just that much harder.[3]

On top of these economic changes, lower-income families have become increasingly complex and unstable. Relationships don't tend

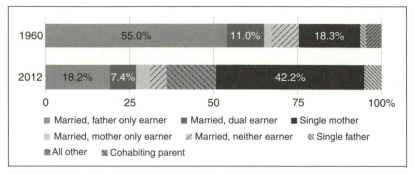

Fig. 3.2 Living arrangements of children aged 14 and under in low-income families, 1960 and 2012. In 1960, over half (55 percent) of low-income children lived in a two-parent family where their father was the sole breadwinner and a fifth (18.3 percent) lived in single-mother families. By 2012, these percentages were mostly reversed. Compare the changes in family composition between 1960 and 2012 of the lower-income families shown here with the changes in composition of middle-class families shown in Fig. 2.3 and professional families in Fig. 4.2. *Note:* Data on cohabitating available only for 2012.

to last as long in low-income families as they do in middle-class or professional families. Compare Figure 3.2 which shows changes between 1960 and 2012 in family composition and work patterns for children in low-income families, with Figure 2.3 on changes in the middle class. Among children age fourteen and under living in families in the bottom third today, nearly half live in a single-parent family—42.2 percent in a single-mother family and 5.2 percent in a single-father family. This wasn't the case in 1960. Most children growing up today in low-income families will spend at least some time living with just one parent or with one parent who changes partners over time. These changes in family structure mean that women's jobs are very important to the economic well-being of low-income families.[4]

Not every low-income family is headed by a single parent—not by a long shot. We also see low-income families with a traditional male breadwinner and a stay-at-home mom. Recently, there has been an uptick in the number of families with a stay-at-home mother, especially in the years after the economic crisis that took hold in 2008.

Most of the increase has been among women who have less than a college degree and are on average younger than working mothers. They are also much more likely than working mothers to be poor: one-third (34 percent) of stay-at-home mothers live in poverty, compared with one in eight working mothers (12 percent). Stay-at-home mothers are also more likely than working mothers to be women of color or immigrants.[5]

It's important to remind ourselves that being stuck isn't the fault of those at the bottom—any more than the eruption of Mount St. Helens was the fault of the park rangers. Even as earnings for low-income families have failed to rise, their qualifications have improved. Today, workers in these families are older and more educated than even a couple of decades ago. In 1979, only 8.4 percent of low-income families had a member with a college degree. Today that figure is about double—16.4 percent of low-income families have a family member with a college degree. These are sobering statistics.[6]

Like middle-class families, low-income families have had to struggle with an economy that's creating fewer good jobs. Their stories, however, differ in important ways. Middle-class families have more options: they face an economy where economic security is elusive yet still possible to attain with two earners. Low-income families too often find unstable, low-paying jobs that put economic security out of reach—even with two breadwinners and especially for those with a single earner.

Too Few Good Jobs

The shift in the balance of power between workers and employers leaves low-income workers even more disadvantaged than middle-class workers. In the decades just after World War II, the U.S. economy produced lots of good jobs for workers without a college degree. Today, without a college degree—and even with one—a good job is increasingly hard to find. We learned in Chapter 2 that the growth of middle-class jobs has slowed. But it's important to

understand how this slowdown affects people in the working class.
The paucity of middle-class jobs means there are fewer jobs for those
trying to *move into* the middle class. It also means that many people
who might once have competed for a middle-class job now compete with less-skilled workers for low-wage jobs.[7]

Many of the jobs that used to be available for less-educated workers
were in the manufacturing industry. In 1979, just over a fifth of al
U.S. workers were employed in manufacturing. These jobs tended
to pay well, thanks to strong unions. A man with a high school diploma could get a manufacturing job and bring home a bigger
paycheck than the average worker. Today, it is still true that manufacturing workers bring home more per week on average than the
typical worker. Yet in 2014, only 9 percent of workers were employed
in manufacturing, compared with around 30 percent in the 1940s
through the 1960s—the heyday of factory-line manufacturing jobs
in our nation. This means that far fewer families can earn a living
from manufacturing employment.[8]

One important reason for the decline in good manufacturing jobs
is that global competition has decimated many U.S. metal-bending
industries. As developing countries—in particular China—built up
their manufacturing capacity with far lower labor costs than those
in the United States, they could outcompete U.S. firms. This was
especially true once capital investment and tariff barriers were lowered. In 2001, the United States opened up its borders to more imports from China, which at the time had labor costs equal to about
one-quarter those of the United States. Since then, the United States
has imported an additional $333.4 billion of Chinese goods per year
on average, while exports to China have grown by only a third, on
average $92.7 billion per year, both in 2014 dollars. In the West
Coast ports, including Seattle, ships enter with full containers and
leave with them half empty.[9]

Economists have found that this increase in Chinese imports explains about a quarter of the overall decline in U.S. manufacturing
employment. It also explains some of the downward wage pressure
on U.S. workers. Globalization has curtailed opportunities for

workers without a college degree and is one reason that many low-income families are stuck on the bottom rungs of the ladder without access to stable jobs.[10]

But manufacturing's demise in the United States wasn't due only to globalization or trade policy. Our economy also shifted toward service industries for a variety of reasons independent of globalization. Professional jobs have increased, as we'll discuss in the next chapter, as have low-paid service jobs, such as in child care and elder care, retail, and temporary work. One reason for this shift is that the changes in how families work and live have led them to demand more services. We've learned that the most important coping mechanism for middle-class families was for women, especially mothers, to increase their hours of work. Families now need to purchase goods and services to replace all the work that women traditionally did for free inside the home, such as caring for children, as well as the sick and the elderly, and cooking and cleaning. Without the time to cook and clean, families focus on buying convenience, such as eating out and picking up prepared foods.[11]

The changes inside families explain why, for some time now, jobs involving care work have been among the fastest growing in our economy. This trend is likely to continue, especially as our nation ages. Every two years, the U.S. Bureau of Labor Statistics identifies what are likely to be the fastest-growing occupations over the next decade. As shown in Figure 3.3, the bureau predicts that between 2012 and 2022, the number of home health aides will increase by 424,000, a nearly 50 percent increase, while the number of child-care workers will rise by 184,000. Given these trends, experts have attributed growing inequality in part to the rise of low-paid service jobs, especially in care work.[12]

Changes within families also help explain the rise of the "24/7 economy." Families without a stay-at-home caregiver or homemaker need to be able to do their buying when they aren't at work. An important coping strategy for addressing work-life conflict is for families to access services and retail opportunities—from grocery stores to doctors' offices—outside the traditional 9-to-5, Monday through

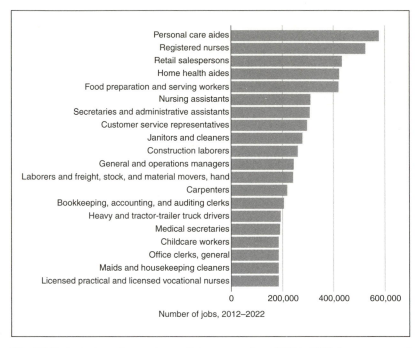

Fig. 3.3 Projected employment growth by occupation, 2012 to 2022. Low-wage and caring-sector jobs rank high among the top 20 occupations that the Bureau of Labor Statistics projects will add the most jobs by 2022.

Friday workdays. While having retail businesses open outside of traditional hours is good for people with traditional jobs, it can wreak havoc on the lives of the people who have to work in those businesses. Workers who put in nonstandard hours—evenings, nights, and weekends—are commonly those at the low-paid end of the labor market. Six in ten workers who have nonstandard schedules earn less than the typical U.S. worker, and four in ten earn less than 75 percent of all workers. While some people choose nonstandard work because it suits their schedule, the majority of workers—55 percent—are at these jobs for involuntary reasons, such as not being able to find another, more family-friendly job.[13]

In addition to nonstandard hours, many low-wage jobs—especially many of those that the Bureau of Labor Statistics predicts will grow the most—have erratic and unpredictable schedules. Complex computer algorithms now allow businesses to analyze large amounts of data very quickly and alter staffing schedules by quickly adapting to consumer demand and keeping down labor costs. This "just-in-time scheduling" pushes the cost of demand fluctuations onto workers rather than firms. In other cases, a boss simply changes his or her mind about needing a worker who is already on the schedule—even without consulting a fancy computer. *New York Times* journalist Steven Greenhouse wrote about workers at Popeye's fast-food restaurant who would show up for work but be sent home without pay. Employees at this company are not alone. According to a 2012 survey of New York City retail workers, more than one-third of respondents reported being sent home early when there wasn't enough work.[14]

While many low-wage employers require their employees to be willing to work unpredictable schedules, they are often inflexible when it comes to the employee's scheduling needs. In many of these jobs, showing up even five minutes late can lead to a demerit or disciplinary measures. Numerous examples of such practices exist, but here's one ripped from the headlines: in 2006 Wal-Mart changed its attendance policy. According to the Associated Press, this meant that "being 10 minutes or more tardy for work three times will earn you a demerit. Too many of those could get you fired." The lack of any flexibility—and penalties for not being on time—are typical of low-paying jobs. One study found that two-thirds of low-wage employees— defined as those earning less than two-thirds of the typical male earner—have no control over their starting or ending times.[15]

Unpredictable schedules, low pay, and inflexible workplaces all take their toll on families. A recent *New York Times* article by journalist Jodi Kantor highlighted many of these problems. Kantor traced the story of Jannette Navarro, a young Starbucks barista and single mother, as she sought to juggle Starbucks's "just-in-time" scheduling software and practices with her child-care arrangements and her desire to finish her education. She often would not know her week's schedule until a day in advance, making it impossible for her to finish school, let alone structure her life in any consistent way. Getting and keeping a job may be critical for family economic security, but for Navarro and others with little scheduling predict-ability, it can wreak havoc on everything else.[16]

The good news for Navarro and her colleagues is that the day after Kantor published that story on the cover of the *New York Times*, Starbucks announced that it would change its scheduling prac-tices. But Starbucks remains the exception, and the policy isn't yet fully in place. These kinds of labor practices are common and legal. As we learned in Chapter 1, the Fair Labor Standards Act does not require employers to provide predictable schedules, options for sched-uling flexibility, minimum hours, or prorated pay or benefits for part-time workers.[17]

On top of the broad shift from manufacturing to services and the move toward a 24/7 economy, many low-wage jobs simply aren't included in the labor standards we have in place. Consider the child-care, elder-care, and domestic-help industries. Many of these jobs were excluded from key aspects of the New Deal, such as minimum wage and overtime requirements. Denied even these most basic standards, workers in these jobs have very little to help them address conflicts between work and family life—even though they need the most workplace flexibility to care for their own families. We have seen some progress on this front. In September 2013, the Depart-ment of Labor extended the protections of the Fair Labor Standards Act to in-home care workers. Under this new rule, the act's minimum-wage and overtime provisions cover about two million direct-care workers.[18]

All of this means that workers like Navarro face a job market with too few good jobs and too few boundaries on how employers can use their time. But three other trends have also limited the oppor-tunities available to workers without a college degree. First, the per-centage of the population on active duty in the U.S. Armed Forces has declined. In the 1960s and 1970s, military service provided stable employment in the short term and a reliable route to good jobs in the future. This is not to say that we should bring back the draft, but it is important to see how changes in military service have affected the route to employment for some young men. In 1968, at the peak of the Vietnam War, more than 5 percent of working-age men in the United States were in the Armed Forces. With the end of the Vietnam War and then the Cold War, the share of the male working-age population in the military has fallen. As of 2013, it was at about 1 percent. Further, while it used to be the case that being a veteran was associated with better employment prospects and higher wages, that's no longer the case. Male veterans now fare no better in the labor market than similarly skilled nonveterans and, in fact, often fare worse.[19]

Second, many men—and increasingly women—are getting caught up in the criminal justice system, with serious consequences for their future job opportunities. The United States has the highest incarceration rate in the developed world. In 2013, about 1.4 percent of all working-age men were in state or federal prison or jail, three times the number in the 1960s. More than half the inmates in state and federal prisons serving a sentence of a year or more—about 53.4 percent—are there for nonviolent offenses. A criminal record seriously impedes a person's ability to find a good job. Researchers have estimated that between 1979 and 2008, as much as 75 percent of the decline in the employment rate of men with less than a high school degree can be explained solely by the large increase in the number of those with a criminal record. Incarceration not only limits future employment prospects but also means time away from family, leaving others to cope with care on their own. A disproportionate share of those with a prison record are African American men.[20]

Finally, the long-term decline in union coverage has lowered job quality and wages in low-wage industries. As noted in Chapter 2, the percentage of U.S. workers who belong to a union has fallen precipitously. Manufacturing has traditionally been the locus of union coverage, and as employment has fallen in that sector, union coverage has fallen as well. Further, as production has moved to states with antiunion laws—such as so-called right-to-work laws, which make it harder for unions to collect dues—new manufacturing jobs are less likely to be unionized. While unions have made progress organizing service workers, they have not been able to match the former clout

of industrial unions. In recent years, the rising number of undoc-
umented workers has likely played a role in the struggle of unions
to organize new members. If people are fearful that their employer
will inform the authorities about their—or their colleagues'—
immigration status, they will be less likely to join a union-organ-
izing campaign.[21]

It's All Unaffordable

Low-income families draw on a variety of strategies to cope with the
demise of good jobs. More of us used to think we were middle class
because the basic elements of a middle-class lifestyle were affordable
to families up and down the income ladder, even to those who may
have statistically been "low income." But if middle-class families are
having trouble affording the basics, then these are almost entirely
out of reach for today's low-income families.

Let's start by getting one issue out of the way. For the most part,
relying on a welfare check to pay the bills isn't a viable coping strategy
for most low-income families. Public opinion and my mother's frustrations about handouts notwithstanding, welfare is available to few
people and it's too stingy. In 2012, only 1.5 percent of families received a cash payment under the Temporary Assistance for Needy
Families program, commonly known as "welfare." In order to encourage work, the payments are meager, time-limited, and typically
include work requirements. It's always been the case that while Netflix can stream seemingly endless movies about the poor family who
becomes rich by striking oil or winning the lottery—or, in the romance department, the Cinderella who marries the prince—moving
out of poverty without access to a good job is about as likely as
meeting a fairy godmother.[22]

Our social policy expects able-bodied adults—with and without
children—to be either at a job or in school. The purpose of the 1996
welfare-reform legislation was to encourage poor and low-income
mothers seeking employment. To this end, at around the same time

as it passed, federal policymakers increased supports for the working poor. They expanded access to health care, increased the subsidies for child-care programs, and both raised the minimum wage and expanded the reach of the Earned Income Tax Credit. After welfare reform, employment increased for less-educated single mothers, so some claimed success. (Immigrant women and women of color, as noted, have always been more likely than white women to work outside the home, legislation aside.) However, what welfare reform didn't do was ensure that those jobs paid a living wage or had the benefits necessary to address conflicts between work and family life.[23]

A variety of government programs reduce the amount that low-income families have to pay for essentials such as food, housing, health care, and child care. But too many families do not get this support. About one in five families nationwide receives nutrition assistance. Fewer than 900,000 families receive child-care subsidies, and about a million children are in a Head Start program, which provides subsidized preschool and other services to very low-income children and their families. These are not large numbers in a nation of more than 315 million people, 24 million of them children under the age of six. Under the Affordable Care Act, as of this writing, twenty-eight states and the District of Columbia have expanded eligibility for Medicaid—the joint federal-state health-care program for the poor and elderly—to include more working families, which has improved their access to health care and cuts down on a large family budget item (but this means that twenty-two states have not done so). The Department of Housing and Urban Development reports that 5.4 million families receive some kind of rental-housing assistance. Nonetheless, we've seen an increase in the number of homeless families; today more than a third of the homeless population are people in families.[24]

Researchers find that these government programs serve too few people because many of those eligible do not take advantage of them—because they don't know about them, cannot figure out how they qualify, or don't think applying is worth their time. Further, many people who do secure a subsidized rental or other benefits find that these can be lost or sharply reduced as soon as a family member gets a decent-paying job. The very benefits that made it possible for them to begin to climb the ladder into the middle class, such as an apartment in a neighborhood with good schools, are taken away or reduced. Researchers call this phenomenon "running in place" or the "benefits cliff" because it imposes real hardship on families, sometimes trapping them in low-wage work. All means-tested programs share this self-defeating feature.[25]

In an interview with Delores (she did not give her last name), a single mom living in Virginia, the journalist Bryce Covert at *Think-Progress.org* found that a pay raise might not make life easier. She reported that Delores got a new job and went from making $8.00 an hour to $10.50 an hour, plus health insurance and other benefits. On paper, this was good news for Delores and her young daughter. Her higher pay, however, disqualified her for food stamp benefits. In economic terms, she paid a high implicit "tax" because as her earnings rose, she lost benefits, thereby lowering the real value of her wage increase. The reduction in benefits meant that in order to afford her new job, Delores had to take a second job. This was, of course, counterproductive. Dolores said, "If I'm working seven days a week, school, plus my daughter, I cannot do it. Right now I'm supposed to go [to computer classes] four days a week but I cannot do it because I need to work." To be clear, she liked her new job. It provided—among other things—schedule stability and vacation time. Yet with the disappearance of food stamps, things weren't necessarily easier for her and her family: "Sometimes I'm feeling like I'm getting sick because I don't sleep well."[26]

Complex Families and the Rise of Female Breadwinners

The erratic nature of the low-wage economy and the paucity of good jobs for those without a college degree make it hard to find and keep the kinds of jobs that pay a consistent living wage with reasonable (and enough) hours and decent benefits to support a stable family life. At the same time, low-income families have become increasingly complex and more prone to instability. High rates of nonmarriage and divorce mean that single parenthood are the norm.[27]

Trends in the economy and family makeup go together. The sociologists Sara McLanahan and Christine Percheski describe a feedback loop between an unequal economy and family complexity. They argue that it's become harder to get all the economic pieces in place—most importantly, a steady job—to feel ready for marriage. If people feel as though they don't meet this "marriage bar" because, among other things, they lack a good job or an adequate paycheck, then they often delay marriage and enter into nonmarital partnerships, which, as research has found, are often more susceptible to economic hardships compared with married families because they lack economic security. As Stephanie Coontz recently wrote in the *New York Times*, "Low-income women consistently tell researchers that the main reason they hesitate to marry—even if they are in love, even if they have moved in with a man to share expenses, and even if they have a child—is that they see a bad marriage or divorce as a greater threat to their well-being than being single."[28] Achieving this goal, however, is increasingly difficult given the shortage of well-paying, stable jobs.[29]

This situation has led to a decoupling of marriage and childbearing within low-income families. Sociologist Kathryn Edin and ethnologist Maria Kefalas report that low-income women tend to have children while they still search for the perfect partner. Thus a new kind of inequality emerges in terms of what families look like—and children's access to parental time and resources—that echoes economic inequality.[30]

It's important to remember—as shown in Figure I.1—that low-income and middle-income families didn't always look so different. Lower marriage rates for low-income families are a relatively new phenomenon and coincide with rising inequality. In his book *Labor's Love Lost*, the sociologist Andrew Cherlin concludes that the last time the marriage gap between workers at the top and bottom of the

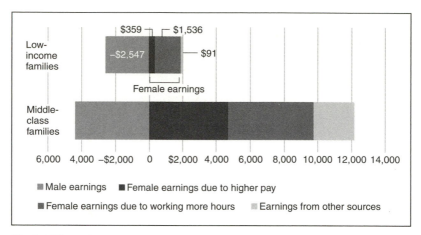

Fig. 3.4 Effect of women's earnings on total income of U.S. low-income and middle-class families, 1979 to 2012. Between 1979 and 2012, low-income families saw their income fall by $561 (in 2013 dollars). The decline happened because men's earnings fell more than women's pay and hours rose. *Note:* Analysis done at the household level. Sample includes households with at least one person aged 16 to 64. Individuals with zero or missing personal income dropped from sample.

income distribution grew as much as it has in recent decades was in the early twentieth century, when income inequality was also rising rapidly. Even just a few decades ago, marriage rates and family structure did not differ so greatly by income. Although Cherlin's categories don't overlap perfectly with mine, the trends are consistent with those shown in Figure 3.2 above.[31]

These trends mean that women's employment and earnings have become increasingly important to low-income families. By 2013, a woman was either the family breadwinner (bringing home at least as much as her husband or a single, working mother) or a cobreadwinner (bringing home at least a quarter of the family's earnings) in 73.9 percent of low-income families. Women's rising pay and added hours kept low-income families from being even more stuck. Figure 3.4 shows that, overall, between 1979 and 2012, low-income families saw their income fall by $561 (in 2013 dollars). The decline happened because men's earnings fell more than women's earnings—broken out into their pay and hours—rose. Men's earnings fell by $2,547, while women's pay rose by $1,536 and their earnings from added hours of work brought in an additional $359 each year. Without the added hours and earnings of women, incomes would have fallen even more for low-income families.[32]

Despite the fact that women's earnings are important to the family's economic well-being, women continue to account for the majority of workers in many of the care and, more generally, service jobs, which are typically low paid. As shown in Table 3.1, from 2012 to 2022, women are expected to make up the majority in thirteen of the top twenty fastest-growing occupations, and in eleven of them, women will constitute more than 80 percent of workers. This isn't news; it has been the case for many years now. For more than a decade, the Bureau of Labor Statistics has predicted that most of the new jobs would be in lower-paid, female-dominated occupations that do not require much higher education. Further, these fast-growing, low-wage jobs typically offer few benefits, such as paid time off, health insurance, or a retirement plan that could make up for the low pay. In 2010, for example, fewer than four in ten personal care and service workers had access to paid sick days. Many argue, however, that female-dominated jobs are not low paid but rather systemically undervalued. Because these are jobs that replace work that women historically did for free, we value them less.[33]

A fundamental problem is that the wages of workers—both men and women—in low-income families haven't grown in step with those of other workers. Between 1979 and 2012, men in low-income families saw their annual earnings fall by 23.3 percent. Women saw theirs rise—by a hefty 34.1 percent—but their starting point was very low, and that's a smaller increase than for women in either middle-income or professional families. Further, the volatility of low-wage work and its incompatibility with the domestic needs of working families too often lead to workers either being fired or quitting their jobs. We can see this in the fact that job tenure is lower in low-paid jobs. In 2014, the typical workers employed in food preparation or serving—often low-paying jobs—held their jobs for

Table 3.1 Low-wage, care-sector jobs have the most projected job growth, 2012–2022

Occupation	Median annual wage, 2012 ($)	Most significant source of postsecondary education or training[1]	Share that is female, 2012 (%)[2]
Personal care aides	19,910	Less than high school	82.9
Registered nurses	65,470	Associate's degree	90.6
Retail salespersons	21,110	Short-term, on-the-job training	51.2
Home health aides	20,820	Short-term, on-the-job training	89.4
Combined food preparation and serving workers, including fast food	18,260	Short-term, on-the-job training	28.1
Nursing assistants	24,420	Postsecondary nondegree award	89.4
Secretaries and administrative assistants, except legal, medical, and executive	32,410	High school diploma or equivalent	94.3
Customer service representatives	30,580	High school diploma or equivalent	65.4
Janitors and cleaners, except maids and housekeeping cleaners	22,320	Short-term, on-the-job training	35.0
Construction laborers	29,990	Short-term, on-the-job training	2.4
General and operations managers	95,440	Bachelor's degree	30.0
Laborers and freight, stock, and material movers, hand	23,890	Short-term, on-the-job training	18.4
Carpenters	39,940	Apprenticeship	2.0
Bookkeeping, accounting, and auditing clerks	35,170	Moderate-term, on-the-job training	89.8
Heavy and tractor-trailer truck drivers	38,200	Postsecondary nondegree award	7.5
Medical secretaries	31,350	Moderate-term, on-the-job training	88.8
Childcare workers	19,510	Short-term, on-the-job training	95.1
Office clerks, general	27,470	Short-term, on-the-job training	83.9
Maids and housekeeping cleaners	19,570	Short-term, on-the-job training	88.2
Licensed practical and licensed vocational nurses	41,540	Postsecondary nondegree award	88.9

Notes: 1. An occupation is placed into 1 of 10 categories that best describes the postsecondary education or training needed by most workers to become fully qualified in that occupation. 2. The ORG data combine home health aides and nursing aides into one category, "Nursing, psychiatric, and home health aides," and we use the share of that workforce for both "Home health aides" and "Nursing assistants."

Data source: Bureau of Labor Statistics, Employment Projections—2012–2022 (U.S. Department of Labor, December 19, 2013), http://www.bls.gov/news.release/pdf/ecopro.pdf, Table 5, and author's analysis of the Center for Economic and Policy Research Extracts of the Current Population Survey Outgoing Rotation Group (ORG) Files, 2012.

2.2 years. This is less than half as long as the typical workers in the economy overall, who hold their jobs for about 4.6 years.[34]

Kin and Care

The combination of high rates of single parenthood, complex families, and low wages and unstable jobs means that low-income families often have limited options to address care needs. Low-income families are more likely than professional families to turn to kin networks to cope with their unstable work-life problems. Some of this is about income and some of this is about culture. But unquestionably it is about their lack of other options.

Few low-income families can afford high-quality care, and few have access to government supports. The U.S. Department of Health and Human Services advises families to spend no more than 10 percent of their income on child care, but low-income families have a hard time making that cut-off. In 2014 dollars, low-income families paid around $2,538 a year in care for each child under age six—about 14 percent of their income. While this is less in total dollars than the amount spent in higher-income families, it's a much larger share of their total income.[35]

High costs are why low-income families often rely on informal kinds of child care, which they may not need to pay for. Among low-income families, roughly one-third—34 percent—rely on relatives for their primary form of child care, a greater percentage than among higher-income families. Low-income families are also more likely than higher-income families to rely on the parents themselves for child care—26 percent. Many are forced to "tag-team," with parents working alternate schedules in order to care for their children themselves. Because of the high cost of care and limited subsidized options, fewer than a third of low-income families—28 percent—use center-based care.[36]

The kind of care that parents choose is influenced not only by cost but also by work schedules. Most child-care centers do not offer around-the-clock care, which poses challenges for low-income parents who have to work nonstandard schedules. In recent years, the number of 24-hour day-care centers has increased to meet the child-care needs of working parents scrambling to find care that aligns with their schedules. But the new child-care services come at a price: families pay roughly $250 a week for just one child—about five times the annual cost of child care for the typical low-income family. Further, nonstandard hours may be hard on children not only because of the odd hours but also because the quality of that care might not be adequate. According to Wen-Jui Han, the reason children of mothers who work nonstandard schedules don't do as well academically or developmentally as other children might be the quality of that child care.[37]

Unpredictable scheduling practices reverberate throughout the economy. Often parents must pay for child care that they do not ultimately need or scramble to find care when an unexpected shift opens up. As anyone who has a child knows, day-care providers require stability in their scheduling. They need to know how many children they will be taking care of week to week, so they know when they'll have openings and what their staffing levels must be. Yet the instability of low-wage jobs means that child-care providers for low-income children have to struggle with the parents' erratic work schedules.[38]

How families cope—and how this may intersect with race and immigration—differs depending on where families sit on the income spectrum. In an essay for the *National Journal*, radio broadcaster Michel Martin wrote about what it was like to be an African American woman with twins and a career. Her argument was that kin play a larger role in the support network for families in communities of color, especially low-income ones, compared with other families. She noted, "It's been my observation that minorities are more likely than whites to be involved with or take financial responsibility for people other than their own children and parents—say, the children of siblings, or even close friends of their own children."[39]

Research confirms that low-income families rely more than others on extended kin networks for emotional and other support, both on and off the job. This is the conclusion of the book *Unequal Time*, by the sociologists Naomi Gerstel and Dan Clawson. They look at the different experiences of people who work in health care—from the high-paid professional to the low-paid emergency medical technicians and nursing assistants—to understand their schedules and concerns about work-life conflict. They specifically make the point that relying on kin for help may appear to be more common among families of color, but that decision is as much about class as culture: women and people of color typically have less control over their schedules and so rely on family for nonstandard care. Although my categories differ in that Gerstel and Clawson look at people in specific occupations and typical wages in those jobs, the trends they reveal are consistent with my findings.[40]

It's not just about care for children. Low-income families also need help caring for aging family members. As our nation ages, there's a long, circuitous path from being an able-bodied adult to being an elder who needs to live in a nursing home. Many seniors live on their own and get help from kin with the activities of daily living. There is little assistance available for those families, however. Medicaid will step in when an aging or disabled family member is destitute and needs to enter a nursing home, but Medicare, the federal health insurance program for the aged, provides little support for in-home care. The low subsidy levels for elder care—and child care—limit not only the availability of affordable care options for families but also the pay and benefits of the care providers. This is a key reason that these jobs—held disproportionately by women and often women of color—typically pay relatively low wages.

Few Good Choices

As Jodi Kantor of the *New York Times* told Jannette Navarro's story, she traced out how challenging Starbucks' scheduling practices were not only for Navarro but also for her child, her child's care providers, and her relationships with other adults. In Navarro's case, she turned to her aunt, her aunt's boyfriend, and her own boyfriend for help. By the end of the story, Navarro's boyfriend had broken up with her. They became yet another unstable low-income family. As Kantor reports, "He had been feeling too weighed down and that he could not do what he wanted—go back to school and get a better job— amid the whirl of Ms. Navarro's last-minute logistics."[41] He just could not cope with her chaotic schedule. Navarro's son Gavin was traumatized by having to move out of her boyfriend's apartment. Starbucks' "flexible scheduling," in practice at the time the story was published, gave all the flexibility to the store manager, not the employees, and corroded a relationship that was providing stability in the life of a child.

Low-income families need flexibility that works for them, not just for their employers. Traditional employers don't provide it, so some look to nontraditional arrangements. The Internet has facilitated the pairing of people who want to work with people who need someone to do something for them. Some call this the "gig economy" or "Task Rabbiting," after a popular software app. The *New York Times* featured a story by journalist Natasha Singer about a working mom, Jennifer Guidry, who, like millions of other working moms, is trying to make a living by performing tasks in this new sharing economy. She has downloaded a number of "apps" to her phone to find short-term jobs and to post her availability to potential employers. These jobs may last a few minutes, an hour, or perhaps a day. She is essentially in a "spot market" for labor, but instead of physically queuing up for job like the longshoremen in the film noir classic *On the Waterfront*, she is using the Internet.[42]

Guidry tells the reporter that she works this way because it gives her some much-needed flexibility. If she wakes up and her child is sick, she does not have to go to work. However, this means she shoulders all the risk of not working a regular job. She does not have a steady income that she can rely on. She does not get health insurance. And if there are no jobs posted on Task Rabbit today, she does not work. Of course, if Guidry does not work she does not get paid.

As the story progresses, it becomes clear that juggling a variety of different apps and clients to make ends meet in this new, so-called sharing economy can be nerve-racking. Further, she needs her own "capital," like a car, a computer, and other supplies, which she has to pay for up front. So while she has the flexibility to choose not to work when she has a conflict, she doesn't always get enough work when she needs it. And managing all these little jobs is both stressful and costly.

Many workers in low-income families face big hurdles trying to keep a job once they find it. Having the right to take a day off to care for oneself, a child, or an elderly parent may make the difference between keeping a job or not, especially in families with a single parent. These stories are all too common. Consider the story of Marianne Bullock, reported on National Public Radio. Bullock is a personal care assistant in Massachusetts. When her toddler woke up with a stomach virus, she faced the tough decision of staying home to take care of her daughter or going to work. She focused on her family and missed work to take her daughter to the hospital. For this, Bullock was fired. Her manager told her that they would rather hire someone without a child.[43]

The private sector has not stepped in to provide policies to address work-life conflict for low-income workers and their families. Workers without access to family-friendly policies are disproportionately in retail, restaurant and food service, and caring occupations, most of which are low-wage jobs that don't have any work-life benefits. For example, among those in the bottom 10 percent of wage earners, eight in ten lack access to paid sick days. Workers whose wages are in the lowest 25 percent of average wages are about four times less likely to have access to paid family leave than those in the highest 25 percent.[44]

Unions could help, but they are too scarce. For those who are in a union, the working conditions are generally better than they are for those who are not. Unions typically address issues such as hours and schedules, pay, and benefits, including family-friendly leave policies in their contracts. Union members also have an advocate on the job who can help them adjudicate conflicts with their manager over scheduling or other issues.[45]

As an alternative to forming a union, many people are turning to new workers' rights organizations. These include Workers' Centers, which exist in communities across the country, the Restaurant Opportunities Center, which is organizing food-service workers nationwide, and the Domestic Workers Alliance, which is fighting for a "domestic worker bill of rights" in cities and states around the nation, and many others. Although the progress is encouraging, the reach of these organizations—so far—isn't wide enough, which is why we also need to consider public action.

In Chapter 2, I talked about the tough choices my sister and a journalist acquaintance both faced. If they chose not to work outside the home, their families would suffer financially. If they stayed home, good career options might not be available to them when they tried to get back into the job market. If they chose work then they might not be around for their families when they needed them, on top of paying high costs for child care. Either choice put their families in an economic bind. At least both women had options, in no small part because they had spouses with decent jobs to help with care and income.

These are middle-class problems and middle-class solutions. Debra Lynn Harrell didn't have such options. She had a nine-year-old daughter and worked at McDonald's. She had been leaving the child at home to play on a laptop, but when it was stolen, the girl begged to be allowed to get out and play with other children. Paying for day care wasn't an option. At Debra's job, the average wage is slightly higher than $8.00 an hour. So Harrell allowed her daughter to stay at a playground while she worked her shift at the McDonalds' nearby. Someone noticed the child in the park and called Child Protective Services. Harrell ended up in jail. Her child was taken from her. She's out now and her child is home. What mother should end up in jail because she's trying to do the best she can for her family? What choices did Harrell really have?[46]

One thing common both to middle-class and low-income families is that while the New Deal–era set of labor standards and government programs for working families remain important, they are insufficient for today's economy and today's families. But whereas middle-class families have options—even if imperfect—low-income families too often have none. They're stuck. Low-income families cannot afford basics, let alone the necessary investments in their families that could boost their economic potential over the long run. And government policy hasn't caught up to their needs. In a world of family-hostile jobs, they often cope by turning to their kin for support.

Low-income families—like middle-income families—need something new. Economic security requires a new way of thinking about what business, government, and households owe one another. We must redefine the boundary between time for work and time for life in a way that recognizes how today's families interact with the economy. While the New Deal laid out a set of standards that worked for families long ago, today's families struggle to engage in work while also providing care for their loved ones. This isn't just a problem for low- and middle-income families. It turns out that money can't buy us enough time. As my friend Zoe, who runs a nonprofit in Washington, DC, said to me over dinner recently, "There's just not enough time and money to do everything."

Soaring above and Sounding the Alarm: Today's Professional Families

In the past two chapters, we learned how economic changes have left middle-class and lower-income families with a new set of conflicts. Families work hard, but the economy hasn't given them much more for their efforts. For middle-class families, the path upward has stalled, while low-income families are stuck in the proverbial mud.

Professional families are the ones for whom the economy has performed relatively well. Recall Figure 3.1, which looked at income growth for families in the middle and at the lower end of the income spectrum. Figure 4.1 shows the same data, adding average income growth for professional families, which I define as families with incomes that put them in the top 20 percent of all U.S. families for that year and in which at least one person has a college degree—13 percent of all families in 2012. Professional families have continued to climb the income ladder. This is starkly different from the situation for families in the middle or at the bottom. Whereas average middle-class family incomes grew by 10.9 percent between 1979 and 2012 and low-income family incomes fell by 2.4 percent, professional families saw their income grow on average by a whopping 48.9 percent. Among professional families, average annual income is $194,000. If we thought that the rungs on the ladder between low-income and middle-class families were getting too far apart, Figure 4.1 shows that the gap is growing much faster between the top and everyone else.[1]

Rising incomes for professional families are the result of rising salaries, an increase in dual-income families, and a greater likelihood of professionals' marrying other professionals. While the salaries of both professional men and women have risen, a central part

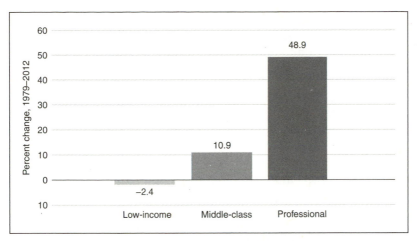

Fig. 4.1 Change in inflation-adjusted family income for professional compared with middle-class and low-income families, 1979 to 2012. Between 1979 and 2012, professional families saw their average incomes rise by 48.9 percent, over four times the pace of middle-class families, while low-income families saw their incomes fall by 2.4 percent. *Note:* Analysis done at the household level. Sample includes households with at least one person aged 25 to 64. Individuals with zero or missing personal income dropped from sample.

of the story is that more women than ever before have professional degrees and work in high-paying occupations, and they tend to marry professional men. As is the case for women across the income spectrum, professional women have seen a sharp uptick in employment and are more likely than in prior generations to stay employed even after they marry and have children. When their greater earnings are added to the already high incomes of their husbands, their family income soars.

Professional families near the top of the ladder have excellent economic opportunities and high incomes, but for many of them maintaining their place in the economic hierarchy requires a great deal of time and effort. In the last chapter, we heard the story of Jannette Navarro and the challenges posed by her unpredictable work hours at Starbucks. While the exact circumstances—and access to resources—are certainly different, we can see echoes of the challenges she faced among workers nearer the top of the income ladder.

Millions of professional workers and their families face erratic schedules and have to miss family milestones because of commitments at
work. It's so common for professionals to put in unanticipated long
hours that some child-care centers and after-school programs have
imposed hefty fines—as much as $5 a minute—as an incentive for
parents to pick up their children on time.[2]

Professionals, of course, put in long hours to bring home those
big paychecks. They work longer hours than families further down
the income ladder, and their jobs sometimes require extensive travel.
Their employers often demand that they be "all in," and they are
frequently tethered to the office at all times via mobile phones,
email, and cloud servers. These jobs seem built around the presumption that there's someone at home to take care of "life." Some employers provide onsite child care, laundry services, and healthful
cafeteria food, but these are solutions to keep professionals at work
even longer. This combination of long hours and dual-earner couples means that today's professional families face high levels of work-
life conflict.

I don't need a research study to tell me any of this. This is my life
and that of many people I know—although mostly without fancy
onsite perks. My husband and I both have PhDs and hold down professional jobs. Long hours and regular travel are the norm. Don't get
me wrong; I think I have the best job in world. I feel lucky to spend
my time writing and speaking about the economic issues facing
our nation. But like many professionals, I don't always have control
over my schedule, and I've had to cancel too much family time. I also
hear directly from people all around me about the challenges of
dual-earner professional couples and the very real everyday stresses
of this lifestyle. Knowing my interest in these issues, people will
often strike up a conversation with me about their workplace benefits or how reasonable—or unreasonable—their bosses are.

I'm also very aware that it is professionals like myself—often
women, but not always, as we'll see—who have used the media to
share their stories about conflicts they face between work and family
life and, in the process, focus policymakers on how to fix it. In the

summer of 2012, when Anne-Marie Slaughter stepped down from a two-year stint as director of policy planning in Secretary Clinton's State Department—the first woman to hold this post—she published an article in the *Atlantic* magazine titled "Why Women Still Can't Have It All." In the article, she said, "I still strongly believe that women can 'have it all' (and that men can too). I believe that we can 'have it all at the same time.' But not today, not with the way America's economy and society are currently structured." Slaughter shared details about her life as compelling as Navarro's, and her experiences echo the kinds of challenges facing earners in low- and middle-class families—albeit with a higher income. She said,

> My workweek started at 4:20 on Monday morning, when I got up to get the 5:30 train from Trenton to Washington. It ended late on Friday, with the train home. In between, the days were crammed with meetings, and when the meetings stopped, the writing work began—a never-ending stream of memos, reports, and comments on other people's drafts. For two years, I never left the office early enough to go to any stores other than those open 24 hours, which meant that everything from dry cleaning to hair appointments to Christmas shopping had to be done on weekends, amid children's sporting events, music lessons, family meals, and conference calls.

Strikingly, Slaughter notes that she "had it better than many," since "Secretary Clinton deliberately came in around 8 AM and left around 7 PM, to allow her staff to have morning and evening time with their families (although of course she worked earlier and later, from home)." Lucky indeed.[3]

Slaughter's piece, recently expanded into the book *Unfinished Business*, was quickly followed by the publication of Sheryl Sandberg's book *Lean In*. Sandberg, chief operating officer of Facebook, offered advice to professional women like herself on how to make changes to resolve day-to-day conflicts between work and family life.

She called for women all across America to create "lean in circles," where they could talk about the challenges they faced in the workplace and how they could take action to boost their chances of individual success. Sandberg was very careful to repeat throughout her book that she was speaking of her own experience—that of a highly paid professional. But she believed that the public—and policymakers—could learn from her experience and find solutions that would work not just for those at the far end of the earnings spectrum but also for others.[4]

Professionals often have to look at the big picture. Certainly, it's the job of the economist to help people understand complicated trends and see the full story—even when what's going on isn't visible to the naked eye. It's our professional responsibility. On Mount St. Helens, professionals—in this case, geologists—saved many lives by identifying the underlying tremors that indicated a potential eruption. Even though the loggers, hikers, and homeowners couldn't know that disaster was imminent, the geologists were able to warn people in time to save lives. The U.S. Geological Survey had installed seismographs on the mountain to track movement below the earth's surface, and in March 1980, after a magnitude 4.2 earthquake struck and ash and steam began venting out the top of the mountain, geologists pushed state authorities to close Mount St. Helens to the public despite heavy pressure to keep it open.[5]

But let's not get too full of ourselves. While we professionals are policymakers in government or corporations and often have access to media platforms to sound the alarm—and perhaps just enough of a sense of entitlement to muster the chutzpah to do so—we don't always have a close-up view of what the economic and family devastation looks like on the ground. We know there's a problem and can see that families all the way down the income ladder also struggle, but from our perch it may be hard to see exactly how the daily conflicts play out.

In the last two chapters we learned how the challenges of finding time for work and for home life affect low-income and middle-class families. In this chapter, we'll learn that, compared with middle-class and low-income families, professional families have more options—often many more options—as well as the money to pay for high-quality solutions. They can afford to outsource what they don't have time to do themselves. They can buy high-quality care for their children and elderly parents. And they are much more likely to have access to the kinds of workplace policies that give them paid time off and some flexibility—even though there is too often a professional cost to using the benefits. Not all professionals, of course, have access to these policies, and even who do may not feel they can make use of them.

And they, too, are short on time. Like low-income and middle-class families, professional families typically have no stay-at-home caregiver. Figure 4.2 shows what this means for families with children. According to Philip Cohen, children in professional families are more likely to have two working parents, compared with middle-class or low-income children. In 2012, more than two-thirds of such children—67.7 percent—lived in a family with two working parents and a quarter lived in the traditional male-breadwinner, stay-at-home-mom family. This more than reverses the trend in 1960, when 78.3 percent of children in professional families had a stay-at-home mother and only 20.1 percent had two working parents. Few professional families are headed by a single parent, in no small part because having only one income makes it hard to rise into the top income group. Like low-income and middle-class families, professional families have lost time.

But Figures 4.1 and 4.2 don't show the full story of what's happened to professional families. We learn from the work of economists Emmanuel Saez and Thomas Piketty that families at the very top of the income ladder have seen the most significant income gains. These economists have compiled detailed U.S. tax record data—data that were not previously available to the public—in order to see what has happened to income for families all the way up into the top .01 percent. One of their most important findings is shown in Figure 4.3. In the United States, since 1979, income gains have been concentrated among families in the top 1 percent. Figure 4.1

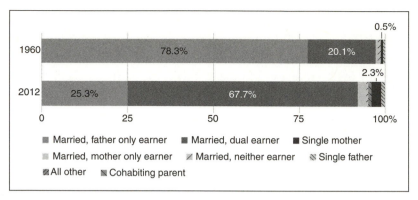

Fig. 4.2 Living arrangements of children aged 14 and under in professional families, 1960 and 2012. In both 1960 and 2012, most children in professional families lived with two parents. However, in 1960, fathers were usually the sole breadwinner, but by 2012 in most families both parents were in the workforce. Compare the changes in family composition between 1960 and 2012 of the professional families shown here with the changes in composition of middle-class families shown in Fig. 2.3 and lower-income families in Fig. 3.2. *Note:* Data on cohabiting available only for 2012.

showed that overall, professional families have done well; Figure 4.3 shows that those gains pale in comparison to those of people at the very peak of the income distribution.

Here's one way to think about this difference. Let's say the top 1 percent and the bottom 90 percent ran a marathon and agreed to celebrate together at the end (while those in the top 2 to 10 percent sat out this particular race). Let's further assume that their paces were equal to their wage growth between 1979 and 2012. If the top 1 percent completed the race at the rapid clip of three hours and thirty minutes, they would be wise to pack a snack—and a sleeping bag. They would be waiting at the finish line for more than twenty-four hours for the bottom 90 percent.

This rising inequality at the very top raises the stakes for professional families. Political scientists Jacob Hacker and Paul Pierson call this a "winner-take-all" economy. A growing body of research shows that the gains from being on top economically are larger than ever before, but that moving into the "winner's circle" is no easier and

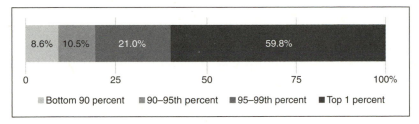

Fig. 4.3 Share of income gains in 2007 going to the top 1 percent of tax filers compared with the remaining 99 percent of Americans. In 2007, taxpayers in the top 1 percent took home the largest share of total income (59.8 percent) while the bottom 90 percent took home only 8.6 percent.

may actually be more difficult than for generations past. Of course, the same data that show little upward mobility also show little downward mobility. Further, downward mobility—like upward—has been relatively stable in recent years. For example, one study found that the sons of high-income fathers are equally likely to be top earners later in life, just as the sons of low-income fathers are to more likely to remain stuck at the bottom of the income ladder. Winner-take-all means that only some reap the outsized gains. It also means that whereas low-income and middle-class families are seeking to move up—or at least attain economic security—those at the top can see how far they could fall down the economic ladder.[6]

To get to the top today, you typically need a high-paying job, not simply rich parents. This is a shift from a century ago. Families with the highest income streams (the top 10 percent) receive a substantial portion of their income—75 percent—from salaried employment, including stock options and other kinds of nonwage remunerations. It's not until we reach the very top of the income ladder—the top 0.01 percent—that income from capital investments (stocks and bonds and other financial instruments) plays as large a role as earnings, as shown in Panel B of Figure 4.4. This is markedly different from the situation in 1929, as shown in Panel A of Figure 4.4. In 1929, capital income as opposed to work effort was the main source of income for the top 0.5 percent. This shift in how the rich earn

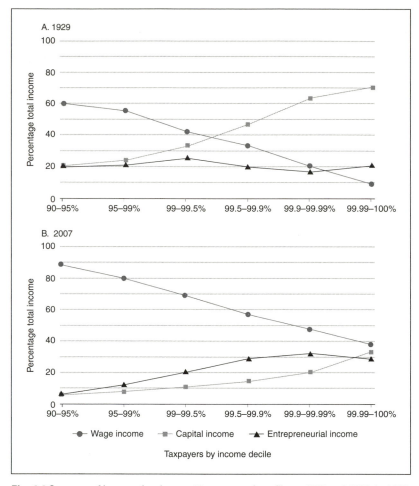

Fig. 4.4 Sources of income for the top 10 percent of tax filers, 1929 and 2007. In 1929, wage income was less important than capital income for those in the top 0.5 percent and above. However, by 2007, wage income was more important than capital income for all families, even those in the top 0.01 percent. *Note:* Capital income does not include capital gains.

their income underscores the importance today of having a job—even for those at the top. A century or two ago, if you grew up in a rich family you were most likely the child of property owners or living off business investments. Your parents did not spend fifty-plus hours a week at work, and you did not expect to either.

The hit British television show *Downton Abbey* captures the lifestyle of this particular kind of wealth in the early twentieth century.

The rich worked so little that they had time to don four or five out-fits over the course of a day. At that time, the young focused on mar-rying well because finding a mate with a fortune was often the only route to economic security. Today, young people are more likely to see their SAT scores as the key to their economic future. In a society where income is based primarily on personal accomplishment—as opposed to an inheritance of land or other assets—educational in-vestments are paramount economic concerns. But this carries with it high stress surrounding individual performance in school and at work.

In this chapter, we'll learn how professional families have adapted to being today's "overworked rich." Long hours and extremely high inequality are both indicators of how the stakes have risen for pro-fessional families. There are real consequences of attending the right school, marrying the right mate, and getting the right job, as well as of raising the next generation to take your place one day at the top of the pecking order. Those aiming for jobs at the top of the economy must put in years of higher education—often accruing lots of debt along the way—and be willing to put in long hours once they land that plum job. They typically delay marriage and children until their thirties and then make significant investments of time and money to raise the next generation to follow in their footsteps. The stakes of winning are extremely high and time is in short supply.

Soaring Above

Let's start by looking at why incomes at the top have risen so high so fast. In Chapters 2 and 3, we learned that structural economic changes, including the move away from manufacturing and toward services and the rise of the 24/7 economy, have led to a decline in good jobs for middle-class and low-income workers. Why is it is that as the incomes of the middle and bottom have stalled or been stuck, the top has soared?

Since many of those at the top get their incomes from salaries, as indicated in Figure 4.4, let's start with the pay of jobs for those at the top. The first important fact is that those with a college degree now earn almost twice as much as those with a high school diploma, compared with only 1.4 times more in 1979. Some economists argue that the higher salaries for those at the top are due to increasing returns on education. Those who have invested in higher skills are better rewarded because the so-called new economy requires ever more highly skilled workers. These experts interpret the rise in returns on education as an indication that people overall are underinvesting in higher education. This fits into the economic narratives in Chapters 2 and 3, where we saw that, in recent decades, technological changes have led employers to seek workers with more specialized or hi-tech skills. At the same time, these changes mean that some workers—often manufacturing workers—have seen their jobs replaced by robots.[7]

Education is important. But it's not the whole story—and certainly not for low-income families, who overall have increased their educational levels but haven't seen corresponding income gains. There are two simple reasons that education alone cannot explain the rise of high-end salaries. First, the rise in wages at the top has been concentrated among the wealthiest earners, which is hard to reconcile with the notion that this is primarily a skills story. Salaries for professional workers have grown rapidly, far outpacing those for workers down the income ladder, but the largest gains have been concentrated in the top 1 percent. Between 1979 and 2012, earnings of men in professional families grew by 28.5 percent while women's grew by 129.9 percent. But among those in the top 1 percent, salary income increased by even more—156.2 percent.[8]

Second, wage trends at the top of the income ladder are not the same across all developed nations, even though all these nations have experienced similar changes in their economies. It would seem reasonable to assume that workers face the same technological innovations across countries comparable to the United States, such as the United Kingdom, Canada, Germany, or Australia. So it's hard to understand why the U.S. economy would be demanding so many more highly skilled workers relative to other developed economies.

How is it that the United States could have so few qualified people that top-end salaries need to rise so much faster, compared with those in other developed economies? Moreover, if the higher salaries for those at the top in the United States were productivity-related, then U.S. economic growth should outpace that of other countries. Yet that's not the case. Not only has the United States registered average economic growth but also our measurable productivity is not rising faster than that of our main economic competitors, such as France and Germany.[9]

This leads to a fundamental question: if rising demand for skill cannot fully explain what's driving salaries at the top of the U.S. income distribution to new heights, what can? A big clue is that most of those earning the highest salaries are senior managers, not technicians, engineers, or doctors.[10] In *Capital in the Twenty-First Century*, Thomas Piketty argues that high-end salaries are rising due to the advent of the "supermanager." As he puts it, "wage inequalities increased rapidly in the United States and Britain because U.S. and British corporations became much more tolerant of extremely generous pay packages after 1970."[11] Corporate boards determine the pay of senior managers, but these boards cannot discern easily the managers' added contribution to the firm's productivity (what economists call someone's "marginal product").

I am sympathetic to Piketty's view. While those at the top contribute to our economy, I find it difficult to take on faith that the very highest earners have contributed so much more to their firm's productivity to justify—on economic grounds—their highly outsized salaries and benefit packages. If our economy had seen phenomenal growth or if that growth had trickled down to the benefit of more people in society, this might be true. But in an era of slower growth, as shown in Figure 4.4, and unshared prosperity, as shown in Figure 4.1, it's hard to see this as anything but those at the top taking more than their work contributions could possibly merit—which is not to the benefit of the economy or families overall.

What is also clear is that the "winner-take-all" economy is extremely competitive, and the high salaries for those at the top don't come easy. This system puts pressure on professional employees who must show their boss that they—perhaps more so than their colleagues—are worth every penny and are useful to the firm. This can be hard to do because an individual employee's productivity can be difficult, if not impossible, to measure within many professions. Employees spend time—and lots of it—to prove their value to the firm. Just like workers further down the income ladder, many professionals have to work in a 24/7 economy.

A simple way that bosses know a professional is working hard is to see them at their desk. There's a term for this: "face time." In a highly competitive, winner-take-all system, face time is something employees can control and use to differentiate themselves from their peers. And it works. Getting to the office early and staying late can lead supervisors to evaluate an employee's work more favorably, even though research shows that focusing on face time doesn't lead to greater productivity. Although personal interaction is important, having people put in hours at their desks just to say they did so does not actually increase productivity. The same is true of electronic face time. The employee who wants to impress his boss by sending emails at midnight and then again at six in the morning wants to show he's very dedicated, but the action of sending emails after hours rather spending time away from work can also harm productivity as the employee isn't getting much-needed downtime.[12]

Face time and the norm of long days mean that professionals devote most of their waking hours to their careers. Hours of work among professional families have been rising over time. By 2012, working men in professional families put in 2,186 hours per year on average—more than forty hours per week, fifty-two weeks a year—while working women put in 1,708 hours. For many people, this means fifty-hour workweeks or more. Such long hours are not as common in middle-class or low-income families, who, as we learned, often face the opposite problem of too few hours. This leaves professional families with all the advantages except the one thing that money cannot (completely) buy: time.[13]

The long hours typical of professional workers isn't the case in other developed economies and isn't even the case in the non-U.S. branches of global firms. Alan, a British lawyer at one of London's top law firms, came to the United States to do a rotation in his company's American office. He knew the reputation of Americans as a hard-working bunch, but he was used to putting in occasional hours at night or on the weekend. That was the norm for lawyers everywhere. What he didn't expect was for the "strong work-ethic" of Americans to translate into a disregard for life outside the office. In London, people would put in long hours, but come Friday at 5:00 PM, everyone would turn off their work phones and head home to be with their families (with the occasional check-in during busy times of year). In the United States, however, the lawyers in Alan's firm were online 24/7. Alan frequently had to work through the weekends, and even when he was "off," he would get "urgent" work emails that were, in fact, not urgent at all.

As a new transplant with few friends and a girlfriend back in London, he was thankful that he didn't have the impossible task of balancing his current job with other obligations. Still, the work felt excessive. Alan had done the same job at the same company both in Britain and in the United States, and in his view, U.S. lawyers worked endless hours because of a cultural norm, not for some social or economic need. The American system seemed inefficient and unnecessary—a good system could help get things done better. Needless to say, he's moving back to London and said he won't do a U.S. rotation ever again.

Since these workers are the elite, sitting at the top of organizations, policymakers have not typically focused on their right to reasonable schedules. Professional workers are not covered by the Fair Labor Standards Act, the federal legislation that governs hours of work. For them, there are no set limits on how many hours an employer can demand. In some professions, such as flying, policymakers concerned about public safety have established rules governing overwork, and in others professional organizations set standards, such as for medical residents, but in general, there's no legal recourse for overworked professional employees. Moreover, because professionals are rarely unionized (airline pilots being a notable exception), they are often left to negotiate their schedules with their supervisors on their own.[14]

The good news is that professional families are more likely than middle-class or low-income workers to have workplace flexibility. To give just one example, Sarah Jane Glynn and Jane Farrell looked at data from the Bureau of Labor Statistics American Time Use Survey and found that among high-wage employees—people earning in the top quarter of all workers—nearly nine in ten (88 percent) report that their employer allows them to earn paid time off or to change their schedule if they have an urgent family issue. Not everyone at this level gets these benefits, however, and they may not be enough to make up for long hours and unpredictable schedules.[15]

One reason professionals have more flexibility is that employers provide these benefits to attract workers. Business journals feature articles about how executives can recruit and retain top talent by encouraging them to address conflicts between work and life. Some firms are heeding that message. In the 1990s, an early leader was the professional services firm Deloitte, which implemented workplace flexibility and now aims for flexibility for all of its employees. Instead of having a policy just for employees who brought up conflicts around work and life, Deloitte took the opposite approach and assumed that every employee has personal priorities that may occasionally conflict with work. Periodically, every one of Deloitte's nearly 46,000 employees fills out a profile detailing whether they want to "dial up" their career by taking on more responsibilities, "dial down" by reducing hours or travel, or just stay where they are. According to Cathy Benko, Deloitte's chief talent officer, this program, called Mass Career Customization, "is about recognizing that an employee's career is a lattice, not a ladder," and this applies to every worker, not just parents and not just those at the top.[16]

This kind of universal flexibility is not available at most firms, but even if their employers don't have formal programs in place, many professionals are often in a better position to request workplace flexibility from their supervisors. In *Lean In* Sheryl Sandberg tells the story of how when she had children, she asked her boss if she could leave work at 5:30 PM. She would get back online after they went to sleep, but she needed to be home for dinner and bedtime. She recalls being afraid to ask for this accommodation. Yet at the time, Sandberg was one of the top employees of the firm. If she felt fear, she surmised, then most people probably felt the same.[17]

For many, even among professionals at the top, fear is in fact common. Given the norm of long hours, professionals who don't have understanding bosses or who are afraid to ask for accommodations often end up pushed out of their careers. The sociologists Pamela Stone and Meg Lovejoy interviewed professional women, whom they defined as women in professional or managerial jobs, who had quit working and found that nearly all of them—86 percent—reported workplace factors such as long workweeks and inflexible jobs as critical reasons they had left their jobs.[18]

Yet journalists often miss this key finding when reporting on stay-at-home moms; as a result, the stories we hear in the news often portray these women as voluntarily leaving good jobs. In a content analysis of U.S. newspapers, Joan Williams and her colleagues found that journalists reported that the "pull of family life" rather than the push of inflexible jobs was the prevailing narrative of why mothers left their jobs to be full-time mothers, especially for women in professional or managerial jobs. The overwhelming majority of professional mothers do work, more so than any other mothers, and there is no evidence that they have been opting out in favor of motherhood. Like my sister, many try to find the right path but get so frustrated—or so bullied—that they leave the workplace if they can afford to do so.[19]

A New Negotiation inside the Family

Incomes within professional families are also rising because professionals tend to marry each other, combining their high salaries. This leads not only to higher incomes but also to serious work-life conflicts.

When both partners work at "all-in" jobs, clashes with the needs of the family are more likely.

A few years ago, I first heard the term "Dink," which according to the Urban Dictionary stands for "Dual-Income, No Kids." This term came into the popular lexicon in the 1980s after the term "Yuppie" (young urban professional) had been around a while. Whereas Yuppie describes a person, Dink describes family life for young professionals. They marry in their late twenties or early thirties and tend to have their children well into their thirties and even forties, when they can more easily afford to pay for high-quality child care and live in the best neighborhoods with the best schools. These marital and childbearing patterns combine with career patterns to ramp up economic inequality across families.[20]

Highly educated women in professional families tend to be employed and stay employed even once they marry and have children. Women now outpace men in completing both college and graduate school. Women are parlaying that education into professional careers and now make up about a third of lawyers, judges, and physicians, and nearly four in ten managers. By 2007, the year before the financial crisis, among women with a college degree, 80.7 percent were in the labor force—as were nearly as many mothers (77.9 percent)—compared with 47 percent of those who stopped their education at a high school diploma. While highly educated women have always been more likely than other women to work—even once they become mothers—the combination of greater numbers of highly educated women and their growing presence in the professional workforce has boosted incomes within these families.[21]

Women's career progress means that professional families tend to have two earners, not one. Adults today are also more likely to marry someone with similar education and therefore someone who brings home a similar paycheck. And while professional families delay childbearing, most still have children. About a quarter of women who graduated from college between 1980 and 1990 had realized the goal of having both career and family by age forty. According to the economist Claudia Goldin, this number is greater than that of any prior cohort. Earlier cohorts of women did one or the other, but less often both.[22]

Women who delay childrearing until their mid-thirties or later have time to establish their careers. By that age, many professionals are nearing the first career peak, no longer the lowest person on the totem pole and more likely the boss—or at least in upper-middle management—with the greater job security that comes from moving up the ladder. They have had time to save up more money, and their seniority at work means that they have had the opportunity to accrue more sick leave and vacation time. Of course by that time, many are also heavily invested in their careers and may fear retaliation or being put on the "mommy track," that is, not given promotions or plum assignments, when they have a family.

Figure 4.5 shows how much of the rise in professional family incomes is due to women's employment and pay raises, male earnings, and other income. As in middle-class and low-income families, women's higher pay and increased hours combined were the most important factor in boosting family income. Of the total gain for professional families, $22,566 was due to women's higher pay and $13,122 was due to women's added hours of work. All of this contributes to the fact that between 1979 and 2012, the share of professional mothers who are breadwinners (bringing home at least as much as their husbands or single, working mothers) or cobreadwinners (bringing home at least a quarter of the family's earnings) almost doubled, from 36.3 percent to 62.6 percent. However, unlike in middle-class or low-income families, in recent decades professional men have helped boost family income. Higher earnings for men in professional families accounted for $24,948 of the total $63,593 increase.[23]

Because both earners are important in professional families, we've seen changes in how men and women think about marriage, housework, and caring labor. One thing is clear: whom you marry matters. Young professionals are encouraged to choose their spouses with an eye to adjudicating between work-life conflicts. Recently, Princeton alumna Susan Patton ('77) wrote an open letter to women at Princeton encouraging them to "find a husband on campus

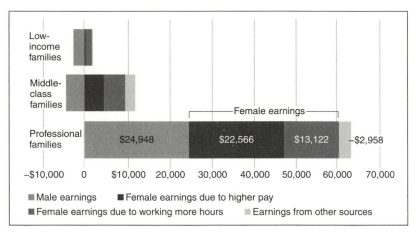

Fig. 4.5 Effect of women's earnings on total income of U.S. professional, low-income, and middle-class families, 1979 to 2012. Between 1979 and 2012, professional family income rose by an average of $63,593. As in middle-class and low-income families, women's higher pay and increased hours combined were the most important factor in boosting family income. Unlike in middle-class or low-income families, however, in professional families, men have helped boost family income. *Note:* Analysis done at the household level. Sample includes households with at least one person aged 16 to 64. Individuals with zero or missing personal income dropped from sample.

before you graduate." She pointed out that their classmates at school would probably be the most impressive group of marriageable partners they would ever be among. She made the point that in today's economy, whom you marry may have just as big an effect on your life prospects as your career decisions, but for reasons very different from those made by the better-off in society a century or more ago.[24]

Patton was widely criticized, but she isn't the only one making such an argument. In *Lean In*, Sheryl Sandberg acknowledged that finding the right partner can make all the difference. She used examples from her own marriage to show how having a partner who is supportive of your career can help you succeed in the workplace. Sandberg is speaking specifically to young women, but this advice certainly goes both ways. It has long been the case that professional men sought to find spouses who could be good "corporate wives," able to host lovely dinner parties and graciously entertain clients.

Today these men may not actively look for women with good educations and promising professional career opportunities, but more and more that's whom they meet and marry while working and living in the same social circles.[25]

As professional women have become more economically independent, they have renegotiated what marriage entails. When we look at all women with a college degree—which overlaps with, but is not exactly the same as, women in professional families—we see that husbands are much more involved in family life. As of 2000, college-educated dads spend an average of 9.1 hours per week on child care, compared with 13.8 hours for college-educated mothers. While men still spend less time than women on child care, this is an improvement. Whereas in the 1970s, many argued that marriage and feminism couldn't go together, today's professional women seem to have found ways to strike a new bargain.[26]

Today's professional men are increasingly comfortable telling their bosses about negotiations with their wives over time and asking for more flexibility—and even talking about this on national television. In 2009, NBC broadcast host David Gregory interviewed Maria Shriver, then the first lady of California, and John D. Podesta, then president of the Center for American Progress and now chairman of Hillary Clinton's campaign for the presidency, about a report I coedited, *The Shriver Report: A Woman's Nation Changes Everything.* During that interview, Gregory talked about how the daily challenges that come with being part of a dual-career couple were exactly the challenges he faced in his own life. His wife, Beth Wilkinson, was a trial lawyer, and—on air—he said the following,

> Just this week I had a conversation at NBC News with a female executive. . . . I said, "Look, I need to factor this in a little bit with my wife's schedule, because she's traveling more as a lawyer." And I thought to myself . . . would that conversation have happened 20 years ago, you'd have a female executive and somebody in my position bringing these issues up?[27]

Gender equity at work requires more gender equity at home, and this is certainly progress, even if we still have a ways to go.

Higher Stakes for the Next Generation

The daily conflicts over work and life within professional families are often due to the tension between earning a high salary today and preparing the next generation to do so in the future. A day in the life of a typical high-end professional family involves a good deal of rushing from home to child care to work and back, always online and connected to the office.

Professionals' high incomes mean that their children—the so-called Generation Z of infants and toddlers and school-age children today—have access to significant resources. Children today who are born into the most advantaged families have seen substantial gains in economic resources, as well as high levels of parental involvement in their emotional needs and development. Sociologist Sara McLanahan describes the new family patterns, documenting how professional families delay marriage and children, are less likely to divorce or have children outside marriage, and have high maternal employment. Relative to their counterparts forty years ago, their mothers are older and more likely to be working at well-paying jobs. These patterns enable families with a mother in the top quartile of educational attainment to bestow the benefits of more stable families on their kids. New gender norms mean that these children get to spend more time with their fathers than was the case for their own parents.[28]

Yet professional families with children struggle with conflicting mandates. On the one hand, their jobs require them to be "all in," while on the other, they are under pressure to prepare the next generation to take their place in the economic hierarchy. The shift away from inherited wealth toward salaried income for those at the top means that making sure you have—and pass on to your children—the skills and training necessary to get a plum job and keep it are of paramount importance. In the nineteenth century and before, most of those in the top income class were there because they were born into it and inherited the fortunes of their families. Today, incomes are overwhelmingly based on what we accomplish in our lifetimes, and these accomplishments are the direct result of our perceived contributions to the production process—basically, how valuable we are to our employers. In this winner-take-all world, success in the workplace becomes everything. Parents who want the best for their children when they enter the workforce focus on what it takes to position them for good jobs rather than on making the right marriage (as used to be the case among the wealthy). This takes time.

This helps explain why professionals, both men and women put in long hours on childrearing as well as at work. In *Unequal Childhoods*, the sociologist Annette Lareau documents this trend, showing how upper–middle-class families in her study focus on what she terms "concerted cultivation," or an emphasis on developing a child's talents. She finds that parents at the top of the income ladder worry about early childhood education because of economic anxiety as well as because of the groundswell of research finding that early childhood matters for future skill development. This concerted cultivation, however, requires a great deal of time, which is one thing professional families too often have in short supply. Families with the income to do so often outsource this work to tutors or enroll children in expensive after-school or summer-enrichment activities, on top of investing time in their children's development.[29]

We see professional parents' anxieties for their children's future playing out especially in concerns about their children's education. They want to get their children into the right educational environments early on so they can attend the right college and get good jobs when they grow up. Given the economic trends over the past forty years, this is eminently logical. Yet it's also crazy-making. In 2008, filmmaker Marc Simon told this story in a documentary entitled *Nursery University*, in which he followed five high-income Manhattan families as they moved through the elite preschool application process. Reportedly, Simon—also a lawyer—got the idea for the film when one of his colleagues rushed out of the office for pre-school interviews. Simon wasn't a parent, and the absurdity of a preschool interview seemed ripe for study. What he showed was that the competition is brutal. Indeed, a recent report from the University of California–Berkeley finds that in fall 2014 there were about four preschool slots for every ten children living in Manhattan, even after the recent expansion of public preschools in New York City. Even if you have the money to pay for high-quality care and educational opportunities, you still have to compete for the most coveted slots.[30]

Another anxiety-producing time is applying for college. It's not enough for professional families to see their children go to college; children must attend the *right* college. The economists Garey Ramey and Valerie Ramey call this competition the "rug rat race." In their research, they find that compared with other families, college-educated parents have increased the time they spend on child care as a result of the heightened competition for college admissions. (Even so, the evidence is mixed on how much going to a specific school matters. According to the economists Stacy Dale and Alan Krueger, "Students who attended more selective colleges earned about the same as students of seemingly comparable ability who attended less selective schools." Actually getting into a school like Princeton doesn't matter as much as being the type of person who could get into Princeton.)[31]

Notably, professional families can afford advantages that low-income and middle-class families cannot. Some call this "opportunity hoarding," where those with money are able to ensure that their children have access to the resources necessary to fill tomorrow's high-paying jobs. To the extent that all children don't have access to the resources and tools they need to become highly skilled, it harms the overall economy. The United States came to be an economic superpower in no small part because we were the first nation to invest in universal access to primary and secondary schools—not just education for those at the very top. The high-stakes race for education may lead to some children getting those choice jobs, but if a good education is reserved for the wealthy, who have seemingly endless resources, then it won't lead to the kind of human capital across the labor force that our economy needs.[32]

A Long Way Down

Evidence shows that rising inequality has made it even more costly for families—even those near the top—to feel economically secure. As inequality has risen, families have engaged in a "keeping-up-with-the-Joneses" escalation of consumption. This trend may take the form of families purchasing too many high-end stainless steel appliances they really cannot afford, but indications are that some increased consumption stems from concerns for their children's education. Economist Robert Frank argues that families higher up the income ladder have been borrowing to purchase a home in a neighborhood with the best schools. As those at the top have shifted the frame upward to get into the best schools, families just below them have struggled to keep up. Frank calls these "expenditure cascades" and finds that as inequality has risen, people spend more to keep up with those just above them.[33]

The sociologist Marianne Cooper conducted in-depth interviews with families at the top that revealed deep anxieties about maintaining their enviable positions despite their high incomes and impressive resumes. She tells of families who are "upscaling" the very idea of what is necessary to feel economically secure. She found that high-income, professional families are acutely aware that to ensure their children's future place in the economic hierarchy, they must invest in developing their skills and talents. They also know that to maintain their lifestyle into old age, they have to save—a lot—for their retirement. Yet they also told her that the benchmarks are constantly rising and slightly out of reach: children are never doing enough to stay in the fast track at school, mothers can't juggle work and life decisions with enough aplomb, and fathers are always concerned about family finances. There is "never-resolved anxiety about goalposts."[34]

Professional families' high incomes allow them to purchase high-quality care and other perks that are out of reach for most middle-class and working-class families. These include housecleaning and healthful prepared foods, which their long hours often necessitate. They have enough money to purchase the best child care and elder care, and while they may bemoan the expense or become frustrated that they are charged extra when they cannot pick up their children promptly by 6 PM, they do not rely on an array of friends and relatives to provide care for their children. They are more likely than those with less income to hire a nanny to care for their children.[35]

One surefire way to beat the time crunch is to eat out or order in. Just because they don't cook doesn't mean they're eating fast food or less nutritious foods. Professional families can afford to rely on freshly prepared food from their local Whole Foods or restaurant meals. They certainly pay more for food. In 2012, families in the top fifth of the income distribution spent 11.4 percent of their annual income on food—a smaller share than among families with lower incomes. But nearly half of their total food spending—46.7 percent—was on food away from home, a larger share than among other income groups.[36]

This kind of outsourcing has led to the rise of many of the service jobs discussed in Chapter 3. It also has fueled the polarization of U.S. jobs. The availability of a pool of workers to be child-care providers, home health aides for the aging, or home-delivery grocers makes it possible for professional families to put in long hours at work. This has driven up employment, especially among low-wage, service-sector workers. As our economy becomes increasingly polarized because professional families have schedules that can work only if they can purchase household help, we're seeing jobs becoming polarized, too.[37]

I am certainly not going to argue that policymakers should focus on raising the salaries of professionals so they can afford better household help. But as long as professionals need household help to put in long hours, we either need to reexamine their working conditions—no more late nights!—or find a better way to ensure that the child-care providers, home health aides, and food-service workers earn a living wage.

In the late nineteenth and early twentieth centuries, a small but growing group of professional women sounded the alarm about the conditions facing working families. Francis Perkins was a part of the Hull House, a settlement house in Chicago that provided services to the local community. In the settlement house movement, which had branches in Great Britain and the United States, educated women committed to live among the poor to provide educational and other services and to learn about their lives. Much of the early sociological research came out of this movement, as those involved studied what caused poverty and how they could empower families to move up and into the economically secure middle class.

Today, professional women don't join settlement houses. They write books and light up the Internet with serious conversations. After the publication of Anne-Marie Slaughter's article and Sheryl Sandberg's book, the debate focused on whether now is the time to change the rules. Having Sandberg and Slaughter step up and share their stories is powerful. They are using their perches to sound the alarm. This is important. Work-life reforms to meet the needs of twenty-first-century families and workplaces won't happen unless those who drive our nation's political process embrace them.

Yet we also need to be watchful. In Chapter 3, I quoted radio broadcaster Michel Martin, who noted that the challenges of balancing career and family are too often seen as a problem for white professionals. She has a point. Our national conversation about how to address conflicts between career and family is often led by professional families—and particularly white professional women. This book is a part of that conversation. My hope is that we can learn from the stories of professionals. These aren't everyone's experiences,

but that doesn't make the problems any less real or any less important for us to consider in the overall economic cycle.

We must ensure, however, that any work-life reforms do not just
help professional families. We've seen that for families up and down
the income spectrum the rules governing what firms, families,
and the government owe one another in determining the boundary
between time for work and time for life are woefully outdated. All
families are struggling to find time. Reforms need to address all of
the work-life problems faced by working-class and middle-class families, as well as professional families.

Making change happen may mean getting the help of professionals. Research shows that legislation in the United States passes
only if the economic elite support it. Professional families who vote
and donate money to political campaigns need to get behind work-
life reforms that apply to low-income and middle-class families for
these reforms to become law. Today's politics requires a coalition
with elites. Even as we might be frustrated by this finding, as it cuts
against our belief in the power of democracy, in the case of the issues around family economic security, the professional class may be
well-placed to help effect change. The good news is that these are
problems everyone faces, which makes finding common ground
easier.[38]

Thinking Like an Economist

In the previous three chapters, we learned that families up and down the income ladder are struggling with an economy that just doesn't work for them and their families. Jobs don't fit today's busy family lives. Families have been left on their own to navigate the day-in, day-out conflicts between work and home life. No set of public policies comes anywhere close to helping them out.

Back in the 1970s, when Nixon missed an opportunity to address budding economic insecurities, his advisers' rationale was cultural. They wanted to preserve their idea of traditional motherhood, even in the face of structural economic changes. Today, the arguments against work-life policies that could meet the needs of twenty-first-century families are often couched in economic language. Take the issue of paid sick days. In many communities, advocates have sought laws giving workers the right to earn a few days of paid sick time that they can use when they or their child becomes ill or needs to see a doctor. Typically, they ask employers to pay the employees for five to seven days a year of earned time off for sickness or routine medical care. Even though these laws provide a minimal, commonsensical benefit, conservative politicians have a long record of opposing this kind of legislation, claiming that it would be bad for the local economy, and so bad for individual businesses that they either might not hire—or have to fire—people.

In 2013 and 2014, for example, eight cities in New Jersey (East Orange, Irvington, Jersey City, Newark, Passaic, Paterson, Montclair, and Trenton)—covering about 140,000 workers—voted paid sick days ordinances into law. In response to the wave of municipalities passing legislation, New Jersey's Republican governor and 2016 presidential hopeful Chris Christie said, "These towns that are doing it just continue to make New Jersey less and less competitive. . . . And then when businesses leave the state, they want to know why."[1]

Self-professed conservatives are not the only ones pushing this economic argument: it has crossed over to liberals as well. In 2010, former New York City council speaker Christine Quinn—a Democrat—was beginning to campaign to become the first woman (and lesbian) mayor of New York City. Like a good liberal, she supported raising the minimum wage. But in October 2010, she drew a line at a bill that would have allowed workers to earn five paid sick days a year. She took the side of her Republican mayor, Michael Bloomberg, who said that the legislation would be "disastrous" for the New York City economy.[2]

In taking this position, both Quinn and Bloomberg were bucking public opinion. Polls showed that three in four New Yorkers backed the legislation, and support was growing.[3] At the time, the majority of the city council—thirty-five out of fifty-one members, according to news reports—did as well, meaning that Quinn could have easily brought up the paid sick day bill for a vote, with the majority able to pass the legislation and override Mayor Bloomberg's veto. At that time, however, Quinn refused to bring the legislation up for a vote.[4] Her press release explained why, articulating her view of how the economy works:

> In an ideal world, we'd be able to provide all benefits to every New Yorker. In a better economy, we might have the financial freedom to both expand benefits and create new jobs. But that's not the reality we live in. . . . Providing sick leave to working New Yorkers is a noble goal, and supporters of this bill have the best of intentions. But now is simply not the right time for a measure that threatens the survival of small business owners.[5]

We could call this Quinn-essential tough love. Quinn agreed that the policy was nice in principle, but in practice, she claimed the mantle of serious-minded economics. (Voters agreed that Quinn was wrong; the eventual winner, Bill de Blasio, made this a campaign issue and signed the Earned Sick Time Act into law in June 2013.)[6]

Chris Christie and Christine Quinn are politicians. They don't claim to be economists. But as Stephen Colbert used to say, there seems to be some "truthiness" behind what they are saying. After all, if businesses have to cough up more money, wouldn't that hurt their bottom line? If their bottom line is hurt, won't they stop hiring or lay people off? These questions are unsettling. Maybe paid sick days are a bad idea, economically speaking. Ask an average citizen on the street, and he may agree that Christie and Quinn make a certain amount of sense.

As it turns out, there is more to economics than this simple story. A firm is not the whole economy. The economy's performance does not hinge only on the short-term interests of business. In this chapter, we will see that what happens inside families is just as important to making the economy hum along as what happens inside firms. We need both, of course, but it starts with families.[7]

Economics Begins with Families

Sure, paying workers for a few days of sick time has a direct cost to companies. If the government requires coffee-shop owners to pay their baristas when they don't come into work, then, in the simplest of frameworks, the firm will have to cut back on how much coffee it sells and earn less in profits or increase the price of coffee to cover the extra expenses. This is what economists call a classic supply-side argument. We use the term "supply" to talk about the amount of something made available at a given price. If costs rise—and everything else stays the same—then this upsets the firm's business plan. If we look only at the supply side, we take into account only the effects of paying sick workers when they stay home on the firm's immediate, cost-side of the ledger.

This analysis—so far—ignores the other effects of paid sick days. Remember demand and supply? Those are the key ideas that many of us learned about in high school economics. Even if your only concern is whether a policy is good for business, you need to look at more than just the supply side of the equation. A key to understanding the economy overall is to find where the supply curve intersects the demand curve. It is essential to consider all the factors that influence demand as well as supply. Indeed, good business-people think about this as much if not more than their own internal costs. Just listen to small business owner Freddy Castiblanco, who owns Terraza 7 Train Café, in Queens, NY, and supported the New York City paid sick days legislation:

> Lack of paid sick days has consequences not only for workers but also for business, particularly in my community. Those workers are my customers. We need to protect salaries. If we protect the salaries, if we give jobs stability, we are going to protect the purchasing power of potential customers. If you give me tax cuts, I won't be able to generate any more jobs. What really creates jobs in my community is customers. We need the capacity of [purchasing] power of our customers, but particularly low-income Latinos who are our customers in Jackson Heights, Elmhurst, and Corona.[8]

Castiblanco grounded his support for paid sick days in a demand-side argument.

Demand is someone's willingness and—just as important—ability to buy a good or service. Many things affect demand. Certainly price matters. We all know how to comparison shop. If the local coffee shop charges $5 for a cup of coffee, I might decide it's a good day to start drinking tea—or I might head to the 7-11 across the street for a big $1.50 cup of Joe. How much I am willing to pay for the quality of the good or service will also be important (do I want to pay for a particular variety of coffee beans from a specific country), as will the tastes or the fashion of the times (am I looking to buy a cup of coffee for my Grandma, who preferred weak coffee—think "instant"—over that "thick black stuff"?). All those choices, however, depend on how much money I have in my pocket (or in my line of credit), which will determine how much I can demand and what level of quality. For the economy overall, demand rises when more people have good-paying jobs.

Allowing workers to earn paid sick days may also affect demand. If the barista seems to have a stuffed-up nose or sneezes on the cash register, that may encourage me to buy my caffeinated beverage someplace else. Without the right to earn paid sick days, when the barista stays home, he loses a day's pay, which means he doesn't eat out Friday night. Maybe this is the third sick day he's taken and the coffee-shop owner fires him—so he misses his rent payment and can buy only rice and beans until he can find another job. All of these possibilities would create some turbulence in demand. Of all the policies we'll examine in this book, paid sick days might have some of the smallest demand-side effects. An increase in the availability of high-quality, affordable child care or elder care may have larger effects on what and how much families consume. Nonetheless, even in the case of paid sick days, we can see an economic effect on both supply and demand.

The story of how the economy works doesn't end with demand and supply. "Labor productivity" is also an important component. Economists use this term to refer to how much better or worse a firm gets at producing goods and services—how the firm seeks to produce more "widgets" per hour, say, or, to keep going with our coffee-shop example, serve more coffee per hour. The concept of productivity helps us move beyond an overly simplistic understanding of the way firms operate. Productivity-enhancing investments might include a faster coffeemaker or a more efficient system for taking orders that reduces customer wait time. Boosting productivity is the key to increasing profits because the firm that can build more—or better—widgets per hour of labor can reduce its prices, sell more, and bring in more money.

Boosting productivity isn't just about improvements in technology. It's also about the qualities of the workers in the economy. Paid sick days are a perfect example of a productivity-enhancing policy. Paid sick time lets people recover when they're ill and care for their sick family members. This boosts productivity. Sick people won't show up for work; they won't waste the day groggily pretending to work; and they won't get the whole office sick. If having paid sick days leads to fewer people quitting—or being fired for not showing up—productivity is enhanced. Baristas who know how to do their jobs—and do them well—save firms money.

We can see how the whole economy works in Figure 5.1, a picture you can find in most standard introductory economics textbooks. The key economic players are households (most of which are families), and firms. Moving clockwise from the top left, we see the four phases of the economic cycle. Families buy goods and services from firms and, in turn, supply firms with workers by selling time. Firms buy people's labor, or time, to produce goods and services, which they then sell to families, completing the cycle.[9]

So far, we are retreading high school economics. Complexities are left out of the standard picture, which doesn't even attempt to distinguish the different ways that men and women typically participate in each quadrant of the economic cycle (let alone other differences, such as age, race or ethnicity, immigration status, or disability). Further, we too often overlook how our future workforce (and the vitality of our future economy) is the product of today's families—their children. As we work our way through each quadrant, we will talk about some of the ways that an explicit focus on different roles of men and women affects how we think about each quadrant.

Figure 5.1 shows us how Christie and Quinn's economic logic wasn't quite right. Work-life policies do more than help families function better; they can help workers be more productive and improve the bottom line of businesses. By tracing out what happens in each of the four quadrants, we can better understand what buying goods and services, selling time, buying time, and selling goods and

Fig. 5.1 The economic cycle.

services are each about, and what factors influence them. In all four areas, we can improve economic outcomes by ensuring that workers and their families have the right kinds of work-life policies in place to be more productive at work and at home.

Buying Goods and Services

Starting from the top left of Figure 5.1, families buy goods and services from businesses. An economist would say that families "demand" firms' outputs. As consumers, we shop for the best quality at the lowest price on the basis of our preferences. When we start with demand for goods and services, this puts the family and its role as consumers at the forefront of the economic cycle. Many economists argue that the economic cycle shown in Figure 5.1 *starts* here, with demand. Although the other components are important, the initial spark that drives the economic cycle is people who need to buy goods and services to meet basic human needs—as well as to satisfy consumerist desires.

There is some truth to this assertion. How well the buying goods and services quadrant works—how much families spend and whether that spending is stable—is a key economic indicator. The total value of what families purchase is by far the largest component of U.S. economic output. Economists measure the sum of all the goods and services produced within our national borders as gross domestic product, or GDP. The National Income and Product Accounts, produced by the U.S. Bureau of Economic Analysis (a government statistical agency), divides our nation's total output (GDP) into four basic categories: consumption, investment, government spending, and net exports. U.S. households (who do the "consuming" in consumption) account for the biggest chunk by far: nearly 70 percent of all spending in the economy. This might contradict what readers take away from the headlines of the business pages of newspapers and websites, which dedicate disproportional attention to the other three categories.[10]

The combination of people in other countries (purchasing our exports), government, and business (which economists refer to as "investment," although this also includes residential investment—that is, buying homes) buy the other 30 percent of economic output. Most household spending is on services—that is, haircuts, dinners out, car washes, education, health care, or dog grooming—with only about a third spent on goods—the tangible things, such as cars, clothing, furniture, knick-knacks, and food.[11]

So what determines how much families spend overall? The answer is that spending depends largely on what you earn—and I'm guessing you didn't need an economist to tell you that. This is what connects the first quadrant to the next. For families up and down the income ladder, finding and keeping a job determine whether they can put food on the table and pay the rent or mortgage. Only families on the highest rung of the income ladder get more than a very small fraction of their income from interest, rent, or capital, while families at the very bottom get a larger share of their income than others from government-support programs such as unemployment or disability payments.[12]

There is a "life hack" that frees families momentarily from needing to earn enough to buy the goods and services they want and need. It's called borrowing. We learned in Chapter 2 that the typical family's income is about the same now as it was in the mid-1990s. As income growth stalled, families saved less and borrowed more. In the early 1980s, households saved just over 10 percent of their income, but by the mid-2000s, this fell to less than 5 percent. In July 2005, the savings rate hit a four-decade low of 1.9 percent. Household debt also rose. Households' debt-to-income ratio almost doubled between 1980 and 2000, and then grew sharply—faster than it had in the past fifty years—between 2000 and 2007. During the early 2000s, debt rose more in families at the lower end of the income distribution than in those at the top. In 2014, six years after the economic crisis, household debt was at late-2007 levels and the savings rate hovered around 5 percent.[13]

From one perspective, less saving and more debt meant that families could maintain their spending and fulfill their role as consumers. If your income rises over your lifetime, borrowing can be a good strategy to smooth out your consumption. But borrowing has its risks. And it has to be paid back. Living on credit is a short-term strategy. If my income grows, then it's easy to pay off the loan. But if my income is the same when I borrow as when my debts are due, then I'll still have to pare back my spending to cover what I borrowed, plus interest, with an unavoidable downward push on my demand.

Thus it's sensible—even savvy—for a young person to borrow to pay for college, as most can be confident that a college degree will

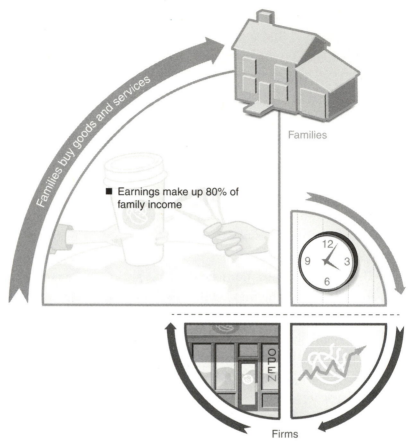

Families

Earnings make up 80% of
family income

Firms

Fig. 5.2 Families buy goods and services, looking for the best-quality products at the
lowest price.

mean a better job and the ability to pay off the loan. For a laid-off
middle-aged worker, however, borrowing in order to keep spending
at the same level as before may not be wise. That person may never
find another job at the same salary level—or even find another
job—and more debt could lead to bankruptcy. As we learned in recent years, when too many families are in too much debt, the foundations of the entire economy are weakened—especially when high
debt is paired with little or no income growth.[14]

Policymakers who counsel tough love expect families to live
within their means, save, and invest in their children and care for

their ailing family members. Yet they scoff—or scold—when families get into too much debt. But the lack of income gains that we learned about in earlier chapters forces many families to borrow just to cover the basics and make necessary investments in their economic future.

We can see the basic elements of buying goods and services in Figure 5.2. Every firm needs customers to buy the products they produce. That's the basic feature of our market economy. For this to happen, customers need to have money to spend. For most of us, earnings from employment constrain our spending and thus our economic demand.

Selling Time

Moving from the top-left section of Figure 5.1 to the top right, we have selling time, or what economists call "labor supply." This is how much time families devote to paid employment. It is measured in terms of how many people have a job or are seeking one, as well as how much each person works or wants to work. In the United States, about 65 percent of the total share of the U.S. population over twenty years of age is in the labor force, and the typical person works 34.5 hours a week. Figure 5.3 shows labor-force participation for adult men and women (age twenty and over), going back to 1948. There are four notable trends. Men's labor-force participation fell steadily from the 1950s through the late 1990s while women's rose. Both men and women had little change in their labor supply between the late-1990s and just before the Great Recession in 2007. Finally, as of this writing, neither men nor women have recovered from the Great Recession, even though the subsequent economic recovery has now been going on for nearly a decade.

How much time is sold—that is, how much labor is supplied—is an important piece of our economic cycle because it determines how much families can buy. A decline in the supply of labor will slow U.S. growth. As William Galston aptly wrote in the *Wall Street Journal*, the decline in labor supply will "eat away at our economic prosperity." We can see this by simply looking at the economic

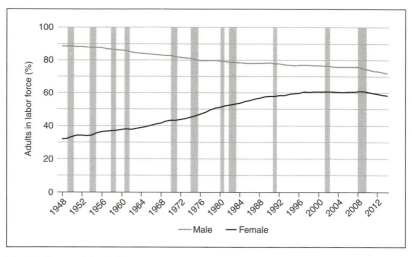

Fig. 5.3 Share of the U.S. adult population in the labor force, by sex, 1948–2014. From the 1950s through the late 1990s, men's labor-force participation fell steadily while women's rose. Between the late-1990s and 2007, neither men's nor women's labor supply changed notably, and neither has recovered from the Great Recession that began in 2008. *Note:* Civilian labor-force share is given for those 20 years and over. Shaded areas indicate recessions as defined by the National Bureau of Economic Research.

importance of the added hours of work and rising wages of women. Economists Eileen Appelbaum, John Schmitt, and I estimated that, between 1979 and 2012, the greater hours of work by women accounted for 11 percent of the growth in gross domestic product. In today's dollars, had women not worked more, families would have spent at least $1.7 trillion less on goods and services—roughly equivalent to the combined U.S. spending on Social Security, Medicare, and Medicaid in 2012. Women's labor supply has serious economic implications.[15]

Many factors affect how much time people want to sell to employers. There is only so much time in the day, and only so much time we could physically work without collapsing from exhaustion. For most of us, how much time we sell is based on how much money we need and how well we are able to sort out our work and life responsibilities. Whereas for some people work is a calling and perhaps we'd be doing our jobs even if we weren't paid (like the pastor who just has to preach), for most of us—even those of us who love our jobs—that's not the case. We get up every morning and fight the traffic to get to our desks or the shop floor or behind the espresso bar because we have to. We need the money. We work to support our families.

Economists also know that people won't work if the pay is too low or the time demands are impossible to meet. Today's economists call this someone's "reservation wage," the wage below which we simply will not take the job, thank you very much. No matter how much we like our coworkers or the doughnuts that the boss brings in every third Friday, if we have a choice at all, most of us won't take a job if the pay is too low. Some people have few options, but we all have a bottom line. This is different for everyone; it's a measure of how we value our time. The unemployed nurse might search for a new job in her field at about the same pay she had before she lost her job, rather than take a job mowing lawns in her neighborhood for a tenth as much pay. But the laid-off textile worker who's looking at being evicted if he doesn't find something—anything—to pay the rent might mow those lawns this month if that would bring in enough money to placate his landlord. But if not, he may also pass.

The reservation wage is tied to the income we need to make ends meet. In *The Wealth of Nations*, first published in 1776, Adam Smith put it this way: "A man must always live by his work, and his wages must at least be sufficient to maintain him. They must even upon most occasions be somewhat more; otherwise it would be impossible for him to bring up a family, and the race of such workmen could not last beyond the first generation."[16]

Wages aren't the only thing we consider when we decide how much time to sell to an employer. We look at the whole package— workplace benefits, working conditions, and whether the job is the right fit for our career plan and our life outside of work. The stories and analysis in the previous three chapters about how families up and down the income ladder are struggling to cope with work-life conflicts show that we need to think more seriously about how these affect how much time to sell. Before the barista can fight the traffic to get to the coffee shop to work his shift, he has to find high-quality child care—care he can afford on his wages. If he cannot afford child care, he may not work. Many of us also have to care for the sick or the aging, which affects when we work, how much we can work, or how much we feel we need to earn.

Evidence shows that the flat labor-supply trends shown in Figure 5.3 are in part linked to our nation's failure to address conflicts between work and life. The United States used to have one of the highest rates of labor-force participation for both men and women across developed economies. Now we're falling behind—far behind. The Organisation for Economic Co-operation and Development reports that as of 2013 (the latest data available) the United States ranks twenty-first out of twenty-two developed nations in terms of men's labor supply and nineteenth out of twenty-two such countries for women's. Economists Francine Blau and Lawrence Kahn point to the lack of family-friendly policies as a likely explanation for the relatively low share of women working: "Unlike the United States, most other economically advanced nations have enacted an array of policies designed to facilitate women's participation in the labor force, and such policies have on average expanded over the past 20 years relative to the United States."[17]

The lag in men's participation may be more surprising, but men now report even more conflict between work and family than do women. As women have increased their time at work, men have had to share in the work of the "second shift" at home. One reason for the greater reporting of work-life conflict among men is that with the once commonplace stay-at-home American Wife typically no longer at home, men and women must often each cope with the caring needs of their ailing parents. In many families, a man cannot assume that his stay-at-home wife will care for his ailing parents. According to data from the U.S. Department of Labor, men take nearly as much leave as women to care for a seriously ill family member. In my own family, both my father and my husband's father provided significant care for their parents as they aged, taking time off from work and coping with the ensuing stress of the conflicting demands of work and care.[18]

To complete our understanding of selling time, we also need to consider the long-term issues. Families raise the people who eventually sell time. This isn't a quick or necessarily easy process—every parent knows that parenting is hard work and can be expensive. Families raise children out of love, but economists also know that all that love and care are what create tomorrow's workforce. An economist will tell you that the years from birth to age five are when we learn the skills that affect our future earnings. These are the years when we acquire what economist and Nobel laureate James Heckman terms "non-cognitive" skills, such as how to sit still, get along with others, and delay gratification in the hopes of better future rewards—all foundations for success at work later on. These early-childhood skills are learned from primary caregivers very early in life—be they mom and dad, grandparents, child-care professionals, some combination of these role models, or, sadly, sometimes hardly anyone at all.[19]

Given the importance of early childhood, you may be wondering why the American Wife doesn't just head back home. First, as we learned in the last few chapters, many families need Mom's earnings. Second, many women want to work—and even some will admit that they don't make the best full-time caregivers. (Check out the *Feminine Mystique*, where in 1963 Betty Friedan opened America's eyes to what she called "the problem that has no name," the widespread unhappiness among middle-class women with their lot in life.) Third, many families know that there's no need to worry. Evidence abounds that nonparental child care can be as enriching for children as a mother's care, so long as it's high-quality care (an issue we'll return to in Chapter 8). Further, while mothers are special (very special!), they aren't the only ones who can ensure a good start: Dad is important to child development, too. In fact, enabling Dad to provide care improves children's outcomes. Children who have an engaged father do better in school, have fewer behavioral issues, and have better adult outcomes than children whose fathers don't actively engage with them.[20]

Figure 5.4 lays out the role of selling time in the economic cycle. Families sell time to earn the money they need. Everyone looks for

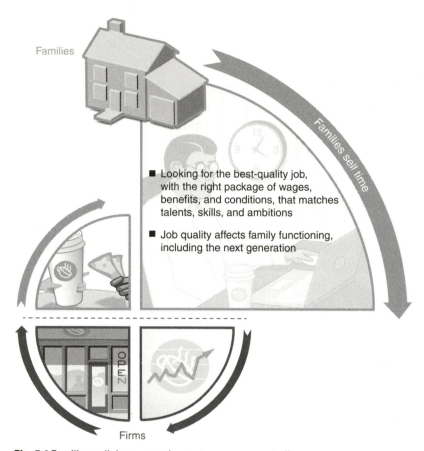

Families

Looking for the best-quality job, with the right package of wages, benefits, and conditions, that matches talents, skills, and ambitions

Job quality affects family functioning, including the next generation

Families sell time

Firms

Fig. 5.4 Families sell time to employers to earn money to live.

the best fit—that perfect job with the best wages, benefits, working conditions, and schedules for his or her life. Work-life policies affect labor supply because they determine how well we can manage the everyday conflicts between our job and our life. Without them, selling time can be a hard sell. For our nation's economy to be as competitive as possible, we want people to be able to make decisions about taking a job on the basis of whether that job is the best fit in terms of productivity. If you're an excellent cook and want to work in a restaurant, the lack of paid sick days isn't a good reason to deprive the economy of your kitchen talent. There are measurable productivity losses associated with poor job fit.

Buying Time

Next let's turn to the bottom right-hand quadrant of the economic cycle to look at the firm side. People may seek jobs, but they need employers to hire them. That's where labor demand comes in. This refers to how much time and what kind of staff an employer wants to hire. Employers bought more than four billion hours of labor last year. Rules of the game govern when and where and under what conditions employers can hire (we'll go through these in later chapters), but in general, employers have a lot of leeway to do whatever works for them. Sometimes they hire someone to be on staff full-time and pay a fixed salary no matter how many hours worked. At other times, they hire "by the hour," pulling staff in for short or long shifts depending on their needs.[21]

The firm's business plan will dictate how much time it needs to buy from its employees and when it wants to have that staff on hand. Going back to our coffee shop, the owner might want to hire five staff people to work in the morning. This is when the shop sells the most coffee, and a five-person team can serve one person his or her coffee (or tea, with doughnut) every two minutes. This means the line will move fast enough to avoid having people queuing out the door, which would encourage potential customers to skip her shop and head for the one across the street. That's the owner's demand for labor. But she wants only two staff people during the evening shift. By then, few people are interested in a caffeine jolt—more likely, folks are hitting the bar down the street—but she needs some people to clean up and prepare for the next day's rush.

The coffee-shop owner doesn't want just any people staffing her coffee counter. She wants to find the best match between a person's skills and talents and the firm's needs. She wants the barista to be a neat freak who will keep the counter tidy at all times. She wants her coffee buyer to have an exquisitely honed nose for the best beans and be able to negotiate fair prices. Her accountant must be very (very) good at math. She needs the right person for the right job. The owner may be willing to pay more for the right talent. She also might

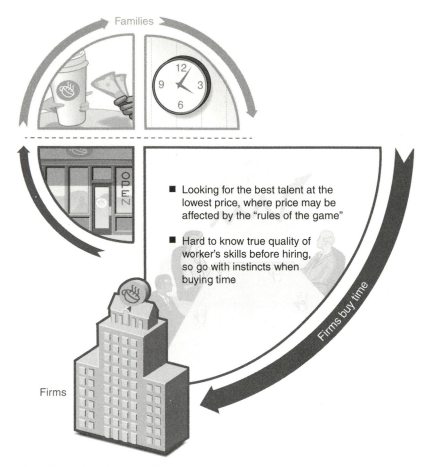

Fig. 5.5 Firms buy time to produce goods and services.

be willing to bargain over working conditions or benefits, if she feels she's getting the perfect fit.

Figure 5.5 shows how buying time fits into the larger economic cycle. Firms buy time to have the staff to make the products. They are looking for the most talented staff at the lowest price who can work the hours the employer needs at the price she can pay. They are looking for the most flexibility so they can make the most money selling goods and services.

Selling Goods and Services

Let's look at the last quadrant, on the lower left of Figure 5.1: the supply of goods and services for sale. In order to produce those delicious cups of coffee, the employer will combine the talents of her employees with inputs—coffee beans, a storefront, a box of doughnuts, and an espresso maker—to make the best, competitively priced cup of coffee in town. If she can get all this right, she'll bring in sufficient profits to keep the shop in business and bring home a tidy income.

Fundamentally, firms are interested in profits, which equal the difference between their revenue—that is, how much they are able to charge for goods and services—and their costs. When selling, it's hard to raise prices. Consumers tend to be price-conscious, especially in low-income and middle-class families, where incomes haven't grown much at all. They will switch up their buying habits if prices rise. In a market economy, consumers have options—they can buy from other firms. If our coffee-shop owner unilaterally decides to charge $6 for a cup of Joe but all the other shops charge $4, she'll soon find her customer base dwindling. That's why the key to selling goods and services is producing the best product at the lowest price. Firms can find ways to control their costs. The cost they have the most control over is typically labor—and how productive that labor is. Firms may not be able to control the price of land or physical capital—the coffee roaster machine, the countertops, or espresso cups—so they typically look to getting productivity high and keeping it there.

High productivity drives firms to look to combine the right talent, at the right price, to work as efficiently as possible. This is how they produce the highest quality goods to sell at the most competitive price. The United States is among the most productive economies in the world. In 2014, the United States produced $67 worth of goods and services per hour worked, the third-highest rate among other developed nations. But we can always do more to boost worker productivity.[22]

So, how do employers do this? There are carrots and there are sticks. The big, juicy carrot is the price of time, that is, what employers have to pay—or what they're willing to concede—to get the work done. One way economists think about this is the idea of an "efficiency wage." Nobel Laureates Joseph Stiglitz and George Akerlof first wrote about this concept in the 1980s, when they argued that one way firms could maximize profit is by using wages to motivate workers so as to induce greater effort and improve productivity. A few pages ago, I quoted Adam Smith saying that wages "must even upon most occasions be somewhat more" than the bare minimum. Employers may pay more than they absolutely must in order to attract—and keep—top talent or to spur greater effort. Sometimes, they will offer benefits that their employees value, such as a terrific health-care plan, a generous 401(k) retirement-savings match, or predictable hours. Putting in place policies to help an employee address conflicts between work and family life is a prime example of how firms can boost the productivity of their employees.[23]

If we listened to Christie and Quinn, we'd see only one aspect of how the price of time affects selling goods and services. Paying people more—or providing more benefits or more flexibility—is a cost, and that's the end of their tale. Their logic is that if the pay package becomes more generous—because the minimum wage goes up or employers have to pay people when they stay home with the flu—maybe our coffee-shop owner will decide that she can do without that fifth staff person in the morning. But that's an extreme step. If she did that, the lines at her shop would be much longer than at other shops and she would lose customers. More likely (and consistent with the evidence, as we'll see in the next chapter), she'll find another way to get more bang for her buck, probably by trying to get a little bit more out of each of her employees.

Further, when every employer has to pay more or provide a new benefit, there's no competitive disadvantage to any one business. Our coffee-shop owner faces the same minimum-wage increase as the owner across the street. Maybe they will both raise the price of doughnuts by ten cents and break even (most doughnut-eaters are too excited about the cakey goodness to change their order because of a ten-cent price increase). Or maybe they will both find a way to improve productivity. The point is, they face the same rise in costs.[24]

We also need to consider the sticks. Bosses can be demanding and drive people to work harder and faster. They can deny them paid sick days or insist on mandatory overtime. Sometimes sticks work. But sometimes they're counterproductive. Sometimes good employees—like my sister—will get fed up and quit. But just because someone stays on the job and shows up to work doesn't mean they are actually being productive—especially in industries where attention to detail matters. A worker with a cold or someone who is worrying about a child in the school nurse's office may not get very much done—and may even make costly mistakes. One study estimated that in 2002 "lost productive time" due to personal or family health reasons cost U.S. employers at least $226 billion, or about $1,685 or more annually per employee, and the majority of this cost—71 percent—was the result of "reduced performance." The authors also note that for some categories of workers, returning to work before they have fully recovered seems to raise costs because they work at a lower level of productivity for a longer period of time.[25]

Policies that keep good people in their jobs can save firms money. Organizations incur a variety of costs when an employee leaves. The cost of staff transitions include advertising, interviewing, hiring, and training a new employee, and the slower productivity until the new employee gets up to speed in his or her new job. Recruiting costs can also include direct expenses such as advertising for someone to fill the new position, the time interviewing those candidates, search fees, referral bonuses, or relocation assistance. (I run an organization and am acutely aware of all these costs!)[26]

These costs can be very high. The consulting firm PriceWaterhouseCoopers LLC estimates that in large firms, hiring costs add up to more than $2,500 for every hire. And it's not just top employees who are expensive to replace. The sociologist Sarah Jane Glynn and I conducted a review of the literature on the cost of job turnover and found that up and down the pay ladder, businesses spend about

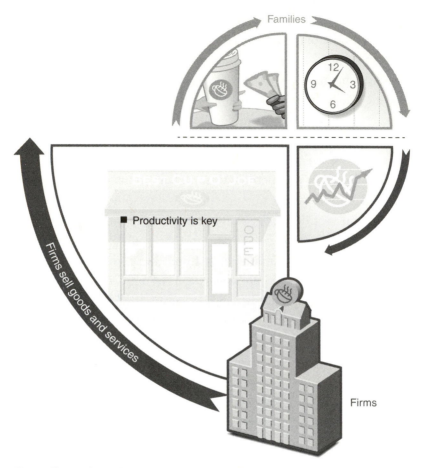

Fig. 5.6 Firms sell goods and services, aiming to produce the best-quality goods and services for the lowest price.

one-fifth of a worker's salary to replace that worker. Among jobs that pay $30,000 or less, the typical cost of turnover was about 16 percent of the employee's annual pay, only slightly below the 19 percent across all jobs paying less than $75,000 a year.[27]

Don't take my word for it. The stock market tends to respond positively when firms introduce workplace flexibility. One study examined the announcements in the *Wall Street Journal* of new work-life balance policies by *Fortune* 500 companies. The researchers found that on average stock prices rose 0.36 percent in the days following these announcements. There's also evidence that a company's profits rise when they give employees access to policies that address conflicts between work and family life. Profits go up because the firms attract higher-quality workers and their employees are not only less likely to quit but also absent and tardy less. All of this boosts productivity and, with it, profits.[28]

Figure 5.6 sums up how firms seek to sell the most goods and services by producing the best-quality product at the lowest price. They do this by being more productive than the other guy. This drives the overall productivity of our nation—that thing called "competitiveness"—and it also makes lots of money for firms. Notably, this is a cycle. It doesn't matter where you start, but you do need to see that each quadrant is connected to the others. And then you need to decide which point in the cycle is the most important arbiter of sustained, competitive economic growth.

Demand and Supply

Chris Christie and Christine Quinn argue that the economic cycle starts—and ends—in the bottom-right quadrant, buying time. Yet as we've seen, this is putting the cart before the horse. Without customers, there is no demand. No one has a reason to invest or hire workers unless they know they can sell what they produce. Listen to Nick Hanauer, founder of the Seattle-based venture capital firm Second Avenue Partners and an original investor in Amazon.com, who said in a recent *Bloomberg Businessweek* column: "Only consumers can set in motion a virtuous cycle that allows companies to survive and thrive and business owners to hire. An ordinary middle-class consumer is far more of a job creator than I ever have been or ever will be." Hanauer is just one of a growing number of business leaders who wholeheartedly agrees that families are the real job creators.[29]

This question of where the economic cycle truly begins is at the core of the most important economic debate of the past two centuries.

In the early 1800s, the argument tilted in favor of the idea that if you make it, they will buy it. At that time, the French businessman and economist Jean-Baptiste Say published *A Treatise on Political Economy; or The Production Distribution and Consumption of Wealth*, in which he argued that once a product is made and ready for market, it will be sold. Otherwise, he argued, the product has no value:

> When the producer has put the finishing hand to his product, he is most anxious to sell it immediately, lest its value should diminish in his hands. Nor is he less anxious to dispose of the money he may get for it; for the value of money is also perishable. But the only way of getting rid of money is in the purchase of some product or other. Thus the mere circumstance of creation of one product immediately opens a vent for other products.[30]

Say's logic was that making something would itself create demand for the goods and services that go into producing an item.

By the early twentieth century, Say's idea was widely influential, and it is still at the foundation of conservative economic argument. To continue with our coffee-shop example, this suggests that when the owner buys the coffee, milk, and sugar (and doughnuts) and combines them into a yummy breakfast item, this creates demand. Having produced a cup of coffee, the coffee-shop owner will pretty much do anything to sell it. Unsold, it has no value. When I think of Say's Law, I hear the mysterious voice from the film *A Field of Dreams* saying, "If you build it, they will come." Of course, in that film, Kevin Costner's character, Ray, did build it (a baseball field), and the ghosts of baseball legends past did come to play.[31]

But that's a movie. What if tomorrow everyone decides to give up coffee in favor of tea? Or if tough economic times lead people to invest in a thermos and make coffee at home? I think that a more apt message comes from the modern-day satirical sitcom *The Simpsons*. In season 4, episode 12, the town invests in a monorail to nowhere, which fails because there are no riders—no demand—for the service. Marge calls this "Springfield's folly."[32]

Springfield's monorail went belly-up because Say's Law is fundamentally flawed. The experience of the Great Depression (and the more recent Great Recession that began in late 2007) led economists to rethink Say's theory. They concluded that the cycle starts in the top-left corner, with buying goods and services. In 1936, economist John Maynard Keynes published his treatise *The General Theory on Interest, Employment, and Money*, in part to refute Say's Law. He put forth the alternate view that demand drives supply. In his words, "All production is for the purpose of ultimately satisfying a consumer."[33] This revolutionized how we think about the economy. All four quadrants of Figure 5.1 are important—it's an interlocking system—but the cycle starts with meeting people's needs.

Thinking about the whole economy and not just the supply-side piece isn't a new idea. Unfortunately, it's not one we've heard much about over the past few decades. We've been driving around in the dark, lost. In 1914, Henry Ford famously announced that he would begin paying his workers the then-princely sum of $5 a day. We often hear this story as an example of an employer who understood that in order to sell his product, he needed a workforce that earned enough to buy it. But the truth is that Henry Ford first implemented this policy to directly boost his bottom line. At the time, assembly line workers had a very high rate of turnover. Ford put in place the $5-a-day wage as a carrot to improve productivity. It worked: the $5-a-day program increased both productive efficiency and the company's profitability.[34]

By the middle of the 1930s, the idea that supporting the middle class was important to our economy was so thoroughly embedded in the popular imagination that President Franklin D. Roosevelt was able to say that the minimum wage brought on "a sounder distribution of buying power," and this was a key reason to enact the Fair Labor Standards Act. By the 1950s, the consensus around this economic model was so solid that Republicans and Democrats were in agreement that government should make the kinds of investments that created economic security for working families and that taxes were a necessary part of the equation.

Yet before the ink was dry on the New Deal policies Roosevelt put in place, a group of business leaders were mobilizing to undo, or at least gut, his signature legislation and reframe the economics of the debate. The arguments are the same ones we hear today, that anything policymakers seek to do to support workers and their family are more likely than not "job killers" or are, at the very least "economically inefficient." As Kimberly Phillips-Fein documents in *Invisible Hands: The Businessmen's Crusade against the New Deal*, beginning in the 1930s, the "money and the organizational connections of businessmen" were used to "espouse the vision of the free market." She points to the founding of the Liberty League in the summer of 1934 by the du Pont family, whose wealth was so outrageously large that they could aim to buy everything from political influence to a U.S. Olympic wrestling team. The Liberty League had the explicit purpose of pushing back on policies that support workers and their families. Their mission was clear. "You can't recover prosperity by seizing the accumulation of the thrifty and distributing it to the thriftless and unlucky," said the chairman of the Illinois division of the Liberty League in 1934. Efforts like these laid the first stones in a decades-long effort to rebuild popular support for the supply-side economic arguments we hear today from people across the political spectrum, like Christie and Quinn.[35]

Three principles emerge from the analysis so far. The first is that the economy is a system in which families and firms matter. To understand what is good for the economy, we must look at demand and supply. This means looking at what happens inside firms and families.

Not just firms. Not just families. Both. We've seen that families' and firms' relationships with the economy are multifaceted. Whereas the very purpose of a firm is to engage in the economy, the purpose of families is both economic and noneconomic. Families are where we raise children and care for one another. These roles may be subjectively more important to family members than their role in the economy. This complication shapes how work-life policies play an important role in our economy.

The second analytic principle is that we need to look at all kinds of costs. We need to look both at out-of-pocket and hidden costs and at benefits for families *and* firms.

Costs and benefits matter, but costs aren't only what firms pay out of pocket, and benefits aren't only about more money. Costs include all the hidden costs that may be hard to see. A change in policy, for example, may require a shift in managerial style, which in turn may require the added cost of retraining supervisors about new rules. Whereas in the past middle managers may have been trained to automatically deny requests for leave, now there may need to be a process for allowing it. Benefits may also be hidden. A flexible work schedule may boost a child's school achievement—a benefit that the Human Resource staff at Dad's job may not be able to see or savor, but this certainly counts for families and for the economy more generally. Even on the so-called cost side of the ledger, work-life policies often don't entail out-of-pocket costs for firms. Moreover, many of the hidden costs provide tangible benefits for firms, once we dig a little deeper. Much depends on productivity—how do firms get the most out of their workforce?

Productivity increases sometimes take a while to show up. This brings us to our third principle: don't just look at the immediate cost or benefit, look at the long-term effects.

Upfront costs might be obvious, but benefits may take a while to show up. Think of the Interstate Highway system. In the thirty-five years after President Dwight D. Eisenhower signed the Federal Aid Highway Act of 1956, our nation invested $114 billion to connect communities across the United States; the benefits are still with us today. Similarly, a shift in managerial style may entail a one-time cost, but after that, training on how to implement the new policy is just part of the package of supervisor training—nothing special, no added cost. The cost of giving workers flexibility to care for a sick child may entail short-term costs to the firm, but that may mean the child gets well sooner and thus the parent is back at work sooner. Further, if parents are better able to provide care and to earn a living, once their children grow up they will enter the labor force with higher levels of skills. When we're thinking about the economy, we have to keep in mind that long-term trends matter just as much as— sometimes even more than—short-term trends.

Putting it all together, we see that a firm might face a direct short-term cost when a new work-life policy becomes law, but that is not true for the economy overall. After the law passes, the store manager will need to find someone to fill in for a sick worker and perhaps pay two workers, one at home sick and one covering for the sick worker on the sales floor. Yet without the law, many other firms and families have to cope with the reverberations of a sick employee who doesn't have the right to a paid day off. Imagine the retail worker has a toddler. The toddler goes to day care sick, making the other children sick. That's an added cost for other families in the day-care center, as well as the day-care center and its employees, who may also fall ill. Alternatively, if the worker stays home and misses a day's pay, she cannot pay her rent on time. That's added economic stress for her landlord. Further, not having paid sick days is associated with higher turnover and other productivity losses, which aren't in the long-term interest of our economy. Businesses and their short-term incentives are important, but they are only a piece of the economy.

The lesson of this chapter is that if you want to sell goods and services, you had better make sure that people can buy them. Whether they will be in a position to do so or not depends on adequate and sustainable selling and buying of time, which is why we have to consider the whole economic cycle, not just one slice of it.

Here at Home: Paid Time off to Care

American business has lost its Silent Partner. When the traditional 1950s American Wife spent her days at home, she could nurse a sick child or an aging parent, or check in on an elderly neighbor while her breadwinner husband went to work. Now that she, too, is in the workforce, that's not possible. Employers can no longer assume that if an employee is healthy, he or she can be at work. Unless a dystopian future of a robot-run society is our destiny, employers will have to cope with the reality that people get sick and that—sometimes—their loved ones need their care. With the American Wife at work, there are times when each of us needs to be Here at Home. Coping with employee absences is part of doing business.

The question is, what are the economic implications of this reality? When an employee needs to be at home, does this harm the economy? In Chapter 5, we heard the claims of Chris Christie and Christine Quinn that paid sick days would be bad for the economy. They said it would cost businesses dearly. But in a world without the American Wife at home, does giving the American Worker some time off mean we're dragging down our economy? How does the economy benefit from paid time off to care—or does it?

This chapter will examine how being here at home—either for a few days or for extended leave—affects all four quadrants of the economic cycle. We'll start with short-term time off, what I'll call "paid sick days," taken when an employee or his immediate family member is ill, and then move on to more extended leave, what I'll call "paid family and medical leave." As we go through the economic cycle, we'll heed the three principles identified in Chapter 5. We'll look at demand and supply by taking into account both firms and families. We'll explore the hidden costs and benefits. And we'll highlight both

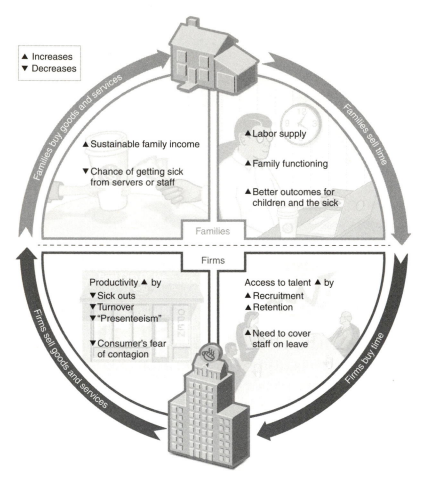

Fig. 6.1 Effects on the economic cycle of policies that let employees be at home.

the long-term and the short-term costs and benefits of these policies.

We'll also bear in mind what we learned in Chapters 2, 3, and 4. There, we saw that for families in the middle, at the bottom, and at the top of the income spectrum, the economic issues are different. Families at the bottom have been stuck with no income growth, while those in the middle have seen slow but fairly limited growth. In both, incomes would have fallen were it not for the added hours and pay of women. At the top, both men and women typically work, and their incomes have soared, but they are still left with too little time to care.

Figure 6.1 provides an overview of how both paid sick days and paid family and medical leave affect our entire economy. Here, we can see how Christie and Quinn were homing in on one specific aspect of the economic cycle: how the cost of buying time affects the price of selling goods and services. They both talked about the direct cost that businesses face when a locality requires employers to pay employees when they stay home sick. But neither focused on the other aspects of the economic cycle. Their comments told an economic story from the firm's perspective as though this was the full economic picture, which simply isn't true. A firm is not the same as the economy; a firm is one important actor in the economic cycle—but families are equally important.

Leave Your Heart in San Francisco: Paid Sick Days

Let's revisit the claims of Christie and Quinn that we heard in Chapter 5. In both of their jurisdictions—the state of New Jersey and New York City, respectively—advocates were calling for legislation to give workers the right to earn paid sick days. Workers with paid sick days can take short, unplanned leave when the worker or his or her family member has an everyday illness. This benefit can be used with little notice—when, for instance, a parent wakes up to a child with the flu. Legislation does not usually allow many days— advocates call for about five to nine days a year—so while paid sick time might help someone who's seriously ill, it's not specifically designed to address that need. Paid sick days are employer-paid because setting up a government agency to pay for such short amounts of time would be very expensive and cumbersome.

A single-minded focus on only one aspect of the economic cycle isn't unique to Christie and Quinn. In 2006, San Francisco was the first place in the United States to pass paid sick day legislation. The initiative became law through a ballot measure and won

59 percent of the vote. Like Christie and Quinn, San Francisco's business community acknowledged the human need to stay home sick but launched a campaign against the policy anyway. In the months leading up to the measure's passage and implementation, leaders in the business community argued that the legislation would either reduce the supply of goods and services or force them to raise their prices, both of which would be bad for business and could lead to job losses.

Just listen to Richard Crain, owner of the Village Grill in San Francisco. In January 2007, Crain told the *San Francisco Chronicle* that if the people passed into law a ballot measure giving workers the right to earn five to nine days of paid sick leave annually—depending on whether they worked for a small or large employer—it would force him out of business. He asked, "How can we afford this? You can only charge so much for a hamburger, and then people will stop coming. I'm 52 and was hoping to do this until I retire, but the city is going to force me out of business."[1]

The Chamber of Commerce and other business organizations also weighed in with their concern that the ordinance would deal a harsh blow to the local economy. Kevin Westlye, executive director of the Golden Gate Restaurant Association, said, "San Franciscans have a history of voting their social conscience as long as someone else writes the check." According to the *New York Times* reporter Steven Greenhouse, Westlye went on to say that "consumers would be hurt, predicting that restaurants would raise prices. . . . The higher prices, he said, might cause some restaurants to lose business—and perhaps close."[2]

To listen to these economic arguments, one might have thought San Francisco was debating a policy that would give workers the right to stay home *every* day and still be paid—which certainly would greatly increase the cost of buying time. But the concerns seem disconnected from the reality of the policy on the table. The proposal was that an employee at a small business could take off 1/52nd of the work year and even then only when sick. At a large business, the employee could take up to nine days a year—a larger share of the work year, but still a minimal amount. Further, the business community seemed oblivious not only to the fact that most employers already offer earned sick time but also to the economic concerns of families and communities. Given that so many firms already find that offering paid sick days makes business sense, what's the evidence behind these dire economic claims?

Notwithstanding the concerns of the business community, in 2006 San Francisco voters chose to go ahead with the ordinance. Workers—including part-time, temporary, and small-business employees—accrue one hour of paid sick time for every thirty hours on the job. We can use San Francisco's experiences—along with those of businesses that have this policy—to have a fact-based conversation about how this policy affects each of the four quadrants of the economic cycle.[3]

When a locality implements a policy to allow workers to earn paid sick days, there are direct, immediate costs. As Figure 6.1 shows—and business owners point out—the cost of buying time rises, and that may affect the price of selling goods and services. Although a single paid sick day is not a substantial cost, it is an added expense. According to the U.S. Bureau of Labor Statistics, when employers provide paid sick days, the direct cost of the policy is thirty-five cents per worker per hour, although it estimates that this amount is less for sales office workers (twenty-one cents per worker per hour) and service workers (fourteen cents per worker per hour). If the firm does not currently provide paid sick days, or does so only for some workers, then there will be a new direct cost to provide this to all those covered by the new legislation.[4]

And it's not just paying the worker to stay home; there are added costs to cover the absence of the sick worker. Employers may need to hire a temporary worker or ask another worker in the firm to work overtime, both of which add out-of-pocket costs. Yet some of these expenses arise even without a sick-day policy. A worker with the flu may stay home simply because he cannot get out of bed.

But we can't think of the cost that earned sick time adds to buying time as simply an extra five, seven, or nine days of paid time off.

First, we shouldn't assume that employees will take all the days available to them. Among those of us whose employers already offer paid sick days, we take an average of two to five per year. Having a state or local policy doesn't change this. In a survey of San Francisco workers, more than a third said they had not used any sick days in the past year; this is about the same as in a survey in Connecticut, the first state to offer paid sick days, after it implemented a paid sick days policy in 2013.[5]

Second, most of us focus on keeping our bosses happy. We need to make a good impression because our livelihoods depend on it. The stakes are higher given that most U.S. workers are not covered by a union contract, and, therefore, annoying our boss can leave us without a job at all. Most workers are subject to what is called "employment-at-will." Unless there is an explicit contract, we can be fired for any reason not expressly prohibited by law. Even if the boss fears she cannot penalize staff for abusing paid sick days, she can do so for any variety of other reasons. Bosses have most of the power. Undoubtedly, this means that most of us don't take advantage of paid sick days unless we need them, which is consistent with employer surveys: nine out of ten (86 percent) employers surveyed in Connecticut reported that they were not aware of any abuse under the state's new paid sick days law.[6]

Thinking through the other pieces of the economic cycle, we can see that the ability to earn paid sick time may make it possible for workers to sell time and, thus, buy goods and services—particularly in an economy where the typical American Worker also has to be a caregiver at times. Some employers offer paid sick leave, presumably because they think it's good for business, but when they do, they tend to give it only to the higher-paid employees, as shown in Figure 6.2. Low-wage workers, like everyone, occasionally get sick, as do their children. These workers may not only be out a day's pay (and depending on how close to the bone their family budget is, a few days lost pay may constrain their spending on goods and services) but also face penalties at work. For some, this even includes losing their job. Further, while opponents of paid sick time argue that workers who have paid vacation or other personal leave are cov-

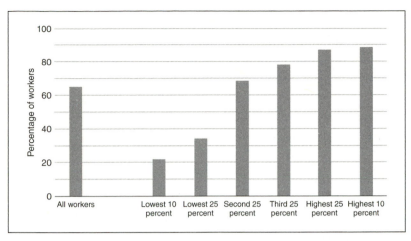

Fig. 6.2 Percentage of workers with employer-provided paid sick leave by average wage, 2014. Relatively few low-wage workers have access to paid sick days, while nearly all high-wage workers have access. *Note:* Includes workers in the private nonfarm economy except those in private households, and workers in the public sector except the federal government.

ered for sick time, many workers cannot take this kind of leave without giving their employer advance notice, making it unusable when a child wakes up with a high fever or other urgent-care needs arise. Paid sick days solve that problem, making it easier for caregivers to sell time.[7]

The ability of parents, and caregivers more generally, to sell time may be especially hampered by a lack of access to paid sick days. In a 2012 survey conducted by University of Michigan's C. S. Mott Children's Hospital, almost half—42 percent—of parents of young children in child care reported having to miss work because of a sick child. About one-quarter of parents—26 percent—reported missing work three or more times during a one-year period because of a sick child. This time at home is good for children: research finds that when parents are there to provide care to their sick children, children get better faster. Sometimes homemade chicken soup is the best medicine. If the employer doesn't allow the employee to stay home, what happens? Too often, the worker is disciplined or fired and loses earnings.[8]

The direct costs do not have a big effect on firms, relative to the other economic effects. After San Francisco implemented the ordinance, employers reported that the new policy was generally a good thing—or had no discernible business consequences. In a 2011 study, the economists Vicky Lovell and Robert Drago at the Institute for Women's Policy Research surveyed nearly 1,200 employers affected by the ordinance. They found that more than two-thirds of employers supported the ordinance and only a third reported any difficulty administering it. In terms of factors that affect the quality of time bought, only one in seven employers reported any negative effect on profitability, 1 in 14 said the policy reduced the predictability of employee absences, 1 in 50 reported any problems with customer service, and just 1 in 100 said it had a negative impact on employee morale.[9] Just listen to Jennifer Piallat, the owner of Zazie Restaurant in San Francisco, quoted after the implementation of the paid sick days ordinance:

> I was concerned it would become more of a Paid Hang-
> over Day! However, I've found that not only have my staff
> not abused the system, it's led to us being much less likely
> to have the horrible "sick-outs" that restaurants are known
> for—where your entire staff is sick at once. Since we work
> in such close quarters and often eat/drink from the same
> plates, we used to have times when we had so many sick
> staff we'd have to close. Now, people stay home when
> they're ill, thus not infecting the customers or the other
> staff members.[10]

An example of the "sick-outs" Piallet mentioned occurred in 2009, when the swine flu swept the nation. Even though about 40 percent of the labor force doesn't have the right to stay home sick, the Centers for Disease Control recommended that people who had the flu stay home. More than a quarter of private-sector employees who contracted this flu nonetheless caught it from coworkers who came to work sick with the disease. Doing the math, this works out to approximately 7 million Americans infected by sick coworkers during that time period. Almost 12,500 individuals died from this flu, most of them infants and the elderly. Although we can't know for certain how many people caught it from a workplace or business contact, certainly some did.[11]

More recently, we've seen concerns about other infectious diseases, such as measles, and far more dangerous ones, such as Ebola, where the public quite reasonably expects ill people to stay away from those they can infect. Often, many workers—especially low-wage workers—don't have the option to stay home. They carry diseases into the workplace, with very little commentary on this problem reported in the news. Yet these are real economic effects.

Then there's the "yuck" factor. I take the bus to work, and one morning I found myself sitting next to a woman who clearly had a cold. She kept coughing and sneezing. Her friend asked if she was feeling better and she said, "No, but I gotta go in. They don't give us sick time at 'Sam's' Deli. (Ah-choo!)" (I've changed the deli's name, but I've never gone there again for lunch.) I'm sure I'm not alone in feeling repulsed by the idea of someone with a nasty cold (or worse) slapping together my tuna sandwich. Yet, those on the front lines of service work, such as food-industry, retail, and child-care and home-care workers, are among those least likely to be covered by a firm's paid sick days policy.[12]

For all these reasons, the paid sick days ordinance feared by some in San Francisco wasn't such a bad idea after all. A couple of years after it went into effect, Jim Lazarus, the senior vice president for policy at the San Francisco Chamber of Commerce, reported that his members were not complaining to him about the ordinance. As he said, "It has not been a huge issue that we have heard from our members about."[13] Lazarus also pointed out that San Francisco's economy was doing well: "By and large, [paid sick days] has not been an employer issue. . . . San Francisco's economy is booming."[14] Indeed, in the first two years after the ordinance went into effect, San Francisco saw employment grow nearly three times faster than in the five surrounding counties of Alameda, Contra Costa, Marin,

San Mateo, and Santa Clara. The number of business establishments in San Francisco grew by 1.6 percent, whereas the number of business establishments in neighboring counties fell by 0.6 percent.[15]

I am not arguing that paid sick days caused employment to rise. But in the face of this kind of evidence, the idea that paid sick days cause businesses to lay off workers or fail to remain profitable is a hard argument to make. As we work through all four quadrants of the economic cycle, we can see that once all the economic effects are examined, paid sick days are not bad for the economy.

Unsurprisingly, given the actual economic effects, the cacophony of complaints about San Francisco's paid sick days ordinance quieted down once the ordinance was in place. As Sam Mogannam, the owner of a Bi-Rite market in San Francisco, put it, "When the San Francisco paid sick days law was first being debated I, like many other local businesses, was concerned; now I appreciate its value. It creates a better, less stressful work environment and increases employee morale."[16]

In the end, the restaurant owner Crain—the businessman who claimed that the paid sick days ordinance would "force" him out of business—seems to have greatly overestimated how bad things would be. His restaurant, the Village Grill, did close its doors, but not for more than seven years after the ordinance went into effect. According to the Bay Area's restaurant magazine *Inside Scoop SF*, he and his partner, Robbie Connolly, sold the restaurant to another local restaurateur, Eddie Naser, who operated three Toast Eatery locations in San Francisco. At the time, Connolly said, "It's been 25 years next month and we'd like to do something different. . . . It's been 25 great years. When it's time to move on, it's time to move on."[17] The Village Grill did not go under because of the paid sick days ordinance. The owners were able to operate a small but apparently profitable local business for another seven years. Further, they successfully sold their business to another local business owner, who had also persevered—and, it seems, flourished—even as he had to offer his workers the right to earn up to five days a year to stay home sick and still get paid.

The success of San Francisco's paid sick days ordinance has spurred communities around the country to follow suit. As of July 2015, twenty-one municipalities, the District of Columbia, and four states have passed paid sick days legislation—including New York City as of June 2013. Nevertheless, many elected officials continue to repeat the inaccurate and incomplete economic logic in opposition to paid sick days. Voters in Milwaukee passed a paid sick time ballot initiative in 2008, but it was held up by court challenges and nullified by Wisconsin's governor, Scott Walker, who enacted a law that "pre-empts local ordinances from requiring businesses to provide paid sick leave to employees for families, medical, or health issues." Philadelphia finally adopted paid sick days in 2015 after Mayor Michael Nutter, for reasons similar to Quinn's, had twice vetoed the measure.[18]

As more communities and states implement paid leave policies, we're learning more about the economic effects. One confirmation that San Francisco's experience is likely to be generalizable is that researchers found that Connecticut's statewide paid sick days policy has also been good for families and the economy, with little negative effects on the economic cycle. As in San Francisco, a year after the law's implementation, when researchers surveyed employers and conducted on-site interviews statewide, they found that employment had risen in several of the sectors most directly affected by the legislation, including hospitality and health services. Similarly, after Seattle's ordinance was put in place, a study by the University of Washington prepared for the Office of the City Auditor found an increase in the number of firms and employees in the city, as well as rising wages. In the year following the ordinance's implementation, employment growth was stronger in Seattle than in the surrounding cities of Bellevue, Everett, and Tacoma, controlling for factors such as seasonal variation. In the District of Columbia, a 2013 audit found no evidence that its law prompted businesses to leave the city or discouraged employers from establishing new businesses in it.[19]

What we've learned is that paid sick days ordinances that address family needs touch all four quadrants of the economic cycle. This policy makes it easier—or in some cases, possible—for people to sell time so they can buy goods and services. As cities and states consider this legislation, most provide at least five days of paid sick leave and some places have higher benefits—some jurisdictions allow workers to earn up to nine days. Not all places cover all workers. In Connecticut, for example, firms with fewer than fifty employees are exempt. In all places, however, the legislation gives workers the ability to use earned sick time without fear of retaliation—an important step forward for local economies and families alike.[20]

Time at Home: Family and Medical Leave Insurance

Sometimes we need a little more time to care. When a new child comes into the family, when a family member is seriously ill, or when a worker himself is ill, an employee needs a few weeks or more to be at home. In response to this need, the first piece of legislation that the newly inaugurated President Clinton signed into law in 1993 was the Family and Medical Leave Act. This act provides up to twelve weeks of job-protected, unpaid leave for employees who need time off to care for a new child (newborn or adopted), to recover from a serious illness, or to care for a seriously ill family member. It was the first national law giving workers job-protected time off to care. This policy is not the same as paid sick days as it is explicitly focused on longer periods of leave for more serious events, and it does not provide pay.

President Clinton argued that family and medical leave was good for families and good for the economy. At the bill signing, he said, "I know that men and women are more productive when they are sure they won't lose their jobs because they're trying to be good parents."[21] Contrast this with the view of President George H. W. Bush, who vetoed the bill twice—once in 1990 and once in 1992—and said at the time of his first veto: "We must ensure that Federal policies do not stifle the creation of new jobs, nor result in the elimination of existing jobs. The Administration is committed to policies that create jobs throughout the economy—serving the most fundamental needs of working families."[22] This statement ignores the evidence that growing our economy means taking into account how both firms and families interact with the economy.

We've now lived with the Family and Medical Leave Act for more than two decades—and even longer in the twenty-three states that before 1993 had laws covering private-sector workers (to varying degrees) and the eleven states covering state employees. We've learned that this kind of leave didn't turn out be a job killer. Jane Waldfogel examined the economic effects of the federal Family and Medical Leave Act. Her analysis shows that after the implementation of the law, more workers took leave, which helped families address their care needs. She did not find that the law reduced women's employment or earnings, even though it increased employees' access to and use of unpaid leave. Similarly, other researchers found that after the implementation of unpaid leave, new mothers returned to work more quickly than before the law was passed and were more likely to go back to work with the same employer they had before their child was born.[23]

So unpaid family and medical leave serves an important purpose—it increases the ability of people to sell time and thus buy goods and services. Job-protected time off is nice to have. But it's not good enough to ensure economic security for today's families. The loss of income—even for just a few months—can cause a serious economic pinch for most families. As described in the preceding chapters, most families' savings will cover barely a few months' expenses. These families must have the money to pay the rent or mortgage and put food on the table (and pay the utility bill, the health insurance copayments, and everything else), which is possible only with a regular paycheck, or at least a portion of it. This leads many to refuse unpaid leave, even when it would help them and their families address their care needs. According to a recent survey by the U.S. Department of Labor and Abt Associates, 46 percent of those who need leave but don't take it cited an inability to afford the time off.[24]

As with paid sick days, some employers have stepped in to provide paid family and medical leave. Most commonly this takes the form of insurance to cover the income lost during a worker's own health issues. Private temporary disability insurance programs that offer benefits for maternity and an employee's own illness cover about 40 percent of all workers. Five states (California, Hawaii, New Jersey, New York, and Rhode Island) have a program that provides insurance coverage to nearly every worker for temporary disabilities, including pregnancy and childbirth. Because of these statewide programs, about a fifth of women in the United States have the right to maternity leave, and the typical mother covered takes ten weeks off to be with her newborn child. Usually, these programs cover about 60 percent of an individual's pay, which can make a real difference in a family budget.[25]

The vast majority of employers, however, do not offer extended paid leave specifically to care for a new child or for an ill family member. A paid family leave program covers only about 13 percent of employees. There are a number of high-profile exceptions, such as Google, which now provides eighteen weeks of paid maternity leave and twelve weeks of paid paternity leave for its employees, but they are rare. There is also Netflix, which on August 4, 2015, announced "an unlimited leave policy for new moms and dads that allows them to take off as much time as they want during the first year after a child's birth or adoption." Not everyone has access to this leave, though; it's a two-tiered policy disproportionately benefiting higher-income employees.[26]

This isn't unusual. When employers offer paid family leave, the employees who are least likely to have access are low-wage workers. Figure 6.3 shows that the higher wages you earn, the more likely you are to have this benefit. Only 5 percent of workers in the bottom quarter of earners have paid family and medical leave through their employer, compared with 21 percent in the top quarter. The trends look similar across educational categories: the U.S. Census Bureau reports that 60 percent of new mothers with a bachelor's degree or higher received some kind of paid maternity leave, compared with

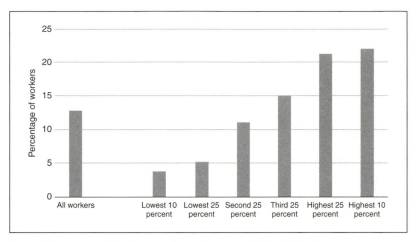

Fig. 6.3 Percentage of workers with employer-provided paid family leave by average wage, 2013. Across the earnings distribution, relatively few workers have access to employer-provided paid family leave, but higher-wage workers are more likely to have access than low-wage workers. *Note:* Includes workers in the private non-farm economy except those in private households, and workers in the public sector except the federal government.

only 22 percent of those without a high school diploma. Unlike pensions and health insurance, uniform leave policies are not mandatory. Thus, even within a given firm, not all employees may have access to the same paid family and medical leave benefits. Low-income families are least likely to be able to afford paid help to care for loved ones, so this lack of leave can quickly lead to an exit from employment or a sharp reduction in family spending.[27]

Young workers also are less likely than others to have access to paid family and medical leave, which makes little sense when we consider that most women have their first child by age twenty-five. Many policymakers fail to consider that young workers not only are in the beginning of their careers and earning less than they are likely to when they are older, but also haven't had time on the job to accumulate time off. When I worked on Capitol Hill, the House of Representatives passed legislation to give federal workers paid parental leave. On the House floor, Congressman Darrell Issa (R-California) argued that federal workers didn't need paid parental leave because they could use their accrued sick time and vacation, saying, "Worker[s] need only borrow from the sick leave that they were eventually going to cash out" in the last six months they're in the federal workforce. This assumes that employees have been on the job long enough to save up leave, which isn't the case for many new parents. In a recent development addressing this issue within the federal workforce, in January 2015, President Obama signed a Presidential Memorandum directing federal agencies to allow an advance of up to six weeks of paid sick leave for employees who are new parents, caring for ill family members, or have other sick leave–eligible needs.[28]

The lack of a specific policy for parental leave certainly disadvantages young parents who haven't had much time on the job to save up leave. It doesn't make sense to punish them for not building up within-firm tenure. While some want to delay parenthood, many people do not (and delay brings with it its own challenges for older mothers and fathers) or are surprised by the pregnancy and want to add a new child to their family. Further, young workers may gain from job switching in their twenties as they find the best fit for their skills.

A few states have put in place programs to provide paid family and medical leave. California in 2002, New Jersey in 2008, and Rhode Island in 2013 passed laws to expand their long-standing statewide temporary disability insurance programs by adding caregiver leave for new parents and workers who need to care for a seriously ill family member. Benefits are for six weeks in California and New Jersey, four weeks in Rhode Island, and typically cover about half or more of an employee's pay, capped at around what the typical worker earns in a week. Benefits are paid for through an employee payroll deduction, spreading the costs of leave so that employers don't bear those costs. In 2007, Washington became the first state to pass legislation establishing a new, stand-alone program for paid parental leave, but the program has yet to be implemented because the administrative and financing mechanisms remain to be worked out.[29]

Mirroring what happens when paid sick days were proposed in San Francisco and elsewhere—and notwithstanding funding mechanisms that do not put costs on employers—the Chambers of Commerce and various employers lobbied hard against bills creating a paid family leave program. In California, the lobbyist for the National Federation of Independent Business predicted, "If it becomes law, it will be the biggest financial burden for small businesses in decades." California Chamber of Commerce President Allan Zaremberg argued that the law would be bad for business, saying, "We're opposed to a lot of bills, but this is one of the worst." In New Jersey, Senator Christopher "Kip" Bateman (R-Somerset) asked, "Why now? This is the wrong time to pass this bill that will send more businesses out of New Jersey. Maybe at the right time, in the right economy, this would be the right bill."[30]

Yet among opponents of these kinds of work-life reforms there never seems to be a "right time" for policies that address the time crunch facing families. As with the issue of paid sick days, the opposition focused on one slice of the economic cycle—how the cost of buying time affects selling goods and services. The focus was on the immediate costs to business, but not on all the other aspects of the economy.

As we consider their effects on the full economic cycle, two very crucial differences become apparent between paid sick days and paid family and medical leave policies. First, in the three states that have it, paid family leave is financed by a tax on *employees* in a risk-pooling insurance program. Employers do not pay the wages of workers who do not show up for work; their direct cost is only the cost of covering the employee's absence. This is important because asking employers to pay would disadvantage some businesses more than others. Some employers have more employees who might need extended time off, such as a mostly twenty-something staff on the cusp of parenthood or a mostly fifty-something staff who might be more likely to need time off for their own illnesses or to care for an aging parent. Requiring those employers to pay for this leave on their own would disadvantage them in the marketplace.[31]

Second, the duration of paid family and medical leave is much longer—up to six weeks in California and New Jersey, four weeks in Rhode Island, and up to twelve weeks in proposed federal legislation—than in the case of paid sick days. This certainly poses a greater burden on employers. Paid family and medical leave undoubtedly encourages absence from work. People need some time at home that's just not negotiable (does anyone voluntarily work the day after their baby is born?), but the policy encourages people to take longer leaves than they would if they did not have paid leave. Whereas this policy may be good for the family—and for the economy more broadly—the employer must cope with the fact that an employee is at home, not at work. Most firms simply make do with existing staff; only about 12 percent of firms hire temporary help when their employers take leave for a week or more. This presents challenges for short-term productivity, but it's also an investment in long-term productivity as employees with paid leave are more likely to return to their jobs.[32]

Since California was the first state to put paid family and medical leave into effect, we know more about the economic results there. We learn that, as with paid sick days, the evidence does not confirm the dire predictions. In an extensive survey of employers and employees, the sociologist Ruth Milkman and the economist Eileen Appelbaum discovered that, contrary to opponents' warnings, the program was not a "job killer." They found that the overwhelming majority of employers—nine out of ten—reported that the program has had either no effect or positive effects on profitability or performance. One reason may be that many longer leaves, such as leave for elective or nonemergency surgery or the birth of a child, can be planned for, making it easier on employers. Further, the researchers found that nine out of ten employers (87 percent) reported no increase in their costs. Based on these kinds of findings and his own research, the economist Christopher Ruhm told Claire Cain Miller, a reporter for the *New York Times*, about paid family leave: "Is it going to be good for the economy? . . . The answer to that, based on the evidence we have, is yes."[33]

Not surprisingly, once we start looking at the family side of the economic cycle, the benefits are quite strong. Family and medical leave insurance can help protect families from suffering financial setbacks when working parents are forced to take unpaid leave or exit the labor force entirely in order to provide care for their children. This can reduce long-term costs for state and local governments. Researchers from Rutgers University's Center for Women and Work found that paid family and medical leave reduced the number of women who relied on public assistance. In the year after they had their child, women who took paid leave were 39 percent less likely to receive public assistance compared with mothers who did not take leave but returned to work.[34]

The economic effects of paid leave are also important for families caring for an elder. According to the Bureau of Labor Statistics, about one in six Americans (16 percent) cares for an elder for an average of 3.2 hours a day. Most unpaid family caregivers—63 percent—also hold down a job; most of those with a job are employed full-time. This means that the "family" part of family and medical leave is important for large swaths of the U.S. workforce. This is especially true since, unlike in other countries, few elders receive support from government—about 6.4 percent of seniors are in long-term care in the United States compared with 12.7 percent across other developed economies.[35]

We also have to think through the economic implications of the specific details of the policies. With American business having lost its Silent Partner—the American Wife—these kinds of benefits became necessary in all types of families. It is encouraging that in the three states that added paid family leave and the five that provide paid medical leave, the coverage is more inclusive than in the federal unpaid Family and Medical Leave Act. That federal legislation, while good to have, provides access to unpaid leave to only about 60 percent of all workers. To be eligible, employees must meet requirements more suited to the traditional breadwinner-model of employment: an employee must put in at least 1,250 hours of work a year at a large company (one with fifty or more employees within a seventy-five-mile radius) and must have worked at that company for at least a year (although not necessarily consecutively). These rules fail to acknowledge that many people work part time for caregiving reasons or that young workers are likely to switch jobs for career reasons. These rules mean that many young parents—disproportionately people of color—are categorically excluded from protected leave. Further, by covering only workers in larger firms, the law leaves out about a third of all U.S. workers—those who tend to earn less and to be less likely to have access to paid benefits than their counterparts in larger companies.[36]

Understanding how economic changes look up and down the income ladder is important especially for buying goods and services because paid family and medical leave improves family budgets, making it more likely that people will join the workforce and stay employed. The legislation also has been important for family well-being and improved job tenure. After California implemented such leave, researchers found that the policy kept people in jobs. Workers, especially low-wage workers, who took paid family leave through the state program were more likely than those who did not to transition back into their job and remain in the labor force. Among workers in low-paying jobs, 88.7 percent of those who used the leave returned to their jobs, compared with 81.2 percent of those who did not use the leave. The economist Tanya Byker found that the paid family and medical leave programs in California and New Jersey increased the number of mothers in the labor force around the time when they had a child. This was particularly the case for women without a college degree. Similarly, access to family leave to care for an elder can keep people in the workforce.[37]

Fundamentally, paid family and medical leave fosters economic security by making it possible to sell time in a way that works for families. Researchers have found that paid family leave improves wages and earnings for caregivers. It increases the employment rate of mothers and increases the economic contribution of wives to family earnings. In my research, I found that women who had access to paid leave when they had their first child had wages years later that were 9 percent higher than similar women who had not had access to paid leave. Other researchers have found that women who had access to job-protected maternity leave were more likely to return to their original employer. This reduced the gap in pay that mothers experience relative to nonmothers. The Rutgers University Center for Women and Work found that working mothers who took paid family leave for thirty days or more for the birth of their child were 54 percent more likely to report wage increases in the year following their child's birth, relative to mothers who did not take leave.[38]

Paid family and medical leave also can help close the gender pay gap and give both men and women time to care for themselves and their families, which also boosts family incomes. The percentage of leave taken by men in California has increased since the institution of the state's paid leave program. Men's share of parent-bonding family leave—as a percentage of all parent-bonding family leave claims—increased from 17 percent in the period from 2004 to 2005 to 30.2 percent in the period from 2011 to 2012. In addition, men in California are taking longer leaves than they did before family and medical leave insurance was available. As my colleague Eileen Appelbaum puts it, "When leave is paid, men think it's for them."[39]

The economic consequences of paid leave for families go beyond the earnings and employment. The policy affects a family's ability to care for the next generation. The economists Raquel Bernal and Anna Fruttero explain that paid parental leave can increase a child's average human capital as parents use their leave to spend time with their new baby, which as research indicates, increases a child's future skill level. Parental leave also enhances children's health and development and is associated with increases in the duration of breast-feeding and reductions in infant deaths and later behavioral issues. Similarly, returning to work later is associated with reductions in depressive symptoms among mothers.[40]

President George H. W. Bush did not think job-protected family and medical leave was sound economic policy, but Bill Clinton made it clear when he was campaigning to be president in 1992 that he was eager to sign the legislation. He kept touting the benefits even after he signed the law. Karen Kornbluh, the former U.S. ambassador to the Organisation for Economic Co-operation and Development, spent a good deal of time with Clinton on the campaign trail four years later, in 1996. She argues that it was partially because of this support that Clinton became the first Democratic contender in at least a decade to win the votes of a majority of married women. As she told me, he brought up the legislation repeatedly on the 1996 campaign trail and mentioned it in every state in the Union.[41]

On the twentieth anniversary of signing the Family and Medical Leave Act into law, President Clinton said, "To this day, I receive more thanks from citizens for the FMLA than any other single piece of legislation I signed into law." Family and medical leave is popular because people use it. The law has been used more than 200 million times to allow workers to care for a new child, a seriously ill family member, or to recover from a serious illness. But our work does not stop there.[42]

Providing only unpaid leave and, even then, not to everyone, sends the signal that either caregiving or workers who provide care to family members aren't economically important. Yet the economic cycle presented in Chapter 5 contradicts both attitudes. We need policies like paid leave that provide help to families up and down the income ladder so they can stay in the workforce. Leaving this to the private market excludes too many people—especially those in low-income and middle-class families. With lower incomes, it can be impossible to take much-needed unpaid leave.

The New Deal left us with no national family and medical leave insurance program. Current federal law requires an employer to hold a person's job only until she or he comes back and only if the employee and his firm meet the law's eligibility criteria. At the federal level, we should build on what we've learned from the states and the Family and Medical Leave Act. Legislation like the Family and Medical Insurance Leave Act, introduced in the House of Representatives by Rosa Delauro (D-Connecticut) and in the Senate by

Kristin Gillibrand (D-New York), does just that, providing near-universal coverage, including for young and intermittent workers.[43]

American business has lost the Silent Partner who could be home all the time and provide care. As a result, there are times when workers need to be at home to take care of a loved one. While employers might wish that they didn't have to cope with absences, they need to adjust to the reality that they are no longer getting a hidden subsidy from their Silent Partner. This isn't a new cost; it's a shift in how families are finding the time to care.

Looking at paid family and medical leave and paid sick time from all four quadrants of the economic cycle makes clear that the advantages vastly outweigh the disadvantages. Once we look at the full economic cycle, we can see that what happens at home when workers aren't at work is not just a private family concern. As we learned in Chapter 5, the time workers spend caring for themselves and their family members is part of the economic cycle. When a worker isn't at work, he's at home, and the care he provides is not only about love and compassion; it's economically important. The care that a child receives from her parents in the first few months of life can make all the difference in what kind of adult she'll eventually grow up to be. Having time at home allows us to recover from an illness faster. What's better for productivity than healthy workers and families?

Yet families up and down the income spectrum have limited access to job-protected time off. Nationally, U.S. workers do not have the right to earn either paid sick days for short-term, often unexpected illnesses, or longer paid family and medical leave for the extended time off that may be necessary in the case of a serious illness or the joy of welcoming a new child into a family. Especially for middle-class and lower-income families, the lack of paid time off creates serious economic challenges. But even professional families sometimes need time off to care, and that shouldn't be held against them at work.

There at Work: Scheduling Time

When employers buy time, like the coffee-shop owner in Chapter 5, they want their employees to be at work when they need them. Employers have a good deal of discretion over the employment contract. The boss can tell us when, where, and how we work. In recent years, employers have increasingly used that discretion to insist that employees accept schedules only on their terms. But that does not fit the realities of family life. Lack of predictable schedules and fluctuating hours would be a challenge even with the American Wife at home to serve all her family's needs. Without her, it's almost impossible.

Chapter 5 showed that from the perspective of the full economic cycle, it's irrational to treat employee time as though it were not attached to a person and a family. Firms no longer have their Silent Partner, and conflicts over when we need to be at work and how employers schedule those hours affect all four quadrants of the economic cycle. Employees want to be at work, but they need a schedule that doesn't prevent them from meeting their family responsibilities. Progressive firms are pointing the way—we'll hear about some of them in this chapter—but in too many cases, firms give perks only to a few employees and not to all. Policymakers need to respond by establishing rules that match today's economic reality.

A century ago, the labor movement's motto was "Eight hours for work, eight hours for rest, eight hours for what we will." That's a nice idea. It fit the economic times. It clearly divided people's days into time for work and time for the rest of life. Today we have a different kind of economy. We have smartphones and other devices that connect many of us to work at all hours. This technology allows workers in some sectors to telecommute as well as to work around the clock, so to speak, since many global companies require some of us to work a schedule that fits daylight in Beijing or London. Because adults all work, the family shopping must get done in the evenings and on weekends, which means more businesses are open evenings and weekends, and they need staff. The economic reality is that "flexibility" is important to both firms and families, but it means very different things to each.

It's also important to see firms' time-buying strategies as part of the larger economic trends. The economist David Weil documents what he calls the "fissured workplace." Whereas we used to have an economy in which large businesses directly employed people, many aspects of production have been subcontracted out to smaller firms. This means that smaller producers directly compete to provide goods and services to big firms—and, as Weil documents, that competition is fierce and pushes down wages and benefits. Someone may appear to be employed by the hotel you've just checked into, but more likely, one contractor provides the front-desk staff and another the janitorial services. Given this new reality, when the larger firm sees its profits go up, there are no longer as many people "in the firm" who can reasonable expect—or have the institutional capacity to demand—a share of the gains. These new ways of working directly affect not only compensation but schedules as well. If everyone's a contractor—or subcontractor—or works for one, who's in charge of putting limits on how we sell and buy time? Is anyone?[1]

This chapter examines what flexibility means for families, what it means for firms, and how it affects our economic cycle, which is summarized in Figure 7.1. We'll begin by looking at how flexibility can work for employers of workers in low-income, middle-class, and professional families. Then, we'll look at how new trends in employer scheduling have been moving in the opposite direction, giving families even less control over their time. Throughout, we will focus on the full economic cycle, rather than viewing issues only through the lens of what families need or whether there's a short-term case for individual businesses. As we look at the employer and employee side, we will apply the three principles of economic

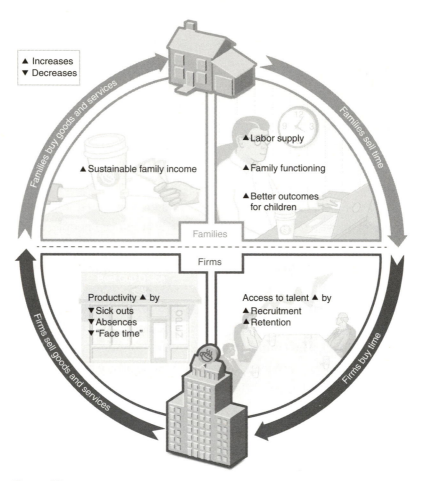

Fig. 7.1 Effects on the economic cycle of policies that allow employees some flexibility in the workplace.

analysis—demand and supply; hidden costs and benefits; and long-term and short-term costs and benefits.

In this way, we can see how the balance has shifted too far toward the needs of employers for flexibility to the detriment of the overall economy. Addressing overwork, underwork, and unpredictable schedules is the key component needed to rebalance this relationship. And we need to figure out how to do this in a world where very few private-sector workers belong to a union. For decades, unions—and union contracts—ensured that employers and employees negotiated scheduling issues. A unionized worker's contract may cover rules about scheduling, and that worker will have a union representative to help him or her navigate scheduling conflicts with the boss. Without unions, employees have no clear guidance on how to negotiate schedules, and many are afraid to even ask about schedules that fit family life.

Can We Talk? Worker Input on Schedules

Everyone needs some control over their time, and for many people, this means some scheduling flexibility. Families don't have another choice. Work schedules are at the heart of the negotiation between families and firms over people's time.

Recall the situation that my sister, Michelle, found herself in just after she had her first child. When her daughter was an infant, she quit her job over scheduling issues. She had been a top employee. In the six months before quitting, she had received an exemplary review. She had clients who liked working with her, and she made money for the firm. Her family lost income when she quit, and her employer lost a good employee. The economy lost out as well. Quitting meant one less talented woman in the labor market bringing home a middle-class salary.

We can see how my sister's decision affected every quadrant of the economic system shown in Figure 7.1. The firm decided that it would be just fine to forgo buying time from a talented employee and risked losing money by alienating clients who had been working closely with her for many years, thus negatively affecting their ability to sell goods and services. There were implications for my sister and her family, too. For her, the way she was locked into selling time wasn't working for her family. Their budget shrank when she quit, lowering the family's economic demand and limiting their capacity to buy goods and services. In her view, the time she spends with her children is important—and economists know that this investment is not just about love (while that is front and center to my sister!), but also about the future competitiveness of the U.S. workforce. Now, with her kids older and in school, she's trying to figure out how find the on-ramp back to work, which hasn't been easy.

Her story isn't at all unique. Every day, all across the United States, people like my sister quit their jobs—or, we should say, are forced out of their jobs—because of work-life conflicts. In Chapter 4, we heard from Sheryl Sandberg, who was able to get an accommodation from her employer, whereas many others—especially nonprofessionals—cannot (a fact Sandberg acknowledged). According to data from the Harris Poll, in 2014, 21 percent of Americans and half of single working parents felt they had at some point in their career been "passed over" for a promotion or raise because they needed a flexible work schedule. Too many workers fear being fired or reprimanded simply for asking for the kinds of accommodations that they need to address the challenges between work and family.[2]

Multiply my sister's exit from the workforce across the millions of other workers trying to cope with caregiving and we start to see the real economic consequences. By simply asking for a different schedule, my sister had taken the first step. Without a union or employment protections, she knew she was risking her job—or at least her reputation on the job—by even asking the question. She was lucky. Even though this is the kind of conversation about schedules that workers and bosses need to have to improve the productivity of our economy, many workers are fearful of even asking these questions. Employees understand that their boss prefers not to have to confront the implications of the loss of America's Silent Partner. Employers have the advantage in conversations about pay and benefits because fewer than one in thirteen private-sector workers is covered by a union contract.[3]

Let's be clear: workplace flexibility isn't just a luxury for families. The outcome of the negotiation over schedules and hours directly affects not only how families function but also all four quadrants of the economic cycle. Researchers now know that even a little control over scheduling can reduce conflicts between a job and family life—and it directly affects workers' ability to sell time. Having access to a schedule that works for the employee and her family reduces stress. It can also improve relationships, both with adults and with children. We learned in Chapters 2, 3, and 4 that those lower on the income ladder tend to have less control over their schedules and fewer resources to high-quality care to make up for workplace inflexibility. Workers from low-income and middle-class families typically have less power in the workplace to negotiate their schedules compared with professionals.[4]

I'm sure I don't need to tell you this, but parental time matters, a lot, during a child's earliest years. Parents are a child's first teachers. The time they have to bond, breastfeed, talk, play, and sing with their young ones before he or she goes to bed matters for a child's success down the road. The sociologists Ronald Bulanda and Stephen Lippmann find that parental time is associated with how well children do in school as well as with the likelihood that they will drop out of high school, become pregnant as teenagers, and develop behavioral issues. Therefore, it should come as no surprise that parents with flexible schedules are better at their job of being parents. In general, researchers have found a strong relationship between parents' abilities to control their work schedules and children's well-being.[5]

The need for some control or flexibility over work schedules is an issue that both men and women face—it's by no means a "woman's issue." According to research by Brad Harrington at Boston College's Center for Work and Family and his colleagues, the vast majority of fathers (95 percent) report that workplace flexibility was an important job characteristic.[6] Josh Earnest, President Obama's White House press secretary beginning in 2014, experienced these work-life conflicts firsthand when his wife gave birth to their first child:

> There is a greater expectation that men will be more involved in the raising and parenting of their children, and that also has inspired I think, it certainly has in me, a desire to be part of that parenting. And that does sometimes come into conflict with the pressures that you have at work to fulfill those work responsibilities.[7]

Earnest's job—like that of many professional workers—requires long and demanding hours. Earnest was able to change his schedule so he could tuck his son into bed once a week. Now, I'm not arguing that workers should expect to see their children just once a week, but we should be encouraged that powerful men are coming forward to talk about their need for flexibility.

Evidence suggests that both men and women make decisions about selling time based on hours of work and how that fits with family time. A recent survey of professional service employees by PricewaterhouseCoopers and others found that schedules—and control over them—are an important piece of employees' wage packages. They found that one in seven male employees and one in five females employees would give up some pay and the frequency of their promotions if they were able to work fewer hours.[8]

This sentiment is especially common among younger cohorts of workers. According to the same PricewaterhouseCoopers survey, two-thirds of millennial workers said that they would like to shift their working hours. This confirms an anecdote from one of my colleagues who spends a lot of time with MBA students. She's found that both men and women tell her that their first question for campus recruiters is whether the firms offer workplace flexibility. If the answer's no, the students—both men and women—tell her that they walk away. Of course, not everyone can afford to do that.[9]

It all comes down to this: employers who refuse to work with employees on schedules will end up buying time only from people who can tolerate those constraints. Firms may have very good business reasons for inflexibility, but with today's technology and a 24/7 economy, they are missing many opportunities. Workplace flexibility increases access to talent and reduces firm turnover. It also improves long-term productivity by giving workers the time to improve their skills through additional training or education, which strengthens the firm's workforce relative to that of the competition.

You might be scratching your head—doesn't federal law prohibit workers from having a flexible schedule? The answer is no. Under federal law, workers are classified into two groups, those who are covered by overtime provisions of the Fair Labor Standards Act, who must be paid time and a half for all hours above and beyond forty in a given workweek, and those who are not; this is the only federal law that addresses employee scheduling. For those covered by the overtime rules—and assuming the employer does not want to pay overtime—an employer can work with the employee to implement any schedule that works for both sides as long as it keeps hours below the forty-per-week threshold. An employer can offer workers the option of varying arrival and departure times, days worked, and shifts, or allow the worker to take time off during the day.[10]

Employers have even more flexibility regarding the hours of workers who are not covered by the overtime rules of the Fair Labor Standards Act, which is estimated to be about a third (33.6 percent) of the total workforce—although that share will fall to somewhere between 23 and 30 percent once new regulations are put into force. Employers can require those employees to work more than forty hours in a given week without paying the worker any extra and therefore can offer these employees a wider variety of schedules. For those workers, there are almost endless combinations of schedules that do not violate current law. One common offer is for workers to compress their workweeks so that they work nine-hour days Monday through Thursday in return for alternating every other Friday between an eight-hour day and getting the day off.[11]

Given the importance of selling and buying time in the economic cycle, finding a solution that works for both employers and employees can mean the difference between firms' tapping into talent and letting it lie fallow. JetBlue has found that by adapting its workplace practices, particularly with respect to telecommuting, it can access highly skilled labor markets. As the economist Nicholas Bloom put it in an interview with *Harvard Business Review*:

> JetBlue allows folks to work as far as three hours from
> headquarters—close enough to come in now and again
> but a much bigger radius from which it can draw appli-
> cants. When I asked the people at JetBlue about this

policy, they said it helped them gain access to educated, high-ability mothers who wanted flexibility in their jobs. The airline believes this policy has improved the quality of its workforce.[12]

JetBlue's practice wasn't just about being nice; it was about adopting management policies that get the most out of a talented workforce by focusing on buying time from an untapped labor pool. JetBlue is just one example. In a large study of more than 700 firms in the United States, the United Kingdom, France, and Germany, Bloom and his colleagues found that employers considered the adoption of workplace flexibility policies to be managerial common sense.[13]

Evidence of the economic effectiveness of flexibility comes from all sorts of places. I go to many events where people talk about the importance of finding ways to address conflicts between work and family. I was not prepared, however, to hear about this issue from the chair of the Joint Chiefs of Staff. At a November 2010 event, Navy Admiral Mike Mullen told the standing room–only audience, "The ability to be the best we can be and carry out our missions is so central to our focus on our people . . . but more than our people, our families, and while we've made significant strides, we still have a long way to go." He argued that allowing workers to have scheduling flexibility and a say in where they work is something leaders can provide. He highlighted compressed workweeks, flextime, part-time work, job sharing, and teleworking as examples of tools managers could use to help workers meet the needs of their employers and their families.[14]

About eight in ten firms allow some employees some flexibility over when they start or end work. But it's still far from the norm in the workplace for all or even most employees to have access to flexible schedules. Only 41 percent of firms allow some of their employees—but not necessary all—to vary their start and end times on a daily basis. Of these firms, slightly more than a quarter allow most of their employees to change their working hours periodically, though that flexibility mostly accrues to high-skilled rather than less-

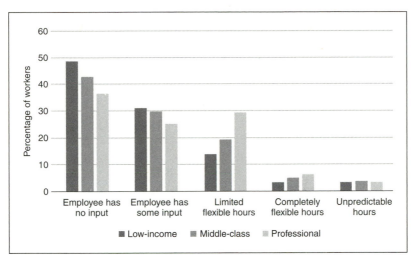

Fig. 7.2 Percentage of young U.S. workers reporting input over schedules, 2012. Most young workers do not have input into their schedules, but those in professional families are more likely to have some control over their starting and ending times, compared with those in middle-class or low-income families. *Note:* Sample includes individuals aged 26 to 32. Individuals who reported being self-employed, in the military, or having zero or missing household income were dropped from the sample. Results are reported as percentages of the cohort population (estimated using sampling weights).

skilled workers. Only about a quarter of workers in manufacturing have a flexible schedule, though evidence shows that it can work in that sector, too. The fact that flexibility is less common in blue- or so-called pink-collar jobs—jobs traditionally held by women in the service sector—doesn't mean it isn't possible there, too.[15]

Workplace flexibility is not evenly distributed across low-income, middle-class, and professional families. In a new survey of young workers, for example, Susan Lambert, Julie Henley, and Peter Fugiel found that half of all hourly workers, including nearly half of parents, say that "their employer decides their schedule without their input." Figure 7.2 shows this data broken down by income group. Young workers in professional families are more likely to have some control over their starting and ending times, compared with those in middle-class or low-income families. To the extent that inflexibility increases turnover, it raises the cost of buying time and lowers productivity, since the cost of replacing a worker is about the same for most workers across the income spectrum, up until those at the very top, as we learned in Chapter 5. To the extent that this is common among parents of young children, the economic effects are amplified.

The lack of widespread flexibility is striking given the large and growing body of evidence that it improves the ability of employers both to buy time and to sell goods and services. The most compelling evidence tends to be from studies looking at specific firms. One example in the retail sector is at The Gap. In order to help employees address work-life conflict, the national clothing retailer is working with researchers Joan Williams at the University of California-Hastings and Susan Lambert of the University of Chicago to test and evaluate how the company can stabilize worker schedules. They have been piloting a multicomponent intervention to improve scheduling practices in hourly jobs in three stores. The managers of these stores reported that, for them, the new system reduced the amount of time they spent scheduling, facilitated shift swapping among store employees, and led them to think more strategically about cross-training associates. Examples like this are useful because often business leaders want to see evidence that a new idea will work for their business or at least in their industry before adopting it—which underscores both the importance of research and the establishment of a set of clear rules for all businesses.[16]

When we put all the evidence together, we see that finding ways to negotiate so that employees have some input into and control over their schedules can lead to fewer absences and less turnover among staff, both of which improve employers' ability to buy time. Overall, estimates are that if every firm in the United States adopted flexible workplace schedules, our economy could save about $15 billion a year—that's just under $100 for every worker in the country. This is a strong argument that employers nationwide should learn from the experience of those who have adopted flexible policies. The policies, research shows, are usually good for business.[17]

Researchers have found strong evidence for lower absenteeism in workplaces with employee flexibility. Dan Dalton and Debra Mesch studied the introduction of flexible schedules inside one large public utility. For one year on a trial basis, the utility adopted a flexible work arrangement in one of its subunits, while retaining its usual scheduling practices in all of its other units. In the year before the implementation of the program, the absence rate for all of the subunits was about the same. During the program, however, the subunit that offered a flexible work schedule had a lower absenteeism rate, 7.8 days per year compared with the more usual 9.9 in the other subunits. After the completion of the one-year trial, all of the subunits reverted to the same inflexible work schedules. The rates of absenteeism rose again. This is strong evidence that the flexible work policy drove absences down. Corporate Voices for Working Families estimated that higher absenteeism costs firms anywhere from about $500 to $2,000 per worker, per year.[18]

The insurance company Aflac has boosted employee retention—and lowered job turnover—by allowing employees to request an alternate work schedule from their supervisor. Since a policy change seven years ago, workers can vary their start times or choose a four-day, ten-hour work week with three days off per week, or a three-day, twelve-hour work week with four days off per week. Tamesia Paschal, who services payroll accounts for the company, has been with Aflac for six years and works a 6 AM to 2:30 PM shift. Paschal took this schedule because it's when she's most productive: "I'm more productive in the early morning, and getting off at 2:30 in the afternoon, I have the option of going to meetings or appointments after work." After implementing this policy, Aflac found that employee retention at its call center operations rose from 87 percent to 94 percent. Every job turnover costs employers money—and creates havoc for the employee who needs to find a new job and for their family who misses out on their income in the meantime.[19]

Given the empirical evidence, economist Nick Bloom has gone so far as to say that it's a "mystery" to him why firms keep turning down the same road instead of adopting flexible scheduling policies—reminding me of my adolescent self repeatedly taking the wrong road as I sought home from downtown Seattle. For one of his research studies, Bloom and his colleagues went to China, where they were able to conduct a randomized controlled trial, or RCT, on the employees of call centers. This study is special because the RCT is considered the gold standard of research methods. It is what doctors do to find out if a new drug works: they randomly assign people into one of two groups: they give patients in one group the new drug and those in the second group a placebo. Then they see whether those who took the drug had a better outcome than those who did not.[20]

Bloom assigned half of a firm's employees to a schedule that had them working from home four days a week and working in the office one day a week. The other half were assigned to a schedule that had them working in the office all five days. After nine months, the researchers found that the workers on the more flexible schedule had been 13 percent more productive than those who had spent the entire week in the office. The researchers also found something else: when *workers* were allowed to choose the place where they worked, at home or at the office, productivity increased by even more—22 percent.[21]

Even the U.S. government has sought to save money through flexible work schedules. As a Chicagoan accustomed to schools staying open even during the constant snows of Illinois winters, President Obama became frustrated with the number of snow days during the long winter of 2009–2010 in the District of Columbia. He instructed the Office of Personnel Management to encourage workers to telecommute, saving the federal government more than $30 million per day—and $150 million in total that winter alone—during days the government was closed due to snow. Of course, flexibility doesn't work for everyone: schools were closed during the snow days, meaning that many of those federal workers had to do their day job in between caring for children—which is not necessarily good for productivity and underscores the importance of both employers and employees having input into devising schedules that actually work.[22]

It's great that many companies offer flexibility, but at far too many companies this opportunity is a perk available only to some employees. This is where public policy can step in. Especially in a world without unions, we need to find ways to get both sides—employers and employees—to talk to each other.

Over the past two years, we've seen increased movement toward workplace flexibility on local, state, and federal levels. On May 14, 2013, Vermont became the first place in the United States to pass a "right-to-request" law, quickly followed by San Francisco. Right-to-request laws give workers the ability to ask their boss for a flexible schedule without fear of retaliation. These rules outline a process for employees and employers to discuss and negotiate workplace flexibility. Vermont's legislation, for example, allows employers to refuse the request for flexibility for reasons such as the burden of additional costs, negative effects on meeting customer demand or business quality and performance, or the inability to reorganize existing staff to make it work. But the law also requires employers to take the request seriously and turn it down only for certain business reasons. At the federal level, President Obama recently established the right-to-request policy for all federal workers.[23]

We know that this kind of "talking cure" between employers and employees works. We've seen companies implement these policies and we've seen similar laws effectively put in place in other countries, including the United Kingdom, New Zealand, and Australia. In two separate studies, researchers found that giving workers the right to request a particular schedule can help limit work-life conflicts. But there's a catch: the right-to-request laws may not look the same on the ground in the United States because we have less union coverage than other countries. In a union setting, an employee could ask his union representative to help him approach his supervisor about a particular schedule. In a nonunion setting, workers don't have an advocate to help them navigate the policy.[24]

Ultimately, workplace flexibility is a management issue. Where workplace flexibility doesn't work, it's usually because the firm has bigger management problems. Take the example of Yahoo. In the summer of 2012, Marissa Mayer was brought in to turn around the troubled company. Seven months into her job as CEO, she reversed the longstanding telecommute policy. A leaked internal memo said that within a couple of months, all employees would need to work on the Yahoo campus. There was an immediate uproar, but Mayer held her ground. At the time, there were reports that telecommuting employees were actually working on side jobs, not on Yahoo projects. Mayer focused on the management issue at hand, which was that Yahoo wasn't as productive or innovative as its competitors; ensuring that the staff was focused on work for Yahoo was imperative. She also made clear that once the performance issues were solved, the option to telecommute might return one day.[25]

One role for policy is to ensure that workplace flexibility isn't available only to professional families. Since there are no rules requiring that if one employee is offered any of these flexible workplace policies all employees must be allowed to take advantage of them, within many firms there is often a wide array of policies available to different workers. The Families and Work Institute Study of a Changing Workforce finds that of employers who permit some employees some flexibility around their starting and quitting times, only a third allow all—or close to all—employees to do so. This is markedly different from the provision of other workplace benefits, such as health insurance or retirement plans, where the firm is legally obliged to provide similar benefits to all workers employed full-time. It makes no sense to assume that workplace flexibility is any less important.[26]

If workplace flexibility becomes more of a policy issue, it will have the added benefit of increasing awareness. Too often, even if employees have the right to these policies on paper, they do not know about it. This explains why we often see very different data coming out of surveys from employers compared with surveys of employees. More than half of employers say that their firm offers some kind of workplace flexibility. But oftentimes no one seems to have told the employees—only about a quarter of employees report having some kind of flexibility. This lack of agreement on what's actually happening in the workplace makes it difficult to study the effects of these policies. It also may make employees feel like these policies are capricious, which could reduce rather than enhance employee morale.[27]

Policymakers could focus on making sure that both sides are at the table and that flexibility doesn't turn into a way for employers to further squeeze employees. For instance, some employers offer "comp time," allowing employees to bank time when they work extra hours and then use those hours later to take time off. If those "extra hours" are more than forty in a given week, employers can only do this for workers who are not covered by the overtime protections of the Fair Labor Standards Act. About a third (36 percent) of employers offer comp time to some workers, and one in five (18 percent) makes it available to all workers. Yet many experts remain unconvinced that this addresses workers' or families' needs for flexibility. Employers can require an employee to work long hours when it suits the firm and then encourage (or require) that the comp time be used when convenient for them, not necessarily for the employee. A review of litigation history on comp time found that within the public sector, employers limit their employees' ability to use comp time at their own discretion. In the private sector, which is less regulated and less unionized than the public sector, employees are likely to be even less able to make use of their comp time when it suits them.[28]

Another important issue is whether employers can subtly—or not so subtly—retaliate against workers who ask for a flexible schedule or who try to use comp time (or any other time off). The right-to-request ideas in place in Vermont and San Francisco prohibit retaliation, an important standard that only policymakers could put in place. The Schedules That Work Act, introduced in both the U.S. House of Representatives and the U.S. Senate, includes right-to-request and provisions to address scheduling predictability. It also prevents retaliation by employers when an employee tries to use the law.[29]

Finally, policymakers could encourage workplaces to offer a wider array of workable flexibility options. One issue is that many workers want—or need—to work part-time as a way of giving themselves some flexibility. Maybe they want to work less than full-time to care for children or other family members, or maybe part-time employment is the right thing for combining work with schooling. Our economy, however, provides too few options for people who want this option. Relatively few jobs tend to offer part-time employment, and those that do tend to pay less—and offer fewer benefits—than full-time jobs requiring the same level of skills. Part-time work is most common among low-wage jobs, with little-to-no upward mobility. Policymakers must make sure that those who choose part-time employment gain access to prorated pay and benefits.

People Aren't Algorithms

In Chapter 3, we heard from Jannette Navarro, the Starbucks employee with the unpredictable schedule. Like her, many of us don't know when we'll be working next week and for how long. Lots of retailers use "just-in-time scheduling" software that can identify—down to the minute—how to create the barest-bones staffing plan. These computer algorithms take into account everything from the usual day-to-day customer base (our coffee-shop owner who knows she gets more coffee customers at 8 AM than at 8 PM), holiday schedules, sporting events, or a myriad of other factors. Firms use these algorithms to save money on buying time. If you buy only exactly what you need, you can save on staffing costs in the short run.[30]

As technology has made these kinds of algorithms more widely accessible, we have seen this buying time strategy emerge in a variety of industries and workplaces. In 2007, Wal-Mart was one of the first retailers to implement just-in-time scheduling. According to a CNNMoney article at the time, this new system—first tested in Pensacola, FL—allowed Wal-Mart to change the number of staff and their hours based on sales. Only managers and what they call "stocking teams" had set schedules.[31]

Many other employers have followed Wal-Mart's lead. For example, Fidelity Investments, a financial services firm with more than 54,000 employees, uses a "transitional staffing model." Their practice is to hire only part-time workers for their call centers. This way, they don't have to pay operators to pick up the phone during times of slow demand. Instead, they can vary the hours of their part-time workers to be staffing the phones only during the times they need them. Sometimes, these schedules are just fine for workers and their families; however, the algorithms typically don't consider the family side of the equation, and this practice has implications not just for families but for the economic cycle as well. Of course, employers can incorporate staff preferences into their algorithms, as in the project The Gap is testing described above.[32]

Just-in-time scheduling is becoming a standard practice in retail, food service, and other sectors. In a study led by the economist Stephanie Luce, the Retail Action Project surveyed 436 nonmanagerial retail workers in New York City. She found that just under half of retail workers surveyed sometimes or always have "on-call" shifts. This means that these employees have to call the store typically within a couple of hours of the beginning of the potential shift, to find out if they have to work that day. This research also found that a whopping 73 percent of workers surveyed said that if they are sent home early they are not paid the minimum amount required by New York State law.[33]

An organization working with food-service workers, Restaurant Opportunities Centers United, recently surveyed more than 200 mothers working in the restaurant industry across five U.S. cities and found that most had unpredictable shifts and had to cope with last-minute schedule changes. Of course, food service depends on nonstandard, customer-driven hours—that's the nature of the industry. But in recent years, as the share of the workforce employed in food service has grown, the necessity and effectiveness of traditional policies have come into question.[34]

We don't have data tracking unpredictable schedules over time, but we do have new data just for 2011 and 2012 from the National

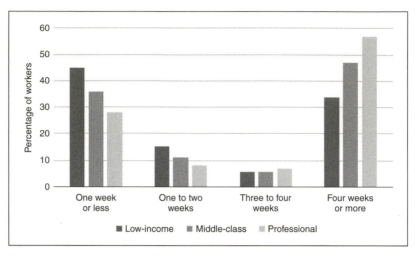

Fig. 7.3 Percentage of young U.S. workers reporting advance notice of schedules, 2012. Young workers in low-income families have less advance notice of their schedules than those in middle-class or professional families. *Note:* Sample includes individuals aged 26 to 32. Individuals who reported being self-employed, in the military, or having zero or missing household income were dropped from the sample. Results are reported as percentages of the cohort population (estimated using sampling weights).

Longitudinal Survey of Youth. These data show that having a predictable schedule isn't common in any income groups but is even less common for workers in low-income families. Figure 7.3 shows that 28.1 percent of young workers in professional families know their schedule less than a week in advance, compared with 45.2 percent of those in low-income families and 35.9 percent in middle-class families. At the other end, most young workers in professional families (57.1 percent) know their schedule at least a month in advance, compared with just a third of those in low-income families (34.0 percent).

While Figure 7.3 shows that unpredictable schedules are more common for (young) workers in low-income families, a not-insubstantial share of middle-class and professional families have to cope with unpredictable schedules as well. There are two common issues, both tied to long hours. Many middle-class workers are compelled to put in "mandatory overtime," that is, work extra hours, often with little or no advance notice, regardless of whether they want to or not. Then there are simply the long hours for many salaried workers, who are often professional employees.[35]

Of course, many families appreciate the extra money that overtime brings in because it can make all the difference to a family budget—so much that it can push a family up into the middle class. Overtime certainly boosts how much families can buy. That was certainly the case in my family: Dad's overtime made all the difference in what we could buy. But when overtime isn't announced in advance or is mandatory—which is legal—and the employee has no option to say no, it can mean scrambling to find child care, canceling family plans, or skipping the night class.[36]

At least those covered by the overtime provisions get extra pay. The Fair Labor Standard Act's overtime provisions cover relatively few salaried employees, and that share has fallen over time. For those employees not covered, employers can demand unlimited hours of work, and, as we learned in Chapter 4, they are willing to push salaried employees to put in as much time as possible. It's not just time in the office; it's all the time made possible by technology—everything from the need to be on email 24/7 to the ability to log into the Internet (and soon be on conference calls) from 30,000 feet in the air (undoubtedly lowering productivity for all of us who use flights to read and write).

Just-in-time scheduling and mandatory overtime push all the responsibility for adjusting to unusual schedules onto workers and their families. This reduces workers' control over their schedules and work time, exacerbating conflicts between work and family life in ways that affect the economy today and into the future. These practices affect the economic cycle through reducing job satisfaction, increasing stress, and limiting—and making unpredictable—time for family, which can affect the ability to sell time as well as turnover and productivity, and thus selling goods and services.

Even though families up and down the income ladder have to cope with unpredictable schedules, those at the lower end have the fewest resources to cope with this instability. Navarro's story brought this home, and she's certainly not alone. One mother in the restaurant industry, Teresa, who gave only her first name and lives and works in Los Angeles, told researchers a similar tale: "I used to have a job that was on-call at hotels [working in banquet service], usually on evenings; I used to have to leave [my children] with [my] sister. But sometimes I would get called in, and my sister was not available, so I would suddenly have to leave them with someone else and I never knew if they had been fed, showered."[37]

Too many workers have schedules that do not allow stability and consistency for their children, which can have negative effects on their parenting and children's outcomes. This also means that too many often cannot make time for their interpersonal relationships, such as time for their spouses and "family dinners," which means those relationships suffer. Low-income workers especially may not have the financial resources to purchase high-quality care or other services that may make an unpredictable schedule a little easier to cope with.

The negative effects on families from unpredictable schedules may not affect an individual firm's profits in the short-run, but economists and policymakers need to be aware of these issues. Research has found that strong job satisfaction—much of which has to do with scheduling issues—improves the quality of marriages and relationships and decreases the chances of a break-up. Poor job satisfaction more often does just the opposite. In Chapter 3 we saw how Jannette's boyfriend said he broke off their relationship because her schedule at Starbucks was wreaking havoc on their lives. This kind of work situation isn't good for couples—something both liberals and conservatives can agree on.[38]

Of course, the economic costs of just-in-time and unpredictable schedules show up in the buying goods and services quadrant as well. An hourly employee with an unpredictable schedule doesn't know how much she'll earn from week to week. The fluctuations may be exacerbated for workers and families with more care responsibilities if the employer retaliates against staff members who refuse to take the shifts offered by giving them fewer hours, or even letting them go. These all add up to a job that doesn't pay the bills, deepening budgeting woes and contributing to the problem of greater variations in income month to month, especially among low-income families.

If an unpredictable schedule leads to more job turnover—which the evidence shows to be the case—then this can also add costs for taxpayers. Unemployed workers may rely on unemployment insurance, public assistance, supplemental nutrition assistance, or housing assistance. We can see the full scope of this problem if we look at the rising number of homeless people who actually have a job. Recent studies have found that about 44 percent of the homeless are now employed. In 2005, New York City commissioned a study from the Vera Institute of Justice which found that "contrary to popular belief," nearly eight in ten homeless heads of family had been employed recently, and that more than half had achieved a level of education—including college degrees—that made them employable. Workers without a home are usually employed in low-wage jobs, as sales clerks or security guards, for example—jobs that often have unpredictable schedules and are paid by the hour.[39]

Just-in-time scheduling may save a firm on their immediate, direct costs, but we have to take into account all of these hidden costs. When employers buy time in a way that gives employees little notice of their schedule, they can only hire people who can make their lives very flexible—or at least think they can because they desperately need the job. This means that their pool of potential employees will not be able to prioritize school, family, or even a second job. The reduced job satisfaction may increase turnover and lead to lower productivity. And it may be that the algorithms—for all the chaos they cause workers and their families—still cannot account for all the vagaries of consumer demand. All of this may mean that relying too much on just-in-time or unpredictable schedules may actually reduce a firm's ability to sell goods and services most profitably, as argued in a recent *Harvard Business Review* article.[40]

Of course, employers use just-in-time scheduling because they believe it's best for their bottom line. A firm's focus is—and should be—on its bottom line. But evidence shows that other ways of scheduling can also be good for a firm's profits, as well as for families and the economy more generally. Zeynep Ton has studied successful low-cost retail companies and found that they don't need to follow this kind of model to make money. Many profitable firms follow what she terms a "good jobs strategy," providing "jobs with decent pay, decent benefits, and stable work schedules." Ton's book, *The Good Jobs Strategy*, is full of examples of firms that take their employees' scheduling needs very seriously in order to improve the quality of the time they buy—with positive effects on their employees' productivity.[41]

The upshot is that employers can use new technology to choose when they buy time in a way that either facilitates better matches between employee and employer needs or makes things more difficult. Cloud servers can facilitate telecommuting or working from home during a snowstorm, but they can also mean that an employee is "always on." Computer algorithms can incorporate worker preferences or they can ignore them. It all depends on how employers choose to manage their employees.

There have been some recent, high-profile reversals of just-in-time scheduling practices. The day after publication of the *New York Times* piece about Jannette Navarro's work-life travails at Starbucks, the company announced a change in their practices. Perhaps the bad press outweighed any gains from how they scheduled workers. Or maybe management just needed an extra push to get them on the right path. Or maybe they'd already figured out they needed to change and the front-page article was just well-timed. Wal-Mart, which pioneered these kinds of scheduling practices, has said that it is changing how it buys time to better accommodate family life. In February 2015, the company announced that, in 2016, some employees will get a fixed schedule, that employees will know their schedule 2.5 weeks in advance, and that they will be able to do some scheduling themselves.[42]

But there is also a role for policy. In today's economy, employers have a good deal of discretion to decide how to schedule their employees. Just-in-time scheduling, mandatory overtime, and long hours for salaried workers are all legal under federal law (although some states do have stricter rules). The Fair Labor Standards Act was put together in a time before computers were invented and when the most important scheduling problem was overwork for hourly employees. Given this, the law says nothing about sufficient hours, predictable hours, or part-time pay. Employers who use just-in-time scheduling can do so without violating federal law, even up to sending an employee home early.

Current law does require, however, that if an employee has to wait around at work to start his shift, then he must be paid for that waiting time. Firefighters, for example, who are playing cards or reading a book at the firehouse while waiting for an alarm are still working and would be paid for their time. But the rules no longer reflect today's technology. In the 1930s when no one had a mobile phone or a computer, an employer had to give advance notice about when he needed a worker to show up because there was no other way to let him know his schedule. Now employers can insist that workers check their schedule in the next couple of hours via the Internet or their mobile phone—neither of which were even a glimmer in the imagination when the Fair Labor Standards Act was passed into law more than seventy-five years ago. This fundamentally changes the definition of what it means to wait to work.[43]

Some states and localities are considering new rules that limit employers' ability to change shifts at the last minute. In November 2014, San Francisco led the way, passing the first legislation in the United States to give some hourly workers schedules that are more predictable. The new ordinance requires major chain-stores to provide hourly employees with two weeks' notice of work schedules, notice of changes to work schedules, and compensation for schedule changes made on less than seven days' notice as well as unused on-call shifts. It also provides part-time employees with the same starting rate of hourly pay, access to time off, and eligibility for promotions as provided to full-time employees. As of this writing, legislators in eleven states introduced similar legislation in 2014 or 2015. This is part of a larger push for a Retail Workers Bill of Rights, promoted by advocates around the country.[44]

In a world where firms have lost America's Silent Partner, we all have to adjust. Firms can no longer assume that they'll benefit from the hidden subsidy that the American Wife used to provide. When they buy time, they have to recognize that the employee has to reconcile that with her life outside of work.

We have to reestablish boundaries between time for work and time for life that fit today's families and today's workplaces. Too many workers don't put in a traditional eight-hour day, working 9-to-5, yet they still need the "time for rest" and "time for what we will" that workers' rights advocates called for a century ago. But they need these rules to match the reality of today, not yesterday.

It comes down to one basic question: what are the rules to sell and buy time? Families offer up their time to firms. In an industrial economy, the boundaries between time at work and time at home were often very clear—you were either at the factory or not. But in our service economy, the lines are often blurry. When am I working and when am I off are questions that many of us—across the income spectrum—cope with every day. Up until now, we haven't put in place employment contracts to control when fidgety or anxious employees answer that vibrating phone or check their email inbox. We should. We need contracts for our mental energy in the same way that we had them for our masculine brawn in the past.

Care: When You Can't Be at Home

The previous two chapters laid out a path to reduce conflict between work and family life and, in doing so, improve our economic performance. Paid time off to provide care and schedules that fit family life would put us on the right path. Both are good for families and the economy. These solutions are important. Yet they don't solve all the problems. They can't make up for the fact that people must be at work for a good deal of their waking hours. They do not address how families ensure that their loved ones are well cared for while they are at work.

By the time the American Wife took a paying job, many aspects of her job in the home had become less time-consuming. The washing machine, the vacuum cleaner, and the dishwasher eliminated some of the hardest work and made it easier to share chores. On top of these modern homemaking marvels, the marketplace began offering the kinds of goods and services that made it possible for families to outsource many aspects of homemaking. For me, the epiphany was the day my mother told me (when I was twenty-five) that if some company had invented "salad in a bag" when I was a child, then we would have had salad every day. Now workers—typically low-paid—use machines to clean lovely lettuces and stuff them in little bags so Mom can just slice it open and dump it in a bowl for dinner. Ten minutes saved.

So far, it remains fictional (and, even if possible, undesirable to most humans!) to think we can outsource the care of our loved ones to machines. If you're a sci-fi fan, you'll be familiar with the fantasy of a robotic future. Sometimes, those machines take on the task of care. In the film *Sleep Dealer*, Tijuana migrants working under sweatshop conditions control the actions of far-off robots in the homes of the global elite, remotely providing "care" for children and the aged. Personally, I'd rather have a Hogwarts house elf magically clean my home and provide care than a robot, but that's not going to happen anytime soon. The point is, for most American families, access to affordable, high-quality care is more the stuff of fantasy than reality.[1]

Employers have fantasies, too. They want their Silent Partner back. Our coffee-shop owner needs the barista to show up on time, not call an hour before his shift to say he'll be late because his child-care provider isn't available or his mom needs him—again—to take her to a doctor's appointment. (Of course, it's worth reiterating the unfairness here as our coffee-shop owner can call the barista and tell him he's needed—or not needed—whenever she wants.) When employers buy time, they want reliable employees. The reality, however, is that business lost its Silent Partner long ago. With few people having an American Wife at home, employers need employees who have a workable system in place to address the daily needs of their children and their aging family members for care.

There's also a new wrinkle. When the American Wife first entered the workplace in force, the public debate focused on what her absence in the home meant for her family's children. This will remain an important issue, especially since the Millennials—the largest cohort since the Baby Boomers—are entering their prime child-bearing years. Yet today, the question of care for the aging is just as important. By 2030, one in five people in the United States will be over age sixty-five, compared with one in seven today. As the Baby Boom generation glides into retirement, many of today's younger families will need to help them. This is important for all kinds of families, but African Americans and Hispanics are slightly more likely to report having to care for an elder compared with whites. This may be due to differences in health problems, cost factors—whites are more likely to be in the middle and professional classes and thus can afford to pay for care—or it may be that they put a higher value on family caregiving.[2]

Whereas Chapters 6 and 7 dealt with the relationship between employers and their employees, in this chapter, we'll look at what happens at home and how that affects employers and the economy more generally. Families have three options to replace the Silent Partner's time spent on care: they can leave the child or elder on their own, with a friend or family member, or with a paid caregiver. These decisions affect the economic cycle today and, indeed, far off into the future. Which path they choose is in no small part tied to whether the family is low-income, middle-class, or professional.

Choosing the right path is often a fraught private decision. Every day in America, millions of people get up, get dressed, and leave their loved ones in the care of a paid caregiver or with hard-pressed relatives or friends. And, just like clockwork, mommies and daddies question whether they've made the right decision while just as many grown-up children fret over who's caring for their aging mom or dad—if anyone.

Which path families choose is also a serious economic issue. We make these choices—fraught as they are—because we need to go to work or school. Without care options, someone in the family must stay home, out of the labor force and earning no income. That may be the right choice for some families, but more often than not, having someone stay at home is simply not a viable economic option. Many of us value the economic independence and personal satisfaction that come with having a job, and as discussed in previous chapters, many family breadwinners need to work.

Whether families have access to affordable, reliable, high-quality care for the young and the aging affects all four quadrants of the economic cycle, as shown in Figure 8.1. Without filling the care-gap left at home when the American Wife entered the labor force, selling one's time can be impossible, especially if the costs of care are high. Care—both for the aging and for children—makes it possible for firms to buy time from those with care responsibilities. But firms need their employees to be reliable, and without good care options, they often cannot be dependable workers. Therefore, the kind of care a family uses—do they juggle schedules, leave the person needing care home alone, rely on friends and family, or do they purchase care?—affects not only the experience of the person being cared for but also the ways the caregiver can sell time. Paid caregivers let family

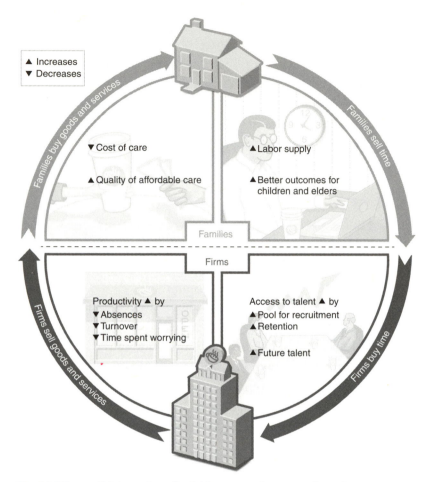

Fig. 8.1 Effects of high-quality, affordable care on the economic cycle.

caregivers take jobs outside the home. Without them, the nation's labor supply would be much smaller, depriving the family of much-needed earnings and the economy of the most productive use of someone's skills and talents.

Care's Role in the Economy

Before we look at the paths families can choose, let's take a moment to remember what we learned in Chapter 5 about what economists call "human capital," that is, the skills and talents of our workforce.

From the point of view of the person seeking to outsource care to a paid or unpaid caregiver, the quality of that care—in terms of reliability, available hours, and the experience of the person being cared for—will affect their ability to do their job or even whether they can sell time. However, from the child's point of view, child care is "education"; no matter which path the family chooses—home alone, friends or family, or a paid caregiver—the child will be learning. And from the elder's point of view, the quality of care will affect their health outcomes and overall quality of life.

When it comes to children, the science today is 100 percent clear that high-quality care is essential for their emotional and intellectual development—and, our economic analysis tells us, their future productivity. We've learned that early childhood education is just as important as later schooling for child development and the child's future skills and employment prospects. The level of skills that children have when they enter kindergarten is correlated with later employment outcomes, even accounting for the quality and quantity of elementary, secondary, and postsecondary schooling. This is not to say that later investments are not important, but recent research in economics points to the conclusion that in order to improve our nation's economic growth and competitiveness policymakers must focus on early childhood.[3]

The economic importance of child care is magnified as more children are in families without a stay-at-home caregiver. Certainly, parents play an important role, but we know that the quality of child care affects early learning and school achievement. The National Institute of Child Health and Human Development Early Child Care Research Network found that among diverse indicators, the quality of child care was the most consistent predictor of young children's behavior. Children who receive high-quality child care have better developmental outcomes in early childhood, including better cognitive, language, and communication development, which, in turn, promotes learning.[4]

The importance of early childhood to learning and future behavior makes the quality of care a national economic issue. Our nation rose to be an economic powerhouse in no small measure because we made investments in education. From compulsory elementary and secondary schooling to the G.I. Bill for college attendance, we've invested in the skills of our workforce in ways that have improved outcomes for children and young adults from across the income spectrum. As the economists Claudia Goldin and Lawrence Katz lay out in their book *The Race between Education and Technology*, these investments and the fact that they were universal—accessible to all—propelled the U.S. economy forward during the twentieth century. To continue to be an economic powerhouse in the twenty-first century, we must also focus on early childhood education and the quality of care. And that means making sure that all children, not just those in professional families, have access to enriching child care and early education.[5]

For all these reasons high-quality, affordable child care is one area where there is consensus on the economics. In 2012, then chairman of the Federal Reserve Ben Bernanke gave a video speech at the Children's Defense Fund National Conference in which he said, "The research shows that effective educations lead to lower rates of poverty, higher lifetime earnings, and greater satisfaction on the job and at home. And specialists in economic development have identified educational attainment as a key source of economic growth and rising incomes in many countries around the world."[6] He went on to point out that investments in early childhood education are more critical for children in lower-income families, since those families cannot afford high-quality care without help. All of these factors affect not only the future human capital available in our country but also, by extension, the productivity of our economy in the decades ahead.

The problem is that most child care in the United States is not of high quality—or even good quality. The economists David Blau and Janet Currie summarize the best-available literature on child-care quality, noting from the outset that there are no nationally representative samples of U.S. day-care centers with such measures. Only two studies with reasonable sample size look at the national landscape and measure quality in site-specific samples of day-care centers using equivalent scales, the Cost, Quality, and Outcomes Study and the National Child Care Staffing Study. Blau and Currie summarize the findings from these studies and show that "the overall average rating in both studies is just under 4, or about halfway between minimal and good."[7]

We aren't doing much better on elder care. Today's elders need different forms of care because life expectancy has increased, many live farther from adult children or do not have children to rely on for help, and medicine has made impressive advances. Most elders cared for by family members live on their own. Some need affordable in-home help with daily activities, such as lifting heavy groceries, changing the light bulb that requires pulling out a ladder, replacing their hearing aid battery, preparing meals, or taking medications. This care can make the difference in the quality of life and how quickly an elder ends up at an expensive nursing home, less connected to friends, church, and community. Too often, however, this kind of care isn't covered by any federal system and families are left both to identify caregivers and to pay for that care on their own. And, increasingly, elders need long-term care—also an area where there are too few high-quality and affordable options.[8]

The importance of caring for children and the elderly makes the workforce providing the care vital. But low wages and lack of adequate training make it difficult to attract and retain well-qualified care providers for young and old alike. Understandably, families are reluctant to entrust the care of their beloved children and elders to substandard providers. If they can afford to do so, many of these families will take on the cost and burden of taking care of a child or an elderly relative by reducing work hours or quitting a job altogether.

Paying for high-quality care—for children or elders—is very expensive and costs have been rising. According to Child Care Aware of America, in 2013, the typical cost to have a four-year-old in full-time day care across the United States ranged from about $4,800 per year to more than $17,000—and four-year-olds are less costly to care for than infants or toddlers. While the costs of infant and toddler care are the highest, parents need afterschool and holiday care for children until at least their preteen years.[9] Families with children end up spending a large percentage of their earnings on care. Joan Williams and I looked at child-care affordability for low-income, middle-class, and professional families. We found that in the late 2000s, the share of income spent to have a preschool-aged child in child care ranged from 3 to 7 percent for professional families to about 14 percent for low-income families. This understates the burden on poor families. Child Care Aware of America reports that the cost of center-based infant care can be above median income for a single mother in some states, among them New York and Massachusetts. Thus, affording care is a significant issue for family budgets—especially when we consider the stalled and stuck incomes of middle-class and low-income families—and affects their ability to buy goods and services.[10]

Elder care is expensive, too, and there's not enough assistance with the high cost. The average yearly cost of nursing home care for a semiprivate room is more than $80,000, three and a half times the earnings of the typical low-income family, and about $10,000 more than the typical middle-class family's income. For care in a one-bedroom unit in an assisted living facility, the average annual costs are about $40,000. Several government programs, such as Medicare and Medicaid, may help pay for some long-term care services under certain circumstances. But not everyone qualifies for these benefits—and when a person does qualify there are restrictions on the services covered and the length of time she can receive benefits. In addition to having to pay for uncovered services, residents have to pay out-of-pocket for a portion of covered services.

These costs are a financial burden for family members providing care, not just for the elder herself. According to a 2015 survey of those providing care to a loved one who's ailing or aged, only a third report having any paid help. For those families who do pay, it can be a large burden. Half of caregivers (47 percent) report having an income under $50,000 a year. A survey from 2010 found that almost half of adult children caring for an elder helped cover the costs and, of those, four in ten (41 percent) reported that their financial contributions were at least "somewhat" burdensome.[11]

The lack of affordable care options not only affects workers' ability to buy goods and services; it also can mean the difference between being able to sell time or not. While we know relatively little about the relationship between the employment of fathers and their contributions to child care, and are only starting to understand the effect of elder care on employment patterns, it is well documented that access to affordable and reliable child care increases the chances of mothers entering into or remaining in the labor force. For every 10 percent reduction in the cost of center-based child care, the research shows that women increase their labor-force participation by about 2 percent or more. This means that if child care were fully paid for, women would increase their working rates by twenty percentage points, and a large number of talented people would be added to the labor force. Data suggest that this employment effect of subsidizing child care is even greater for mothers with children under the age of six.[12]

Making up for Lost Time

Let's turn to how families cope, given the cost of high-quality care. As we learned in Chapters 2, 3, and 4, the loss of America's Silent Partner means that life has changed for everyone—working women and men, children, and the aging. Because the American Wife has her own job now, more men also have to take on the responsibility of caring for children and their own aging parents. In my family, both my parents and my husband's parents have needed time off to care for their parents. The ability to have paid leave and some of the workplace flexibility described in the last two chapters made all the difference in being able to keep a job. But adequate care matters, too.

Caring takes time—time that the Silent Partner used to be able to give. Families facing the need to care for someone—a child or an elder—have to decide how to manage that. Do they juggle work schedules so that one person is always home? Is that possible, given their employers? Do they leave the person who needs care home

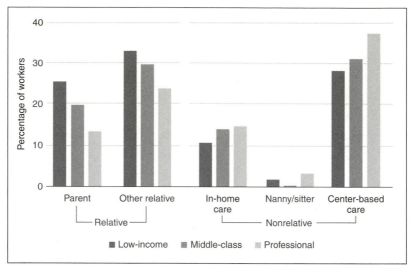

Fig. 8.2 Type of child care used, by income group, 2004. Professional families are more likely than others to use a formal day-care center or a nanny and pay for child care. Low-income and middle-class families are more likely to use "parental care," meaning that the parents tag-team, with one parent providing care while the other works, or rely on friends or family.

alone? Do they ask a friend or another family member to help? Or can they afford a paid care provider?

Of course, families do all of the above. Where a family sits— whether they are a low-income, middle-class, or professional family—affects which option they choose. In my research with Joan Williams, we examined the kind of child care used by families across low-income, middle-class, and professional families. I've reproduced the results in Figure 8.2, which shows that professional families are more likely than others to pay for child care, using a formal day-care center or a nanny. Low-income and middle-class families are more likely to use "parental care," meaning that the parents tag-team, with one parent providing care while the other works, or rely on friends or family. Although I do not have a breakdown for the same income groups for elder care, evidence shows that families with less income also end up choosing less formal kinds of care, and those who provide unpaid care tend to have lower income.[13]

Whichever choice families make, it affects the economy in some way. Each of these choices means a different level of quality of care, which influences whether that care is the kind of option that can ensure the stability necessary for a worker to hold down a job. The quality also, of course, affects what children learn and whether they and their elders are well cared for.

These are questions that my family—like many—has experienced firsthand. As my grandmother Jean aged, we struggled to find good options for her care. She was independent enough to live in her own home, but we feared for her safety and comfort, my grandfather having passed away long ago. She had troubling signs of dementia, but more important, she had macular degeneration, which slowly robbed her of her sight. She lived on Lopez, one of the San Juan Islands, just south of Vancouver, British Columbia, only a few hours from Mukilteo (depending on the ferry line), but too far from our home for my dad to be able to check in on her as often as he would have liked.

In my family, the care of my grandmother began with my dad's time. He spent many weekends, and a day off from work here and there, to check on her or take her to doctors' appointments. Doing a second shift as a family caregiver is now common: workers in the prime of their careers may spend more years caring for their parents than they do caring for their children. As with my Dad, most of this care is added to the responsibility of holding down a job. A 2010 survey by the Families and Work Institute found that 17 percent of workers were providing elder care and that those caregivers were employed forty-five hours a week on average on top of caregiving, an hour more each week in paid work than noncaregivers.[14]

Many families aim to avoid delegating care of children and elders. They juggle schedules or use up all their evenings and weekends providing care. For many, this is an important family value; for others, it's an economic necessity. In practice, this means that many families have coped with the loss of hidden time by doing less of everything else. In Chapter 2, I showed a figure documenting that both mothers and fathers still spend just as much—or more—time with their children today as in 1965. Mothers put in more time at work, but their overall time with children has stayed about the same, while fathers are spending more time caring for children, adding about seven hours a week. Although we don't have the kind of time series data on elder care, new research finds that caregivers spend an average of 24.4 hours a week providing care, and nearly one in four provides more than forty hours a week.[15]

The weight of managing elder care—on top of a full-time job— usually falls on one adult sibling—more often than not, the daughter, although that's not always the case. As Ai-jen Poo, the director of the National Domestic Workers Alliance and co-director of the Caring across Generations campaign, explains, the typical caregiver is "a fifty-year-old woman who provides 19 hours of care per week . . . for an average of four years."[16] This may be the common story, but it didn't apply to my dad, who is an only child.

My dad was lucky in that he was both eligible for caregiver leave under the Family and Medical Leave Act and had paid vacation he could use. Workers who have flexibility from their employer will be better able to manage the demands of also being a caregiver. As the last two chapters documented, however, those who have the most access to paid leave and to some say in their schedules are in professional or, to a lesser extent, middle-class families. These families are also more able than low-income families to have the resources to pay for care. Those most likely to need to juggle because they cannot afford to pay for child- or elder care are those least likely to have the workplace policies to make that possible.

The option of providing care oneself may save money—meaning the family still has that money to buy other goods and services—but it certainly affects how the caregiver sells time. Taking on what is essentially a second job adds significant stress to the caregiver's day, which can affect employment. The National Alliance for Caregiving's 2015 survey found that among those caring for an aging or ailing loved one, 61 percent reported that this negatively affected their paying job, because they needed leaves of absence, had to reduce their work hours, or received performance warnings. They also found that 38 percent of caregivers reported feeling high stress.[17]

When juggling schedules doesn't work—or when an unpredictable work schedule makes juggling impossible—some families choose to leave their loved ones on their own and hope for the best. That's what my parents did once they thought I was old enough. Sometime in the early 1980s, I saw a magazine lying around our house that labeled my sister and me as "latch-key kids." I recall wondering what all the fuss was about. Of course, years later, my mom told me how stressful it was for her and my dad. As with many families, the fact that they worried about whether I was safe at home alone added a layer of stress that my parents didn't need.[18]

But we were lucky—nothing at all scary happened at my house. That's not always the case. Children and elders left on their own are more likely to have accidents—sometimes life-threatening ones. And some families live in neighborhoods where they fear for the physical safety of a child or elder. Years ago, when I was working at the New York City Housing Authority, I conducted focus groups with mothers. I can still vividly recall the strict tone of one mother as she outlined the instructions she gave her eleven-year-old daughter to go directly home and lock the door—and not open it for anyone—while home alone after school.[19]

Professional families have more resources and are less likely to have these kinds of tough choices over leaving someone who needs care on their own. When they do, their child (or elder) is typically in a safer neighborhood. Nor do they often appear in the news because they left their child alone while they went to work; when they do, lately it's been because allowing their child to roam freely is a conscious choice. But in Chapter 3, we learned the story of Debra Lynn Harrell, who ended up in jail because she left her nine-year-old daughter to spend her day at the playground across the street from her worksite, which is sadly more and more a parental necessity. Jail is the extreme outcome; more often, parents just have to live with the everyday anxiety of knowing their child is home alone.[20]

Increasingly, technology allows caregivers to monitor the child or elder they've left on their own. Families buy mobile phones for their preteens and teens; some go so far as to install home-monitoring devices. Families pay to renovate their elder parent's home to accommodate age-related disabilities. My grandmother bought an "Alert" service so that if she fell or needed help, all she had to do was push the red button hanging around her neck. (These aren't always optimal solutions: she would accidently set it off while doing the dishes or rolling over when she slept, then get discombobulated by The Voice asking, "Jean, are you okay?") But this technology costs money, affecting the ability of the aged person's family to buy goods and services, and possibly could lead them into debt.

If you can't work out your schedule and you don't want to leave your junior or senior home alone, then you may look to friends or family. As mentioned in Chapter 3, this strategy is more common among low-income and middle-class families than among professionals. Such so-called informal care arrangements might be a good solution—and for many families, more than a good solution. The doting aunt or good friend—or Dad while Mom works the early shift—may be the perfect solution. But what happens when Aunt Lucy has something else she needs to do and—oops—she forgot to let you know? Research shows that formal child-care options, such as a day-care center or a full-time nanny, where providing care is someone's day job, tend to be the most reliable. Relying on friends and family can solve the family budget, or the problem of buying goods and services, but it may lead to a problem with selling time.

The alternative, of course, is for someone to "choose" to leave his or her job to provide care. That may be an option for some. In a survey of elder caregivers, four in ten (37 percent) reported that their caregiving responsibilities led them to quit their jobs or cut back on hours. But there are implications for the full economic cycle. My parents certainly couldn't afford for my dad to quit his job to care for his mom. Those forced to dial-back and quit in their prime working years to care for an ailing elder lose out on peak earnings, while employers lose valuable, experienced employees. We spend a lot of time debating how much we should allocate to the elderly through Social Security and Medicare, but we need to bear in mind that those dollars don't only support the aged, they affect the budgets of the families of the aged and their stability when the next generation retires. According to a recent study by the MetLife Mature Market Institute, women who leave the labor force before they retire because of elder-care responsibilities lose a total $324,044 in lifetime earnings and Social Security benefits. Men who leave the labor force lose $283,716—less than women, but still significant. This certainly affects a family's ability to buy goods and services.[21]

Leaving the workforce to care for loved ones also has long-term effects on selling time and, as a result, buying goods and services. When a young worker leaves the labor force to care for a child, it may well affect her entire career trajectory. In Chapter 2, I told the story of the journalist who called to tell me that her family questioned the sanity of her spending all "her" earnings on her toddler's day care. (I again put "her" in quotes because, as she pointed out, if it takes two to make a baby, the responsibility for caring for that child isn't all "hers," even if her family couldn't help thinking of it that way.) She was doing so because she felt that if she stopped working, she'd have a hard time getting back into the labor force later on, limiting her ability to support her family years down the road. The evidence certainly supports this decision.

To be clear, the lack of viable care options hasn't stopped people from working, but it does seem that we're at our limit. In Chapter 1, we learned how President Nixon vetoed universal child care in the hopes that women would not choose employment. We know how that turned out. Between 1971 and 2015, forty-one million women entered the labor force. In recent years, however, U.S. employment rates have flatlined or fallen, which has not happened in other developed economies. There are indications that this is due to some combination of lack of workplace flexibility, as in those situations described in Chapters 6 and 7, and inadequate and unaffordable care options. American families are tapped out.[22]

The Fantasy and Reality of Paying for Care

Paying a caregiver to make up for the lost time of America's Silent Partner is often the best solution for families, firms, and the economy.

The problem is that most families cannot afford the cost of high-quality care. Even so, according to the U.S. Census Bureau, nearly two-thirds of children under the age of five—12.5 million children—regularly spend time in some type of child-care arrangement. For elders, the statistics are a little more muddled: only about a quarter of people who care for an elder report also paying for a caregiver, but the costs of long-term care are large and significant, especially when compared with family incomes.[23]

If you ask caregivers what they are looking for in a care situation, they'll likely describe a location that is convenient, is open for the hours they need, provides nutritious meals and an enriching environment, and is affordable (as well as an employer who provides a supportive office environment through the ideas discussed in Chapters 7 and 8). We had a system of care like this once upon a time in America—at least for children. In Chapter 1, I mentioned that during World War II, federal policymakers interpreted the Lanham Act as authorizing "public works" to include child-care facilities for mothers employed in the war effort. While the men were off at war, domestic industries needed to find a new labor force, and they saw child care as a key piece of the puzzle. Women couldn't march into factories just because they saw a "Rosie the Riveter" poster. So the federal government went about setting up child-care centers. Every state except New Mexico had centers that cared for infants and children up to age twelve, with eligibility open so anyone could access care.[24]

Interpreting the Lanham Act to include child-care facilities made it possible for mothers to sell time. By the program's peak in July 1944, more than 130,000 children were enrolled in over 3,100 child-care centers across the country. The cost was reasonable and included meals, so Mom didn't have to worry about packing a lunch. The centers accommodated local labor schedules, too. If factories or bases were open twenty-four hours, the centers provided evening and overnight care. This program worked for parents and children. Between 1942 and 1945, women's labor-force participation rose from 25 to 36 percent. Lanham centers helped boost employment and earnings for women workers. Just as important, later studies showed that children who attended these centers saw positive short-term and long-term outcomes, affecting the economy for decades to come.[25]

A modern-day model can be found in the U.S. military. It has the largest employer-sponsored child-care program in the United States. It also has some of the best child-care programs in the United States. The goal of the program is to make sure that parents working on military bases have affordable child-care options and can do their jobs without worrying about whether their children are in good care. The centers are open during the hours that personnel need to work and are staffed by highly trained and well-paid professionals—they are paid about $15 an hour, compared with the industry average of $10 an hour. The best part for parents is that the cost is subsidized: about two-thirds of costs are covered by the military.[26]

This kind of program is good for the family side of the equation, especially for low-income and middle-class families who otherwise cannot afford such high-quality and easy-to-use care. But the U.S. military and Lanham Act's programs aren't just good for families; they solve problems for the firm's side of the equation as well.

If you ask an employer what his fantasy care situation is, after he gets over his frustration that his Silent Partner isn't coming back, he is likely to describe something that looks similar to the parents' and caregivers' ideal. Employers want every employee to have access to reliable child- and elder care that leaves them free to focus on their job. Like workplace flexibility, predictable schedules, paid sick days, and paid family and medical leave, reliable child care or elder care reduces absences and saves firms money. For families, what's often most important is "quality" and "affordability," but the key word for employers is "reliability." From the employer's perspective, formal care options—such as a day-care center or a nanny with set hours—can be especially important to making sure employees can get to work on time.

Some firms step in and provide care onsite. Employers do this because it makes sense for the bottom line. Onsite care reduces turnover, reduces employee absences, and can make it easier to have an employee work extra hours (so long as the care facility works this out with the employer). All of this can save the firm money. In a survey of 120 employers in upstate New York, Reagan Baughman, Daniela DiNardi, and Douglas Holtz-Eakin found that "employers who offer flexible sick leave and child care assistance experience measurable reductions in turnover."[27]

Even so, onsite care is rare, in no small part because there are large upfront costs and the employer needs to be sufficiently large to have enough employees use the facility. According to the National Study of Employers, in 2014, only 7 percent of firms provided onsite or nearby child care, down from 9 percent in 2008. Even firms that do provide onsite care may see this as a perk only for employees at the very top. Only 2 percent of employers subsidized such care. And a firm can change its mind at any time. To the chagrin of many employees (at least according to news reports), Google recently shut down its "Kinderplex" care center and replaced it with an expensive facility to meet the care needs of the firm's top brass, but not really anyone else.[28]

Instead of meeting the needs of all employees, some employers focus their attention specifically on the issue of reliability and provide help for their employees only when their primary-care arrangement breaks down. The housing finance company Fannie Mae, for example, reimburses employees who need emergency back-up care for an aging loved one up to $40 a day. But here, too, the numbers are small: only about one in twenty employers provides any help with back-up care for the aging.[29]

Given that very few employers provide help with care and less than 2 percent of the population is in the military, most of us are left to fend for ourselves. It can be very difficult to afford the kind of care we need—in terms of cost, quality, or ease of service for children or for aging family members. Because the United States does not provide a system of care for the young, the ill, or the aged, families must patch together various, mostly private, solutions.

There are limited government programs to help defray the costs of care, typically aimed at the very poor, and some tax relief for middle-income and professional families. The federal programs to defray the costs for families who buy care for children and the aging are listed in Table 8.1. Although the list may seem long, it's woefully insufficient to address the economic issues of families. It's also important to note that this entire list accounts for 0.7 percent of total federal outlays. (I know that seems like an error, but I've fact-checked it twice!)

Let's start with the simplest: tax relief. There are two types of tax breaks available to families for care-related expenses, and families may use one or the other but not both. Working families can get a tax credit of up to 35 percent of what they spend on child or dependent care, although the credit shrinks to 20 percent for families who earn above about $43,000 per year. This program, called the Child and Dependent Care Tax Credit, is for families with a child under the age of thirteen or for a mentally or physically handicapped spouse or dependent, which can include an elder. The federal government also allows firms to set up Flexible Spending Accounts for their employees to spend on either child care or elder care. If their firm sets one up, employees can set aside up to $5,000 pretax dollars a year to pay for child or dependent care. In 2014, 61 percent of surveyed employers provided such accounts for child care and 41 percent for elder care. But let's remember that tax breaks presume that families can find high-quality care to buy, which as discussed above isn't always the case. Thus from the get-go, this cannot be the full solution.[30]

Further, while these tax breaks are nice, not everyone can actually make use of them. The more your family earns, the more valuable are these programs, although they are capped. Even if you pay lots in Social Security, property, and sales taxes, if you have no federal income tax liability, then these tax breaks provide absolutely no benefit. Therefore, middle-class and some professional families are the ones who benefit from these tax programs. It's the same for the Flexibility Spending Account: the married couple who earns $50,000 a year could save $750, whereas if that family earned $175,000 a year, they could save $1,250. But if your family doesn't

Table 8.1   Federal spending on child care and elder care

Program	Amount (in millions of dollars)	As share of total federal outlays (%)	Fiscal year
Child and Dependent Care Tax Credit	4,400	0.13	2014
Dependent Care Assistance Plan	*		
Head Start	8,598	0.25	2014
Child and Adult Care Food Program	2,900	0.08	2013
Child Care and Development Block Grant (discretionary)	2,348	0.07	2014
Child Care and Development Block Grant (entitlement)	2,917	0.08	2014
Temporary Assistance for Needy Families (direct)	73	0.00	2013
Temporary Assistance for Needy Families (transferred to Child Care and Development Fund)	1,367	0.04	2013
Social Services Block Grant	1,699	0.05	2012
Preschool (development block grants)	250	0.01	2014
Total	24,552	0.71	

*Data unavailable.

Data source: Data compiled by Maryam Adamu and Katie Hamm using Early Childhood Learning and Knowledge Center, "Head Start Program Fact Sheet Fiscal Year 2014," Head Start, April 2015, http://eclkc.ohs.acf.hhs.gov /hslc/data/factsheets/2014-hs-program-factsheet.html; National Conference of State Legislatures, "Child and Adult Care Food Program (CACFP)," April 14, 2015, http://www.ncsl.org/documents/statefed/CACFP_Report .pdf; Administration for Children and Families, "All Purpose Table (APT) FY 2014 and FY 2015," https://www.acf .hhs.gov/sites/default/files/olab/2014_and_2015_acf_apt.PDF; Social Security Administration, "Funding for Child Care," accessed May 27, 2015, http://www.ssa.gov/OP_Home/ssact/title04/0418.htm; Administration for Children and Families, "Fiscal Year 2013 Expenditures"; Administration for Children and Families, "Social Services Block Grant Program: Annual Report 2012" (U.S. Department of Health and Human Services, 2014); U.S. Department of Education, "Preschool Development Grants: Funding," August 2014, http://www2.ed.gov/programs /preschooldevelopmentgrants/funding.html. Federal budget data from U.S. Congressional Budget Office, "Budget Data and Projections," accessed August 21, 2015, https://www.cbo.gov/publication/45069.

earn enough to owe any federal income taxes (although all working families still pay federal Social Security taxes and a host of state and local taxes such as sales and property taxes), then these accounts won't help you at all. Further, the Flexible Spending Account has to be set up by your employer and therefore mostly benefits professional families with more stable employment patterns, who also tend to be higher earners.[31]

These tax-based programs are built on traditional ideas of family, where the caregiver is the "primary" caregiver. This doesn't make sense in a world of complex families, where a child's care costs may be split between the households of two separate parents or where siblings aim to share the cost of caring for an aging parent. The tax benefit can only go to one person—the "primary caregiver," when in fact care is being provided by the proverbial family village. The benefits are out of the reach of the millions of families who provide occasional support to an ailing or elderly family member who is not a dependent, as well as extended families who share the financial and emotional costs of care but cannot share the credit.

The federal government also provides direct subsidies to help low-income families left out of the tax-relief programs afford child care and elder care, also shown in Table 8.1. Let's begin with Head Start, on which the federal government spends nearly twice as much as on the tax credits described above. Even so, the program is under-funded—so much so that it serves less than half of the more than two million children living in poverty who are eligible for the program. The Child Care and Development Block Grant provides federal funds to the states, which have considerable leeway in setting provider-payment levels, parent copayment levels, and income-eligibility requirements, as well as authority to regulate their own programs. Some provisions in the Temporary Assistance for Needy Families program enable those in the program seeking to reenter the workforce to tap child-care funds. But these programs also serve a fraction of the low-income and working families who need child-care assistance. In 2013, nineteen states had a waiting list or had stopped signing up new children for their child-care assistance programs.[32]

Typically, for a family to be eligible for child-care subsidies though the federal programs—even if administered by the state—total earnings must fall below the state's median income, but the threshold varies widely. The economist Randy Albelda and I, with a team of other scholars, found wide variation disparities in the income thresholds for eligibility—varying from just over $14,000 per year in Texas to about $41,500 per year in the District of Columbia, in 2014 dollars. However, we also found something else: in none of the ten states we looked at did more than half of eligible families actually receive the subsidy.[33]

This means that waiting lists are long and growing. As a part of our research, Albelda and I traveled the country, talking to advocates and policymakers in ten states. In Cincinnati, Ohio, during a meeting with a local policymaker in charge of one of the city's largest subsidized child-care facilities, I listened to one of the most nonsensical policy conversations I've ever sat in on. The policymaker spent about fifteen minutes telling us that her child-care program had a variety of positive outcomes. I asked how long the waiting list was, and she cheerfully replied, "There's no waiting list. Only families with incomes well below the poverty line are eligible, so we are constantly having to search to find eligible families." Of course there was no waiting list! The very low threshold meant that thousands of Cincinnati working families lacked access to this program because they were earning just enough to be ineligible for such high-quality care. As the kids today would say, hashtag-policy-fail.

The failure to help families extends to the area of elder care. The Families and Work Institute reports that while families get some help paying for the costs of elder care from a variety of sources, it's not always the right help at the right time. Sixty percent report getting some help from Medicare, the federal health insurance program for those over age sixty-five, 44 percent get help from their private medical insurance, 34 percent get partial assistance in paying for care from the elders themselves, and 8 percent of families get help from Medicaid, which provides insurance for those with limited finances.[34]

Medicaid and Medicare benefits, however, typically do not cover the costs of long-term care in people's own homes. You typically have to be in a nursing home—which is overall more expensive than having a home health aide come to the elder's house. In order to get help paying for a home health aide, the elder must spend down all his assets. Once he's done that, there are more options and Medicaid will help pay for residential or nursing home care. Our family could not tap these programs to help defray the costs for my grandmother so long as she lived on her own, even though a nursing home was far more costly than living in her own home with a little help. And of course, she wanted to stay in her home, where she could remain active in her church, say hello to every passing neighbor, and watch the otters play in the Straits of Juan de Fuca as the sun set each evening.[35]

Finally, neither tax subsidies nor programs limited to the poorest families promote widespread access to high-quality care. There are, however, some new ideas brewing. Forty states and the District of Columbia provide public prekindergarten programs. These programs help families manage work-life conflict by offering safe, enriching, and affordable—and most often free—care for children aged three and four. But most of these programs (like most elementary and secondary schools) operate for less than a typical full workday. Oklahoma was one of the first states to implement this kind of program and has been well studied. The state enrolls 76 percent of all four-year-olds, and as of 2008, 99 percent of its school districts offered prekindergarten programs. Research at Georgetown University found that "Tulsa's pre-kindergarten program produced substantial academic benefits for all children in the program, regardless of race or ethnicity." Still, in 2014, nationwide only 29 percent of four-year-olds and 4 percent of three-year-olds attended state prekindergarten programs.[36]

The reality is that if children are going to be in child care, someone has to pay. Right now, most of the costs are borne by families, which means that mostly professional families—and to a lesser extent middle-class families—can afford high-quality care. As states take on the role of these programs, they have to take on the costs—just like we do with primary and secondary education. I won't mince words: the costs to states are high. In 2014, state prekindergarten programs cost an average of $4,125 per child. The National Institute for Early Education Research, however, has found that only fifteen of the forty statewide universal prekindergarten programs have sufficient funding to meet all of their benchmarks for quality standards. To address this gap at the state level, President Obama's proposed universal prekindergarten program would receive $75 billion in federal funding over ten years, which is about $24 for every person, per year, in the United States.[37]

A New and Improved Industry to Get You out the Door

The economics of care is not just about finding the cheapest spot to park a child or elder family member while you're at work. While salad-in-a-bag can be cheap because machines can do the work, child care and elder care still require humans. The price we pay for care is important because it affects the quality, which matters more than ever. This is why child care and elder care are expensive. Care-sector jobs need to be a destination—a career—not a low-paid way station.

Experts understand the link between the quality of care providers' jobs and the quality of care. Nearly four decades ago, the renowned child-care specialists Richard Ruopp and Nancy Irwin documented that the cognitive skills and emotional development of young children in day-care centers were higher the more training that care-givers received. Over the past few decades, carefully documented reports from the National Research Council and the Institute of Medicine have summarized the extensive research that establishes the link between high-quality caregiving from birth to age five and future success of children. The *National Child Care Staffing Study* showed that the quality of care depended largely on turnover rates and the education, training, and wages of staff. Studies such as the *Cost, Quality, and Child Outcomes Study* and the *National Institute of Child Health and Human Development Study of Early Child Care* found that the well-being of children and their future success depended largely on the quality of child care they received. As *The Early Childhood Care and Education Workforce* report noted: "The research picture is clear—quality of care and education matters to the lives of young children, and teachers and caregivers are central to providing that quality. . . . Yet, the problems identified more than

30 years ago—inadequate training and education, low wages, and high turnover—are still vexing today."[38] Staffing matters. Regardless of whether we go with private or public solutions, the jobs created in the care sector must be good jobs.[39]

Child-care and elder care workers make up a small share of the total workforce—less than about 3 percent—but they are critical for the economy and families. We know that these kinds of jobs are the jobs of the future. As described in Chapter 3, the U.S. Bureau of Labor Statistics projects that the jobs that will grow the most are in services, with many of them related to caring, such as nursing or home health aides. These are jobs that tend to pay far below the median wage and are primarily held by women and people of color. As a result, there is very high turnover. Estimates range from place to place but can be as high as 100 percent staff turnover each year. According to research by the family demographer Kristin Smith and the economist Reagan Baughman, turnover is associated with low earnings—although they can't say for sure which way the causality goes. For every 10 percent jump in pay, the chance that a direct-care worker stays in her job rises by 2.1 percent.[40]

High turnover can also be harmful for elders—research shows that in long-term care centers, the churn of employees has negative effects on patient outcomes. Geriatricians are some of the lowest-paid doctors and, unsurprisingly, in short supply. As the surgeon and writer Atul Gawande notes, "It's foolish: These are folks that keep people out of hospitals, out of emergency rooms, out of nursing homes. And not only that, they help people achieve more fulfilling lives. We've clearly got the priorities wrong."[41]

In today's economy, families need high-quality and affordable solutions for caring for children, the elderly, and the ailing. The American Wife is no longer at home to take care of everyone. This means that day-in and day-out, families all across the income spectrum need affordable, high-quality options for child care and elder care. The lack of affordable-care options reduces our nation's labor supply and adds stress to those in the workforce, crimping productivity.

Business leaders and the Chamber of Commerce are encouraging investments in early childhood education. A 2010 report by the U.S. Chamber of Commerce's Institute for a Competitive Workforce concludes, "The research is clear. Early learning opportunities for children from birth to age five have great impact on a child's development and build a strong foundation for learning and success later in life."[42] In May 2013, more than 300 business leaders, including thirteen local Chambers of Commerce, signed onto a statement saying,

> We have examined the research and drawn our own conclusions: quality early childhood programs have a significant and positive impact on the skilled workforce, customer base, economy and nation we need. . . . We rarely have the luxury of making business investment decisions with as much evidence as we have to support the economic value of investing in early care and education. . . . Early care and education is not a partisan issue. It is an American competitiveness issue that impacts all of us.[43]

Given this consensus, we should be able to make progress on providing universal child care.

Yet too often our national debate still tends to see child care as a "handout." As a nation, we are failing to see that child care is an investment in early childhood education. And this lack of focus crosses party lines. In the midst of the Great Recession of 2007–2009, then-Speaker of the House Nancy Pelosi invited me and five other economists to a closed-door forum with the House of Representative's leadership—all those in leadership positions, including the chairs of all the House committees—to discuss what the Democratic-controlled Congress could do to create more jobs. My remarks included a paragraph about how investments in child care could help spur recovery. Many members nodded their heads in agreement, but the conversation quickly shifted to other topics, and there were no questions on that section of my remarks.

After the forum was over, Speaker Pelosi—one of the most powerful women in the United States—clasped my hands in hers, looked directly into my eyes, and said, "Heather, we must find a way to do something on child care. These men, they just don't get it."

This isn't the case in other developed economies. A couple of years ago, I had the opportunity to meet with British policymakers in London's House of Commons in Westminster. We were there to brainstorm ideas for an upcoming speech that would present the Labour Party's agenda for the U.K. economy. The conversation began with an anticipated list of economic policy ideas—the need for infrastructure investments, energy use and climate change, and manufacturing. But about ten minutes into the meeting, out of the blue, the man sitting to my left said, "We should definitely include investments in child care," and the man across the table replied, "Yes, of course. It boosts the economy and people need it."

You could have pushed me over with a feather. I was in a country that had only changed the rules of succession to the crown from men-first to first-born a year before, but they were ahead of us on grasping that what happens inside families is serious economic stuff. I've been in many economic policy conversations in Washington, DC, but at that time, never one in which the conversation turned to the importance of child care as a serious economic issue.

The Labour Party's economic advisers—all but two of the dozen or so men—saw child care for what it is writ large. Access to care increases productivity for today's workers and improves outcomes for the future generation of workers who are still children today. Workers aren't automatons; they have families. How the United States addresses care for the young and the old is perhaps the most underappreciated economic issue facing policymakers today.

Fair: Finding the Right Path

In this book, I've shown that helping families isn't just about being nice; it's about being serious about the performance of our economy. Our society and our economy are better off with both women and men in the workforce. Because of this, paid leave, schedules that work for employers and employees alike, and affordable, high-quality family care options can—and do—improve our economy.

If my argument has been that such policies make good economic sense, then why have I chosen to end the book with a chapter called "Fair"? There are two reasons. First, to be effective at improving the overall performance of our economy, all workers must be able to avail themselves of the work-life policies that I've outlined. They cannot be afraid to speak up out of fear of retribution or the damage it may do to their career or job security. In today's workplace, all caregivers who want a job should have the opportunity to contribute to the economy and excel for the good of their firms and their families. In reality, too many worker-caregivers experience what can only be called caregiver bias.

Asking tough questions about what is fair is especially important in our era of high—and seemingly ever-rising—inequality. As shown in the preceding chapters, inequality isn't measured only in wages and incomes; it's reflected in access to jobs with paid leave, workplace flexibility, a predictable schedule, and access to high-quality and affordable care. Families in all income groups have faced challenges since the American Wife moved into the workforce, but access to solutions is highly unequal. Caregiver bias is another layer of inequality that affects both paid and unpaid caregivers. It pushes the cost of losing the Silent Partner back onto the family. Too often, that burden then falls onto the shoulders of working women.

This kind of bias is easy to spot, once we know where to look. One of my former colleagues recalls having a terrific boss who was generally a good and fair manager. Her boss was respectful of the new moms on the team and their need for parental leave. Then one of the male staff members took parental leave. During the twelve weeks he was out, the boss made it widely known how much he missed him. More than once, he popped out of his office to proclaim (jokingly?), "Is he *still* on Daddy leave? Isn't that kid grown already?" The boss seemed to wish he still had a Silent Partner. He clearly missed the world in which the American Wife would do most of the work at home and seemed to think that wishing for it would bring it back.

Of course the new dad, like most new dads, had a working wife. If he hadn't taken leave then his wife would have had to take more time off from her job—or maybe even had to quit entirely. We won't have gender equality until both men and women are seen as the caregivers they are. Until men aren't mocked—even gently—for taking leave, the pressure will remain on women to do so. It's important to recognize the progress we've already made: the new dad had the right to take family leave. It wasn't a perk; it was a right. Now he—and everyone—needs to be able to access these benefits without fear of retaliation—or public shaming.

Expecting America's Silent Partner to return isn't sound policy—for bosses or for our economy. Like my adolescent self who kept hoping to find the fast way home by going down the same wrong road, our nation can't afford to keep holding onto the fantasy that families have an American Wife at home to provide care. Doing so isn't good for families, firms, or the economy. Yet this fantasy shows up every day in America through outdated notions of who does the care work inside homes.

We cannot expect employers to consider caregiver bias a problem until we all do. When our nation's labor-market standards and social insurance programs were first laid out, care work and care workers were left out. Policymakers at the time knew that these were issues back in the 1930s, but amid the Great Depression they didn't seem as urgent as unemployment insurance and fair labor standards. Today, in a world where the once ubiquitous stay-at-home American Wife is now in the workplace, the New Deal's agenda doesn't go far enough. The purpose of the previous three chapters was to outline the path to update it. I showed you the evidence that this was sound economic policy. Yet most workers and their families remain without these vital work-life choices because our social contract continues to fail to meet the needs of today's working families. They must navigate through a world where it's fair to leave out caregivers from our compact over what governments, firms, and families owe one another.

So why haven't we fixed this already? Why haven't we charted a new course? It's possible to do so, as many examples have shown. If these are such good ideas—and such good economic ideas—then why aren't expanded work-life laws already in place? For one thing, a firm may not feel that addressing this issue is in its best interest. Maybe it would save money, but perhaps management does not see enough evidence to warrant changing—or maybe they don't even see caregiver bias at all. This is where policy comes in. This is the second reason I've ended with a chapter called "Fair." We haven't made all the necessary changes because doing so would require all of us—employees across the work spectrum and our business leaders, politicians, and policymakers at all levels of government—to redefine what we consider fair for today's workplace.

Many politicians and businesses now accept the workers' rights enshrined in the New Deal but are more suspicious of new rights. It was the same eight decades ago. As we saw in Chapter 1, businesses began opposing the New Deal as soon as it was passed into law. But once they lost the fight, most accepted the reforms. So what was once considered a huge imposition on business has become just part of the wallpaper of capitalist life. Besides a few on the fringe, most people accept the need for a minimum wage, child labor bans, and a decent retirement. But there was nothing natural or automatic about any of these policies. Someone had to propose them, and then they had to be passed. As we've seen in earlier chapters, once a new policy is in place, it becomes just another part of doing business. If we put in place the complete agenda outlined in Chapters 6, 7, and 8, I would be willing to bet that twenty-five years from now—if not much sooner—these policies, too, would seem just as natural as requiring children to attend primary and secondary school.

Another part of the story is a little darker. Many people see new laws that mostly benefit men in the workplace, or at least benefit men and women equally, as more legitimate than new laws that seem to favor women. The three areas where we need new solutions to the everyday economic problems facing low-income, middle-class, and professional families—Here, There, and Care—have historically been seen as women's issues. It would be offensive in our society today to deny the importance of an issue just because women. The economic evidence is in—these new work-life reforms are good for women, good for men, good for families, and good for the economy.

This chapter will examine the economic effects of caregiver bias in our workplaces and our social policies. In many ways, these biases are similar to not having any policies in place—except that our biases affect whether we even embark on policy reform in the first place and who gains access to benefits. This discussion starts by looking at how bias against caregivers in the workplace affects all four quadrants of the economic cycle, as laid out in Figure 9.1. As with all the issues we've discussed, we have to think of caregiver bias not as private problem but as an economic one. Then we will look at how the vision of fairness embedded in the New Deal affects economic performance today. By not acting, are we doing what's best for our economy?

Nostalgia can be fun, but it's not a good way to make policy. In earlier chapters, I pointed to the eruption of Mount St. Helens as a metaphor for the implosion of the American Dream for all but the very top earners. I'll say it again: we'll never restore that specific mountaintop, nor should we want to. The years when incomes rose more or less equally up and down the income ladder—when the trajectory of the typical family income looked like a climb up pre-eruption Mount St. Helens—were indeed good for many families.

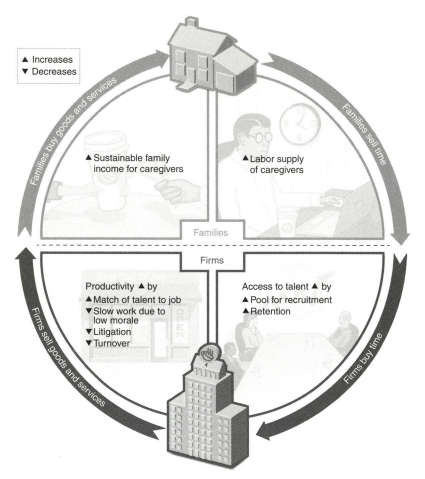

Fig. 9.1 Effects of fair work-life policies on the economic cycle.

Yet these were also the years when African Americans, women, gays and lesbians, and other minorities didn't have access to the full panoply of rights and job opportunities that opened up after the Civil Rights and Women's Rights movements of the 1960s and 1970s.

Part of what's changed—albeit often too slowly—is that in polite society, it's no longer okay to say you want to exclude some people from economic opportunity. But that doesn't mean that everyone actually has access to opportunity. As President Obama put it, "It's time to do away with workplace policies that belong in a 'Mad

Men' episode." That he had to say this in 2014 should indicate that it's not a foregone conclusion. Bias remains against caregivers in our workplaces and in our thinking about what's fair for workplace policy. The forces below the earth's surface have already begun pushing forth a new peak for Mount St. Helens; we need to do the same for the American family.[1]

Caregiver Bias: It's Real and It's Costly

Economists have done a lot of research on discrimination. In 1957, the economist and future Nobel Laureate Gary Becker published *The Economics of Discrimination*, which walks the student through the field he spearheaded. For economists, discrimination is when people—employers, customers, and other workers—bestow preferences on one group or person over another based on characteristics that are not tied to that person or group's economic contribution. There are two kinds of discrimination. A person can have a discriminating "taste," which perhaps means they prefer that white men brew the coffee at their local coffee shop. Or a person could practice what economists call "statistical" discrimination, where they believe their preference for a white male barista is evidence-based (maybe they believe that women aren't strong enough to lift big bags of coffee). There's no accounting for taste, and statistical discrimination may sound rational, but it may not be grounded in real facts or be applicable to the individual in front of you.[2]

Becker quickly dismissed the idea that discrimination could persist in a competitive marketplace. It's not rational. Successful employers would hire the best, most productive person for the job. Firms who practiced discrimination would be driven out of business because they weren't making rational economic decisions. They would not hire based on tastes or statistical discrimination that didn't hold up economically. Or, as Nobel Laureate Kenneth Arrow famously said, the employer discrimination model "predicts the absence of the phenomenon it was designed to explain."[3]

There's an old joke in which a physicist, a chemist, and an economist are stranded on a desert island with only a crate of canned soup. The physicist and the chemist each devise an ingenious mechanism for getting the cans open using shark's teeth and coconuts. The economist merely says, "Assume we have a can opener." In the case of discrimination, assuming everyone—even employers—acts in his or her best *economic* interest is like assuming a can opener. Nice in theory, but not so relevant in practice. We all have biases and preferences and some—many—of these are not economically rational. This is especially the case when it comes to how we think about the family.

Evidence suggests that caregivers experience a good deal of workplace discrimination and that this affects their ability to sell time. The phrase "family responsibilities discrimination" describes the unfair treatment at work of "pregnant women, mothers and fathers of young children, and employees with aging parents or sick spouses or partners." This kind of discrimination, which is also known as caregiver bias, can take many forms. According to the Center for WorkLife Law at the University of California-Hastings, workers "may be rejected for hire, passed over for promotion, demoted, harassed, or terminated—despite good performance— simply because their employers make personnel decisions based on stereotypical notions of how they will or should act given their family responsibilities."[4]

Consider this case: Kevin Knussman, a Maryland state trooper, requested unpaid leave under the Family and Medical Leave Act to care for his newborn child. His wife had had a difficult delivery, and he needed the time away from work to care for the child while she recovered. His supervisor told him, "God made women to have babies" and that in order for him to qualify for unpaid family leave, his wife would have to be "dead or in a coma." This is a clear case of caregiver bias, which is why he won his case. The Center for WorkLife Law has documented that within a span of ten years, cases such as these have increased by 400 percent.[5]

Caregiver bias isn't just a women's issue. Men—like Knussman— who stray from the "male breadwinner" stereotype also experience it. In their research on middle-class workers, Jennifer L. Berdahl and Sue H. Moon found that fathers with caregiving roles experienced more harassment and mistreatment than did traditional breadwinner fathers and men without children. The costs for men of taking time off from work to care for a loved one can have a lasting downward pull on employment and earnings. The sociologist Scott Coltrane and his co-authors found that, over time, men who have ever quit work or are unemployed for family reasons earned significantly less than others. This affects both men and women's ability to sell time. If men are not allowed time to care, then women will have to morph back into being America's Silent Partner—or we had better find a faster way to figure out that cyborg technology.[6]

It's especially important to consider how caregiver bias affects selling time (and buying goods and services) up and down the income spectrum. The sociologist Lisa Dodson has followed low-income families over time—those with incomes below 200 percent of the poverty line, or about $38,000 a year for a single mother and two children in 2014—to understand how they cope with work-life issues. She found that mothers often had trouble finding stable child care, an issue we discussed in the last chapter. The lack of access to affordable and reliable child care leads their employers to see them as "irresponsible" employees, when they are just trying to be good parents. Although some employers in her study expressed sympathy for the plight of their caregiving employees, many dismissed low-wage mothers' difficulties with reliable child care as a problem of their own making. This is a form of caregiver bias that makes it challenging for low-wage workers to stay employed. Another study of low-income working parents—those below 200 percent of the poverty line—found that the majority reported that they did not expect to be able to adjust their work schedules or create arrangements to better balance work and family life other than through finding another job. This is a pretty extreme way to have to cope with conflicts between work and life.[7]

Addressing caregiver bias is made more challenging because most U.S. workers don't have an advocate to help them negotiate with their employers or to help them when they feel they are treated unfairly. This is especially true for those in low-income and middle-class families. Workers with care responsibilities who want to request flexible work arrangements or need time off typically have no job-protected mechanism even for asking their employer to help them resolve the conflict.

This means that sorting out how caregivers can sell time to their employers is challenging. Let me be very clear—there are many employers who do a good job hiring, promoting, and fairly treating their employees with care responsibilities. We've heard many of those stories in the preceding chapters. But workplace policies are only as good as the manager who implements them, and the evidence is that too many caregivers experience or fear discrimination in the workplace as they struggle to convince employers that they are productive employees. Economic models predict that discrimination will magically disappear as the economic irrationality becomes visible, but in everyday reality, workers experience caregiver bias.

When employers buy time, they want to know, "Which applicant will be the most productive?" This gets at the question of how we measure productivity—especially in jobs that don't produce measureable goods, like cars or bales of hay—which is at the root of discrimination. It's especially hard to evaluate "true productivity" during the hiring process. The coffee-shop owner we met in Chapter 5 doesn't know if Job Applicant #15 is a neat freak who will keep the counter clean and tidy at all times or a total slob who will hand customers cups with coffee oozing out the top. Will Applicant #15 get defensive and argue with customers or is he the kind of person who charms even the grumpiest among the caffeine-deprived standing in line?

There is lots of evidence that we all walk around with all sorts of biases that are unrelated to productivity characteristics. The owner's perception of which applicant is likely to be a good fit for her team will be based on some facts—the applicant's resume, references, and her impressions from the twenty-minute job interview—as well as her gut instinct, which may or may not turn out to be right. The question is, can she see beyond her bias if the prospective new hire reveals that he has two toddlers at home and a wife with a high-stress, low-flexibility job as an emergency room nurse?

Let me give you an out-of-the-box example of how bias clouds our judgment and affects the selling of goods and services. If you're a basketball fan, particularly a New York Knicks fan, I'm sure you've heard of Jeremy Lin—the first American of Chinese or Taiwanese descent to play for the NBA. When Lin started his first NBA basketball game in early February 2012, he gave a much-needed productivity boost to the Knicks. In the twelve games that followed, Lin averaged 22.5 points and 8.7 assists, and in one game, he outscored Kobe Bryant on the Los Angeles Lakers 38 to 34 points. The media buzzed with questions asking why this talent had been sitting on the bench for months. As the story unfolded, it became clear that racial bias and stereotypes had clouded the views of coaches and recruiters.[8]

It was plain to see that in the months Lin sat on the bench, the Knicks lost out on his productivity. They probably "sold" fewer winning games. In most cases, an employer's underutilization of talent is not as clear-cut as this. But this story shows how productivity depends on whether a firm—or society—can make the most of its skills and talent. If employers don't see caregivers as the kind of people who can contribute to their workplace, they'll miss out.

The truth is, we tend to see caregivers as less competent, even when they aren't. Sadly, this is now well documented. When people are faced with a slate of job candidates, identical except that one is clearly a mother (knowable because she has "PTA member" listed on her resume) and the other is not ("Lions Club member"), respondents tend to downgrade the mother's skills, while ramping up expectations. The findings are unsettling. According to the sociologists Shelley Correll, Stephen Benard, and In Paik, among two groups of job candidates with identical credentials, the group identified as mothers were perceived to be less competent, less promotable, less likely to be considered for management, and less likely to be recommended for hire; they also had lower recommended starting salaries than nonmothers. Their study also found that people expect more

from moms: a mother needed a higher test score or more experience to get the exact same job or promotion as someone else. That's
not just bias, that's expecting mom to be a Superwoman.[9]

Let me give you an example from my own experience. I like to
think that I'm a good manager, especially on the issues I've discussed
in this book. One of my top-performing staff members has small
children, and when I hired her, she was very clear about her schedule.
We are a start-up where job descriptions can evolve quickly. I assumed that she wasn't interested in taking on more responsibilities
as we grew, even though I wanted to ask her to do more because she's
so good at what she does. When a senior hire fell through at a time
when we had too much on our plates, I suggested the "crazy" idea
of her taking the task of supervising a junior person to do that job.
To my surprise—and delight—she jumped at the opportunity. She
couldn't put in extra hours, but she was willing to do more in the
hours she put in and to take on hiring and training a staff person.
I had let my assumptions blind me to having the kind of open and
honest dialogue that got our organization to a more productive place.

The other side of the coin, of course, is that we also walk around
with expectations of how men should act and what roles they play at
work and home. In 1977, Rosabeth Moss Kanter published a land-
mark study of managers at Indsco, where she documented how a
"masculine ethic" dominated perceptions of how workers should be-
have, a point echoed in feminist economics where our ideas of how
we act in the economy are modeled on an idea of "rational economic
man." More recently, the sociologist Marianne Cooper interviewed
Silicon Valley workers to understand their workplace norms. As she
put it, her interviewees

> work in order to become "real men" and become "real
> men" by working. The masculinity created and con-
> structed by the labor process borrows from, but is not
> identical to, traditional masculinity. It does not empha-
> size physical strength, but mental toughness. It does not
> require hazing women but does require a willingness to

be absorbed in one's work that, by effect if not design,
excludes both women and family responsibilities.[10]

Cooper concludes that while men said they believed in gender equity, a "masculine mystique" permeated how they talked about the
workplace.[11]

Not every player on the bench is a Jeremy Lin, of course, but evidence abounds that employers discriminate against those with care
responsibilities. They may not see it—or want to deal with it—but
those who look at the economywide effects see the evidence. Research by the economists Chang-Tai Hsieh, Erik Hurst, Charles
Jones, and Peter Klenow confirms the high cost to the economy
of not allowing people to access jobs they have the skills and talent
to do. They find that between 1960 and 2008, upward of a fifth (between 15 percent to 20 percent) of U.S. economic growth was due
to women and people of color entering professional occupations
and making use of their talent. Before the rise of women and people
of color in those jobs, the economy suffered because they were
being prevented from making the most of their abilities. As the famous multibillionaire investor Warren Buffett put it, "We had all
this marvelous progress in the time we became a country until today.
It's incredible what's happened. And for over half of that period, we
wasted half our talent."[12]

When the employer fails to make the most of talent, this reduces
productivity and the firm's ability to profitably sell goods and services. As we learned in Chapter 5, ask any economist what drives
economic growth and the answer will include "human capital"—
that is, the level of skills, education, and talents of the potential
workforce. Economists may use this rather off-putting technical
term to describe people, but what they mean is that the skills and
talents of workers are the real power behind a competitive economy.
Progress comes from the inventions of the innovator as well as the
methods of the machinist, the talent of the teachers, and the practiced smiles of the sales clerk. Without us—people—coming up with
new ideas, we don't have a better mousetrap, salad-in-a-bag, taller

buildings, or "just-in-time-production." If employers cannot see the value of someone because they're blinded by their biases—be it a Harvard-educated Asian American who can really play basketball or a caregiver who can be a reliable employee—we all lose.[13]

Employers have a lot of leeway in their buying-time decisions. Caregiver bias isn't technically illegal at the federal level. However, while federal law does not require employers to accommodate caregivers nor explicitly prohibit discrimination on the basis of family responsibilities, a framework based on growing case law on sex stereotype discrimination is emerging. The Equal Employment Opportunity Commission (EEOC)—the federal agency tasked with enforcing antidiscrimination laws—has provided guidance for employers on how caregiver bias might be illegal according to current law. This starts with a foundation for equitable treatment at work in the United States, which is laid out in Title VII of the 1964 Civil Rights Act. As originally passed, Title VII protected individuals against employment discrimination on the basis of sex, race, color, national origin, and religion; it has been amended to include pregnant women, and other legislation has expanded the rights of disabled and older workers. Employers are violating current law if they, for example, treat men and women with care responsibilities differently, such as presuming that mothers do all the child rearing and men bring home the earnings.

The EEOC Caregiver Guidance also provides "best-practice" recommendations, which go beyond the letter of the law. These include that employers not subject employees to a hostile work environment, treat them differently once they develop caregiver responsibilities, or hold them to stricter standards (for example, about requesting leave or timeliness) than other workers. This means that loudly complaining about a father's parental leave—but not a mother's—is not the best practice.[14]

Without changes in federal law, the EEOC, however, cannot mandate that employers give workers the time and flexibility they need to handle caregiving obligations. All employees have an equal opportunity within the structures that already exist, but an employer does not have to address issues that *only* affect caregivers. For example, while the Pregnancy Discrimination Act amendments to Title VII prohibit discrimination on the basis of pregnancy, they do not mandate that employers take any specific positive actions; they must only offer pregnant women the same benefits that they offer any other worker.[15] It remains the case that, as Ann O'Leary, Secretary Clinton's policy adviser, and Karen Kornbluh, former ambassador to the Organisation for Economic Co-operation and Development, put it, "Equal protection laws are only as good as the nature and quantity of benefits the employer provides to other workers."[16] That's why the definition of what's fair matters for the economy. We have a system where people can sell time only if they—for the most part on their own—find a way to cope with the lack of an American Wife.

Fair implementation is just as important a part of the solution as having good policies in place. I've stressed throughout the book that anyone can have care responsibilities—and most of us will at some point. Yet on the ground, it can seem like work-life rules are available only to some, and their access to those benefits burdens everyone else. The single person feels grumpy about always having to stay late while the moms get to leave at 5 PM because they have to pick up their children at child care. I've done more call-in radio shows than I count where a frustrated or angry caller shares a tale of how his co-worker gets all the breaks because she has care responsibilities, while he has to pick up the slack. I've also told you about how my sister asked her boss for a flexible schedule, and he gave it to her, but he wouldn't give it to everyone. This irritated her colleagues, who felt that she was getting special treatment, and they lashed out at her.

Workplace flexibility that is inconsistently administered—provided only to some workers at a manager's discretion or contingent on having a particular manager—isn't a fair way to go. It needs to be universal. If everyone has access to these kinds of policies, it's easier for firms to administer and it builds political consensus—these aren't special perks for some, they're rights for all. Employers who implement these policies have made this argument—such as the big services firm Deloitte, which, as we learned in Chapter 7, requires all of its employees to talk with their supervisor about their work-life concerns.

While legal, caregiver bias is an economic problem that affects more than how employers buy time. With the American Wife in the workforce, if caregiver bias lowers pay—or reduces opportunities—this affects a family's ability to buy goods and services. The majority of today's gender pay gap is really a caregiving pay gap. The sociologists Michele Budig and Paula England found that most of the gap in pay among women is due to a "motherhood pay penalty." Women with the same work history and personal characteristics are paid differently depending on whether they are mothers. Think of it like this: two similar women take four months off. One, not a mom, uses that time off to travel the world; the other, a mom, takes maternity leave. The nonmom earns more, even when she has similar credentials, a similar job, and, like the mom, took four months off. What's more, we still live in a world where men get a "baby bonus." Fathers get, on average, a 6 percent bonus when they have children in the home. Mothers, in contrast, see their earnings fall by 4 percent for every child they have, all else equal.[17]

This analysis is important. But these estimates of the motherhood pay penalty are a conservative estimate of the true cost to families. They take into account what's already happened, that is, the reported employment and earnings of men and women and moms and dads. What they cannot tell us is whether and how caregiver bias affected people's decisions about their education, such as college major, or what kinds of jobs they considered. They cannot tell us how caregiver bias might affect the hours that people work. Most part-time jobs are in a small number of occupations, which tend to pay less than others. If caregivers "choose" those jobs because they need shorter hours, this adds to the long-term pay penalties. They also cannot tell us anything about the fairness of past pay and promotions—we know that too many women, like Lilly Ledbetter, end up experiencing a career-long pay gap relative to their male colleagues.[18]

The gender pay gap affects how much women—and their families—can buy. We learned in earlier chapters that most families have a working wife because they need the income. Yet if she's earning less because she's a mother, or if he's penalized when he steps up to do his part at home, then this lowers the benefit of having the American Wife at work. The pay penalties add up. The Institute for Women's Policy Research looked at how much money women lose over a lifetime due to the gender pay gap. The cohort of women born between 1955 and 1959 who have worked full-time, year-round through age fifty-nine have earned over half a million dollars less than their male peers. For college-educated women, the losses are even higher, averaging nearly $800,000 by age fifty-nine. Not all of this is due to the caregiving pay gap, but most of it is.[19]

We probably won't make much more progress on closing the gender pay gap until we deal with how employers and employees alike treat caregivers in the workplace. The available research on all kinds of U.S. workers—from low-wage single parents to professional dual-income couples—finds that workplace flexibility for workers with no stigma attached can improve earnings. Steps to improve options for workplace flexibility at the firm level improve not only access to talent for workers with care responsibilities generally but also the pay of women relative to men. For example, Budig and her co-authors found that work-life policies such as child care and moderate parental leave have decisively positive effects on mothers' employment hours and wages.[20]

Evidence also suggests that where these work-life changes are happening inside workplaces, the gender pay gap is shrinking. In her 2014 Presidential Address to the American Economic Association, the economist Claudia Goldin argued that now gender pay parity is not fundamentally about changes in policy—although important—but about changes at the firm level. She said that the solution must involve changes in "how jobs are structured and remunerated to enhance temporal flexibility." She found that the sectors—such as technology, science, and health—that had adapted the kinds of workplace practices around time that I've described in earlier chapters were seeing a greater convergence in the earnings of men and women. But not all jobs have been similarly restructured. Jobs in the corporate, financial, and legal worlds still had workplace practices that made it difficult for caregivers.[21]

It may be that caregiver bias is good for some businesses—or that some bosses and politicians think it is. But it's not good for families or the overall economy. And so long as it remains, it promotes a race-to-the-bottom, rather than addressing a core economic issue. One possible solution would be to transform the Equal Employment Opportunity Commission's Caregiver Guidance into legislation. Some policymakers are doing just that. A growing number of state and local laws explicitly prohibit caregiver bias. Many of these laws focus exclusively on discrimination aimed at parents of dependent children, but a handful go further and allow protection for workers caring for other dependents such as a disabled adult child or a dependent elderly relative. As of the summer of 2104, two states— Alaska and Minnesota—and the District of Columbia had laws in place that prohibit employment discrimination for people with family responsibilities.[22]

Stopping at the New Deal Is Another Form of Caregiver Bias

Fairness undergirds our vision of what governments, firms, and families owe one another. Today, our labor and social policies define fairness as ensuring that everyone earns a wage at or above a certain minimum, that there are limits on overwork, that there are prohibitions on child labor, and that workers who are too old or too sick to work—or unemployed through no fault of their own—deserve a helping hand. This system encourages people to find jobs. It also presumes that families alone cope with the need for an American Wife.

In the 1930s, when the foundations of our current labor and social policies were being crafted, care as a job and as a responsibility was left out. At the time, this seemed fair. This should come as no surprise given that the 19th Amendment to the U.S. Constitution giving women the right to vote wasn't ratified until August 18, 1920, just a little over a decade before. The 1930s were also the height of Jim Crow in the South, which made it possible for the New Deal to exclude jobs typically held by African Americans. But this means we're left with a system that supports some kinds of workers—those who tend to have the employment pattern of (white) men—but not others.

Today, the debate is over whether the current set of rules is fair. In Chapter 5, I quoted Chris Christie and Christine Quinn making arguments about how helping workers and their families would be a job killer. While neither thought that paid sick days made sound economic sense, both supported some increase in the minimum wage, Quinn more so than Christie. Quinn backed a $1.75-an-hour increase, and though Christie vetoed a $1.25-an-hour increase, he counterproposed a $1-an-hour increase. Why would they be okay with forcing businesses to dole out more money to each of their workers in the form of higher minimum wages (adding to employers' pay-outs on paydays), but be averse to a bill that would disrupt the employee-employer relationship no more than a handful of times a year? They didn't say. But I have a few hunches.[23]

My guess is that both Christie and Quinn felt more comfortable with the "tried and true" ideas, like the minimum wage, than the new ideas in this book. I also wonder whether it's the case that, since policies like paid sick days weren't part of the original deal, they view them as less important. As Quinn put it, paid sick days are "a noble goal," but "now is simply not the right time." The consensus (now) is that the New Deal gave help-outs to families so they could cope with the glaring realities of the industrial economy. In the 1930s, when U.S. policymakers—led by President Roosevelt and Secretary Perkins—put the New Deal in place, they made the case that those were the policies necessary to support workers and their families. These policies were necessary for families, firms, and the economy. We've accepted these standards. Very few politicians stand up and say that the abolition of child labor is a "job killer." (Of course, there are exceptions. Former congressman Newt Gingrich said child labor laws were "stupid" when he was running for president in 2012.) [24]

However, we run into roadblocks when it comes to envisioning and implementing new standards, especially ones that address the loss of America's Silent Partner and recognize the value of women and their economic contributions. Too often, policies like those in this book are seen, at best, as nice to have but not necessary, or, at worst, as a handout. This is caregiver bias in our social policy. For today's families and today's economy, we need to move beyond an argument that sees addressing care as akin to a handout. The policies discussed in the last three chapters are help-outs that make it possible to work.

Christie and Quinn agreed that paid sick days were nice to have, but not good for the economy. They bought the argument on fairness, but not on the economics. I've laid out an alternate argument. Workers with care responsibilities can't sell time without the full array of policies laid out in Chapters 6, 7, and 8. If they cannot sell time, they cannot buy the goods and services their families need. We must evaluate the full economic implications of policies that address family needs and make it possible for caregivers, often women, to fully participate in the economy. We've seen the economic evidence. Here's one final statistic: even the International Monetary Fund (IMF) is making the case that "unleashing" the potential of women and addressing work-life issues is economically important. An IMF study found that if women were employed at the same level as men, U.S. gross domestic product would rise by 5 percent.[25]

Still, too often, care is seen as a private matter, outside the market. Some contend that the market can decide or that it isn't the role of the state to lay down these kinds of "rules of the road." But there are good economic reasons to intervene. What's good for one business may not be good for the whole economy. I hope you've concluded from the last eight chapters that this isn't true; what happens inside families isn't "outside" the market.

We also need to pause and reflect on whether, even after reading my arguments here, a person could still harbor some doubts that work-life balance policies are not just "handouts," "perks," or some-thing "nice for the ladies." Let's pause and consider why a reader might think that. Could it be that things that women have tradition-ally done inside the home—for free—aren't seen as part and parcel of what we think of as "the economy"?

Part of the problem is that when it comes to families, many see a help-out and a handout as the same thing. Policies such as Social Security's retirement benefits or overtime protections are defensible economic policy because they are about workers and their individual situations. They aren't about how the worker both supports a family financially and has time to care. But the presumption is often dif-ferent for work-life policies. Perhaps our collective bias is that these are handouts for those who don't really belong in the labor force. I think this is why when I say work-life, people often hear that the kinds of policies I'm advocating are "welfare." Throughout this book, all I've talked about are working people. Yes, to be clear, this agenda is about helping people who work for a living and who get and keep jobs.

This is why the passage of the Family and Medical Leave Act was such an important milestone. In that law, our nation decided that men *and* women are equally important workers *and* caregivers. Un-like in many other countries, under FMLA (as well as in the three states that have put in place paid leave), leave is tied to the worker. Parental leave is evenly divided between Mom and Dad, and can similarly be divided between those caring for a sick loved one. To put this another way, if a child has two parents and both are covered and eligible for FMLA leave, that child has access to twenty-four weeks of his parents' time in his first year of life, half from Mom and half from Dad (or half from each of his two Moms or two Dads). Men and women have equal access to the right to care for their family and to the right to return to their paid job.[26]

Considering work-life policies as handouts rather than as help-outs taps into another deep-seated economic trope. To see this, let's revisit the discussion in Chapter 1. As I described, there have tradi-tionally been two poles in the debate over social policy. On one side

are those who argue that supporting families reduces an individual's incentives to work, which reduces economic efficiency and, ultimately, growth. If policymakers insist that firms provide too high a
wage or impose onerous regulations, this reduces profits, the only
economic variable considered. In this view, we should not address
unequal economic outcomes that mean some families are doing
well and others are not because this distorts the market mechanisms.
We must accept unequal—and often unfair—market outcomes
rather than muck up the market's logic.

Yet we know that the market is imperfect, and this logic means
that not everyone can participate in the economy. By teeing up the
debate this way, we're left with an either/or decision—help families
or help the economy—which doesn't match reality. It's a myopic
shorthand about what actually makes the economy hum. Sadly, I
can say that after fifteen years working on economic policy in Washington, DC, this isn't ancient history. Pitting what's good for families against what's good for the economy is a path many still choose
today.

Many of today's policymakers use the mantra from Okun's book
Equality and Efficiency: The Big Trade-Off as a roadmap for how to
think about policy. A couple of sentences from his conclusion make
his key point: "I do, however, hope to persuade others to share my
views about the preconditions for optimization—a more focused
public dialogue on the intensities of preferences for equality and a
greater research effort by social scientists on the measurement of the
leakages. In short, I am pleading for us all to face up to the tradeoff
between equality and efficiency."[27] Okun's concern was focused on
when and how policymakers should tax the rich to give to the poor.
The ideas in this book do not touch on that trade-off; they are about
how we can address families' conflicts between work and home life
so that we can improve overall economic outcomes. It we want to
use Okun's language, we have to consider how "optimization" requires us to let go of the old notion of what it means to support
workers and their families. We cannot ignore how the loss of America's Silent Partner reshapes what families need to function in today's
economy.

Okun lived in a world where "the relative distribution of family income has changed very little in the past generation," and where he could argue that the most pressing question was how much equality was enough. The problem is, in the forty years since Okun's book was published, the gains of economic growth in the United States have not been shared as widely as they were in the immediate postwar era that Okun examined. While our economy has grown and productivity has improved—that is, American workers produce more goods and services per hour worked—wages and incomes have failed to keep pace. As we've learned, the middle class has seen little growth and the bottom has seen no growth, while incomes at the top have exploded.

I am not saying there are never trade-offs. At some point, we cannot add so many paid sick days that people never have to show up to work. A key economic research question is where the right line is. Researchers need to ask at what point raising the minimum wage turns from helping to hurting, or at what point consumer gains from more trade with other countries—cheaper goods and services— outweigh the costs to our native workforce. These are important questions, without a doubt.

But we've taken this claim about a trade-off between equity and efficiency way too far. We've used the idea of an inherent, non-negotiable trade-off between what's nice to do for families and what's good for the economy as a shorthand for *all* policymaking. In doing so, we too often end up with arguments that rely only on one aspect of the economic cycle, the bottom-left corner of the economic cycle, selling stuff—and only in the short-term—missing the full picture. We've overemphasized the supposed trade-offs to the detriment of families and our economy. Not everything can be summed up by a supposed equity-efficiency trade-off, nor is this a useful way to think about all economic policymaking.

It is clear that we must blaze the trail anew, just as policymakers did in the early part of the twentieth century. This will require letting go of the bleeding heart and tough love tropes we're so used to falling back on. Too often, we're told that the bleeding hearts are putting values or fairness above practical concerns, while the tough love crowd are the ones serious about the economy. This isn't correct. For today's economy, the question is how to help families so they can thrive as workers *and* as consumers.

We all are attached to our way of thinking. We keep taking the same turn, even when we know it's not the fastest way home. For too many, the rule of thumb on what's good for the economy isn't the best route to long-term profitability.

Because of these economic changes—and because of the opening up of new opportunities for women—the American family interacts with the economy in a new way. Throughout this book, I've emphasized that as the American Wife left the home, American business lost a Silent Partner. Since she was a *silent* partner, it was hard to see how the work she did in the home made what happens inside workplaces possible. But understanding the role she played lets us see the economic importance of charting a new path about what governments, firms, and families owe one another.

Conclusion

I hope by now I have convinced you of the economics of the case for work-life reforms to match the needs of families and firms in our new, twenty-first-century economy.

In this book, we looked at the economy as an economist would. Economists talk of demand and supply together because neither can exist on its own. So families enter into the picture not only through the cost of hiring them, but also as consumers and reservoirs of talent. We looked beyond the short-term and obvious metrics and into the out-of-pocket and hidden costs and benefits.

When we did all that, we learned that the basket of policies that address work-life conflict have many positive economic effects. Because these policies address the ways our economy and society have transformed in recent decades, they can improve economic outcomes in all four quadrants of the economic cycle.

We also learned that a firm is not the economy. That now discredited idea that helping families is a handout stems from an economic analysis that looks only at one side of the economic cycle—the short-term profits of selling goods and services. One business's short-term interest is not—by a long shot—the whole story of the economy. Firms and families work together to complete the economic cycle; not attending to the very real issues facing families as they seek to find and keep jobs means that firms face more challenges both buying time and selling goods and services. Many of these don't show up immediately, but that doesn't make them any less real.[1]

These economic insights underpinned the system that President Roosevelt and Secretary Perkins put in place. These policies served our nation's families and economy well for many decades. They created economic security for millions of families and a solid foundation for economic growth. Putting families at the core of the economic model was economically successful. In the decades that followed implementation, the United States experienced growth in productivity and earnings that was the envy of the world. Gross domestic product grew at a healthy pace of 3.8 percent per year, and incomes for rich and poor families alike grew at about 2 percent per year. In those decades, a bipartisan consensus emerged around the policies of the New Deal.

But these are no longer enough. The first step in blazing a new path is to acknowledge that recent economic and demographic transformations mean that we need a new set of pillars to address economic insecurities caused by today's work-life challenges. Families up and down the income ladder struggle to find time. The hodgepodge of work and family policies that has evolved over the years does not address how people can have the time to deal with conflicts between work and home life. This is not to say the system in place is not critical to maintain. We need to build upon the edifice we have. Families will continue to need the pillars of retirement security, minimum wage, overtime protection, and unemployment insurance.

If Frances Perkins were alive today, what would her list of new reforms look like? Given what we know about how families work and live today, what would be on those little slips of paper hidden in her desk drawer?

In this book, I've suggested some possibilities. I started by seeking to understand what families need and listened to leaders from around the nation to see how they are addressing the day-in, day-out challenges to find time. What I've found is that there is not one magic fix. We need solutions in four areas that fall under the headings Here, There, Care, and Fair:

- Policies to address when we need to be Here (at home), including paid leave for short-term and long-term family and medical needs and when a new child comes into the family.

- Schedules for when we need to be There (at work) that fit family life and work for families, as well as for employers. This means schedules that are predictable and don't require too many—or too few—hours each week.
- Comprehensive systems for high-quality and affordable Care for children and the aging.
- Finally, policies must be Fair. Everyone up and down the economic ladder must have access to these new work-life arrangements, and those who have care responsibilities must be treated fairly, not as second-class workers.

Like Secretary Perkins, I included on this list only items that have already proven both pragmatic and doable. Every one of these ideas is already in place somewhere in the United States. We can learn from the communities—and businesses—that are leading the way. We can also see that a new government program is not the solution to every problem. Some problems require private-sector solutions, and many employers are leading the way.

Those standing in opposition to work-life reforms will probably continue to tell us that we cannot afford to help the breadwinners of low-income, middle-class, and professional families care about their jobs and care for their families. Sometimes, they'll try to sidestep the economics and say these are values issues, as President Nixon did when he vetoed child care. They will argue that what happens inside a family is a private concern, not the purview of government. Or, like presidential hopeful Carly Fiorina, they will invoke a different kind of values argument and say that paid leave is important, but that it should be left up to employers to decide whether or not to offer it, not the government.

But I believe that the most insidious—and compelling—argument against this agenda is the one invoked by Chris Christie and Christine Quinn. Recall that they argued that these policies would be nice to have, but that we "cannot afford" them. This argument is effective because it's based on fear. In an economy where middle-class and low-income families are barely making ends meet or failing to do so, and where professional families are overworked and struggling to compete with the exceedingly wealthy, it's easy to sow fear about a loss of jobs. While polls show that policies to address conflicts between work and life are popular among Democrats and, to a lesser extent, among Republicans, what can diminish support the most is to claim that acting will hurt the economy and lead to job loss.

This book has shown that these fears are misplaced. Those who claim the mantle of serious economics need to get the economics right. America has lost its Silent Partner, and the best thing for the economy is not to tell families that they alone must pay up; what's good for the economy is to solve the problem. We know this to be true both because it fits the theory of how the economy works and because the research supports it.

Yet still too often, the new realities of how we work and live have left us seemingly lost as to the next steps. We can now plainly see that women's increased labor supply has been good for our economy—and the evidence is that it's not women's employment that harms families, it's inflexible, family-hostile workplaces and the paucity of high-quality, affordable care options for children and seniors. Too often, we continue to take the well-trod path instead of focusing on the full economic effects.

There is hope. In communities all across the United States and in forward-thinking businesses, leaders are paving the way to addressing conflicts between work and life. They are doing this because it's the right thing to do, but many also point to the economic evidence for why this is the smart thing to do. The 2014 midterm elections included ballot initiatives on paid sick days in three cities and one state—Trenton and Montclair, New Jersey; Oakland, California; and Massachusetts—and passed in all places. Over the past couple of years, new mayors such as Bill de Blasio in New York City, Betsy Hodges in Minneapolis, Ed Murray in Seattle, Marty Walsh in Boston, and Bill Peduto in Pittsburgh have all sought to implement pieces of this agenda. In August, Montgomery

County, Maryland, became the first county to put in place a paid sick days standard.[2]

We also have evidence that some businesses are showing not only that this agenda can be put into action, but that it is good for the economy. In May 2015, Facebook chief operating officer Sheryl Sandberg announced that every Facebook employee and contractor would receive at least a $15-an-hour minimum wage; at least fifteen paid days off for holidays, vacation, and sick time; and a $4,000 child benefit so long as they do not also receive maternity or paternity leave. This was just a couple of months after Microsoft announced that its contractors would receive at least fifteen days of paid leave. At a White House Champions of Change event in April 2015, Microsoft CEO Satya Nadella said, "It's simple for us . . . paid time off is good for business. It leads to increased productivity, employee retention, and lower health care costs." Netflix, for its part, recently announced that some (but not all) of its employees will have access to up to a year of paid parental leave. And in August, the Gap announced that it would give workers ten days' notice of their schedules.[3]

We can see a broad coalition uniting around this agenda. Policy reform can address the loss of time in families up and down the income ladder. Workers' rights groups, parents, grandparents, the disabled, children, immigrants, people of color, gays and lesbians—we all benefit from policies that give us back our time. This creates an opportunity to craft a set of reforms for which professionals are advocating and which, if thoughtfully constructed, can address the needs of families in the middle, bottom, *and* top. As I noted at the end of Chapter 4, new research in political science shows that in today's political climate, getting all income groups on board is one way to break through the roadblocks.

These kinds of coalitions are necessary to chart a new path. A few years ago, I coedited a book with three wonderful social scientists— Annette Bernhardt, Laura Dresser, and Chris Tilly. One of the contributors was the economist David Weil, who is now heading the

Wage and Hour Division at the Department of Labor. In his chapter, he outlined how the U.S. business community has opposed every piece of progressive labor legislation in the U.S. Congress for more than half a century. His analysis focused on what was special about the two pieces of workplace legislation that did pass into law. One was the Family and Medical Leave Act of 1993, giving workers the right to unpaid leave when they need to be at home. He showed that this legislation became law because advocates built a new coalition. Historically, employment rights looked to traditional workers' rights groups and unions, but in this case, the coalition included those advocating on behalf of women, the elderly, the disabled, children, and people of faith, alongside traditional workers' rights groups. Advocates brought together people from across the United States to focus on an issue affecting all of us: the time we need to care for our loved ones. I hope this book can lead us toward more of that kind of success.

Maybe it's no accident that the first bill signed into law by President Barack Obama when he took office in 2009 was the Lilly Ledbetter Fair Pay Act, which redefined the statute of limitations for workers filing equal-pay lawsuits. There was bipartisan support for this law: five Senate Republicans and every Senate Democrat voted for this bill, while three House Republicans voted for it (and five House Democrats voted against it). Although this legislation did not introduce new policies to address conflicts between work and family, it did allow workers who experience discrimination to seek redress in the courts. Maybe the reality that America's Silent Partner is no longer at home is sinking in.

The ideas laid out in this book are only the tip of the iceberg for a new vision for America. The organization I lead, the Washington Center for Equitable Growth, is spearheading a campaign to fund new research to better understand how inequality affects our economy. A key way inequality plays out in the United States is through job quality, including access to policies that address conflict between work and home life. Clearly, there is much evidence that taking steps to reduce inequality would improve economic outcomes. If you want to know more about this, I encourage you visit our website, www.equitablegrowth.org, and engage with us on the issues.

Thirty-five years later, the hikers have returned to Mount St. Helens. According to the Washington Trail Association, there are more than 200 marked trails where families can spend a holiday walking through the landscape. Flowers, grasses, and trees have begun to return, growing on top of the piles of ash in the shadow of the re-shaped mountain's dome. The U.S. Forest Service even allows climbers to go all the way to the peak (of a live volcano!). These are new paths. They take us through a new landscape. Let's help families find time by blazing a new path for our nation's labor standards and social policy.

APPENDIX

Data and Methods

Throughout this book, I look across families using precise definitions for low-income, middle-class, and professional families. These categories are based on research I conducted with Joan Williams, a professor of law at the University of California-Hastings and the Director of the Center for WorkLife Law, for our 2010 report *The Three Faces of Work-Family Conflict: The Poor, the Privileged, and the Missing Middle* (Washington, DC: Center for American Progress and the Center for WorkLife Law, University of California, Hastings College of the Law, 2010).

Here I continue to use these definitions for low-income, middle-class, and professional families. The three income groups are as follows. Low-income families are those in the bottom third of families by income. Professional families are those families that are in the top 20 percent by income and have at least one member of the family holding at least a college degree. Middle-class families are everyone else, a little over half of all families in 2012.

In order to make the best use of the depth and breadth of the research literature, I also draw on a wide range of sources that use different definitions for each income group. I note throughout the book where the data are based on my definitions of low-income, middle-class, and professional families and clarify how other researchers' definitions differ from mine. To avoid confusion, if the source note does not point to this Appendix, I am using secondary material.

In general, while the precise definitions are conceptually important, they do not drive the trends. In a paper I wrote with Eileen Appelbaum and John Schmitt in 2014, *The Economic Importance of Women's Rising Hours of Work* (Washington, DC: Center for

American Progress and Center for Economic and Policy Priorities, 2014), we examined the differences across three ways to categorize families by income: (1) low-income, middle-class, and professionals, as defined above; (2) household income between 75 percent and 200 percent of the median, compared with those above and below; and (3) households in the middle three quintiles of the income distribution, compared with those above and below. Our analysis showed there were slight differences in the point estimates, but the overall trends in employment and earnings were similar across definitions.

For ease of composition, throughout the book I use the term "family," even when the analysis is done at the household level. The precise definition is always noted in the source note or endnote. According to the U.S. Census Bureau, in 2014, two-thirds of households were made up of families, defined as at least one person related to the head of household by birth, marriage, or adoption (U.S. Census Bureau, "Table H1. Households by Type and Tenure of Householder for Selected Characteristics," 2014, http://www.census.gov/hhes/families/data/cps2014H.html).

I have been fortunate in that a number of scholars have overlaid the low-income, middle-class, and professional family definitions onto their data and analysis for use in this book. Table A.1 below summarizes the key data and differences in samples, followed by information that is more detailed about each of the four unpublished analyses. Because of differing datasets, the samples differ due both to the constraints of the particular survey and to the concept of interest (e.g., the sample for child care is children, not households).

1. For data on income trends, earnings, and hours of work, my colleagues John Schmitt and Kavya Vaghul and I used the Center for Economic and Policy Research extracts of the Current Population Survey Annual Social and Economic Supplement. The CPS provides annual income and the analysis bases the income groups on household income. All dollar values are reported in 2013 dollars, adjusted for inflation using the Consumer Price Index Research Series available from the U.S. Bureau of Labor Statistics.

Table A.1 Data sources, samples, and key tables

Source	Data	Sample
Previously unpublished analysis		
1. Analysis by Heather Boushey, John Schmitt, and Kavya Vaghul	Household income and earnings, decomposition	Households with someone between the ages of 16 and 64
2. Analysis provided by Philip Cohen based on his paper "Family Diversity Is the New Normal for America's Children," Brief Reports (College Park, MD: Council on Contemporary Families, September 4, 2014)	Children's living arrangements	Children aged 0 to 14
3. Analysis provided by Sarah Jane Glynn based on her paper "Breadwinning Mothers, Then and Now" (Washington, DC: Center for American Progress, June 2014)	Share of mothers who are breadwinners	Women aged 18 to 60, with a child under 18 at home
4. Analysis provided by Susan J. Lambert and Peter J. Fugiel based on their paper with Julia R. Henly, "Schedule Unpredictability among Early Career Workers in the US Labor Market: A National Snapshot" (Chicago, IL: Employment Instability, Family Well-Being, and Social Policy Network, 2014)	Scheduling notice and whether employees have any say over their schedules	Households with someone between the ages of 26 and 32
Previously published analysis		
5. Eileen Appelbaum, Heather Boushey, and John Schmitt, "The Economic Importance of Women's Rising Hours of Work" (Washington, DC: Center for Economic and Policy Research and Center for American Progress, April 2014)	Women's share of total household hours of work (Table 3); Women's share of earnings (Table 4).	Households with someone between the ages of 16 and 64
6. Joan C. Williams and Heather Boushey, "The Three Faces of Work-Family Conflict: The Poor, the Privileged, and the Missing Middle" (Washington, DC: Center for American Progress and the Center for WorkLife Law, University of California, Hastings College of the Law, 2010)	Kind of child care used (Figure 3); Cost of child care (p. 8).	All children under age six with a mother using a child-care arrangement

In our analysis, we limit the universe to households that have positive total incomes and at least one person aged 16 to 64 present. For calendar year 2012, the last year for which we have data at the time of this analysis, the cut-offs are as follows:

- Low-income households are those at the bottom third of the income distribution; in 2012, these included households that had a size-adjusted income of below $24,806. In 1979, 28.3 percent of all households were low-income, increasing to 30 percent in 2012. These percentages are slightly lower than one-third because the cut-off for low-income households is based on household income data that includes persons of all ages, while our analysis is limited to households with at least one person between the ages of 16 and 64. The working-age population (16 to 64) typically has higher incomes than older workers, and as a result, the working-age population has somewhat fewer households that fall into this low-income category.

- Professional households are those at the top fifth of the income distribution with at least one household member with a college degree or higher. In 2012, those in the top fifth had an income of $69,423 or higher. In 1979, 10.2 percent of households were considered professional, and in 2012, this share grew to 16.4 percent.

- Everyone else falls in the middle-income category. For this group, the household income ranges from $24,806 to $69,423 in 2012; the upper threshold, however, may be higher for those households without a college graduate but with a member who has an extremely high-paying job. This explains why within the middle-income group, the share of households exceeds 50 percent: the share of middle-income households declined from 62 percent in 1979 to 54.1 percent in 2012.

These data are decomposed into income changes between 1979 and 2012 (and between 1979 and 2007 for comparison below) for low-income, middle-class, and professional families.

The household income decomposition uses a simple shift-share analysis to find the differences in earnings between 1979 and 2012 [2007] and calculate the extra earnings due to increased hours worked by women.

We first calculate the male, female, and other earnings by the three income categories. To calculate the sex-specific earnings per household, we sum the income from wages and income from self-employment for men and women, respectively. The amount for other earnings is derived by subtracting the male and female earnings from total household earnings. We average the household, male, female, and other earnings by each income group for 1979 and 2012 [2007] and take the differences between the two years to show the raw changes in earnings by each income group.

To find the change in hours, for each year, by household, we sum the total hours worked by men and women. We average these per-household male and female hours, by year, for each of the three income groups.

Next, we find the counterfactual earnings of women; we calculate the 2012 [2007] earnings per hour for women and multiply it by the 1979 hours worked by women. Finally, we subtract this counterfactual earnings from the female earnings in 2012 [2007], arriving at the female earnings due to additional hours.

Because of the nature of this shift-share analysis, the averages don't exactly tally up to the raw data. Therefore, when presenting average income, we use the sum of the decomposed parts of income. Further, I show averages in the Figures 3.1 and 4.1, rather than medians, although the medians are also shown in Table A.2 for comparison. While economists typically show median income, for ease of composition and the constraints of the decomposition analysis, I show the averages so that the data are consistent across figures and tables.

One question that must be addressed is how to measure economic progress. To isolate the trend from the business cycle, economists aim to measure trends from one business cycle peak (or trough) to another peak (or trough). The National Bureau of Economic Research dates the most recent economic peak in December 2007 and the last economic trough at the end of the Great Recession in June 2009. Technically, this means that when looking at economic trends from the peak year of 1979, we should compare it to 2007. However, as of this writing, we are six years into a recovery, and I did not want to leave out six years of economic progress. Therefore, throughout the book, I use 2012 or latest-year data, even though this conflates trend and cycle.

The decision to show data that are more recent affects the story I tell, and the reader should be aware of these differences. Tables A.2 and A.7 below show key income-related data and analysis in this book comparing the trends using 2007 and 2012 as the end point. Table A.2 shows average income, and earnings and hours for men and women for 1979, 2007, 2012, and the change from 1979 to 2007 and 1979 to 2012. Table A.7 shows the breadwinner analysis for 1979, 2007, and 2012 (described below). In Table A.2, the end year matters—2007 was a higher peak for income, earnings, and hours across the income distribution, but especially for low-income and middle-class families. In Table A.7, however, the end year does not substantively alter the analysis.

Throughout the book this analysis is cited as Heather Boushey, John Schmitt, and Kavya Vaghul's analysis of the CEPR extracts of the CPS Annual Social and Economic Supplement.

2. Philip Cohen, professor of sociology at the University of Maryland-College Park, graciously provided breakdowns for low-income, middle-class, and professional families using his analysis of data from the 1960 U.S. Census and the 2012 American Community Survey, with data from IPUMS.org.

The sample includes children aged 0 to 14. As he notes, the Census data identify only one parent per child, so married and cohabiting parent couples are identified by the relationship status of

Table A.2 Earnings, income, and hours of work, by income group, 1979, 2007, and 2012

	Year			Change		Percent change	
	1979	2007	2012	1979–2007	1979–2012	1979–2007	1979–2012
Average household income							
Low-income	$23,261	$25,246	$22,699	$1,985	−$562	8.5%	−2.4%
Middle-class	70,839	83,634	78,536	12,795	7,697	18.1	10.9
Professional	130,053	198,502	193,646	68,450	63,593	52.6	48.9
Median household income							
Low-income	21,824	23,512	21,224	1,688	−600	7.7	−2.7
Middle-class	65,489	74,737	70,173	9,248	4,684	14.1	7.2
Professional	122,890	166,275	159,730	43,385	36,840	35.3	30.0
Average annual earnings							
Men							
Low-income	10,947	10,302	8,399	−644	−2,547	−5.9	−23.3
Middle-class	46,421	45,387	42,019	−1,034	−4,402	−2.2	−9.5
Professional	87,585	116,370	112,533	28,785	24,948	32.9	28.5
Women							
Low-income	5,552	8,656	7,448	3,104	1,895	55.9	34.1
Middle-class	16,975	28,795	26,657	11,820	9,682	69.6	57.0
Professional	27,476	60,640	63,163	33,164	35,687	120.7	129.9
Average household work hours							
Men							
Low-income	1,013	950	828	−63	−185	−6.2	−18.3
Middle-class	2,020	1,961	1,866	−59	−154	−2.9	−7.6
Professional	2,372	2,228	2,186	−145	−187	−6.1	−7.9
Women							
Low-income	629	875	792	246	163	39.2	26.0
Middle-class	1,184	1,525	1,461	340	277	28.7	23.4
Professional	1,353	1,688	1,708	335	355	24.7	26.2

Notes: Dollar values in 2013 dollars. Sample includes households with at least one person aged 16 to 64. Average household income is equal to the sum of the household male, female, and other earnings shown in Table A.3.

Data source: Heather Boushey, John Schmitt, and Kavya Vaghul's analysis of Center for Economic and Policy Research extracts of the Current Population Survey Annual Social and Economic Supplement.

Table A.3 Change in average household income by source, 1979 to 2007 and 1979 to 2012

	Men	Change in earnings	Women		Change other than earnings	Total change in household income
	Total change in men's earnings	Due to higher pay per hour	Due to more hours	Total change in women's earnings		
1979–2007						
Change in dollars						
Low-income	−$644	$668	$2,436	−$3,104	−$474	$1,985
Middle-class	−$1,034	$5,393	$6,428	$11,820	$2,009	$12,795
Professional	$28,785	$21,139	$12,025	$33,164	$6,500	$68,450
Percent change						
Low-income	−32.5%	33.7%	122.7%	156.3%	−23.9%	100.0%
Middle-class	−8.1%	42.1%	50.2%	92.4%	15.7%	100.0%
Professional	42.1%	30.9%	17.6%	48.5%	9.5%	100.0%
1979–2012						
Change in dollars						
Low-income	−$2,547	$359	$1,536	$1,895	$91	−$562
Middle-class	−$4,402	$4,625	$5,057	$9,682	$2,417	$7,697
Professional	$24,948	$22,566	$13,122	$35,687	$2,958	$63,593
Percent change						
Low-income	453.7%	−63.9%	−273.6%	−337.5%	−16.2%	100.0%
Middle-class	−57.2%	60.1%	65.7%	125.8%	31.4%	100.0%
Professional	39.2%	35.5%	20.6%	56.1%	4.7%	100.0%

Notes: Dollar values in 2013 dollars. Sample includes households with at least one person aged 16 to 64.

Data source: Heather Boushey, John Schmitt, and Kavya Vaghul's analysis of Center for Economic and Policy Research extracts of the Current Population Survey Annual Social and Economic Supplement.

Table A.4   Characteristics of low-income, middle-class, and professional families, 1979 and 2012

	Low-income		Middle-class		Professional	
	1979	2012	1979	2012	1979	2012
Race and ethnicity						
White	67.7%	50.1%	86.1%	67.2%	92.5%	78.6%
African American	20.8	19.6	7.9	11.2	3.5	5.9
Hispanic	9.2	24.1	4.4	14.8	1.9	5.7
Other	2.3	6.2	1.7	6.8	2.1	9.8
With a college degree						
Men	8.5	12.8	15.1	25.1	82.6	80.7
Women	5.5	13.9	12.0	31.6	59.0	81.8
In household	8.4	16.4	18.6	38.4	100.0	100.0
With an earner						
Men	53.6	44.1	84.4	76.3	91.4	85.9
Women	48.4	48.7	66.9	69.8	68.8	77.5

Notes: For race and ethnicity, sample is persons aged 16 to 64 within a household, by income group. For college degree holders, sample is persons aged 25 to 64 within a household, by income group. For earners, sample is households with at least one person aged 16 to 64.

Data source: Author's analysis of Center for Economic and Policy Research extracts of the Current Population Survey Annual Social and Economic Supplement.

the parent (a married mother, for example, may be married to the biological, adopted, or step-father of the child). Single fathers include never-married and formerly married fathers who are not co-habiting or married.

In his analysis, in 1960, 32.9 percent of children aged 0 to 14 lived in a low-income family, 60.7 were in a middle-class family, and 6.4 percent were in a professional family. In 2012, those break-downs were 30.6 percent of children in a low-income family, 54.6 in a middle-class family, and 14.8 percent in a professional family. Table A.6 provides the share of children living in different family types, across the three income groups.

Throughout the book this analysis is cited as Philip Cohen's analysis of 1960 U.S. Census and the 2012 American Community Survey, with data from IPUMS.org.

Table A.5   Top-five most common occupations for low-income, middle-class, and professional families, 1979 and 2012

1979		2012	
Occupation	Share of income group	Occupation	Share of income group
Low-income			
Office and administrative support	9.3%	Sales and related	12.2%
Food preparation and serving	8.2	Office and administrative support	11.8
Durable goods manufacturing	5.8	Food preparation and serving	11.4
Nondurable goods manufacturing	5.5	Transportation and material moving	8.3
Building and grounds cleaning	5.1	Building and grounds cleaning	8.3
Middle-class			
Office and administrative support	11.7	Office and administrative support	14.5
Salaried (other industries)	7.3	Sales and related	10.3
Secretaries, stenographers, and typists	5.6	Management	9.6
Other professional (salaried)	5.2	Transportation and material moving	6.8
Durable goods manufacturing (other)	5.1	Production	6.7
Professional			
Other professional (salaried)	17.4	Management	20.4
Salaried (other industries)	14.9	Healthcare practitioners and technical	10
Teachers, except college and university	8.9	Sales and related	9.3
Clerical (other)	6.9	Education, training, and library	9.2
Engineer	5.2	Business and financial operations	8.8

Notes: Dollar values in 2013 dollars. Sample includes all persons aged 16 to 64 within a household, by income group.

Data source: Author's analysis of Center for Economic and Policy Research extracts of the Current Population Survey Annual Social and Economic Supplement.

Table A.6   Family type and earner arrangement of children in low-income, middle-class, and professional families, 1960 and 2012

	Low-income	Middle-class	Professional	All
1960				
Married, father only earner	55.0%	69.5%	78.3%	65.3%
Married, dual earner	11.0	21.3	20.1	17.8
Married, mother only earner	1.8	1.0	0.2	1.2
Married, neither earner	8.0	2.1	0.5	3.9
Single mother	18.3	2.7	0.5	7.7
Single father	1.6	1.0	0.4	1.1
All other	4.4	2.5	0.0	3.0
Total	*100.0*	*100.0*	*100.0*	*100.0*
Share of sample population	32.9	60.7	6.4	100.0
2012				
Married, father only earner	18.2	24.2	25.3	22.2
Married, dual earner	7.4	43.7	67.7	34.2
Married, mother only earner	3.9	3.8	2.4	3.6
Married, neither earner	4.3	1.1	0.5	2.2
Cohabiting parent	14.3	3.7	0.6	7.1
Single mother	42.2	14.0	2.3	22.5
Single father	5.2	4.7	1.3	4.4
All other	4.6	4.8	0.0	4.0
Total	*100.0*	*100.0*	*100.0*	*100.0*
Share of sample population	30.6	54.6	14.8	100.0

Note: Children aged 0 to 14.

Data source: Philip Cohen's analysis of the 1960 U.S. Census and the 2012 American Community Survey.

3. Sarah Jane Glynn, a sociologist and director for Women's Economic Policy at the Center for American Progress, graciously provided breakdowns for low-income, middle-class, and professional families using our analysis of women breadwinners on data from the 1980 to 2013 Current Population Survey Annual Social and Economic Supplement, which includes calendar years 1979 to 2012. These data are shown in Table A.7.

The sample includes families with a mother who is between the ages of 18 and 60 and who has children under age 18 living with her. Breadwinner mothers include single mothers who work and bring home earnings and married mothers who earn as much as or more

Table A.7   Share of mothers who are breadwinners or cobreadwinners within low-income, middle-class, and professional families, 1979, 2007, and 2012

	Year			Percentage point change	
	1979	2007	2012	1979–2007	1979–2012
Breadwinners					
Low-income	61.7%	72.3%	71.3%	10.6	9.6
Middle-class	20.0	35.8	38.5	15.8	18.5
Professional	13.4	32.6	36.2	19.2	22.8
Cobreadwinners					
Low-income	3.1	3.0	2.6	−0.1	−0.5
Middle-class	21.4	26.7	22.3	5.3	0.9
Professional	22.9	27.6	26.4	4.7	3.5
Breadwinners or cobreadwinners					
Low-income	64.8	75.3	73.9	10.5	9.1
Middle-class	41.4	62.5	60.8	21.1	19.4
Professional	36.3	60.2	62.6	23.9	26.3

Note: Sample limited to married couples with children and single-mother households, with at least one child under age 18, mothers between the ages of 18 and 60.

Data source: Sarah Jane Glynn's analysis of the Annual Social and Economic Supplement.

than their husbands. Cobreadwinners are married mothers who earn less than their husbands but still bring home at least 25 percent of the couple's earnings. For this analysis, we provided Glynn with the nominal, size-adjusted household income ranges for each of the three income groups according to their definitional criteria described earlier in this appendix.

Throughout the book this analysis is cited as Sarah Jane Glynn's analysis of the Annual Social and Economic Supplement.

4. Susan Lambert, associate professor in the School of Social Service Administration at the University of Chicago, and her colleague Peter Fugiel, a doctoral candidate at the University of Chicago, graciously provided breakdowns for low-income, middle-class, and professional families using their analysis of scheduling notice and whether employees have any say over their schedules on data from the National Longitudinal Survey of Youth (NLSY97), Round 15, fielded in 2011–2012. This analysis is shown in Table A.8.

Table A.8   Employee schedule notice and control over schedules, by young workers
in low-income, middle-class, and professional families, 2012

	Low-income	Middle-class	Professional	All
Schedule notice				
1 week or less	45.2%	35.9%	28.1%	37.4%
Between 1 and 2 weeks	15.0	11.1	8.1	11.8
Between 3 and 4 weeks	5.7	5.7	6.7	5.8
4 weeks or more	34.0	47.2	57.1	45.0
Control over schedule				
Employer decides	48.3	42.7	36.3	43.4
Employer with some employee input	31.0	29.8	24.9	29.4
Employee decides within limits	13.9	19.0	29.2	19.1
Employee decides freely	3.4	5.0	6.4	4.7
Outside control of employer and employee	3.4	3.5	3.2	3.4
Addendum				
Share of cohort population	28.4	56.7	14.9	100.0

Notes: Sample includes persons aged 26 to 32 who reported having household income greater than zero, and who are not self-employed or in the military.

Data source: Peter Fugiel and Susan Lambert's analysis of data from the National Longitudinal Survey of Youth (NLSY97), Round 15, fielded in 2011–2012.

The sample includes individuals who are aged 26 to 32. Individuals who reported being self-employed, in the military, or having zero or missing household income were dropped from the analysis. In their analysis, 28.4 percent of people are in low-income families, 56.7 percent are in middle-class families, and 14.9 percent are in professional families. Again, for this analysis, Fugiel and Lambert applied the same criteria we use to define our three groups (see above), but calculated the income thresholds relative to the NLSY97 cohort (people born in the United States between 1980 and 1984) rather than the larger adult population. Their results are reported as percentages of the cohort population (estimated using sampling weights).

Throughout the book this analysis is cited as Peter Fugiel and Susan Lambert's analysis of data from the National Longitudinal Survey of Youth (NLSY97), Round 15, fielded in 2011–2012.

FIGURE SOURCES

Frontispiece: Courtesy of Ricardo Levins Morales.

Figure I.1: Philip Cohen's analysis of 1960 U.S. Census and the 2012 American Community Survey, with data from IPUMS.org.

Figure 2.1: U.S. Census Bureau, "Table F-7. Type of Family, All Races by Median and Mean Income: 1947 to 2013" (Current Population Survey, Annual Social and Economic Supplements), https://www.census.gov/hhes /www/income/data/historical/families/.

Figure 2.2a and b: Courtesy Harry Glicken, U.S. Geological Survey.

Figure 2.3: Philip Cohen's analysis of 1960 U.S. Census and the 2012 American Community Survey, with data from IPUMS.org.

Figure 2.4: U.S. Census Bureau, "Table F-7. Type of Family, All Races by Median and Mean Income: 1947 to 2013" (Current Population Survey, Annual Social and Economic Supplements), https://www.census.gov/hhes /www/income/data/historical/families/, and Bureau of Labor Statistics, Productivity—Major Sector Productivity and Costs Database.

Figure 2.5: Heather Boushey, John Schmitt, and Kavya Vaghul's analysis of the CEPR extracts of the CPS Annual Social and Economic Supplement.

Figure 2.6: Suzanne M. Bianchi, John P. Robinson, and Melissa A. Milkie, *Changing Rhythms of American Family Life* (New York: Russell Sage Foundation, 2006): American Time Use Survey, from Council of Economic Advisers, Work-Life Balance and the Economics of Workplace Flexibility, June 2014, http://www.whitehouse.gov/sites/default/files/docs/updated _workplace_flex_report_final_0.pdf.

Figure 3.1: Heather Boushey, John Schmitt, and Kavya Vaghul's analysis of the CEPR extracts of the CPS Annual Social and Economic Supplement.

Figure 3.2: Philip Cohen's analysis of 1960 U.S. Census and the 2012 American Community Survey, with data from IPUMS.org.

Figure. 3.3: Bureau of Labor Statistics, Employment Projections—2012–2022 (U.S. Department of Labor, December 19, 2013), http://www.bls.gov/news .release/pdf/ecopro.pdf, Table 5, and author's analysis of the Center for Economic and Policy Research Extracts of the Current Population Survey Outgoing Rotation Group (ORG) Files, 2012.

Figure 3.4: Heather Boushey, John Schmitt, and Kavya Vaghul's analysis of the CEPR extracts of the CPS Annual Social and Economic Supplement.

Figure 4.1: Heather Boushey, John Schmitt, and Kavya Vaghul's analysis of the CEPR extracts of the CPS Annual Social and Economic Supplement.

Figure 4.2: Philip Cohen's analysis of 1960 U.S. Census and the 2012 American Community Survey, with data from IPUMS.org.

Figure 4.3: Thomas Piketty and Emmanuel Saez, "Income Inequality in the United States, 1913–1998," *Quarterly Journal of Economics* 118, no. 1 (February 2003): 1–39. Tables and figures updated to 2013 in Excel format, January 2015; see http://elsa.berkeley.edu/~saez/TabFig2013prel.xls.

Figure 4.4: Piketty and Saez, "Income Inequality in the United States, 1913–1998," Table A4, rows 1929 and 2007.

Figure 4.5: Heather Boushey, John Schmitt, and Kavya Vaghul's analysis of the CEPR extracts of the CPS Annual Social and Economic Supplement.

Figure 5.3: Bureau of Labor Statistics, Labor Force Statistics from the Current Population Survey, http://www.bls.gov/data/.

Figure 6.2: U.S. Bureau of Labor Statistics, "Table 6. Selected Paid Leave Benefits: Access, National Compensation Survey, March 2015" (U.S. Department of Labor, 2015), http://www.bls.gov/news.release/pdf/ebs2.pdf.

Figure 6.3: U.S. Bureau of Labor Statistics, "Table 32. Leave Benefits Access, Private Industry Workers, National Compensation Survey, March 2014" (U.S. Department of Labor, 2014), http://www.bls.gov/ncs/ebs/benefits/2014 /ownership/civilian/table32a.htm.

Figure 7.2: Peter Fugiel and Susan Lambert's analysis of data from the National Longitudinal Survey of Youth (NLSY97), Round 15, fielded in 2011–2012.

Figure 7.3: Peter Fugiel and Susan Lambert's analysis of data from the National Longitudinal Survey of Youth (NLSY97), Round 15, fielded in 2011–2012.

Figure 8.2: Joan C. Williams and Heather Boushey, "The Three Faces of Work-Family Conflict: The Poor, the Privileged, and the Missing Middle" (Washington, DC: Center for American Progress and the Center for WorkLife Law, University of California, Hasting College of the Law, 2010), Fig. 3, https://cdn.americanprogress.org/wp-content/uploads/issues/2010/01 /pdf/threefaces.pdf.

NOTES

Preface

1 Some—but by no means all—of the scholars who have influenced my thinking on these issues include Judith Warner, *Perfect Madness: Motherhood in the Age of Anxiety*, rpt. ed. (New York: Riverhead Books, 2006); Brigid Schulte, *Overwhelmed: Work, Love, and Play When No One Has the Time* (New York: Sarah Crichton Books, 2014); Arlie Russell Hochschild and Anne Machung, *The Second Shift* (New York: Penguin USA, 2003); Stephanie Coontz, *The Way We Never Were: American Families and the Nostalgia Trap* (New York: Basic Books, 2000); Nancy Folbre, *The Invisible Heart: Economics and Family Values* (New York: The New Press, 2001); Jerry Jacobs and Kathleen Gerson, *The Time Divide: Work, Family, and Gender Inequality* (Cambridge, MA: Harvard University Press, 2005); Anne-Marie Slaughter, *Unfinished Business: Women Men Work Family* (New York: Random House, 2015); Ruth Milkman and Eileen Appelbaum, *Unfinished Business, Paid Family Leave in California and the Future of U.S. Work-Family Policy* (ILR Press, 2013), http://www.cornellpress.cornell.edu/book /?GCOI=80140100480110.

Introduction

1 Mondale quote from Walter Mondale, *The Good Fight: A Life in Liberal Politics* (New York: Simon and Schuster, 2010), 98; Joseph G. Colmen and Corazon Sandoval, "Pre-Primary Education: Needs, Alternatives, and Costs, 1971–1980" (Washington, DC: Education and Public Affairs, Inc., September 1971), 31; Nixon quote from Richard Nixon, "Special Message to the Congress on the Nation's Antipoverty Programs" (Washington, DC, February 19, 1969), http://www.presidency.ucsb.edu/ws/?pid=2397. See also Bryce Covert, "Why America Gave up on the Fight for a Family-Friendly Workplace, and Why It's Starting Again," *ThinkProgress*, July 31, 2014, http://thinkprogress.org/economy/2014/07/31/3466326/work-family-history/.

2 Quote from President Richard Nixon, "Veto of the Economic Opportunity Amendments of 1971" (The American Presidency Project, December 9, 1971), http://www.presidency.ucsb.edu/ws/?pid=3251. For background on this veto, see Nancy L. Cohen, "Why America Never Had Universal Child Care," *New Republic*, April 24, 2013, http://www.newrepublic.com /article/113009/child-care-america-was-very-close-universal-day-care; Covert, "Why America Gave up on the Fight for a Family-Friendly Workplace, and Why It's Starting Again."

3 On Buchanan's role, see Covert, "Why America Gave up on the Fight for a Family-Friendly Workplace, and Why It's Starting Again."

4 Barack Obama and Mitt Romney, "Remarks by the President and Governor Romney in Second Presidential Debate" (Hempstead, NY, October 17, 2012), http://www.whitehouse.gov/the-press-office/2012/10/17/remarks-president-and -governor-romney-second-presidential-debate.

5 There's a rich literature on the family wage. Deborah M. Figart summarizes the importance of this concept for today's families in her 2007 address: "Social Responsibility for Living Standards: Presidential Address, Association for Social Economics, 2007," *Review of Social Economy* 65, no. 4 (December 1, 2007): 391–405, http://www.jstor.org/stable/29770432.

6 On the importance of paying close attention to the middle class, see Theda Skocpol, *The Missing Middle: Working Families and the Future of American Social Policy* (New York: W. W. Norton and Company, 2000).

7 David Weil makes a compelling argument for why policies that address work-life conflict are so politically resonant. See David Weil, "Mighty Monolith or Fractured Federation? Business Opposition and the Enactment of Workplace Legislation," in *The Gloves-Off Economy: Workplace Standards at the Bottom of America's Labor Market*, ed. Annette Bernhardt et al. (Ithaca, NY: Cornell University Press, 2008), 287–314.

8 These categories are based on research I conducted with Joan C. Williams. See Joan C. Williams and Heather Boushey, "The Three Faces of Work-Family Conflict: The Poor, the Privileged, and the Missing Middle" (Washington, DC: Center for American Progress and the Center for WorkLife Law, University of California, Hastings College of the Law, 2010), https://cdn.americanprogress.org/wp-content/uploads/issues/2010/01/pdf /threefaces.pdf. I have been fortunate that a number of scholars—Phillip Cohen, Susan Lambert, Peter Fugiel, and Sarah Jane Glynn—have overlaid these definitions of low-income, middle-class, and professional families onto their data and analysis for use in this book.

I. Our Roots

1 Arthur M. Okun, *Equality and Efficiency: The Big Tradeoff*, 2nd ed. (Washington, DC: Brookings Institution Press, 2015), 14.

2 See E. P. Thompson, *The Making of the English Working Class* (London: Penguin Books, 1980); Fred Block and Margaret Somers, *The Power of Market Fundamentalism* (Cambridge, MA: Harvard University Press, 2014), chap. 6; Paul Slack, *Poverty and Policy in Tudor and Stuart England* (London: Longman, 1988); Neil S. Rushton and Wendy Sigle-Rushton, "Monastic Poor Relief in Sixteenth Century England," *Journal of Interdisciplinary History* 32, no. 2 (Autumn 2001): 193–216, http://crcw.princeton.edu/workingpapers /WP01–20-Rushton.pdf.

3 See Adam Smith, *An Inquiry into the Nature and Causes of the Wealth of Nations*, 1776. It wasn't until 1822 that power looms were produced in large numbers by Roberts, Hill, and Co. Robert Ayres, *Technological Transformations and Long Waves* (Lazenburg, Austria: International Institute for Applied

Systems Analysis, 1989), 18, http://webarchive.iiasa.ac.at/Admin/PUB
/Documents/RR-89–001.pdf.

4 In his poem "Jerusalem," William Blake wrote, "And was Jerusalem builded
here, / Among these dark Satanic Mills?" Scholars argue that Blake was
referring to the mill towns of the Industrial Revolution. See John Hinshaw
and Peter N. Stearns, *Industrialization in the Modern World: From the
Industrial Revolution to the Internet* (Washington, DC: ABC-CLIO, 2013),
583. On the Poor Laws, see *An Act for the Amendment and Better Administration of the Laws Relating to the Poor in England and Wales*, 1834, http://www
.workhouses.org.uk/poorlaws/1834act.shtml.

5 Thomas Malthus, *An Essay on the Principle of Population*, 1st ed.
(London: J. Johnson, in St. Paul's Church-Yard, 1798), 21, http://www.esp.org
/books/malthus/population/malthus.pdf.

6 David Ward, "Population Growth, Migration, and Urbanization, 1860–1920,"
in *North America: The Historical Geography of a Changing Continent*, ed.
Thomas F. McIlwraith and Edward K. Muller, 2nd ed. (Lanham, MD:
Rowman and Littlefield, 2001), Table 13.1.

7 Martha May, "The Historical Problem of the Family Wage: The Ford Motor
Company and the Five Dollar Day," *Feminist Studies* 8, no. 2 (July 1, 1982):
402, doi:10.2307/3177569.

8 See, for example, the seminal economic texts on this topic: Heidi I. Hart-
mann, "The Unhappy Marriage of Marxism and Feminism: Towards a
More Progressive Union," *Capital & Class* 3, no. 2 (June 1, 1979): 1–33,
doi:10.1177/030981687900800102; Jane Humphries, "Class Struggle and the
Persistence of the Working-Class Family," *Cambridge Journal of Economics*
1, no. 3 (September 1, 1977): 241–258, http://www.jstor.org/stable/23596633.

9 Frances Fox Piven and Richard Cloward, *Regulating the Poor: The Functions
of Public Welfare*, updated ed. (New York: Vintage, 1993); Ira Katznelson,
Fear Itself: The New Deal and the Origins of Our Time (New York: Liveright,
2014). U.S. presidential election data are from "United States Presidential
Election of 1932 / United States Government," *Encyclopedia Britannica*,
accessed May 9, 2015, http://www.britannica.com/EBchecked/topic/1753014
/United-States-presidential-election-of-1932. Unemployment data are from
Stanley Lebergott, "Annual Estimates of Unemployment in the United
States, 1900–1954," in *The Measurement and Behavior of Unemployment*
(Cambridge, MA: National Bureau of Economic Research, 1957), 211–242,
http://www.nber.org/chapters/c2644.

10 See, for example, Jacob S. Hacker, *The Divided Welfare State: The Battle over
Public and Private Social Benefits in the United States* (New York: Cambridge
University Press, 2002); Gøsta Esping-Andersen, *The Three Worlds of Welfare
Capitalism* (Princeton, NJ: Princeton University Press, 1990).

11 I highly recommend the excellent biography by Kristin Downey, *The
Woman behind the New Deal: The Life of Frances Perkins, FDR's Secretary of
Labor and His Moral Conscience* (New York: Nan A. Talese, 2009).

12 Ibid., 6, 11. In 1902, just under 5 percent of women and just over 5 percent of men graduated from college. See Claudia Goldin, Lawrence Katz, and Ilyana Kuziemko, "The Homecoming of American College Women: The Reversal of the College Gender Gap," *Journal of Economic Perspectives* 20, no. 4 (Fall 2006): Fig. 1.

13 Leah W. Sprague, "Frances Perkins: The Woman behind the New Deal," *Frances Perkins Center*, June 1, 2014, http://francesperkinscenter.org/?page _id=574.

14 Louise C. Wade, "The Heritage from Chicago's Early Settlement Houses," *Journal of the Illinois State Historical Society (1908–1984)* 60, no. 4 (Winter 1967): 414.

15 Downey, *The Woman behind the New Deal*, 37, 52.

16 Ibid., 118–123.

17 Perkins said in her memoir, "It ought to be on the record that the President did not take part in developing the National Labor Relations Act and, in fact, was hardly consulted about it. It was not a part of the President's program. It did not particularly appeal to him when it was described to him. All the credit for it belongs to [Senator] Wagner." Democratic senator Robert F. Wagner of New York sponsored the legislation and played such an important role in its conception and passage that it is often referred to as "the Wagner Act." Frances Perkins and Adam Cohen, *The Roosevelt I Knew*, rpt. ed. (New York: Penguin Classics, 2011), 226; For Perkins's list, see Downey, *The Woman behind the New Deal*, 121–123.

18 Michael B. Katz, *The Undeserving Poor* (New York: Pantheon Books, 1989).

19 See, for example, Deborah M. Figart, "Social Responsibility for Living Standards: Presidential Address, Association for Social Economics, 2007," *Review of Social Economy* 65, no. 4 (December 1, 2007): 391–405, http://www .jstor.org/stable/29770432.

20 Teresa L. Amott and Julie A. Matthaei, *Race, Gender, and Work: A Multi-Cultural Economic History of Women in the United States* (Brooklyn, NY: South End Press, 1996), Table 9-2.

21 This was contested, as the historian Linda Gordon documents in *Pitied but Not Entitled: Single Mothers and the History of Welfare, 1890–1935* (New York: Free Press, 1994), 107.

22 See, for example, Ira Katznelson, *When Affirmative Action Was White: An Untold History of Racial Inequality in Twentieth-Century America* (New York: W. W. Norton and Company, 2005); Cybelle Fox, *Three Worlds of Relief: Race, Immigration, and the American Welfare State from the Progressive Era to the New Deal* (Princeton, N.J.: Princeton University Press, 2012).

23 For the basics of what is included in the law, see U.S. Social Security Administration, "Social Security Programs in the United States," July 1997, http://www.ssa.gov/policy/docs/progdesc/sspus/.

24 The federal pension program is known as Title II in the original Social Security Act. Social Security Administration, "Contributions and Benefit Base," 2013, http://www.ssa.gov/oact/cola/cbb.html.

25 Theda Skocpol, *Protecting Soldiers and Mothers: The Political Origins of Social Policy in the United States* (Cambridge, MA: Belknap Press of Harvard University Press, 1995), 132; U.S. Social Security Administration, "Social Security Programs in the United States."

26 Jill Quadagno, "Welfare Capitalism and the Social Security Act of 1935," *American Sociological Review* 49 (1984): 632–647; Larry DeWitt, "The Decision to Exclude Agricultural and Domestic Workers from the 1935 Social Security Act," *Social Security Bulletin* 70, no. 4 (2010): 49–68, http://www.ssa.gov/policy/docs/ssb/v70n4/v70n4p49.pdf; Jill Quadagno, *The Color of Welfare: How Racism Undermined the War on Poverty* (New York: Oxford University Press, 1994), 20. For a list of extensions to the Social Security Act, see Table 7 of Heather Boushey and Sarah Jane Glynn, "Comprehensive Paid Family and Medical Leave for Today's Families and Workplaces: Crafting a Paid Leave System That Builds on the Experience of Existing Federal and State Programs" (Center for American Progress, August 2012), http://www.americanprogress.org/wp-content/uploads/2012/09/Boushey UniversalFamilyLeavePaper.pdf.

27 U.S. Department of Labor, "History of Unemployment Insurance in the United States," August 10, 2010, http://www.dol.gov/ocia/pdf/75th -Anniversary-Summary-FINAL.pdf; New York State Department of Labor, "A History of UI Legislation in the United States and NYS, 1935–2014" (Albany, NY, July 2014), https://labor.ny.gov/stats/PDFs/History_UI_Legislation.pdf; Sprague, "Frances Perkins: The Woman behind the New Deal."

28 See Heather Boushey and Jordan Eizenga, "Toward a Strong Unemployment Insurance System: The Case for an Expanded Federal Role" (Washington, DC: Center for American Progress, February 2011), http://www .americanprogress.org/wp-content/uploads/issues/2011/02/pdf/ui_brief.pdf; DeWitt, "The Decision to Exclude Agricultural and Domestic Workers from the 1935 Social Security Act"; Department of Labor, "Unemployment Insurance Data Summary: 4th Quarter 2011."

29 U.S. Department of Health and Human Services, "A Brief History of the AFDC Program" (Washington, DC, 1998), 6, http://aspe.hhs.gov/hsp/afdc /baseline/1history.pdf; Abe Bortz, "Historical Development of the Social Security Act," Social Security Administration, http://www.ssa.gov/history /bortz.html.

30 Mark H. Leff, "Consensus for Reform: The Mothers'-Pension Movement in the Progressive Era," *Social Service Review* 47, no. 3 (September 1, 1973): 397–417.

31 Susan Blank and Barbara B. Blum, "A Brief History of Work Expectations for Welfare Mothers," *The Future of Children* 7, no. 1 (Spring 1997): 28–38;

Isabelle Sawhill and Ron Haskins, "Welfare Reform and the Work Support System," *Welfare Reform and Beyond* (Washington, DC: Brookings Institution, March 2002); Karen Schulman and Helen Blank, "Downward Slide: State Child Care Assistance Policies 2012" (Washington, DC: National Women's Law Center, October 10, 2012), http://www.nwlc.org/resource /downward-slide-state-child-care-assistance-policies-2012.

32 If an employer fires or retaliates against a worker for exercising a right under the act, the National Labor Relations Board (NLRB) has the authority to instruct the employer to reverse the action, rehire the worker, and pay him or her for any lost wages. See National Labor Relations Board, "How to Enforce Your Rights," accessed July 1, 2015, https://www.nlrb.gov/rights-we-protect /whats-law/employees/i-am-represented-union/how-enforce-your-rights; National Labor Relations Board, "The 1935 Passage of the Wagner Act," accessed April 16, 2015, http://www.nlrb.gov/who-we-are/our-history/1935 -passage-wagner-act; Franklin D. Roosevelt Presidential Library and Museum, "FDR and the Wagner Act: 'A Better Relationship between Management and Labor,'" accessed January 21, 2015, http://www.fdrlibrary .marist.edu/aboutfdr/wagneract.html.

33 National Labor Relations Board, "Pre-Wagner Act Labor Relations," accessed January 21, 2015, http://www.nlrb.gov/who-we-are/our-history/pre -wagner-act-labor-relations; Congressional Digest, "Federal Labor Laws" (Washington, DC, 1993), http://history.eserver.org/us-labor-law.txt.

34 Ruth Milkman, *Gender at Work: The Dynamics of Job Segregation by Sex during World War II* (Urbana: University of Illinois Press, 1987), 34.

35 Labor Project for Working Families, "About Us," accessed February 8, 2015, http://www.working-families.org/about/; Union coverage data are author's calculations of 2013 data from Bureau of Labor Statistics, "Table 1. Union Affiliation of Employed Wage and Salary Workers by Selected Characteristics" (U.S. Department of Labor, January 2015), 1, http://www.bls.gov/news .release/union2.t01.htm.

36 U.S. Wage and Hour Division, "Handy Reference Guide to the Fair Labor Standards Act" (U.S. Department of Labor, September 2010), http://www.dol .gov/whd/regs/compliance/hrg.htm.

37 Howard D. Samuel, "Troubled Passage: The Labor Movement and the Fair Labor Standards Act," *Monthly Labor Review* (December 2000): 33, http://www.bls.gov/opub/mlr/2000/12/art3full.pdf; U.S. Bureau of Labor Statistics, "Chapter 2: Child Labor Laws and Enforcement," in *Report on the Youth Labor Force* (U.S. Department of Labor, 2000), http://www.bls .gov/opub/rylf/pdf/chapter2.pdf; Vivien Hart, *Bound by Our Constitution: Women, Workers, and the Minimum Wage* (Princeton, NJ: Princeton University Press, 1994).

38 "National Recovery Administration (NRA)," *Encyclopedia Britannica*, January 5, 2014, http://www.britannica.com/EBchecked/topic/405302 /National-Recovery-Administration-NRA.

39 See, for example, Quadagno, *The Color of Welfare.*

40 For a list of amendments to the Fair Labor Standards Act, see Table 1 of
Heather Boushey and Alexandra Mitukiewicz, "Family and Medical Leave
Insurance: A Basic Standard for Today's Workforce" (Washington, DC:
Center for American Progress, 2013), http://cdn.americanprogress.org/wp
-content/uploads/2014/04/FMLA-reportv2.pdf. On changes to the min-
imum wage, see U.S. Wage and Hour Division, U.S. Department of Labor,
"Minimum Wage Laws in the States," accessed August 18, 2015, http://www
.dol.gov/whd/minwage/america.htm. As of this writing, the new overtime
regulations have not yet gone into effect. U.S. Wage and Hour Division, "Fact
Sheet #17A: Exemption for Executive, Administrative, Professional, Computer and outside Sales Employees under the Fair Labor Standards Act
(FLSA)" (U.S. Department of Labor, July 2008), http://www.dol.gov/whd/regs
/compliance/fairpay/fs17a_overview.pdf; U.S. Wage and Hour Division, "29
CFR Part 541" (U.S. Department of Labor, April 23, 2004), http://www.dol
.gov/whd/regs/compliance/fairpay/preamble.pdf; Office of the Press Secretary,
"Fact Sheet: Middle Class Economics Rewarding Hard Work by Restoring
Overtime Pay" (The White House, June 30, 2015), https://www.whitehouse
.gov/the-press-office/2015/06/30/fact-sheet-middle-class-economics-rewarding
-hard-work-restoring-overtime. The home care worker rule was to become
effective January 2015, but it was appealed. In August 2015, a federal court
ruled that the regulation should be put in place. See Wage and Hour
Division, "Application of the Fair Labor Standards Act to Domestic Service;
Announcement of Time-Limited Non-Enforcement Policy" (Washington,
DC: U.S. Department of Labor, October 6, 2014), http://www.dol.gov/whd
/homecare/non-enforcement-fr.pdf; Noam Scheiber, "U.S. Court Reinstates
Home Care Pay Rules," *New York Times*, August 21, 2015, http://www.nytimes
.com/2015/08/22/business/us-court-reinstates-home-care-pay-rules.html.

41 The economists Andrew Glyn, Alan Hughes, Alain Lipietz, and Ajit Singh
argue that many of the policies passed during the New Deal made this
linkage possible. See Andrew Glyn et al., "The Rise and Fall of the Golden
Age," in *The Golden Age of Capitalism: Reinterpreting the Postwar Experi-
ence,* ed. Stephen A Marglin and Juliet B. Schor, WIDER Studies in
Development Economics (Oxford: Clarendon Press, 1992), 39–125. See also
Wayne Vroman, "The Role of Unemployment Insurance as an Automatic
Stabilizer during a Recession" (Washington, DC: U.S. Department of
Labor, July 2010), http://wdr.doleta.gov/research/FullText_Documents
/ETAOP2010–10.pdf; Daniel Aaronson, Sumit Agarwal, and Eric French,
"The Spending and Debt Response to Minimum Wage Hikes," *American
Economic Review* 102, no. 7 (December 2012): 3111–3139, doi:10.1257/
aer.102.7.3111.

42 Philip Cohen's analysis of the 1960 U.S. Census and the 2012 American
Community Survey, with data from IPUMS.org. See Appendix for more
information on data and methods.

43 Abby J. Cohen, "A Brief History of Federal Financing for Childcare in the United States," *Future of Children*, 6, no. 2 (Summer/Fall 1996), http://futureofchildren.org/publications/journals/article/index.xml?journalid=56&articleid=326&sectionid=2180; Bryce Covert, "Here's What Happened the One Time When the U.S. Had Universal Childcare," September 30, 2014, http://thinkprogress.org/economy/2014/09/30/3573844/lanham-act-child-care/.

44 Ellen Reese, "Maternalism and Political Mobilization: How California's Postwar Child Care Campaign Was Won," *Gender & Society* 10, no. 5 (October 1996): 566–589, http://www.jstor.org.libproxy.wustl.edu/stable/pdf/189883.pdf?acceptTC=true.

45 *Hearing on Care and Protection of Children of Employed Mothers* (Washington, DC, 1943); See Cohen, "A Brief History of Federal Financing for Child Care in the United States."

46 Claudia Goldin and Lawrence Katz, "The Power of the Pill: Oral Contraceptives and Women's Career and Marriage Decisions," *Journal of Political Economy* 110, no. 4 (2002): 730–770. See also Robert O. Self, *All in the Family: The Realignment of American Democracy since the 1960s* (New York: Hill and Wang, 2012).

II. Stalled

1 Heather Boushey, John Schmitt, and Kavya Vaghul's analysis of the CEPR extracts of the CPS Annual Social and Economic Supplement. See Appendix for more information on data and methods. Note that while the figure shows median income, the text gives the average in order to be comparable with data shown in Figure 2.5.

2 See "On This Day: May 18," *New York Times: The Learning Network* (May 18, 2014), http://learning.blogs.nytimes.com/on-this-day/may-18/; John Watson, "Mount Saint Helens: Mudflows and Floods," *U.S. Geological Survey*, June 25, 1997, http://pubs.usgs.gov/gip/msh/mudflows.html; John Watson, "Mount Saint Helens: Impact and Aftermath," *U.S. Geological Survey*, June 25, 1997, http://pubs.usgs.gov/gip/msh/impact.html.

3 Calculated from U.S. Bureau of Economic Analysis, "Real Gross Domestic Product [GDPC1], Retrieved from FRED, Federal Reserve Bank of St. Louis," accessed May 13, 2015, https://research.stlouisfed.org/fred2/series/GDPC1/; U.S. Bureau of Economic Analysis, "Profit per Unit of Real Gross Value Added of Nonfinancial Corporate Business: Corporate Profits after Tax with IVA and CCAdj (unit Profits from Current Production) [A466RD3Q052SBEA], Retrieved from FRED, Federal Reserve Bank of St. Louis," accessed May 13, 2015, https://research.stlouisfed.org/fred2/series/A466RD3Q052SBEA/; see Appendix Table A.2 for middle-class family median income growth.

4 The gap between income and productivity derives from the gap between pay and productivity. For a nice discussion of the technical details, see Lawrence

Mishel, "Inequality Is Central to the Productivity-Pay Gap," *Economic Policy Institute*, accessed August 8, 2015, http://www.epi.org/blog/inequality-central -productivity-pay-gap/.

5 John Schmitt and Janelle Jones, "Low-Wage Workers Are Older and Better Educated Than Ever," Issue Brief (Washington, DC: Center for Economic and Policy Research, April 2012); John Schmitt and Janelle Jones, "Where Have All the Good Jobs Gone?" (Washington, DC: Center for Economic and Policy Research, July 2012), http://www.cepr.net/documents/publications /good-jobs-2012–07.pdf.

6 Heather Boushey, John Schmitt, and Kavya Vaghul's analysis of the CEPR extracts of the CPS Annual Social and Economic Supplement. See Appendix for more information on data and methods.

7 Author's calculation of labor-force participation of male workers ages twenty-five to fifty-four, for countries in the OECD as of January 2010, from Organisation for Economic Co-operation and Development, "OECD. StatsExtracts," 2015, http://stats.oecd.org/. Data on share of middle-class families with an earner from Appendix Table A.4.

8 Bureau of Labor Statistics, "Consumer Price Index (CPI)," *U.S. Department of Labor*, accessed August 27, 2015, http://bls.gov/cpi/.

9 The importance of fixed costs is brought to life in Elizabeth Warren and Amelia Warren Tyagi, *The Two-Income Trap: Why Middle-Class Mothers and Fathers Are Going Broke* (New York: Basic Books, 2003).

10 The importance of school financing on children's outcomes is an issue of debate, but new research points in the direction that money matters. See C. Kirabo Jackson, Rucker Johnson, and Claudia Persico, "The Effect of School Finance Reforms on the Distribution of Spending, Academic Achievement, and Adult Outcomes," Working Paper (Cambridge, MA: National Bureau of Economic Research, May 2014), http://www.nber.org/papers/w20118; Leah Platt Boustan, "Local Public Goods and the Demand for High-Income Municipalities," *Journal of Urban Economics* 76 (July 2013): 71–82, http://www.econ.ucla.edu/lboustan/research_pdfs/research01_publicgoods .pdf. The Washington Center for Equitable Growth is funding research by the economist Jesse Rothstein to use data of state-level school-finance reforms intended to increase funding for schools serving poor children over the past several decades to study the effects of these reforms on test scores of students in low-income districts (http://diversity.berkeley.edu/uc-berkeley -economist-jesse-rothstein-awarded-research-grant).

11 See World Bank, "Health Expenditure per Capita (current US$)," accessed July 7, 2015, http://data.worldbank.org/indicator/SH.XPD.PCAP/countries /US-CA?display=graph; Karen Davis et al., "Mirror, Mirror on the Wall: How the Performance of the U.S. Health Care System Compares Internationally" (New York: The Commonwealth Fund, June 2014); Council of Economic Advisers, "Trends in Health Care Cost Growth and the Role of

the Affordable Care Act" (Washington, DC: White House, November 2013), https://www.whitehouse.gov/sites/default/files/docs/healthcostreport_final _noembargo_v2.pdf.

12 MetLife Mature Market Institute, "The MetLife Study of Caregiving Costs to Working Caregivers: Double Jeopardy for Baby Boomers Caring for Their Parents" (Westport, CT: MetLife Mature Market Institute, June 2011); Ai-jen Poo, *The Age of Dignity: Preparing for the Elder Boom in a Changing America* (New York: The New Press, 2015), 27; "Senior Care Cost Index," *Caring.com*, accessed July 24, 2015, http://caring.com/support-groups/senior -care-cost-index-2014; Dorothy A. Miller, "The 'Sandwich' Generation: Adult Children of the Aging," *Social Work* 26, no. 5 (September 1, 1981): 419–423, doi:10.1093/sw/26.5.419.

13 Author's calculations, all in nominal dollars. The federal minimum wage was multiplied by 40 hours/week by 50 weeks/year (with two weeks off without pay), equaling $2,500 after the September 3, 1965, increase of the minimum wage to $1.25, and $14,500 in 2013 at the prevailing $7.25 minimum wage. Average annual tuition, room, board, and fees for a four-year public institution was $996 in the 1965–66 school year and $18,110 in the 2013–14 school year. See Institute of Education Sciences National Center for Education Statistics, "Digest of Education Statistics" (U.S. Department of Education, 2014), sec. 330.10, http://nces.ed.gov /programs/digest/2014menu_tables.asp; U.S. Department of Labor, "History of Federal Minimum Wage Rates under the Fair Labor Standards Act, 1938–2009," *Wage and Hour Division (WHD)*, accessed June 4, 2015, http://www.dol.gov/whd/minwage/chart.htm.

14 Among men, only those with a college degree had earnings higher in 2012 than in 1979. Among women, those with at least a college degree have seen faster growth than those without, but even those with a high school degree or some college have seen earnings increases. See David H. Autor, "Skills, Education, and the Rise of Earnings Inequality among the 'Other 99 Percent,'" *Science* 344, no. 6186 (May 23, 2014): 843–851, doi:10.1126/science.1251868; David Leonhardt, "Is College Worth It? Clearly, New Data Say," *New York Times*, May 27, 2014, http://www .nytimes.com/2014/05/27/upshot/is-college-worth-it-clearly-new-data-say .html; Heather Boushey and John Schmitt, "Why Don't More Young People Earn College Degrees," *Challenge*, June 28, 2012.

15 Child Care Aware of America, "Parents and the High Cost of Child Care: 2014 Report" (Arlington, VA, 2014), https://www.ncsl.org/documents/cyf /2014_Parents_and_the_High_Cost_of_Child_Care.pdf; Institute of Education Sciences National Center for Education Statistics, "Digest of Education Statistics 2013" (Washington, DC: U.S. Department of Education, 2013), sec. 330.10, https://nces.ed.gov/programs/digest/d13 /tables/dt13_330.10.asp?current=yes.

16 Calculated using civilian labor-force data for women ages sixteen and over. Retrieved from Bureau of Labor Statistics, "Current Population Survey" (U.S. Department of Labor, n.d.), http://www.bls.gov/data/. See also Chinhui Juhn and Simon Potter, "Changes in Labor Force Participation in the United States," \iThe Journal of Economic Perspectives 20, no. 3 (Summer 2006): 27–46.

17 Nicholas Kulish, "Editorial Observer: Changing the Rules for the Team Sport of Bread-Winning," *New York Times*, September 23, 2005, http://www .nytimes.com/2005/09/23/opinion/23fri4.html.

18 Up until the late 1960s, physicians could not prescribe the Pill to an unmarried woman below the age of consent without her parent's permission. After passage of the 26th Amendment to the Constitution, most states lowered the age of consent to eighteen. Claudia Goldin and Lawrence Katz, "The Power of the Pill: Oral Contraceptives and Women's Career and Marriage Decisions," *Journal of Political Economy* 110, no. 4 (2002): 730–770; See also Barbara Bergmann, *The Economic Emergence of Women*, 2nd ed. (New York: Palgrave Macmillan, 2005).

19 Heather Boushey, John Schmitt, and Kavya Vaghul's analysis of the CEPR extracts of the CPS Annual Social and Economic Supplement. See Appendix for more information on data and methods.

20 See Stephanie Coontz, *A Strange Stirring: The Feminine Mystique and American Women at the Dawn of the 1960s* (New York: Basic Books, 2011); Judith Warner, "The Women's Leadership Gap: Women's Leadership by the Numbers" (Washington, DC: Center for American Progress, March 7, 2014), http://cdn.americanprogress.org/wp-content/uploads/2014/03/Women Leadership.pdf.

21 Robert O. Self, *All in the Family: The Realignment of American Democracy since the 1960s* (New York: Hill and Wang, 2012), 25; Louis Menand, "The Sex Amendment," *New Yorker*, July 21, 2014, http://www.newyorker.com /magazine/2014/07/21/sex-amendment.

22 Real hourly wages in 2011 dollars. Lawrence Mishel et al., "Table 4.6—Hourly Wages of Women, by Wage Percentile, 1973–2011," in *The State of Working America*, 12th ed. (Ithaca, NY: Cornell University Press, 2012); Carmen DeNavas-Walt and Bernadette D. Proctor, "Income and Poverty in the United States: 2013" (Washington, DC: U.S. Department of Commerce, Economics and Statistics Administration, U.S. Census Bureau, September 2014), http://www.census.gov/content/dam/Census/library /publications/2014/demo/p60–249.pdf; "By the Numbers: A Look at the Gender Pay Gap," AAUW: *Empowering Women since 1881*, accessed July 23, 2015, http://www.aauw.org/2014/09/18/gender-pay-gap/; National Partnership for Women and Families, "America's Women and the Wage Gap" (Washington, DC, September 2014), http://www.nationalpartnership.org/research -library/workplace-fairness/fair-pay/americas-women-and-the-wage-gap.pdf.

23　Eileen Appelbaum, Heather Boushey, and John Schmitt, "The Economic Importance of Women's Rising Hours of Work" (Washington, DC: Center for Economic and Policy Research and Center for American Progress, April 2014). Breadwinners data are from Sarah Jane Glynn's analysis of the Annual Social and Economic Supplement. See Appendix for more information on data and methods.

24　Dan Witters, "U.S. Adults with Children at Home Have Greater Joy, Stress," *Gallup*, October 20, 2014, http://www.gallup.com/poll/178631/adults-children-home-greater-joy-stress.aspx?version=print; See also Jacobs and Gerson, *The Time Divide*, Figure 4.1; Arlie Russell Hochschild, *The Time Bind: When Work Becomes Home and Home Becomes Work* (New York: Metropolitan Books, 1997).

25　Heather Boushey, John Schmitt, and Kavya Vaghul's analysis of the CEPR extracts of the CPS Annual Social and Economic Supplement. See Appendix for more information on data and methods. This specific data point is not shown in the Appendix. On stress, see Witters, "U.S. Adults with Children at Home Have Greater Joy, Stress"; American Psychological Association, "Stress in America: Paying with Our Health," February 4, 2015, http://www.apa.org/news/press/releases/stress/2014/stress-report.pdf.

26　U.S. Census Bureau, "Table F-7: Type of Family (All Races) by Median and Mean Income, 1947–2013; Current Population Survey, Annual Social and Economic Supplements," n.d., https://www.census.gov/hhes/www/income/data/historical/families/.

27　Chad Newcomb, "Distribution of Zero-Earning Years by Gender, Birth Cohort, and Level of Lifetime Earnings," Research and Statistics Note (Washington, DC: U.S. Social Security Administration, Office of Policy, November 2000), http://www.ssa.gov/policy/docs/rsnotes/rsn2000–02.html.

28　Ellen Galinsky, Kerstin Aumann, and James T. Bond, "Times Are Changing, Gender and Generation at Work and at Home" (New York: Families and Work Institute, August 2011), http://familiesandwork.org/site/research/reports/Times_Are_Changing.pdf.

29　See Christian Weller and Jessica Lynch, "Household Wealth in Freefall: Americans' Private Safety Net in Tatters" (Washington, DC: Center for American Progress, 2009); Christian E. Weller and Jackie Odum Friday, "Economic Snapshot: July 2015" (Washington, DC: Center for American Progress, July 31, 2015), https://www.americanprogress.org/issues/economy/report/2015/07/31/118604/economic-snapshot-july-2015/.

30　Rising home values from U.S. Bureau of the Census, "1990 Census of Housing: General Housing Characteristics, United States" (Washington, DC: U.S. Department of Commerce, 1990); Ellen Wilson, "Property Value: 2007 and 2008 American Community Surveys," American Community Survey Reports (September 2009), https://www.census.gov/prod/2009pubs/acsbr08–6.pdf. Annual average cash-out refinances from Federal Housing Finance Agency, "Loan Purposes by Quarter," *House Price Index Datasets,* n.d., http://www.fhfa.gov/DataTools/Downloads/Pages/House-Price-Index -Datasets.aspx; "The House Price Index is based on transactions involving conforming, conventional mortgages purchased or securitized by Fannie Mae or Freddie Mac. Only mortgage transactions on single-family properties are included," see Question 2: Federal Housing Finance Agency, "Housing Price Index Frequently Asked Questions," August 26, 2014, http://www.fhfa .gov/Media/PublicAffairs/Pages/Housing-Price-Index-Frequently-Asked -Questions.aspx. See also Atif Mian and Amir Sufi, *House of Debt: How They (and You) Caused the Great Recession, and How We Can Prevent It from Happening Again* (Chicago, IL: University of Chicago Press, 2014).

31 See Federal Reserve Board of Governors, "Consumer Credit—G.19" (Washington, DC, May 2015), http://www.federalreserve.gov/releases/g19 /current/default.htm; College Board, "Trends in Student Aid: 2012" (University of Texas, Austin, 2012), http://advocacy.collegeboard.org/sites /default/files/student-aid-2012-full-report.pdf; Heather Boushey, "Student Debt: Bigger and Bigger" (Washington, DC: Center for Economic and Policy Research, 2005).

32 David U. Himmelstein et al., "Medical Bankruptcy in the United States, 2007: Results of a National Study," *American Journal of Medicine* 122, no. 8 (August 2009): 741–746; Christina LaMontagne, "NerdWallet Health Finds Medical Bankruptcy Accounts for Majority of Personal Bankruptcies," *NerdWallet*, March 26, 2014, http://www.nerdwallet.com /blog/health/2014/03/26/medical-bankruptcy/. See also: Atif Mian and Amir Sufi, *House of Debt*.

33 Federal Reserve Bank of New York, "Quarterly Report on Household Debt and Credit" (New York, February 2015), http://www.newyorkfed.org /householdcredit/2014-q4/data/pdf/HHDC_2014Q4.pdf.

34 Suzanne M. Bianchi, "Changing Families, Changing Workplaces," *Future of Children* 21, no. 2 (Fall 2011): 15–36.

III. Stuck

1 Andrew Dugan, "Americans Most Likely to Say They Belong to the Middle Class: Fewer College Graduates Say They Belong to the Middle Class" (Gallup, November 9, 2012).

2 U.S. Geological Survey, "Mount St. Helens: 1980 Cataclysmic Eruption," 2013, http://volcanoes.usgs.gov/volcanoes/st_helens/st_helens_geo_hist_99 .html; John Watson, "Mount Saint Helens: Impact and Aftermath," *U.S. Geological Survey*, June 25, 1997, http://pubs.usgs.gov/gip/msh/impact.html; John Watson, "Mount Saint Helens: Mudflows and Floods," *U.S. Geological Survey*, June 25, 1997, http://pubs.usgs.gov/gip/msh/mudflows.html.

3 Raj Chetty et al., "Is the United States Still a Land of Opportunity? Recent Trends in Intergenerational Mobility," Working Paper (Cambridge, MA: National Bureau of Economic Research, January 2014), 1, http://www.nber .org/papers/w19844; According to Miles Corak and colleagues, among U.S.

sons born in the bottom quintile, 42.2 percent stayed there and 24.5 percent moved to the second quintile, while among daughters, the corresponding figures are 25.6 and 23.2 percent. See Miles Corak, Matthew Lindquist, and Bhashkar Mazumder, "A Comparison of Upward and Downward Intergenerational Mobility in Canada, Sweden and the United States," *Swedish Institute for Social Research*, March 21, 2014, http://www.sofi.su.se/polopoly_fs/1.172434.1395847283!/menu/standard /file/WP14no5.pdf. See also Bhashkar Mazumder, "Is Intergenerational Economic Mobility Lower Now Than in the Past?" (Chicago, IL: Federal Reserve of Chicago, 2012); Markus Jantti et al., "American Exceptionalism in a New Light: A Comparison of Intergenerational Earnings Mobility in the Nordic Countries, the United Kingdom, and the United States," IZA Discussion Paper (Bonn, Germany: Institute for the Study of Labor, January 2006), http://ftp.iza.org/dp1938.pdf.

4 Philip Cohen's analysis of 1960 U.S. Census data and the 2012 American Community Survey, with data from IPUMS.org. See Appendix for more information on data and methods. See also Andrew J. Cherlin, *Labor's Love Lost: The Rise and Fall of the Working-Class Family in America* (New York: Russell Sage Foundation, 2014), chaps. 5 and 6; Kathryn Edin and Maria J. Kefalas, *Promises I Can Keep: Why Poor Women Put Motherhood before Marriage*, 1st ed. (Berkeley, CA: University of California Press, 2005); Sara McLanahan and Christine Percheski, "Family Structure and the Reproduction of Inequalities," *Annual Review of Sociology* 34, no. 1 (2008): 257–276, doi:10.1146/annurev.soc.34.040507.134549.

5 D'Vera Cohn, Gretchen Livingston, and Wendy Wang, "After Decades of Decline, a Rise in Stay-at-Home Mothers," *Pew Research Center's Social & Demographic Trends Project*, accessed April 30, 2015, http://www .pewsocialtrends.org/2014/04/08/after-decades-of-decline-a-rise-in-stay-at -home-mothers/.

6 Heather Boushey, John Schmitt, and Kavya Vaghul's analysis of the CEPR extracts of the CPS Annual Social and Economic Supplement. See Appendix for more information on data and methods. See also John Schmitt and Janelle Jones, "Low-Wage Workers Are Older and Better Educated Than Ever," Issue Brief (Washington, DC: Center for Economic and Policy Research, April 2012).

7 Marshall Steinbaum and John Schmitt, "Would Graduating More College Students Reduce Wage Inequality?," Washington Center for Equitable Growth, accessed May 30, 2015, http://equitablegrowth.org/research /graduating-college-students-reduce-wage-inequality/.

8 Author's calculation of manufacturing as a share of total nonfarm employment and average weekly earnings of total and manufacturing production and nonsupervisory employees from Bureau of Labor Statistics, "Employment, Hours, and Earnings Statistics from the Current

Employment Statistics Survey (National)" (U.S. Department of Labor), accessed May 21, 2013, http://data.bls.gov/timeseries/CES4244100001?data_tool=XGtable.

9 Trade data are author's analysis of U.S. Department of Commerce and U.S. International Trade Commission, "U.S. Imports for Consumption, Annual Data," accessed May 29, 2015, https://www.census.gov/foreign-trade/Press-Release/current_press_release/index.html; U.S. Department of Commerce and U.S. International Trade Commission, "U.S. Domestic Exports, Annual Data," accessed May 29, 2015, https://www.census.gov/foreign-trade/Press-Release/current_press_release/index.html; U.S. Bureau of Economic Analysis, "Gross Domestic Product: Implicit Price Deflator," FRED, Federal Reserve Bank of St. Louis, January 1, 1947, https://research.stlouisfed.org/fred2/series/GDPDEF/; Thomas Fuller, "China Trade Unbalances Shipping," New York Times, January 29, 2006, http://www.nytimes.com/2006/01/29/business/worldbusiness/29iht-ships.html?pagewanted=all&_r=0; Janet Ceglowski and Stephen Golub, "Just How Low Are China's Labor Costs?" (Bryn Mawr, PA: Bryn Mawr College, November 5, 2005), http://www.swarthmore.edu/SocSci/sgolub1/chinaslaborcosts11_7_2005.pdf.

10 David H. Autor, David Dorn, and Gordon H. Hanson, "The China Syndrome: Local Labor Market Effects of Import Competition in the United States," American Economic Review 103, no. 6 (October 2013): 2121–2168, doi:10.1257/aer.103.6.2121.

11 Richard B. Freeman and Ronald Schettkat, "Marketization of Household Production and the EU-US Gap in Work," Economic Policy Journal 20, no. 4 (2005): 5–50.

12 Rachel E. Dwyer, "The Care Economy? Gender, Economic Restructuring, and Job Polarization in the U.S. Labor Market," American Sociological Review 78, no. 3 (June 2013): 390–416.

13 Maria E. Enchautegui, "Nonstandard Work Schedules and the Well-Being of Low-Income Families" (Washington, DC: Urban Institute, July 2013), http://www.urban.org/UploadedPDF/412877-nonstandard-work-schedules.pdf.

14 The specific question is whether workers can "choose their own starting and quitting time access within a range of hours periodically." Susan J. Lambert and Julia R. Henly, "Scheduling in Hourly Jobs: Promising Practices for the Twenty-First Century Economy" (The Mobility Agenda, May 2009), http://www.mobilityagenda.org/home/file.axd?file=2009%2f5%2fscheduling.pdf; Steven Greenhouse, "A Push to Give Steadier Shifts to Part-Timers," New York Times, July 15, 2014, http://www.nytimes.com/2014/07/16/business/a-push-to-give-steadier-shifts-to-part-timers.html; Stephanie Luce and Naoki Fujita, "Discounted Jobs: How Retailers Sell Workers Short" (New York: Murphy Institute, City University of New York, and the Retail Action Project, 2012), http://retailactionproject.org/wp-content/uploads/2012/03/7-75_RAP+cover_lowres.pdf.

15 Associated Press, "Wal-Mart Implements Tougher Attendance Policy for Workers," *Fox News*, November 2, 2006, http://www.foxnews.com/story/2006 /11/02/wal-mart-implements-tougher-attendance-policy-for-workers. Data on low-wage employees' access to flexibility from James Bond and Ellen Galinsky, "Workplace Flexibility and Low-Wage Employees," National Study of the Changing Workforce (New York: Families and Work Institute, 2011).

16 Jodi Kantor, "Working Anything but 9 to 5," *New York Times*, August 13, 2014, http://www.nytimes.com/interactive/2014/08/13/us/starbucks-workers -scheduling-hours.html.

17 Jodi Kantor, "Starbucks to Revise Policies to End Irregular Schedules for Its 130,000 Baristas," *New York Times*, August 14, 2014, http://www.nytimes.com /2014/08/15/us/starbucks-to-revise-work-scheduling-policies.html.

18 Wage and Hour Division, "Application of the Fair Labor Standards Act to Domestic Service; Announcement of Time-Limited Non-Enforcement Policy" (Washington, DC: U.S. Department of Labor, October 6, 2014), http://www.dol.gov/whd/homecare/non-enforcement-fr.pdf. As noted in Chapter 2, this rule had been contested in the courts, but in August 2015, it was upheld by a federal appeals court: Noam Scheiber, "U.S. Court Reinstates Home Care Pay Rules," *New York Times*, August 21, 2015, http://www.nytimes.com/2015/08/22/business/us-court-reinstates-home-care -pay-rules.html.

19 Unpublished analysis of CPS data from John Schmitt.

20 On U.S. incarceration, see Human Rights Watch, "Nation behind Bars: A Human Rights Solution" (Washington, DC, 2011), http://www.hrw.org /sites/default/files/related_material/2014_US_Nation_Behind_Bars_0.pdf; Tyjen Tsai and Paola Scommegna, "U.S. Has World's Highest Incarceration Rate" (Population Reference Bureau, August 2012), http://www.prb.org /Publications/Articles/2012/us-incarceration.aspx; estimate of the prison population from U.S. Census Bureau, "Annual Estimates of the Resident Population by Single Year of Age and Sex for the United States, States, and Puerto Rico Commonwealth: April 1, 2010 to July 1, 2013," June 2014, http://factfinder.census.gov/faces/tableservices/jsf/pages/productview.xhtml ?pid=PEP_2013_PEPSYASEX&prodType=table; E. Ann Carson, "Male Prisoners under the Jurisdiction of State or Federal Correctional Authorities, December 31, 1978–2013" (Bureau of Justice Statistics, January 7, 2015), http://www.bjs.gov/index.cfm?ty=nps; E. Ann Carson and Daniela Golinelli, "Prisoners in 2012" (Washington, DC: U.S. Department of Justice, Bureau of Justice Statistics, September 2, 2014). On the employment effects of incarceration, see John Schmitt and Kris Warner, "Ex-Offenders and the Labor Market," *WorkingUSA* 14, no. 1 (2011): 87–109, doi:10.1111/j.1743–4580 .2011.00322.x; John Schmitt, Kris Warner, and Sarika Gupta, "The High Budgetary Cost of Incarceration" (Washington, DC: Center for Economic

and Policy Research, June 2010), http://www.cepr.net/documents/publications /incarceration-2010–06.pdf.

21 See, for example, Immanuel Ness, *Immigrants, Unions, and the New U.S. Labor Market* (Philadelphia: Temple University Press, 2005).

22 Data on Temporary Assistance for Needy Families from U.S. Census Bureau, "Survey of Income and Program Participation," Fig. 3, accessed February 14, 2015, http://www.census.gov/programs-surveys/sipp/publications /tables/hsehld-char.html.

23 On historical patterns of employment by race, ethnicity, and gender, see Teresa L. Amott and Julie A. Matthaei, *Race, Gender, and Work: A Multi-Cultural Economic History of Women in the United States* (Brooklyn, NY: South End Press, 1996). Barbara Ehrenreich and Arlie Russell Hochschild, eds., *Global Women: Nannies, Maids, and Sex Workers in the New Economy* (New York: Metropolitan / Henry Holt, 2004).

24 For nutrition assistance, author's calculations for 2013 data from U.S. Department of Agriculture, "Supplemental Nutrition Assistance Program: Average Monthly Participation (Households)," March 6, 2015, http://www.fns .usda.gov/sites/default/files/pd/16SNAPpartHH.pdf; U.S. Census Bureau, "Table H1. Households by Type and Tenure of Householder for Selected Characteristics: 2013," 2013, http://www.census.gov/hhes/families/data /cps2013H.html. For child-care subsidies data, see Office of Child Care—Administration for Children & Families, "Characteristics of Families Served by Child Care and Development Fund (CCDF) Based on Preliminary FY 2013 Data" (U.S. Department of Health and Human Services, November 17, 2014), http://www.acf.hhs.gov/programs/occ/resource/characteristics-of -families-served-by-child-care-and-development-fund-ccdf. For Head Start, see Early Childhood Learning and Knowledge Center, "Head Start Program Fact Sheet Fiscal Year 2014," *Head Start*, April 2015, http://eclkc.ohs.acf.hhs .gov/hslc/data/factsheets/2014-hs-program-factsheet.html. For Medicaid data, see U.S. Centers for Medicare and Medicaid Services, "Medicaid Expansion and What It Means for You," *HealthCare.gov*, accessed April 23, 2015, https://www.healthcare.gov/medicaid-chip/medicaid-expansion-and-you/. For housing-subsidy and voucher data, see U.S. Department of Housing and Urban Development, "Fiscal Year 2013 Program and Budget Initiatives: The Population HUD Serves," accessed May 1, 2015, http://portal.hud.gov /hudportal/documents/huddoc?id=FY13BudFSHUDClients.pdf. For homelessness data, see Meghan Henry et al., "The 2014 Annual Homeless Assessment Report (AHAR) to Congress" (Washington, DC: U.S. Department of Housing and Urban Development, October 2014), https://www .hudexchange.info/resources/documents/2014-AHAR-Part1.pdf.

25 On benefits cliffs, see Randy Albelda et al., "Bridging the Gaps: A Picture of How Work Supports Work in Ten States" (Center for Economic and Policy Research, The Center for Social Policy, October 2007), http://www.cepr.net

/index.php/publications/reports/bridging-the-gaps-a-picture-of-how-work
-supports-work-in-ten-states/; National Center for Children in Poverty,
"Family Resource Simulator," accessed September 24, 2013, http://www.nccp
.org/tools/frs/.

26 Bryce Covert, "Meet a Woman Whose Raise Cost Her Money," *ThinkProgress*, August 19, 2014, http://thinkprogress.org/economy/2014/08/19/3472981
/benefits-cliff/.

27 For recent data on family formation patterns, see Alison Aughinbaugh,
Omar Robles, and Hugette Sun, "Marriage and Divorce: Patterns by
Gender, Race, and Educational Attainment," *Monthly Labor Review*,
October 2013, http://www.bls.gov/opub/mlr/2013/article/marriage-and
-divorce-patterns-by-gender-race-and-educational-attainment.htm, Table 3.

28 Stephanie Coontz, "The New Instability," *New York Times*, July 26, 2014,
http://www.nytimes.com/2014/07/27/opinion/sunday/the-new-instability
.html.

29 McLanahan and Percheski, "Family Structure and the Reproduction of
Inequalities," 261. See also Ariel Kalil and Rebecca M. Ryan, "Mothers'
Economic Conditions and Sources of Support in Fragile Families," *The
Future of Children* 20, no. 2 (Fall 2010): 39–61.

30 Edin and Kefalas, *Promises I Can Keep.*

31 Cherlin, *Labor's Love Lost.*

32 Breadwinner data from Sarah Jane Glynn's analysis of the Annual Social
and Economic Supplement. See Appendix for more information on data
and methods.

33 Bureau of Labor Statistics, "Employment Projections—2010–2020" (Wash-
ington, DC, February 1, 2012), http://www.bls.gov/news.release/archives
/ecopro_02012012.pdf. For more on looking back over a decade's worth of
Bureau of Labor Statistics employment projections, see Heather Boushey, "A
Woman's Place Is in the Middle Class," in *The Shriver Report: A Woman's
Nation Pushes Back from the Brink*, ed. Olivia Morgan and Karen Skelton
(Washington, DC: Center for American Progress, 2014). On the share of
"good jobs," see John Schmitt and Janelle Jones, "Where Have All the Good
Jobs Gone?" (Washington, DC: Center for Economic and Policy Research,
July 2012), http://www.cepr.net/documents/publications/good-jobs-2012–07
.pdf. On paid sick days, see Claudia Williams, Robert Drago, and Kevin
Miller, "44 Million U.S. Workers Lacked Paid Sick Days in 2010: 77 Percent
of Food Service Workers Lacked Access" (Washington, DC: Institute for
Women's Policy Research, 2011). On devaluing women's work, see Christine
Alksnis, Serge Desmarais, and James Curtis, "Workforce Segregation and
the Gender Wage Gap: Is 'Women's' Work Valued as Highly as 'Men's'?,"
Journal of Applied Social Psychology 38, no. 6 (June 1, 2008): 1416–1441,
doi:10.1111/j.1559–1816.2008.00354.x; Shankar Vedantam, "The Wage
Gap—Unconscious Bias in Judging the Value of Predominantly 'Female'

Professions," *Psychology Today*, February 18, 2010, http://www
.psychologytoday.com/blog/the-hidden-brain/201002/the-wage-gap
-unconscious-bias-in-judging-the-value-predominantly-female.

34 Earnings data from Heather Boushey, John Schmitt, and Kavya Vaghul's
analysis of the CEPR extracts of the CPS Annual Social and Economic
Supplement. See Appendix for more information on data and methods.
Job tenure data from U.S. Bureau of Labor Statistics, "Table 6. Median
Years of Tenure with Current Employer for Employed Wage and Salary
Workers by Occupation, Selected Years, 2004–2014" (U.S. Department of
Labor, September 18, 2014), http://www.bls.gov/news.release/tenure.t06.htm.

35 Joan C. Williams and Heather Boushey, "The Three Faces of Work-Family
Conflict: The Poor, the Privileged, and the Missing Middle" (Washington,
DC: Center for American Progress and the Center for WorkLife Law,
University of California, Hastings College of the Law, 2010), https://cdn
.americanprogress.org/wp-content/uploads/issues/2010/01/pdf/threefaces.pdf.

36 Ibid., Fig. 3.

37 Alissa Quart, "The Rise of Extreme Daycare," *Pacific Standard*, November
10, 2014, http://www.psmag.com/business-economics/rise-extreme-daycare
-working-24-hour-children-school-93860; Wen-Jui Han, "Maternal Nonstandard Work Schedules and Child Cognitive Outcomes," *Child Development*
76, no. 1 (February 2005): 137–154.

38 Julia Henly and Susan Lambert have conducted a wide array of studies on
this topic. See Julia R. Henly and Susan Lambert, "Nonstandard Work and
Child-Care Needs of Low-Income Parents," in *Work, Family, Health, and
Well-Being*, ed. Suzanne Bianchi, Lynne Casper, and Rosalind Berkowitz
(Mahwah: Lawrence Erlbaum Associates, 2005), 473–492.

39 Michel Martin, "On Balancing Career and Family as a Woman of Color,"
National Journal, July 26, 2014, http://www.nationaljournal.com/magazine
/when-the-conversation-about-having-it-all-begins-and-ends-with-white
-women-20140725.

40 Dan Clawson and Naomi Gerstel, *Unequal Time: Gender, Class, and Family
in Employment Schedules* (New York,: Russell Sage Foundation, 2014).

41 Kantor, "Working Anything but 9 to 5."

42 Natasha Singer, "In the Sharing Economy, Workers Find Both Freedom and
Uncertainty," *New York Times*, August 16, 2014, http://www.nytimes.com
/2014/08/17/technology/in-the-sharing-economy-workers-find-both-freedom
-and-uncertainty.html.

43 Jennifer Ludden, "Working Moms' Challenges: Paid Leave, Child Care,"
Morning Edition (National Public Radio, April 20, 2012), http://www.npr.org
/2012/04/20/150967376/working-moms-challenges-paid-leave-child-care.

44 U.S. Bureau of Labor Statistics, "Table 32. Leave Benefits: Access, Private
Industry Workers, National Compensation Survey, March 2014" (U.S.
Department of Labor, 2014), http://www.bls.gov/ncs/ebs/benefits/2014

/ownership/civilian/table32a.htm; U.S. Bureau of Labor Statistics, "Employee Benefits in the United States—March 2015" (Washington, DC: U.S. Department of Labor), accessed August 19, 2015, http://www.bls.gov/news .release/pdf/ebs2.pdf; National Partnership for Women and Families, "Quick Facts," *Support Paid Sick Days*, accessed July 11, 2014, http://paidsickdays .nationalpartnership.org/site/PageServer?pagename=psd_toolkit_quickfacts.

45 Rachel L. Swarns, "Some Retail Workers Find Better Deals with Unions," *New York Times*, September 7, 2014, http://www.nytimes.com/2014/09/08 /nyregion/some-retail-workers-find-better-deals-with-unions.html; Janelle Jones, John Schmitt, and Nicole Woo, "Women, Working Families, and Unions" (Center for Economic and Policy Research, June 2014), http://www .cepr.net/index.php/publications/reports/women-working-families-and -unions.

46 "McDonald's Hourly Pay," *Glassdoor*, accessed October 31, 2014, http://www .glassdoor.com/Hourly-Pay/McDonald-s-Hourly-Pay-E432.htm; Bryce Covert, "McDonald's Fires Mom Who Was Arrested for Letting 9-Year-Old Play in Park Alone," *ThinkProgress*, accessed August 1, 2014, http:// thinkprogress.org/economy/2014/07/22/3462704/debra-harrell-fired/.

IV. Soaring above and Sounding the Alarm

1 Heather Boushey, John Schmitt, and Kavya Vaghul's analysis of the CEPR extracts of the CPS Annual Social and Economic Supplement. See Appendix for more information on data and methods.

2 See, for example, Beau Yarbrough, "Etiwanda After-School Late Fees Five Times as High as Malibu's," *Inland Valley Daily Bulletin*, April 21, 2015, http://www.dailybulletin.com/social-affairs/20150421/etiwanda-after-school -late-fees-five-times-as-high-as-malibus.

3 All quotes from Anne-Marie Slaughter, "Why Women Still Can't Have It All," *Atlantic*, August 2012, http://www.theatlantic.com/magazine/archive /2012/07/why-women-still-cant-have-it-all/309020/. See also her book *Unfinished Business: Women Men Work Family* (New York: Random House, 2015).

4 Sheryl Sandberg, *Lean In: Women, Work, and the Will to Lead* (New York: Alfred A. Knopf, 2013).

5 M. Greene, R. Perry, and M. Lindell, "The March 1980 Eruptions of Mt. St. Helens: Citizen Perceptions of Volcano Threat," *Disasters* 5, no. 1 (March 1981): 49–66; San Diego State University, "Mount St. Helens Eruption (1980)," *How Volcanoes Work*, accessed April 11, 2015, http://www .geology.sdsu.edu/how_volcanoes_work/Sthelens.html.

6 Jacob S. Hacker and Paul Pierson, *Winner-Take-All Politics: How Washington Made the Rich Richer and Turned Its Back on the Middle Class* (New York: Simon & Schuster, 2010), 19. On economic mobility in the United States, see Raj Chetty et al., "Where Is the Land of Opportunity? The Geography of Intergenerational Mobility in the United States," Working Paper (Cam-

bridge, MA: National Bureau of Economic Research, January 2014), http://www.nber.org/papers/w19843; Miles Corak, "Income Inequality, Equality of Opportunity, and Intergenerational Mobility," *Journal of Economic Perspectives* 27, no. 3 (August 2013): 79–102.

7 The college wage premium is from Lawrence Mishel et al., "Table 4.14—Hourly Wages by Education, 1973–2011 (2011 Dollars)," in *The State of Working America*, 12th ed. (Ithaca, NY: Cornell University Press, 2012), http://stateofworkingamerica.org/chart/swa-wages-table-4–14-hourly-wages -education/. On technological change, see Claudia Dale Goldin and Lawrence F Katz, *The Race between Education and Technology* (Cambridge, MA: Belknap Press of Harvard University Press, 2010); Erik Brynjolfsson, Andrew McAfee, and Jeff Cummings, *The Second Machine Age: Work, Progress, and Prosperity in a Time of Brilliant Technologies*, MP3 Una edition (Brilliance Audio, 2014).

8 Heather Boushey, John Schmitt, and Kavya Vaghul's analysis of the CEPR extracts of the CPS Annual Social and Economic Supplement. See Appendix for more information on data and methods. For incomes of those in the top 1 percent, see Thomas Piketty and Emmanuel Saez, "Income Inequality in the United States, 1913–1998," *Quarterly Journal of Economics* 118, no. 1 (February 2003): 1–39.

9 Facundo Alvaredo et al., "The World Top Incomes Database," 2012, http://g-mond.parisschoolofeconomics.eu/topincomes; David Howell, "The Great Laissez-Faire Experiment" (Washington, DC: Center for American Progress, December 4, 2013), https://www.americanprogress.org/issues /economy/report/2013/12/04/80408/the-great-laissez-faire-experiment/.

10 Carter C. Price, "Who Are Today's Supermanagers and Why Are They So Wealthy?," July 16, 2014, http://equitablegrowth.org/research/todays -supermanagers-wealthy/.

11 Thomas Piketty, *Capital in the Twenty-First Century*, trans. Arthur Goldhammer (Cambridge, MA: Harvard University Press, 2014), 332.

12 Kimberly D. Elsbach, Dan M. Cable, and Jeffrey W. Sherman, "How Passive 'Face Time' Affects Perceptions of Employees: Evidence of Spontaneous Trait Inference," *Human Relations* 63, no. 6 (June 1, 2010): 735–760, doi:10.1177/0018726709353139; Maura Thomas, "Your Late-Night Emails Are Hurting Your Team," *Harvard Business Review*, March 16, 2015, https://hbr.org/2015/03/your-late-night-emails-are-hurting-your-team. See also, for example: Nicholas Bloom, "To Raise Productivity, Let More Employees Work from Home," *Harvard Business Review*, January 2014, https://hbr.org/2014/01/to-raise-productivity-let-more-employees-work-from -home; Erin Reid, "Why Some Men Pretend to Work 80-Hour Weeks," *Harvard Business Review*, April 28, 2015, https://hbr.org/2015/04/why-some -men-pretend-to-work-80-hour-weeks.

13 Data on hours from Heather Boushey, John Schmitt, and Kavya Vaghul's analysis of the CEPR extracts of the CPS Annual Social and Economic

Supplement. See Appendix for more information on data and methods. See also Joan C. Williams and Heather Boushey, "The Three Faces of Work-Family Conflict: The Poor, the Privileged, and the Missing Middle" (Washington, DC: Center for American Progress and the Center for WorkLife Law, University of California, Hastings College of the Law, 2010), https://cdn.americanprogress.org/wp-content/uploads/issues/2010/01 /pdf/threefaces.pdf; Jerry Jacobs and Kathleen Gerson, *The Time Divide: Work, Family, and Gender Inequality* (Cambridge, MA: Harvard University Press, 2005).

14 See U.S. Wage and Hour Division, "Handy Reference Guide to the Fair Labor Standards Act" (U.S. Department of Labor, September 2010), http://www.dol.gov/whd/regs/compliance/hrg.htm; U.S. Wage and Hour Division, "Fact Sheet #17A: Exemption for Executive, Administrative, Professional, Computer & Outside Sales Employees under the Fair Labor Standards Act (FLSA)" (U.S. Department of Labor, July 2008), http://www .dol.gov/whd/regs/compliance/fairpay/fs17a_overview.pdf; Accreditation Council for Graduate Medical Education, "Common Program Require-ments," July 1, 2011, https://www.acgme.org/acgmeweb/Portals/0/PDFs /Common_Program_Requirements_07012011%5B2%5D.pdf; U.S. Govern-ment Publishing Office, *E-CFR: Title 14: Aeronautics and Space, Part 91—General Operating and Flight Rules, Subpart K—Fractional Ownership Operations, Electronic Code of Federal Regulations*, accessed July 28, 2015, http://www.ecfr.gov/cgi-bin/text-idx?SID=ca9f20ece6a9d0ff90 d84ec2f2bf2fef&mc=true&node=se14.2.91_11059&rgn=div8.

15 Sarah Jane Glynn and Jane Farrell, "Workers Deserve Equal Access to Paid Leave and Workplace Flexibility" (Washington DC: Center for American Progress, November 2012), Fig. 3A, http://www.americanprogress.org/issues /labor/report/2012/11/20/45589/workers-deserve-equal-access-to-paid-leave -and-workplace-flexibility/.

16 Amy Richman, Arlene Johnson, and Karen Noble, "Business Impacts of Flexibility: An Imperative for Expansion" (Washington, DC: Corporate Voices for Working Families, 2011), https://www.wfd.com/PDFS/Business ImpactsofFlexibility_March2011.pdf; Jessica Toonkel Marquez, "The Perfect Fit," *Workforce Management*, January 2010, https://latticemcc.com/downloads /PDFs/WorkforceManagement_ThePerfectFit.pdf; Cathleen Benko and Anne Weisberg, *Mass Career Customization: Aligning the Workplace with Today's Nontraditional Workforce*, 1st ed. (Boston, MA: Harvard Business Review Press, 2007).

17 Sandberg, *Lean In.*

18 Pamela Stone and Meg Lovejoy, "Fast-Track Women and the 'Choice to Stay Home,'" *Annals of the American Academy of Political and Social Science* 596 (November 2004): 62–83.

19 Joan C. Williams, Jessica Manvell, and Stephanie Bornstein, "'Opt Out' or Pushed Out?: How the Press Covers Work / Family Conflict" (University of California, Hastings College of the Law, the Center for WorkLife Law, 2006).

20 "Dink," *Urban Dictionary*, accessed March 27, 2015, http://www.urban dictionary.com/define.php?term=dink; Steven P. Martin, "Delayed Marriage and Childbearing: Implications and Measurement of Diverging Trends in Family Timing," Working Paper (Russell Sage Foundation, October 2002).

21 Bureau of Labor Statistics, "America's Young Adults at 27: Labor Market Activity, Education, and Household Composition: Results from a Longitudinal Survey Summary" (Washington, DC: United States Department of Labor, March 26, 2014), http://www.bls.gov/news.release/pdf/nlsyth.pdf; Judith Warner, "The Women's Leadership Gap: Women's Leadership by the Numbers" (Washington, DC: Center for American Progress, March 7, 2014), http://cdn.americanprogress.org/wp-content/uploads/2014 /03/WomenLeadership.pdf; U.S. Bureau of Labor Statistics, "Women in the Labor Force: A Databook" (Washington DC: U.S. Department of Labor, February 2013); U.S. Bureau of Labor Statistics, "Table 11. Employed Persons by Detailed Occupation, Sex, Race, and Hispanic or Latino Ethnicity," Labor Force Statistics from the Current Population Survey (Washington, DC, February 12, 2015), http://www.bls.gov/cps/cpsaat11.htm.

22 Robert D. Mare, "Five Decades of Educational Assortative Mating," *American Sociological Review* 56, no. 1 (February 1, 1991): 15–32; Claudia Goldin, "The Long Road to the Fast Track: Career and Family," NBER Working Paper Series (Cambridge, MA: National Bureau of Economic Research, March 2004), http://scholar.harvard.edu/files/goldin/files/the_long _road_to_the_fast_track_career_and_family.pdf.

23 Sarah Jane Glynn's analysis of the Annual Social and Economic Supplement. See Appendix for more information on data and methods.

24 Susan Patton, "Letter to the Editor: Advice for the Young Women of Princeton: The Daughters I Never Had," *Daily Princetonian*, March 29, 2013, http://dailyprincetonian.com/opinion/2013/03/letter-to-the-editor -advice-for-the-young-women-of-princeton-the-daughters-i-never-had/.

25 Sandberg, *Lean In*, chap. 5. Sadly, we've just learned of the death of Sandberg's husband, David Goldberg, which is made all the more heartbreaking given how much Sandberg shared of their partnership.

26 Suzanne M. Bianchi, John P. Robinson, and Melissa A. Milkie, *Changing Rhythms of American Family Life* (New York: Russell Sage Foundation, 2006); Stephanie Coontz, "Sharing the Load," in *The Shriver Report: A Woman's Nation Changes Everything*, ed. Ann O'Leary and Heather Boushey (Washington, DC: Center for American Progress, 2009). On

1970s feminist perspectives, see Shulamith Firestone, *The Dialectic of Sex: The Case for Feminist Revolution* (New York: Farrar, Straus and Giroux, 2003).

27 *Meet the Press Netcast: Jarrett, Dodd, Kyl, Shriver, Podesta*, accessed March 14, 2015, http://www.nbcnews.com/video/meet-the-press-netcast /33368508.

28 Sara McLanahan, "Diverging Destinies: How Children Are Faring under the Second Demographic Transition," *Demography* 41, no. 4 (2004): 607–627, doi:10.1353/dem.2004.0033. According to data from Andrew Cherlin, Elizabeth Talbert, and Suzumi Yasutake, among women aged twenty-six to thirty-one who gave birth by 2011, of those with a college degree, less than one in three women was unmarried, compared with 63 percent of those without a college degree. Andrew J. Cherlin, Elizabeth Talbert, and Suzumi Yasutake, "Changing Fertility Regimes and the Transition to Adulthood: Evidence from a Recent Cohort" (Johns Hopkins University, May 3, 2014).

29 Annette Lareau, *Unequal Childhoods: Class, Race, and Family Life*, 2nd ed. (Berkeley, CA: University of California Press, 2011).

30 Marc H. Simon and Matthew Makar, *Nursery University*, Documentary (2009). See also Institute for Human Development, "Expanding Preschool in New York City—Lifting Poor Children or Middling Families?" (Washington, DC: University of Berkeley, February 2015), Fig. 1, http://gse.berkeley .edu/sites/default/files/users/bruce-fuller/NYC_PreK_Expansion_Berkeley _Study_25_Feb_2015.pdf; Susan Dominus, "Cutthroat Preschool Ritual Isn't Like Prison, or Is It?," *New York Times*, November 14, 2008, sec. New York Region.

31 Garey Ramey and Valerie Ramey, "The Rug Rat Race" (San Diego, CA: University of San Diego, April 2010), http://econ.ucsd.edu/~vramey/research /Rugrat.pdf. Overall, they found that the time spent on child care by the entire adult population in 2008 was equal to nearly 20 percent of the time spent on work. See also Stacy Dale and Alan B. Krueger, "Estimating the Return to College Selectivity over the Career Using Administrative Earnings Data," Working Paper (Cambridge, MA: National Bureau of Economic Research, June 2011), http://www.nber.org/papers/w17159.

32 Charles Tilly, *Durable Inequality* (Berkeley and Los Angeles, CA: University of California Press, 1998); Richard V. Reeves and Kimberly Howard, "The Glass Floor: Education, Downward Mobility, and Opportunity Hoarding" (Washington, DC: Brookings Institution, November 2013), http://www .brookings.edu/~/media/research/files/papers/2013/11/glass-floor-downward -mobility-equality-opportunity-hoarding-reeves-howard/glass-floor-downward -mobility-equality-opportunity-hoarding-reeves-howard.pdf.

33 Adam Seth Levine, Robert H. Frank, and Oege Dijk, "Expenditure Cascades," SSRN Scholarly Paper (Rochester, NY: Social Science Research

Network, September 13, 2010), http://papers.ssrn.com/abstract=1690612. See also Marianne Bertrand and Adair Morse, "Trickle-Down Consumption," Working Paper (Cambridge, MA: National Bureau of Economic Research, March 2013), http://www.nber.org/papers/w18883; N. Gregory Mankiw et al., "I Just Got Here, but I Know Trouble When I See It," *New York Times*, 2011, http://www.nytimes.com/2012/01/01/business/from-6-economists-6-ways-to -face-2012-economic-view.html?pagewanted=all; Thorstein Veblen, *The Theory of the Leisure Class* (New York: Penguin Classics, 1994).

34 While Cooper's categories are not the same as mine, the high-income families she profiles seem to fit my definitions, that is, they have income in the top quintile and at least one person with a college degree. See Marianne Cooper, *Cut Adrift: Families in Insecure Times* (Oakland, CA: University of California Press, 2014), 97.

35 See Williams and Boushey, "The Three Faces of Work-Family Conflict," Fig. 3.

36 Randy Schnepf, "Consumers and Food Price Inflation" (Washington, DC: Congressional Research Service, September 13, 2014), http://fas.org/sgp/crs /misc/R40545.pdf.

37 Rachel E. Dwyer, "The Care Economy? Gender, Economic Restructuring, and Job Polarization in the U.S. Labor Market," *American Sociological Review* 78, no. 3 (June 2013): 410.

38 Martin Gilens and Benjamin I. Page, "Testing Theories of American Politics: Elites, Interest Groups, and Average Citizens," *Perspectives on Politics* 12, no. 3 (September 2014): 564–581.

V. Thinking Like an Economist

1 Jill Colvin, "Paid Sick Leave Gathers Momentum in New Jersey," *Daily Record*, December 27, 2014, http://www.dailyrecord.com/story/news/local /2014/12/27/paid-sick-leave-gathers-momentum-new-jersey/20939213/. See also National Partnership for Women and Families, "State and Local Action on Paid Sick Days" (Washington, DC, July 2015), http://www.national partnership.org/research-library/campaigns/psd/state-and-local-action-paid -sick-days.pdf.

2 Patrick McGeehan, "Council Speaker Shelves a Sick-Leave Bill," *New York Times*, October 14, 2010, http://www.nytimes.com/2010/10/15/nyregion /15sick.html.

3 Nancy Rankin, "Paid Sick Days: Support Grows for a Work Standard Most Low-Wage Earners Still Lack in New York City," The Unheard Third 2012: CSS Policy Update (New York: Community Service Society, October 2012), http://b.3cdn.net/nycss/c061ce1681b7950b87_nzm6i2o1l.pdf, Chart 3.

4 McGeehan, "Council Speaker Shelves a Sick-Leave Bill."

5 New York City Council, Christine C. Quinn, Speaker, "Council Speaker Christine C. Quinn's Prepared Remarks on Proposed Paid Sick Leave

Legislation," October 14, 2010, http://council.nyc.gov/html/pr/10_15_10
_paid_sick.shtml.

6 Ginia Bellafante, "Why Quinn Angers Voters," *New York Times*, September
   5, 2013, http://www.nytimes.com/2013/09/08/nyregion/why-quinn-angers
   -voters.html.

7 Or, as Nobel Laureate Paul Krugman put it, "a country is not a company."
   Paul Krugman, "A Country Is Not a Company," *Harvard Business Review*,
   February 1996.

8 Community Service Society of New York, "The Impact of Paid Sick Days on
   Jobs: What's the Real Story? Highlights from a Policy Roundtable Discussion
   Hosted by the Community Service Society of New York" (New York:
   Community Service Society of New York, September 2012), http://b.3cdn
   .net/nycss/d53aaf5763daaa089b_8bm6bluvr.pdf.

9 For simplicity, this model leaves out international trade and government.
   Figure 5.1 is from Karl E. Case and Ray C. Fair, *Principles of Microeco-
   nomics*, 8th ed. (Upper Saddle River, NJ: Prentice Hall, 2006).

10 See Bureau of Economic Analysis, "Table 1.1.5. Gross Domestic Product:
    National Income and Product Accounts," January 30, 2015, http://www.bea
    .gov/national/pdf/SNTables.pdf.

11 Bureau of Economic Analysis, "Table 2.3.5. Personal Consumption
    Expenditures by Major Type of Product: National Income and Product
    Accounts Tables" (U.S. Department of Commerce, January 30, 2015),
    http://www.bea.gov/iTable/iTable.cfm?ReqID=9&step=1#reqid=9&step=3
    &isuri=1&903=65.

12 Author's calculation of the share of adjusted gross income (less than
    $100,000 a year) from salaries and wages. Includes returns with no adjusted
    gross income. See Internal Revenue Service, "Table 1. All Returns: Sources
    of Income, Adjustments, Deductions and Exemptions, by Size of Adjusted
    Gross Income, Tax Year 2011," n.d., http://www.irs.gov/uac/SOI-Tax-Stats
    -Individual-Income-Tax-Returns.

13 U.S. Bureau of Economic Analysis, "Personal Saving Rate [PSAVERT],
    Retrieved from FRED, Federal Reserve Bank of St. Louis," accessed July 13,
    2015, https://research.stlouisfed.org/fred2/series/PSAVERT/; Atif Mian
    and Amir Sufi, "Consumers and the Economy, Part II: Household Debt
    and the Weak U.S. Recovery," *Economic Letter* 2011–02 (January 18, 2011),
    http://www.frbsf.org/economic-research/publications/economic-letter/2011
    /january/consumers-economy-household-debt-weak-us-recovery/; Atif Mian
    and Amir Sufi, *House of Debt: How They (and You) Caused the Great
    Recession, and How We Can Prevent It from Happening Again* (Chicago,
    IL: University of Chicago Press, 2014); Federal Reserve Bank of New York,
    "Quarterly Report on Household Debt and Credit" (New York, February
    2015), http://www.newyorkfed.org/householdcredit/2014-q4/data/pdf
    /HHDC_2014Q4.pdf.

14 On reemployment after being laid off, see Henry S. Farber, "Job Loss in the Great Recession: Historical Perspective from the Displaced Workers Survey, 1984–2010," Working Paper (Cambridge, Massachusetts: National Bureau of Economic Research, May 2011), http://www.nber.org/papers/w17040. See also Mian and Sufi, *House of Debt*.

15 William A. Galston, "How to Reverse the Looming Economic Slide," *Wall Street Journal*, February 10, 2015, sec. Opinion, http://www.wsj.com/articles/william-galston-how-to-reverse-the-looming-economic-slide-1423614007; Eileen Appelbaum, Heather Boushey, and John Schmitt, "The Economic Importance of Women's Rising Hours of Work" (Washington, DC: Center for Economic and Policy Research and Center for American Progress, April 2014).

16 Adam Smith, *An Inquiry into the Nature and Causes of the Wealth of Nations*, 1776.

17 Francine D. Blau and Lawrence M. Kahn, "Female Labor Supply: Why Is the US Falling Behind?" (Bonn, Germany: Institute for the Study of Labor, January 2013). Labor supply rankings are author's calculation for 2013 for countries within the Organisation for Economic Co-operation and Development as of January 2010 from "OECD.StatsExtracts," 2015, http://stats.oecd.org/.

18 Researchers like the sociologist Arlie Hochschild have well documented that working women have long faced a "second shift," putting in a full day at work, then taking on all the care and housework at home. See Jason Furman, "The Economics of Fatherhood and Work" (Council of Economic Advisers, Washington, DC, June 9, 2014), http://www.whitehouse.gov/sites/default/files/docs/working_fathers_presentation.pdf; Arlie Russell Hochschild and Anne Machung, *The Second Shift* (New York: Penguin USA, 2003); Jacob Alex Klerman, Kelly Daley, and Alyssa Pozniak, "Family and Medical Leave in 2012: Technical Report" (Cambridge, MA: Abt Associates Inc., September 7, 2012), Fig. 7.2.3, http://www.dol.gov/asp/evaluation/fmla/FMLA-2012-Technical-Report.pdf.

19 James J. Heckman, "Schools, Skills, and Synapses," Working Paper (National Bureau of Economic Research, June 2008), http://www.nber.org/papers/w14064; James J. Heckman and Lakshmi K. Raut, "Intergenerational Long Term Effects of Preschool—Structural Estimates from a Discrete Dynamic Programming Model," NBER Working Paper (National Bureau of Economic Research, May 2013), http://www.nber.org/papers/w19077.

20 See Centre for Families, Work & Well-Being, "The Effects of Father Involvement: An Updated Research Summary of the Evidence Inventory" (Guelph, Ontario, Canada: University of Guelph, 2007); Paul Raeburn, *Do Fathers Matter?: What Science Is Telling Us about the Parent We've Overlooked* (New York Scientific American / Farrar, Straus and Giroux, 2014); Paul Raeburn, "How Fathers Boost Toddlers' Language Development," *Today*,

June 10, 2014, http://www.today.com/parents/how-fathers-boost-toddlers
-language-development-2D79783877; Nadya Pancsofar and Lynne Vernon-
Feagans, "Children Living in Rural Poverty: The Continuation of the Family
Life Project," *Early Childhood Research Quarterly* 25 (2010): 450–463.

21 Person hours are from author's analysis of U.S. Bureau of Labor Statistics,
"Employment, Hours, and Earnings from the Current Employment
Statistics Survey, Series ID CES0500000002" (Washington, DC, July
2015); U.S. Bureau of Labor Statistics, "Employment, Hours, and Earnings
from the Current Employment Statistics Survey, Series ID CES0500000001"
(Washington, DC, July 2015).

22 Estimated value for productivity. See Organisation for Economic Co-Operation
and Development, "Level of GDP per Capita and Productivity," *OECD.
StatExtracts*, n.d., http://stats.oecd.org/Index.aspx?DataSetCode=PDB_LV.

23 George A. Akerlof and Janet Yellen, *Efficiency Wage Models of the Labor
Market* (Cambridge, MA: Cambridge University Press, 1986); Joseph E.
Stiglitz, "Theories of Wage Rigidity," Working Paper (Cambridge, MA:
National Bureau of Economic Research, 1984), http://www.nber.org/papers
/w1442.pdf. See also Kenneth Matos and Ellen Galinsky, "2014 National
Study of Employers" (New York: Families and Work Institute, 2014), Table 23;
MetLife, "Benefits Breakthrough: How Employees and Their Employers
Are Navigating an Evolving Environment," Annual U.S. Employee
Benefit Trends Study (New York: MetLife, 2014), https://benefittrends
.metlife.com/assets/downloads/benefits-breakthrough-summaries-2014
.pdf; MetLife, "Boosting the Retention Power of Benefits around the
Globe," 2014 & 2015 Employee Benefit Trends Study, n.d.; MetLife, "8th
Annual Study of Employee Benefits Trends: Findings from the National
Survey of Employers and Employees," 2010.

24 Of course, this doesn't take into account the differences in labor costs across
countries. The reality is that the United States is far behind other countries
in providing work-life benefits, so for the most part the United States is
catching up rather than moving ahead of other countries. Even so, as U.S.
labor costs rise because of new benefits, the relative price of labor will rise.

25 Walter F. Stewart et al., "Lost Productive Work Time Costs from Health
Conditions in the United States: Results from the American Productivity
Audit," *Journal of Occupational and Environmental Medicine / American
College of Occupational and Environmental Medicine* 45, no. 12 (December
2003): 1234–1246, doi:10.1097/01.jom.0000099999.27348.78.

26 Heather Boushey and Sarah Jane Glynn, "There Are Significant Costs
to Replacing Employees" (Washington, DC: Center for American
Progress, November 16, 2012), http://www.americanprogress.org/issues
/labor/report/2012/11/16/44464/there-are-significant-business-costs-to
-replacing-employees/.

27 PwC, "2008/2009 US Human Capital Effectiveness Report Executive Summary," US Human Capital Effectiveness Report, 2008, http://www .pwc.com/en_US/us/hr-saratoga/assets/human_capital_effectiveness_report _0809.pdf; Boushey and Glynn, "There Are Significant Costs to Replacing Employees."

28 Michelle M. Arthur and Alison Cook, "Taking Stock of Work-Family Initiatives: How Announcements of 'Family-Friendly' Human Resource Decisions Affect Shareholder Value," *ILR Review* 57, no. 4 (July 2004): 599–613, http://digitalcommons.ilr.cornell.edu/cgi/viewcontent.cgi?article =1099&context=ilrreview; Christine Siegwarth Meyer, Swati Mukerjee, and Ann Sestero, "Work-Family Benefits: Which Ones Maximize Profits?," *Journal of Managerial Issues* 13, no. 1 (Spring 2001): 28–44.

29 Nick Hanauer, "Raise Taxes on Rich to Reward True Job Creators," *Bloomberg View*, November 30, 2011, http://www.bloombergview.com /articles/2011–12–01/raise-taxes-on-the-rich-to-reward-job-creators-commentary -by-nick-hanauer.

30 Jean-Baptiste Say, *A Treatise on Political Economy; or the Production, Distribution, and Consumption of Wealth*, trans. C. R. Prinsep, New America Edition (Ontario, Canada: Batoche Books, 2001), 57.

31 Phil Alden Robinson, *Field of Dreams*, Drama, Family, Fantasy (1989).

32 Rich Moore, "Marge vs. the Monorail," *The Simpsons*, January 14, 1993. For a giggle, see this recent take on Seattle's monorail, which I thought was the inspiration for the plot of season 4, episode 12, not the other way around: Stuart Eskenazi, "Springfield's Advice to Seattle on Monorail: D'oh!," *Seattle Times*, July 8, 2005, http://old.seattletimes.com/html/living/2002367563 _simpsons08.html.

33 John Maynard Keynes, *The General Theory of Employment, Interest, and Money* (New York: Harcourt Brace Jovanovich, Inc., 1953), 46.

34 Daniel Raff and Lawrence Summers, "Did Henry Ford Pay Efficiency Wages?," *Journal of Labor Economics* 5, no. 4 (1987): S57–S86, http://www .jstor.org/discover/10.2307/2534911?uid=3739584&uid=2&uid=4&uid =3739256&sid=21103455575693.

35 Kim Phillips-Fein, *Invisible Hands: The Businessmen's Crusade against the New Deal*, rpt. (W. W. Norton & Company, 2010), Chap. 1.

VI. Here at Home

1 Ilana DeBare, "S. F. Businesses Scramble over Sick Leave Law," *San Francisco Chronicle*, January 12, 2007, http://www.sfgate.com/news/article /S-F-businesses-scramble-over-sick-leave-law-2657697.php.

2 Steven Greenhouse, "With the Democratic Congress, Groups Gear up for Fight over Paid Sick Days," *New York Times*, December 5, 2006, http://www .nytimes.com/2006/12/05/washington/05labor.html.

3   City and County of San Francisco, "San Francisco Paid Sick Leave Ordinance—Fact Sheet," 2007, http://sfgsa.org/modules/ShowDocument .aspx?documentid=7528.

4   Bureau of Labor Statistics, "Employer Costs for Employee Compensation— December 2014" (U.S. Department of Labor, March 11, 2015), http://www .bls.gov/news.release/pdf/ecec.pdf, Table 1; Christopher Flavelle, "Sick Leave Doesn't Hurt Business, Says Business," *BloombergView*, February 4, 2015, http://www.bloombergview.com/articles/2015–02–04/sick-leave-doesn-t-hurt -business-says-business.

5   Averages for private-sector workers only. Sick leave usage differs by industry. See Ross O. Barthold and Jason L. Ford, "Paid Sick Leave: Prevalence, Provision, and Usage among Full-Time Workers in Private Industry" (Washington, DC: Bureau of Labor Statistics, February 29, 2012); Eileen Appelbaum et al., "Good for Business? Connecticut's Paid Sick Leave Law" (Washington, DC: Center for Economic and Policy Research, February 2014), 9, http:// .cepr.net/documents/good-for-buisness-2014–02–21.pdf; Robert Drago and Vicky Lovell, "San Francisco's Paid Sick Leave Ordinance: Outcomes for Employers and Employees" (Washington, DC: Institute for Women's Policy Research, February 2011), http:// .iwpr.org /publications/pubs/San-Fran-PSD.

6   All fifty states honor employment-at-will, although all but four (Florida, Georgia, Louisiana, and Rhode Island) have statutory exceptions to the at-will doctrine. See Jane Whitney Gibson and Lester Lindley, "The Evolution of Employment-at-Will: Past, Present, and Future Predictions," *American Journal of Business Education* 3, no. 2 (February 2010): 89–100, http://www.cluteinstitute.com/ojs/index.php/AJBE/article/view/388/377. In Montana, employees are subject to at-will employment only during their probationary period. See Montana Department of Labor and Industry, "Frequently Asked Questions," accessed July 7, 2015, http://dli .mt.gov/resources/faq. On Connecticut's paid sick days program, see Appelbaum et al., "Good for Business? Connecticut's Paid Sick Leave Law."

7   Institute for Women's Policy Research, "Paid Sick Days and Employer Penalties for Absence" (Washington, DC, July 2011); Joan C. Williams, "One Sick Child Away from Being Fired: When 'Opting Out' Is Not an Option" (San Francisco, CA: Center for WorkLife Law, University of California Hastings College of the Law, 2006), http:// .worklifelaw.org/pubs /onesickchild.pdf.

8   C. S. Mott Children's Hospital, "National Poll on Children's Health: Sick Kids, Struggling Parents" (Ann Arbor, MI: University of Michigan, October 2012), http://mottnpch.org/sites/default/files/documents/10222012ChildCa- reIllness.pdf. See also S. Jody Heymann, Alison Earle, and Brian Egleston, "Parental Availability for the Care of Sick Children," *Pediatrics* 98, no. 2 (August 1, 1996): 226–230, http://pediatrics.aappublications.org/content

/98/2/226; Jody Heymann, *Forgotten Families: Ending the Growing Crisis Confronting Children and Working Parents in the Global Economy* (Oxford: Oxford University Press, 2006); S. J. Palmer, "Care of Sick Children by Parents: A Meaningful Role," *Journal of Advanced Nursing* 18, no. 2 (February 1993): 185–191; M. R. Taylor and P. O'Connor, "Resident Parents and Shorter Hospital Stay," *Archives of Disease in Childhood* 64, no. 2 (February 1989): 274–276.

9 Drago and Lovell, "San Francisco's Paid Sick Leave Ordinance: Outcomes for Employers and Employees," 17.

10 Seattle Coalition for a Healthy Workforce, "WSJ Article: Small Business Owners Write in to Support Paid Sick Days," May 24, 2011, http:// seattlehealthyworkforce.org/2011/05/24/wsj-article-small-business-owners -write-in-to-support-paid-sick-days/. See Emily Maltby, "Seattle Considers Mandatory Paid Sick Leave," *WSJ Blogs*, May 19, 2011, http://blogs.wsj.com /in-charge/2011/05/19/seattle-considers-mandatory-paid-sick-leave/.

11 Sundar S. Shrestha et al., "Estimating the Burden of 2009 Pandemic Influenza A (H1N1) in the United States (April 2009–April 2010)," *Clinical Infectious Diseases* 52 (January 1, 2011): S75–82, http://cid.oxfordjournals. org/content/52/suppl_1/S75; Robert Drago and Kevin Miller, "Sick at Work: Infected Employees in the Workplace during the H1N1 Pandemic," Briefing Paper (Washington, DC: Institute for Women's Policy Research, February 2010); Drago and Lovell, "San Francisco's Paid Sick Leave Ordinance: Outcomes for Employers and Employees."

12 For the most recent breakdowns of who has access to paid sick days, see U.S. Bureau of Labor Statistics, "Employee Benefits in the United States— March 2015" (Washington, DC: U.S Department of Labor), accessed August 19, 2015, http://www.bls.gov/news.release/pdf/ebs2.pdf.

13 Aaron Rutkoff, "Will Sick Days Cost Billions for NYC Businesses? San Francisco Says No," *WSJ Blogs—Metropolis*, May 13, 2010, http://blogs.wsj .com/metropolis/2010/05/13/will-sick-days-costs-billions-for-businesses-san-fra ncisco-says-no/.

14 Rachel L. Swarns, "Despite Business Fears, Sick-Day Laws Like New York's Work Well Elsewhere," *New York Times*, January 26, 2014, http://www. nytimes.com/2014/01/27/nyregion/despite-business-fears-sick-day-laws-like -new-yorks-work-well-elsewhere.html.

15 Between 2006 and 2007, civilian employment increased 4.0 percent in San Francisco, and 1.4 percent in the surrounding counties. Kevin Miller and Sarah Towne, "San Francisco Employment Growth Remains Stronger with Paid Sick Days Law Than Surrounding Counties" (Washington, DC: Institute for Women's Policy Research, September 2011). On the growth in business establishments, see John Petro, "Paid Sick Leave Does Not Harm Business Growth or Job Growth" (New York: Drum Major Institute for Public Policy, 2011).

16 Seattle Coalition for a Healthy Workforce, "WSJ Article"; See Maltby, "Seattle Considers Mandatory Paid Sick Leave."

17 Paolo Lucchesi, "West Portal Staple Village Grill to Close, Become Toast Eatery," *Inside Scoop SF,* May 19, 2014, http://insidescoopsf.sfgate.com/blog/2014/05/19/west-portal-staple-village-grill-to-close-become-toast-eatery/.

18 As of August 5, 2015, the four states are Connecticut (2011) (dates are as of passage, not necessarily implementation); Massachusetts and California (2014); and Oregon (2015). The municipalities are San Francisco, CA (2006); Washington, DC (2008); Seattle, WA (2011); Portland, OR, New York City, NY, and Jersey City, NJ (2013); Newark, Passaic, Paterson, East Orange, Irvington, Montclair, and Trenton, NJ, Portland and Eugene, OR, and San Diego and Oakland, CA (2014); Tacoma, WA, Philadelphia and Pittsburgh, PA, and Bloomfield, NJ (2015). National Partnership for Women and Families, "State and Local Action on Paid Sick Days" (Washington, DC, July 2015), http://www.nationalpartnership.org/research-library/campaigns/psd/state-and-local-action-paid-sick-days.pdf.

19 See the studies by Jennifer Romich et al., "Implementation and Early Outcomes of the City of Seattle Paid Sick and Safe Time Ordinance" (University of Washington, April 23, 2014); Appelbaum et al., "Good for Business? Connecticut's Paid Sick Leave Law"; Office of the District of Columbia Auditor, "Audit of the Accrued Sick and Safe Leave Act of 2008" (Washington, DC, June 19, 2013), http://dcauditor.org/sites/default/files/DCA092013.pdf.

20 Fore more information on paid sick days laws, see National Partnership for Women and Families, "Paid Sick Days Statutes" (Washington, DC: National Partnership for Women and Families, April 2015), http://www.nationalpartnership.org/research-library/work-family/psd/paid-sick-days-statutes.pdf.

21 Bill Clinton, "Remarks at the Signing of the Family Medical Leave Act," February 5, 1993, http://millercenter.org/president/clinton/speeches/speech-4562.

22 Dorothy E. McBride and Janine A. Parry, *Women's Rights in the USA: Policy Debates and Gender Roles* (New York: Routledge, 2014), 236.

23 Jane Waldfogel, "Family Leave Coverage in the 1990s," *Monthly Labor Review* 10 (October 1999): 13–21; Jane Waldfogel, "The Impact of the Family and Medical Leave Act," *Journal of Policy Analysis and Management* 18 (1999): 281–303; see also Sandra L. Hofferth and Sally C. Curtin, "Parental Leave Statutes and Maternal Return to Work after Childbirth in the United States," *Work and Occupations* 33 (2006): 73–105.

24 Jacob Alex Klerman, Kelly Daley, and Alyssa Pozniak, "Family and Medical Leave in 2012: Technical Report" (Cambridge, MA: Abt Associates Inc., September 7, 2012), ii, http:// .dol.gov/asp/evaluation/fmla/FMLA-2012-Technical-Report.pdf. On the instability of family income more generally, see Gregory Acs, Pamela Loprest, and Austin Nichols, "Risk and Recovery: Documenting the Changing Risks to Family Incomes," Brief (Washington,

DC: The Urban Institute, May 2009); Gregory Acs, Pamela Loprest, and Austin Nichols, "Risk and Recovery: Understanding the Changing Risks to Family Incomes," Low-Income Working Families (Washington, DC: The Urban Institute, October 2009).

25 On private temporary disability insurance, see Workplace Flexibility 2010 and Urban Institute, "Fact Sheet on Extended Time Off (EXTO)" (Washington, DC, February 16, 2011), http://workplaceflexibility2010.org/images /uploads/EXTO_Fact_Sheet.pdf. On state temporary disability insurance programs, see Social Security Administration, "Social Security Programs in the United States—Temporary Disability Insurance," accessed July 16, 2013, http://www.ssa.gov/policy/docs/progdesc/sspus/tempdib.pdf. Author's calculations of the share of the female populations, ages twenty and over, of California, Hawaii, New Jersey, New York, and Rhode Island divided by total U.S. female population, ages twenty and over, from U.S. Census Bureau, "Population Estimates," accessed April 27, 2015, http://www.census. gov/popest/data/index.html. Hawaii, New Jersey, and New York offer a maximum of twenty-six weeks, Rhode Island offers a maximum of thirty weeks, and California offers a maximum of fifty-two weeks of temporary disability insurance. However, workers typically do not take the full amount of time. Additionally, workers in Rhode Island, New Jersey, and California who are eligible for family leave are able to take paid leave up to a maximum of four weeks (Rhode Island) or six weeks (California and New Jersey). See National Partnership for Women and Families, "Expecting Better: A State-by-State Analysis of Laws That Help New Parents," June 2014.

26 For data on access to paid leave nationwide, see U.S. Bureau of Labor Statistics, "Table 32. Leave Benefits: Access, Private Industry Workers, National Compensation Survey, March 2014" (U.S. Department of Labor, 2014), http://www.bls.gov/ncs/ebs/benefits/2014/ownership/civilian/table32a .htm. On Google's announcement, see Susan Wojcicki, "Paid Maternity Leave Is Good for Business," *Wall Street Journal*, December 16, 2014, sec. Opinion, http://www.wsj.com/articles/susan-wojcicki-paid-maternity-leave-is -good-for-business-1418773756. On Netflix, see Marlee Moseley, "Starting Now at Netflix: Unlimited Maternity and Paternity Leave," *Netflix US and Canada Blog*, accessed August 13, 2015, http://blog.netflix.com/2015/08/start ing-now-at-netflix-unlimited.html; Bryce Covert, "This Pregnant Netflix Employee Won't Get Any Paid Maternity Leave," *ThinkProgress*, accessed August 13, 2015, http://thinkprogress.org/economy/2015/08/12/3690718/netflix -family-leave-left-out/.

27 See Ann O'Leary, "How Family Leave Laws Left out Low-Income Workers," *Berkeley Journal of Employment and Labor Law* 28, no. 1 (2007): 1–62, http://www.law.berkeley.edu/files/OLearyArticle-BJELL.pdf. For data on paid maternity leave, see Tallese Johnson, "Maternity Leave and Employment Patterns of First-Time Mothers: 1961–2003" (Washington, DC: U.S.

Department of Commerce Economics and Statistics Administration, February 2008), https://www.census.gov/prod/2008pubs/p70–113.pdf. The Employee Retirement Income Security Act of 1974 sets minimum standards for pension plans in private industry, requiring that an employer that provides a retirement plan to some employees must provide the same plan to employees generally. See *Employee Retirement Income Security Act of 1974*, 1974, http://legcounsel.house.gov/Comps/Employee%20Retirement%20 Income%20Security%20Act%20Of%201974.pdf. In a study of the Fortune 100, the Joint Economic Committee found that "many firms responded with a minimum and maximum number of weeks of paid leave, depending on the employee's job category or tenure or other requirements and our analysis provides measures of both the minimum and the maximum weeks provided." See Joint Economic Committee Majority Staff, "Paid Family Leave at Fortune 100 Companies: A Basic Standard but Still Not the Gold Standard" (Washington, DC: United States Congress, March 5, 2008), 5, http://www.jec.senate.gov/archive/Documents/Reports/03.05.08PaidFamily Leave.pdf.

28 Carolyn Maloney, *Flexibility for Working Families Act*, 2013, https://www .congress.gov/bill/113th-congress/house-bill/2559; "Congressional Record" (daily edition, June 19, 2008), p. H5600; Office of the Press Secretary, "Modernizing Federal Leave Policies for Childbirth, Adoption and Foster Care to Recruit and Retain Talent and Improve Productivity" (Washington, DC: The White House, January 15, 2015), https://www.whitehouse.gov/the -press-office/2015/01/15/presidential-memorandum-modernizing-federal -leave-policies-childbirth-ad.

29 California's benefit cap is larger than a worker's median weekly wage in 2013. See National Partnership for Women and Families, "First Impressions: Comparing State Paid Family Leave Programs in Their First Years—Rhode Island's First Year of Paid Leave in Perspective," Issue Brief (Washington, DC, February 2015), http://www.nationalpartnership.org/research-library /work-family/paid-leave/first-impressions-comparing-state-paid-family-leave -programs-in-their-first-years.pdf.

30 Donald Cohen, "Chamber of Commerce Was Wrong about Family and Medical Leave Law," *Huffington Post*, February 4, 2013, http://www .huffingtonpost.com/donald-cohen/chamber-of-commerce-was-w_b_2608961 .html; John M. Broder, "Family Leave in California Now Includes Pay Benefit," *New York Times*, September 24, 2002, sec. U.S., http://www.nytimes .com/2002/09/24/us/family-leave-in-california-now-includes-pay-benefit .html; Susan K. Livio, "Divided NJ Senate Approves Family Leave Bill," *NJ .com*, April 8, 2008, http://www.nj.com/business/index.ssf/2008/04/divided _nj_senate_approves_fam.html.

31 See National Partnership for Women and Families, "First Impressions: Comparing State Paid Family Leave Programs in Their First Years—Rhode Island's First Year of Paid Leave in Perspective." Even if the tax burden is

nominally on employers (as proposed in the FAMILY Act of 2013), research indicates that the tax will be passed through to employees in the form of lower wages. For an overview of tax incidence, see Don Fullerton and Gilbert E. Metcalf, "Tax Incidence," in *Handbook of Public Economics*, ed. A. J. Auerbach and M. Feldstein, vol. 4 (Washington, DC: Elsevier Science B. V., 2002).

32 On using temporary workers, see Klerman, Daley, and Pozniak, "Family and Medical Leave in 2012: Technical Report," Exhibit 8.1.1. On increasing the probability of returning to jobs post–paid leave, see Eileen Appelbaum and Ruth Milkman, "Leaves That Pay: Employer and Worker Experiences with Paid Family Leave in California" (Washington, DC: Center for Economic and Policy Research, 2011), http://www.cepr.net/documents/publications /paid-family-leave-1–2011.pdf; Heather Boushey, "Family Friendly Policies: Helping Mothers Make Ends Meet," *Review of Social Economy* 66 (2008): 51–70.

33 Ruth Milkman and Eileen Appelbaum, *Unfinished Business: Paid Family Leave in California and the Future of U.S. Work-Family Policy* (Ithaca, NY: ILR Press, 2013), http://www.cornellpress.cornell.edu/ book/?GCOI=80140100480110; Claire Cain Miller, "Can Family Leave Policies Be Too Generous? It Seems So," *New York Times*, August 9, 2014, http://www.nytimes.com/2014/08/10/upshot/can-family-leave-policies-be-too -generous-it-seems-so.html. See also Edward Zigler, Susan Muenchow, and Christopher J. Ruhm, *Time Off with Baby: The Case for Paid Care Leave* (Washington DC: Zero to Three, 2012).

34 Linda Houser and Thomas P. Vartanian, "Pay Matters: The Positive Economic Impacts of Paid Family Leave for Families, Businesses and the Public" (New Brunswick, NJ: Center for Women and Work, January 2012), 8.

35 Organisation for Economic Co-operation and Development, "Informal Carers," in *Health at a Glance 2013*, Health at a Glance (OECD Publishing, 2013), http://www.oecd-ilibrary.org/social-issues-migration-health/health -at-a-glance-2013_health_glance-2013-en.

36 Among workers aged eighteen to twenty-five with a small child at home, 43.3 percent of women, 31.2 percent of men, 38.5 percent of whites, 48.0 percent of blacks, and 31.5 percent of Hispanics have been at their job less than a year. See Heather Boushey and John Schmitt, "Job Tenure and Firm Size Provisions Exclude Many Young Parents from Family and Medical Leave" (Washington, DC: Center for Economic and Policy Research, June 2007). On eligibility for FMLA more generally, see Klerman, Daley, and Pozniak, "Family and Medical Leave in 2012: Technical Report"; *Family and Medical Leave Act of 1993*, 1993, http://www.govtrack.us/congress /bills/103/hr1.

37 Milkman and Appelbaum, *Unfinished Business: Paid Family Leave in California and the Future of U.S. Work-Family Policy*; Tanya Byker, "The Role of Paid Parental Leave in Reducing Women's Career Interruptions:

Evidence from Paid Leave Laws in California and New Jersey," Job Market
Paper (Ann Arbor, MI: University of Michigan, April 14, 2014). On the issue
of older workers and how paid leave can improve labor-force attachment, see
MetLife Mature Market Institute, "The MetLife Study of Caregiving Costs
to Working Caregivers: Double Jeopardy for Baby Boomers Caring for Their
Parents" (Westport, CT: MetLife Mature Market Institute, June 2011); Ai-jen
Poo, *The Age of Dignity: Preparing for the Elder Boom in a Changing
America* (New York: The New Press, 2015).

38 Margarita Estévez-Abe and Tanja Hethey-Maier, "Women's Work, Family
Earnings, and Public Policy," in *Income Inequality: Economic Disparities and
the Middle Class in Affluent Countries*, ed. Janet C. Gornick and Markus
Jantti (Redwood City, CA: Stanford University Press, 2013); Boushey, "Family
Friendly Policies: Helping Mothers Make Ends Meet"; Jane Waldfogel,
"The Family Gap for Young Women in the United States and Britain: Can
Maternity Leave Make a Difference?," *Journal of Labor Economics* 16, no. 3
(1998): 505–545; Houser and Vartanian, "Pay Matters: The Positive Economic
Impacts of Paid Family Leave for Families, Businesses and the Public," 2.

39 Leonor Ehling, "California's Paid Family Leave Program: Ten Years after the
Program's Implementation, Who Has Benefited and What Has Been
Learned?" (California Senate Office of Research, July 1, 2014), http://sor
.senate.ca.gov/sites/sor.senate.ca.gov/files/Californias%20Paid%20Family%20
Leave%20Program.pdf.

40 Raquel Bernal and Anna Fruttero, "Parental Leave Policies, Intra-Household
Time Allocations and Children's Human Capital," *Journal of Population
Economics* 21, no. 4 (October 2008): 779–825. For a review of this literature,
see Heather Boushey, Ann O'Leary, and Alexandra Mitukiewicz, "The
Economic Benefits of Family and Medical Leave Insurance" (Washington,
DC: Center for American Progress, December 12, 2013), http://www
.americanprogress.org/wp-content/uploads/2013/12/PaidFamLeave-brief.pdf;
Pinka Chatterji and Sara Markowitz, "Does the Length of Maternity Leave
Affect Maternal Health?," Working Paper (January 2004), http://www.nber
.org/papers/w10206.pdf?new_window=1.

41 Karen Kornbluh, former ambassador to the Organisation for Economic
Co-Operation and Development, personal correspondence. See also Karen
Kornbluh, "Families Valued," *Democracy: A Journal of Ideas*, no. 2 (2006),
http://www.democracyjournal.org/2/6484.php?page=all.

42 Bill Clinton, "Why I Signed the Family and Medical Leave Act,"
POLITICO, February 5, 2013, http://www.politico.com/story/2013/02/the
-family-and-medical-leave-act-20-years-later-87157.html; National
Partnership for Women and Families, "The Family and Medical Leave
Act at 22: 200 Million Reasons to Celebrate and Move Forward," February
2015, http://www.nationalpartnership.org/research-library/work-family
/fmla/the-family-and-medical-leave-at-22.pdf.

43 Rosa DeLauro, *Family and Medical Insurance Leave Act*, 2015, https://www
.congress.gov/bill/114th-congress/house-bill/1439; Kirsten Gillibrand, *Family
and Medical Insurance Leave Act*, 2015, https://www.congress.gov/bill/114th
-congress/senate-bill/786. On setting up a program like this, see Heather
Boushey and Alexandra Mitukiewicz, "Family and Medical Leave Insurance: A Basic Standard for Today's Workforce" (Washington, DC: Center
for American Progress, 2013), http://cdn.americanprogress.org/wp-content
/uploads/2014/04/FMLA-reportv2.pdf; Sylvia Ann Hewlett, Nancy Rankin,
and Cornel West, *Taking Parenting Public: The Case for a New Social
Movement* (Lanham, MD: Rowman & Littlefield Publishers, 2002); Karen
Kornbluh, "Families Valued," *Democracy—A Journal of Ideas*, no. 2 (2006),
http://www.democracyjournal.org/2/6484.php?page=all.

VII. There at Work

1 David Weil, *The Fissured Workplace: Why Work Became So Bad for So Many
and What Can Be Done to Improve It* (Cambridge, MA: Harvard University
Press, 2014).

2 This was an online poll of 4,096 adults in May 2014. Harris Interactives,
"Vast Majority of Americans Favor Flexible Workplace Policies," June 19,
2014, http://www.harrisinteractive.com/NewsRoom/HarrisPolls/tabid/447/ctl
/ReadCustom%20Default/mid/1508/ArticleId/1453/Default.aspx. On fear
see, for example, Joan C. Williams, Rachel Dempsey, and Anne-Marie
Slaughter, *What Works for Women at Work: Four Patterns Working Women
Need to Know* (New York: New York University Press, 2014), http://www
.amazon.com/What-Works-Women-Work-Patterns/dp/1479835455%3F
SubscriptionId%3D0JJEH4PKQM4ZHS8QY102%26tag%3Dthehuffing
top-20%26linkCode%3Dxm2%26camp%3D2025%26creative%3D165953
%26creativeASIN%3D1479835455; Pamela Stone and Lisa Ackerly Her-
nandez, "The All-or-Nothing Workplace: Flexibility Stigma and 'Opting
Out' among Professional-Managerial Women," *Journal of Social Issues* 69,
no. 2 (2013): 235–256, doi:10.1111/josi.12013.

3 Bureau of Labor Statistics, "Table 3. Union Affiliation of Employed Wage
and Salary Workers by Occupation and Industry" (U.S. Department of
Labor, January 23, 2015), http://www.bls.gov/news.release/union2.t03.htm.

4 See, for example, Robert Tuttle and Michael Garr, "Shift Work and Work to
Family Fit: Does Schedule Control Matter?," *Journal of Family Economic
Issues* 33 (2012): 261–271.

5 There is a growing literature on this issue. See, for example, Ronald E.
Bulanda and Stephen Lippmann, "Wrinkles in Parental Time with
Children: Work, Family Structure, and Gender," *Michigan Family Review* 13
(2009): 5–20; Sarah Beth Estes, "Work–Family Arrangements and Parenting:
Are 'Family-Friendly' Arrangements Related to Mothers' Involvement in
Children's Lives?," *Sociological Perspectives* 48, no. 3 (Fall 2005): 310; Sara

McLanahan and Gary Sandefur, *Growing Up with a Single Parent: What Hurts, What Helps* (Cambridge, MA: Harvard University Press, 1994); Pamela Joshi and Karen Bogen, "Nonstandard Schedules and Young Children's Behavioral Outcomes among Working Low-Income Families," *Journal of Marriage and Family* 69, no. 1 (February 1, 2007): 139–156, http://onlinelibrary.wiley.com/doi/10.1111/j.1741-3737.2006.00350.x/abstract; Elizabeth C. Cooksey and Michelle M. Fondell, "Spending Time with His Kids: Effects of Family Structure on Fathers' and Children's Lives," *Journal of Marriage and Family* 58, no. 3 (August 1, 1996): 693–707, doi:10.2307/353729; Lyndall Strazdins et al., "Around-the-Clock: Parent Work Schedules and Children's Well-Being in a 24-H Economy," *Social Science and Medicine* 59 (2004): 1517–1527, doi:10.1016/j.socscimed.2004.01.022; Lyndall Strazdins et al., "Unsociable Work? Nonstandard Work Schedules, Family Relationships, and Children's Well-Being," *Journal of Marriage and Family* 68, no. 2 (May 2006): 394–410, https://researchers.anu.edu.au/publications/15817.

6 Brad Harrington et al., "The New Dad: Take Your Leave. Perspectives on Paternity Leave from Fathers, Leading Organizations, and Global Policies" (Boston, MA: Boston College Center for Work and Family, 2014), http://www.thenewdad.org/yahoo_site_admin/assets/docs/BCCWF_The_New_Dad_2014_FINAL.157170735.pdf.

7 Tessa Berenson, "Working Dads Struggle to Balance Demands of Home Too," *Time*, February 4, 2015, http://time.com/3695887/fatherhood-work-life-balance/.

8 PwC, University of Southern California, and London Business School, "PwC's NextGen: A Global Generational Study: Evolving Talent Strategy to Match the New Workforce Reality" (PwC, 2013), http://www.pwc.com/en_GX/gx/hr-management-services/pdf/pwc-nextgen-study-2013.pdf.

9 For millennial worker data, see ibid. and Kathleen Christensen, personal correspondence.

10 Workplace Flexibility 2010, "Flexible Work Arrangements: The Overview Memo," Memo (Washington, DC: Georgetown University Law Center, Spring 2006), http://workplaceflexibility2010.org/images/uploads/FWA_OverviewMemo.pdf.

11 The rule is in the comment period and will likely be challenged in the courts before it actually goes into effect. Estimates based on: Department of Labor, "Defining and Delimiting the Exemptions for Executive, Administrative, Professional, Outside Sales and Computer Employees; Proposed Rule," *Federal Register* 80, no. 128: fig. 2, accessed July 22, 2015, http://www.gpo.gov/fdsys/pkg/FR-2015-07-06/pdf/2015-15464.pdf; See also: Ross Eisenbrey and Lawrence Mishel, "The New Overtime Salary Threshold Would Directly Benefit 13.5 Million Workers: How EPI's Estimates Differ from the Department of Labor's" (Washington, D.C.: Economic Policy Institute,

August 3, 2015), http://www.epi.org/publication/overtime-threshold-would
-benefit-13-5-million/; Heidi Shierholz, "Increasing the Overtime Salary
Threshold Is Family-Friendly Policy: Women, Minorities, and Younger and
Less-Educated Workers Would Be Most Helped," Issue Brief (Washington,
DC: Economic Policy Institute, August 20, 2014); On the variety of flexible
work arrangements, see: Workplace Flexibility 2010, "Flexible Work
Arrangements: The Overview Memo" State laws, such as in California, can
be more stringent than federal law.

12 Nicholas Bloom, "To Raise Productivity, Let More Employees Work from
Home," *Harvard Business Review,* January 2014, https://hbr.org/2014/01/to
-raise-productivity-let-more-employees-work-from-home.

13 Nicholas Bloom, Tobias Kretschmer, and John Van Reenan, "Work-Life
Balance, Management Practices and Productivity," in *International
Differences in the Business Practices and Productivity of Firms,* ed. Richard
Freeman and Kathryn Shaw (Chicago, Ill.: University of Chicago Press,
2009), 15–54, http://www.nber.org/chapters/c0441.pdf. See also Council of
Economic Advisers, "Work-Life Balance and the Economics of Workplace
Flexibility," June 2014, http://www.whitehouse.gov/sites/default/files/docs
/updated_workplace_flex_report_final_0.pdf.

14 Cheryl Pellerin, "Mullen: Military Workplace Needs More Flexibility,"
DoD News, November 30, 2010, http://www.defense.gov/news/newsarticle
.aspx?id=61881.

15 Kenneth Matos and Ellen Galinsky, "2012 National Study of Employers"
(New York: Families and Work Institute, 2012), Table 3; Eileen Appelbaum,
Manufacturing Advantage: Why High-Performance Work Systems Pay Off
(Ithaca: Cornell University Press, 2000). See also Brad Harrington and Jamie
Ladge, "Got Talent? It Isn't Hard to Find," in *The Shriver Report: A Woman's
Nation Changes Everything,* ed. Heather Boushey and Ann O'Leary
(Washington, DC: Center for American Progress, 2009).

16 Correspondence with Joan Williams. See also Washington Center for
Equitable Growth, "Washington Center for Equitable Growth Grantees
for 2014," July 24, 2014, http://d3b0lhre2rgreb.cloudfront.net/ms-content
/uploads/sites/10/2014/07/grantee-announcement.pdf; Bridget Ansel,
"The Pitfalls of Just-in-Time-Scheduling," Washington Center for
Equitable Growth, *Value Added* (January 27, 2015), http://equitablegrowth.
org/news/pitfalls-just-time-scheduling/; Heather Boushey, "Schedules
That Work for Families and the U.S. Economy," *Equitable Growth,*
September 2, 2015, http://equitablegrowth.org/schedules-work-families
-u-s-economy/.

17 Author's calculation using U.S. labor force in 2014, approximately 156
million. Council of Economic Advisers, "Work-Life Balance and the
Economics of Workplace Flexibility." Also see Sean Nicholson et al., "How
to Present the Business Case for Healthcare Quality to Employers," *Applied*

Health Economics and Health Policy 4, no. 4 (2005): 209–218, http://link
.springer.com/article/10.2165/00148365-200504040-00003.

18 These numbers are not in the original report. Council of Economic
Advisers, "Work-Life Balance and the Economics of Workplace Flexibility,"
20. The utility's decision to end the program created the opportunity to
study the before and after effects of absenteeism and turnover. Dan R.
Dalton and Debra J. Mesch, "The Impact of Flexible Scheduling on
Employee Attendance and Turnover," *Administrative Science Quarterly* 35,
no. 2 (1990): Fig. 1, https://workfamily.sas.upenn.edu/wfrn-repo/object
/4wy6cp6we8jx6n1c; Corporate Voices for Working Families, "After
School for All: A Call to Action from the Business Community" (Washington, DC, 2004).

19 Ken Giglio, "Case Studies: Workplace Flexibility Case Studies," *Work and
Family Researchers Network,* accessed September 12, 2014, https://workfamily
.sas.upenn.edu/static/casestudy.

20 Thomas E. Perez et al., "Second Plenary: A 21st Century Economy That
Works for Business and Workers" (The White House Summit on
Working Families, Washington, DC, June 23, 2014), https://www.youtube
.com/watch?v=vkj4w0Ov6Zw; Aaron E. Carroll, "The Placebo Effect
Doesn't Apply Just to Pills," *New York Times,* October 6, 2014, http://www
.nytimes.com/2014/10/07/upshot/the-placebo-effect-doesnt-apply-just-to
-pills.html.

21 Nicholas Bloom et al., "Does Working from Home Work? Evidence from a
Chinese Experiment," NBER Working Paper (Cambridge, MA: National
Bureau of Economic Research, March 2013), http://www.stanford.edu
/~nbloom/wl8871.pdf.

22 Council of Economic Advisers, "Work-Life Balance and the Economics of
Workplace Flexibility."

23 Liz Ben-Ishai, "State, Local Policies Make Important Steps Forward for
Workplace Flexibility," *CLASP: Policy Solutions That Work for Low-Income
People,* June 25, 2013, http://www.clasp.org/issues/work-life-and-job-quality
/pages/state-local-policies-make-important-steps-forward-for-workplace
-flexibility; *An Act Relating to Equal Pay,* 2013, http://www.leg.state.vt.us
/docs/2014/Acts/ACT031.pdf; Office of the Press Secretary, "FACT SHEET:
The White House Summit on Working Families" (The White House,
June 23, 2014), http://m.whitehouse.gov/the-press-office/2014/06/23/
fact-sheet-white-house-summit-working-families.

24 Ariane Hegewisch and Janet Gornick, "The Impact of Work-Family Policies
on Women's Employment: A Review of Research from OECD Countries,"
Community, Work and Family 14, no. 2 (May 2011): 119–138. See also
Karen S. Lyness et al., "It's All about Control: Worker Control over Schedule
and Hours in Cross-National Context," *American Sociological Association* 77,
no. 6 (December 2012): 1023–1049.

25 See Claire Cain Miller and Catherine Rampell, "Yahoo Orders Home Workers Back to the Office," *New York Times*, February 25, 2013, sec. Technology, http://www.nytimes.com/2013/02/26/technology/yahoo-orders -home-workers-back-to-the-office.html; Kara Swisher, "'Physically Together': Here's the Internal Yahoo No-Work-from-Home Memo for Remote Workers and Maybe More," *AllThingsD*, accessed August 29, 2015, http://allthingsd .com/20130222/physically-together-heres-the-internal-yahoo-no-work- from-home-memo-which-extends-beyond-remote-workers/; Nicholas Carson, "Ex-Yahoos Confess: Marissa Mayer Is Right To Ban Working from Home," *Business Insider*, February 25, 2013, http://www.businessinsider.com/ex -yahoos-confess-marissa-mayer-is-right-to-ban-working-from-home-2013-2.

26 The Employee Retirement Income Security Act of 1974 sets minimum standards for pension plans in private industry, requiring that an employer that provides a retirement plan to some employees must provide the same plan to employees generally. For data on workplace flexibility, see Kenneth Matos and Ellen Galinsky, "2014 National Study of Employers" (New York: Families and Work Institute, 2014). See also Council of Economic Advisers, "Work-Life Balance and the Economics of Workplace Flexibility."

27 See Lonnie Golden, "The Flexibility Gap: Differential Access to Flexible Work Schedules and Location in the U.S.," in *Flexibility in Workplaces: Effects on Workers, Work Environment and the Unions*, ed. Isik Urla Zeytinoglu (Geneva: IIRA/ILO, 2005), 38–56; Ellen Galinsky, James T. Bond, and E. Jeffrey Hill, "When Work Works: A Status Report on Work- place Flexibility" (New York: Families and Work Institute, April 4, 2004).

28 For example, the 2013 Working Families Flexibility Act, which passed the House of Representatives on May 8, 2013, by a vote 223–204, allows firms to pay "comp" time instead of overtime pay, but it does not include strong language on retaliation. That bill lets employees subject to the Fair Labor Standards Act overtime provision choose whether to bank the overtime hours they work to use later as compensation or take their overtime pay. Employers, however, could choose to give extra hours only to those picking the comp- time option. Further, people who agree to work comp time cannot necessarily take their owed time when they want it. They can use it only when it's convenient for the employer—which may or may not work for the employee. See David J. Walsh, "The FLSA Comp Time Controversy: Fostering Flexibility or Diminishing Worker Rights," *Berkeley Journal of Employment and Labor Law* 20, no. 1 (March 1999): 74–137; Dave Jamieson, "Working Families Flexibility Act Passes House over Opposition of Democrats, Labor," *Huffington Post*, July 8, 2014, http://www.huffingtonpost.com/2013/05/08 /working-families-flexibility-act-passes_n_3231385.html; Teresa Tritch, "The Family Unfriendly Act," *Taking Note*, May 10, 2013, http://takingnote.blogs. nytimes.com/2013/05/10/the-family-unfriendly-act/. For data on the share of workers with comp time, see Ellen Galinsky et al., "2008 National Study of

Employers" (New York: Families and Work Institute, 2008), http://familiesandwork.org/site/research/reports/2008nse.pdf.

29 Democrats, Committee on Education and the Workforce, U.S. House of Representatives, "Scott, Warren, Delauro, Murray, Murphy Introduce Schedules That Work Act to End Unstable Scheduling Practices," July 15, 2015, http://democrats.edworkforce.house.gov/press-release/warren-delauro-murray-scott-murphy-introduce-schedules-work-act-end-unstable; National Women's Law Center and National Partnership for Women and Families, "The Schedules That Work Act: Section-by-Section Summary" (Washington, DC, September 2014), http://www.nwlc.org/sites/default/files/pdfs/section-by-section_fact_sheet_house_9.9.14.pdf.

30 For more on these scheduling practices, see Nancy K. Cauthen, "Scheduling Hourly Workers: How Last Minute, 'Just-in-Time' Scheduling Practices Are Bad for Workers, Families and Business" (New York: Demos, 2011), http://www.demos.org/sites/default/files/publications/Scheduling_Hourly_Workers_Demos.pdf.

31 Parija Bhatnagar, "Wal-Mart Seeks to 'Organize' Labor Its Own Way—Apr. 25, 2006," *CNNMoney.com*, April 25, 2006, http://money.cnn.com/2006/04/25/news/companies/walmart_labor/.

32 SHRM Foundation, "Leveraging Workplace Flexibility for Engagement and Productivity," 2014, http://www.shrm.org/about/foundation/products/Documents/9–14%20Work-Flex%20EPG-FINAL.pdf; Seth Freed Wessler, "Shift Change: 'Just-in-Time' Scheduling Creates Chaos for Workers," *NBC News*, May 10, 2014, http://www.nbcnews.com/feature/in-plain-sight/shift-change-just-time-scheduling-creates-chaos-workers-n95881.

33 Stephanie Luce and Naoki Fujita, "Discounted Jobs: How Retailers Sell Workers Short" (New York: Murphy Institute, City University of New York, and the Retail Action Project, 2012), 8, http://retailactionproject.org/wp-content/uploads/2012/03/7–75_RAP+cover_lowres.pdf.

34 Restaurant Opportunities Centers United, "The Third Shift: Child Care Needs and Access for Working Mothers in Restaurants" (New York, July 9, 2013), http://rocny.org/wp-content/uploads/2013/05/ChildCare-Report-Final.pdf; Saru Jayaraman and Eric Schlosser, *Behind the Kitchen Door* (Ithaca: ILR Press, 2014).

35 Lonnie Golden and Barbara Wiens-Tuers, "Mandatory Overtime Work in the United States: Who, Where, and What?," *Labor Studies Journal* 30, no. 1 (March 1, 2005): 1–25, doi:10.1177/0160449X0503000102.

36 Yuki Noguchi, "Part-Time Workers Struggle with Full-Time Juggling Act" (National Public Radio, March 6, 2015), http://www.npr.org/2015/03/06/390730056/part-time-workers-struggle-with-full-time-juggling-act. For more on how schedules need to match the needs of "working learners," see Louis Soares, "Working Learners: Educating Our Entire Workforce for Success in the 21st Century" (Washington, DC: Center

for American Progress, June 2009), http://louissoares.com/wp-content /uploads/2013/03/working_learners.pdf.

37 Restaurant Opportunities Centers United, "The Third Shift: Child Care Needs and Access for Working Mothers in Restaurants," 10.

38 On job satisfaction and relationships, see Paul R. Amato et al., *Alone Together: How Marriage in America Is Changing* (Cambridge, MA: Harvard University Press, 2009). For views on this issue from opposite ends of the political spectrum, see Shawn Fremstad and Melissa Boteach, "Valuing All Our Families: Progressive Policies That Strengthen Family Commitments and Reduce Family Disparities" (Washington, DC: Center for American Progress, January 2015), https://cdn.americanprogress.org/wp-content /uploads/2015/01/FamilyStructure-report.pdf; Robert I. Lerman and W. Bradford Wilcox, "For Richer, For Poorer: How Family Structures Economic Success in America" (Washington, DC: American Enterprise Institute and Institute for Family Studies, 2014), http://www.aei.org/wp-content/uploads/2014/10 /IFS-ForRicherForPoorer-Final_Web.pdf.

39 National Coalition for the Homeless, "Employment and Homelessness," July 2009, http://www.nationalhomeless.org/factsheets/employment.html; Mireya Navarro, "In New York, Having a Job, or 2, Doesn't Mean Having a Home," *New York Times*, September 17, 2013, http://www.nytimes.com/2013/09/18 /nyregion/in-new-york-having-a-job-or-2-doesnt-mean-having-a-home.html.

40 Ethan Bernstein, Saravanan Kesavan, and Bradley Staats, "How to Manage Scheduling Software Fairly," *Harvard Business Review*, December 2014, https://hbr.org/2014/09/how-to-manage-scheduling-software-fairly.

41 Zeynep Ton, *The Good Jobs Strategy: How the Smartest Companies Invest in Employees to Lower Costs and Boost Profits* (Amazon Publishing, 2014), vii.

42 Jodi Kantor, "Starbucks to Revise Policies to End Irregular Schedules for Its 130,000 Baristas," *New York Times*, August 14, 2014, http://www.nytimes .com/2014/08/15/us/starbucks-to-revise-work-scheduling-policies.html; Shane Ferro, "Wal-Mart Just Made Another Promise to Employees, and It Could Be a Bigger Deal Than the Raise," *Business Insider*, February 19, 2015, http://www.businessinsider.com/wal-marts-fixed-scheduling-promise-2015-2.

43 U.S. Wage and Hour Division, "Fact Sheet #22: Hours Worked under the Fair Labor Standards Act (FLSA)" (U.S. Department of Labor, July 2008), http://www.dol.gov/whd/regs/compliance/whdfs22.pdf.

44 National Women's Law Center, "Recently Introduced and Enacted State and Local Fair Scheduling Legislation" (Washington, DC, July 2015), http://www.nwlc.org/sites/default/files/pdfs/recently_introduced_and_enacted _state_local_7.21.15.pdf; Next Generation and California Work and Family Coalition, "Summary: The San Francisco Predictable Scheduling and Fair Treatment for Formula Retail Employees Ordinance" (San Francisco, CA: Next Generation, November 2014); Jobs with Justice San Francisco, "Everything You Need to Know about San Francisco's Retail Workers

Bill of Rights," November 26, 2014, http://retailworkerrights.com
/everything-you-need-to-know-about-san-franciscos-retail-workers-bill
-of-rights/.

VIII. Care

1 Alex Rivera, *Sleep Dealer*, Drama, Romance, Sci-Fi (2008). In case you
   aren't familiar with the Harry Potter books, you can learn more about
   house-elves here: "House-Elf," *Harry Potter Wiki*, accessed August 23, 2015,
   http://harrypotter.wikia.com/wiki/House-elf.
2 Richard Fry, "This Year, Millennials Will Overtake Baby Boomers," *Pew
   Research Center*, January 16, 2015, http://www.pewresearch.org/fact-tank
   /2015/01/16/this-year-millennials-will-overtake-baby-boomers/; U.S. Department of Health and Human Services, Administration on Aging, "Projected
   Future Growth of the Older Population," 2015, http://www.aoa.acl.gov
   /Aging_Statistics/future_growth/future_growth.aspx#age; National Alliance
   for Caregiving, "Caregiving in the U.S. 2015" (Bethesda, MD: National
   Alliance for Caregiving, June 2015), Fig. 2, http://www.caregiving.org
   /wp-content/uploads/2015/05/2015_CaregivingintheUS_Final-Report
   -June-4_WEB.pdf.
3 This literature is large and growing. See, for example, Sean F. Reardon, "The
   Widening Academic Achievement Gap between the Rich and the Poor: New
   Evidence and Possible Explanations," in *Whither Opportunity? Rising
   Inequality, Schools, and Children's Life Chances*, ed. Greg J. Duncan and
   Richard J. Murnane (New York: Russell Sage Foundation, 2011). Later
   interventions still matter. See, for example, Sara Heller et al., "Preventing
   Youth Violence and Dropout: A Randomized Field Experiment," Working
   Paper (National Bureau of Economic Research, May 2013), http://www.nber
   .org/papers/w19014.pdf.
4 See Committee on Integrating the Science of Early Childhood Development
   et al., *From Neurons to Neighborhoods: The Science of Early Childhood
   Development*, ed. Jack P. Shonkoff and Deborah A. Phillips (Washington,
   DC: National Academies Press, 2000); NIHCD Early Child Care Research
   Network, "Early Child Care and Self-Control, Compliance, and Problem
   Behavior at Twenty-Four and Thirty-Six Months," *Child Development*
   69 (1998): 1145–1170; Margaret R. Burchinal et al., "Relating Quality of
   Center-Based Child Care to Early Cognitive and Language Development
   Longitudinally," *Child Development* 71 (2000): 338–357; Kathleen Mc-
   Cartney et al., "Quality Child Care Supports the Achievement of Low-
   Income Children: Direct and Indirect Pathways through Caregiving and
   the Home Environment," *Journal of Applied Developmental Psychology* 28
   (2007): 411–426.
5 See Claudia Dale Goldin and Lawrence F Katz, *The Race between Educa-
   tion and Technology* (Cambridge, MA: Belknap Press of Harvard University
   Press, 2010).

6   Ben Bernanke, "Early Childhood Education" (Children's Defense Fund National Conference, Cincinnati, OH, July 24, 2012), http://www.federal reserve.gov/newsevents/speech/bernanke20120724a.htm.

7   The Early Childhood Environment Rating Scale (ECERS) and its infant-toddler counterpart (ITERS) "rate each observed classroom on 30–35 items using a scale of 1–7 for each item. As a guide to the intended interpretation of the scores, ratings of 1, 3, 5, and 7 are designated by the instrument designers as representing inadequate, minimal, good, and excellent care, respectively. Summary scores are obtained by averaging over the items." David Blau and Janet Currie, "Pre-School, Day Care, and After-School Care: Who's Minding the Kids?," NBER Working Paper (Cambridge, MA: National Bureau of Economic Research, August 2004), 17.

8   According to a survey of caregivers, two-thirds cared for an elder who lived on their own: Kerstin Aumann et al., "The Elder Care Study: Everyday Realities and Wishes for Change" (Washington, DC: Families and Work Institute, 2010).

9   Child Care Aware of America, "Parents and the High Cost of Child Care: 2014 Report" (Arlington, VA, 2014), https://www.ncsl.org/documents/cyf /2014_Parents_and_the_High_Cost_of_Child_Care.pdf; Afterschool Alliance, "America After 3 pm: Afterschool Programs in Demand," 2014, http://afterschoolalliance.org/documents/AA3PM-2014/AA3PM_National _Report.pdf.

10 Joan C. Williams and Heather Boushey, "The Three Faces of Work-Family Conflict: The Poor, the Privileged, and the Missing Middle" (Washington, DC: Center for American Progress and the Center for WorkLife Law, University of California, Hastings College of the Law, 2010), https://cdn .americanprogress.org/wp-content/uploads/issues/2010/01/pdf/threefaces.pdf. See also Child Care Aware of America, "Parents and the High Cost of Child Care: 2014 Report."

11 Data on the costs of rooms are from the SCAN Foundation, "Who Pays for Long-Term Care in the U.S.?" (Long Beach, CA, January 2013), http://www .thescanfoundation.org/sites/thescanfoundation.org/files/who_pays_for_ltc _us_jan_2013_fs.pdf. Family incomes are from Heather Boushey, John Schmitt, and Kavya Vaghul's analysis of the CEPR extracts of the CPS Annual Social and Economic Supplement. See Appendix for more informa-tion on data and methods. For more information on what federal programs pay for, see "Who Pays for Long-Term Care?," U.S. Department of Health and Human Services, LongTermCare.gov (2013), http://longtermcare.gov /the-basics/who-pays-for-long- term-care/. For data on caregiver incomes, see National Alliance for Caregiving, "Caregiving in the U.S." For data on the burden of care, see Aumann et al., "The Elder Care Study: Everyday Realities and Wishes for Change."

12 See Michael Baker, Jonathan Gruber, and Kevin Milligan, "Universal Childcare, Maternal Labor Supply and Family Well-Being," July 2005;

Patricia M. Anderson and Phillip B. Levine, "Child Care and Mothers' Employment Decisions," Working Paper (Cambridge, MA: National Bureau of Economic Research, March 1999); Pierre Lefebvre and Phil Merrigan, "Low-Fee ($5/day/child) Regulated Childcare Policy and the Labor Supply of Mothers with Young Children: A Natural Experiment from Canada," SSRN Scholarly Paper (Rochester, NY: Social Science Research Network, March 1, 2005), http://papers.ssrn.com/abstract=695161; Jonah B. Gelbach, "Public Schooling for Young Children and Maternal Labor Supply," *American Economic Review* 92, no. 1 (March 1, 2002): 307–322, http://www.jstor.org /stable/3083335.

13 Ann Bookman and Delia Kimbrel, "Families and Elder Care in the Twenty-First Century," *Future of Children* 21, no. 2 (Fall 2011): 117–140.

14 Ibid.; Aumann et al., "The Elder Care Study: Everyday Realities and Wishes for Change."

15 National Alliance for Caregiving, "Caregiving in the U.S."

16 Ai-jen Poo, *The Age of Dignity: Preparing for the Elder Boom in a Changing America* (New York: The New Press, 2015), 46.

17 National Alliance for Caregiving, "Caregiving in the U.S."

18 I'm fairly certain it was this cover: Ken Huff, "The Lonely Life of 'Latchkey' Children, Say Two Experts, Is a National Disgrace," *People Magazine*, September 20, 1982, http://www.people.com/people/archive/article /0,,20083140,00.html.

19 Heather Boushey, "'This Country Is Not Woman-Friendly or Child-Friendly': Talking about the Challenge of Moving from Welfare-to-Work," *Journal of Poverty* 6, no. 2 (2002): 81–115.

20 A recent spate of news articles have focused on "free-range" children. See, for example, Donna St George, "Md. Officials: Letting 'Free Range' Kids Walk or Play Alone Is Not Neglect," *Washington Post*, June 11, 2015, http://www.washingtonpost.com/local/education/state-seeks-to-clarify-views -about-young-children-walking-alone/2015/06/11/423ce72c-0b99–11e5–95fd -d580f1c5d44e_story.html.

21 Survey data on caregivers' time from Evercare and National Alliance for Caregiving, "Family Caregivers—What They Spend, What They Sacrifice: The Personal Financial Toll of Caring for a Loved One" (Bethesda, MD, November 2007), http://www.caregiving.org/data/Evercare_NAC_Care giverCostStudyFINAL20111907.pdf. Estimates of lifetime costs of retiring early from MetLife Mature Market Institute, "The MetLife Study of Caregiving Costs to Working Caregivers: Double Jeopardy for Baby Boomers Caring for Their Parents" (Westport, CT: MetLife Mature Market Institute, June 2011).

22 Number of women in the labor force calculated from Bureau of Labor Statistics, "Current Population Survey" (U.S. Department of Labor, n.d.), http://www.bls.gov/data/.

23 Lynda Laughlin, "Who's Minding the Kids? Child Care Arrangements: Spring 2011" (Washington, DC: U.S. Census Bureau, April 2013); Aumann et al., "The Elder Care Study: Everyday Realities and Wishes for Change," 13.

24 Abby J. Cohen, "A Brief History of Federal Financing for Child Care in the United States," *Financing Child Care* 6, no. 2 (Summer/Fall 1996): 26–40, http://futureofchildren.org/publications/journals/article/index.xml?journalid=56&articleid=326&sectionid=2180; Bryce Covert, "Here's What Happened the One Time When the U.S. Had Universal Childcare," *ThinkProgress*, September 30, 2014, http://thinkprogress.org/economy/2014/09/30/3573844/lanham-act-child-care/.

25 See Emilie Stoltzfus, *Citizen, Mother, Worker: Debating Public Responsibility for Child Care after the Second World War* (Chapel Hill, NC: The University of North Carolina Press, 2003); Chris M. Herbst, "Universal Child Care, Maternal Employment, and Children's Long-Run Outcomes: Evidence from the U.S. Lanham Act of 1940," IZA Discussion Paper (Washington, DC: Institute for the Study of Labor, December 2013), http://ftp.iza.org/dp7846.pdf; Ruth Pearson Koshuk, "Developmental Records of 500 Nursery School Children," *Journal of Experimental Education* 16, no. 2 (December 1, 1947): 134–148, http://www.jstor.org/stable/20153770; Jone Johnson Lewis, "Women of World War II at Work in Offices and Factories," *About Education*, November 27, 2014, http://womenshistory.about.com/od/warwwii/a/women_work.htm.

26 The military's child care program significantly improved after the Military Child Care Act of 1989, which aimed to address—among other things—the program's costs and quality of care. See National Public Radio, "Military's Preschool Program Considered a National Model" (National Public Radio, January 1, 2015), http://wvpe.org/post/militarys-preschool-program-considered-national-model. See also Kate Pomper et al., "Be All That We Can Be: Lessons from the Military for Improving Our Nation's Child Care System," 2004 Follow Up Report (Washington, DC: National Women's Law Center, 2004), http://www.nwlc.org/sites/default/files/pdfs/BeAllThatWeCanBe_2004FollowUp.pdf; Karen Schulman, "The Military Child Care System Remains a Model for Improvement," *National Women's Law Center*, February 8, 2012, http://www.nwlc.org/our-blog/military-child-care-system-remains-model-improvement.

27 Reagan Baughman, Daniela DiNardi, and Douglas Holtz-Eakin, "Productivity and Wage Effects of 'Family-Friendly' Fringe Benefits," *International Journal of Manpower* 24, no. 3 (May 1, 2003): 247–259, doi:10.1108/01437720310479723.

28 Kenneth Matos and Ellen Galinsky, "2014 National Study of Employers" (New York: Families and Work Institute, 2014); "Google Daycare Now a Luxury for Larry and Sergey's Inner Circle," *Gawker*, accessed May 30, 2015,

http://gawker.com/5016355/google-daycare-now-a-luxury-for-larry-and
-sergeys-inner-circle.

29 Brigid Schulte, "Aging Population Prompts More Employers to Offer
Elder-Care Benefits to Workers," *The Washington Post*, November 16, 2014,
http://www.washingtonpost.com/local/aging-population-prompts-more
-employers-to-offer-elder-care-benefits-to-workers/2014/11/16/25f9c8e6
–6847–11e4-a31c-77759fc1eacc_story.html; Matos and Galinsky, "2014
National Study of Employers."

30 Internal Revenue Service, "Tax Topics—Topic 602 Child and Dependent
Care Credit," accessed July 19, 2015, http://www.irs.gov/taxtopics/tc602.html;
Tax Policy Center, "How Does the Tax System Subsidize Child Care
Expenses?," *Tax Policy Center Briefing Book*, accessed July 19, 2015,
http://www.taxpolicycenter.org/briefing-book/key-elements/family
/child-care-subsidies.cfm; Matos and Galinsky, "2014 National Study of
Employers." See also Internal Revenue Service, "Publication 969 (2014),
Health Savings Accounts and Other Tax-Favored Health Plans," accessed
July 19, 2015, http://www.irs.gov/publications/p969/ar02.html.

31 Tax Policy Center, *Taxation and the Family: How Does the Tax System
Subsidize Childcare Expenses?* (Washington, DC: Urban Institute and
Brookings Institution, 2007).

32 In 2014, only 852,900 families (1.4 million children) received assistance from
Child Care and Development funding. See Office of Child Care, "FY 2014
CCDF Data Tables (Preliminary)," May 26, 2015, http://www.acf.hhs.gov
/programs/occ/resource/fy-2014-ccdf-data-tables-preliminary. For Head Start,
see Early Childhood Learning and Knowledge Center, "Head Start Program
Fact Sheet Fiscal Year 2014," *Head Start*, April 2015, http://eclkc.ohs.acf.hhs
.gov/hslc/data/factsheets/2014-hs-program-factsheet.html. On waiting lists,
see Karen Schulman and Helen Blank, "Pivot Point: State Child Care
Assistance Policies, 2013" (Washington, DC: National Women's Law
Center), accessed July 22, 2015, final_nwlc_2013statechildcareassistance
report.pdf.

33 Randy Albelda et al., "Bridging the Gaps: A Picture of How Work Supports
Work in Ten States" (Center for Economic and Policy Research; The
Center for Social Policy, October 2007), http://www.cepr.net/index.php
/publications/reports/bridging-the-gaps-a-picture-of-how-work-supports
-work-in-ten-states/.

34 Aumann et al., *The Elder Care Study: Everyday Realities and Wishes for
Change*. This study was done before the implementation of the Affordable
Care Act, which extends Medicaid to more individuals under age sixty-five.

35 Centers for Medicare and Medicaid Services, "Medicaid Eligibility," 2004,
http://www.cms.hhs.gov/medicaid/eligibility/criteria.asp; Centers for
Medicare & Medicaid Services, "Medicare and Home Health Care"
(Baltimore, MD: U.S. Department of Health and Human Services, May

2010), https://www.medicare.gov/Pubs/pdf/10969.pdf; Centers for Medicare & Medicaid Services, "Paying for Nursing Home Care," accessed August 23, 2015, https://www.medicare.gov/what-medicare-covers/part-a/paying-for-nursing-home-care.html.

36 On the Oklahoma program, see William T. Gormley and Ted Gayer, "Promoting School Readiness in Oklahoma: An Evaluation of Tulsa's Pre-K Program," *Journal of Human Resources* XL, no. 3 (July 1, 2005): 533–558, doi:10.3368/jhr.XL.3.533. For more information on prekindergarten programs, see W. Steven Barnett et al., "The State of Preschool 2014: The State Preschool Yearbook" (Graduate School of Education at Rutgers, The National Institute for Early Education Research, 2015), http://nieer.org/sites/nieer/files/yearbook2014_full.pdf.

37 Barnett et al., "The State of Preschool 2014: The State Preschool Yearbook"; U.S. Department of Education, "Early Learning," March 8, 2013, http://www.ed.gov/early-learning.

38 Committee on Early Childhood Care and Education Workforce: A Workshop; Institute of Medicine and National Research Council, *The Early Childhood Care and Education Workforce: Challenges and Opportunities: A Workshop Report* (Washington, DC: The National Academies Press, 2012), ix, http://www.nap.edu/catalog/13238/the-early-childhood-care-and-education-workforce-challenges-and-opportunities.

39 There is now a rich literature connecting the quality of jobs of caregivers and the quality of care. See Richard Ruopp and Nancy Irwin, *Children at the Center: Summary Findings and Their Implications* (Cambridge, MA: Abt Books, 1979); C. D. Hayes, J. L. Palmer, and M. J. Zaslow, *Who Cares for America's Children?* (Washington, DC: National Academy Press, 1990); Marcy Whitebook, Carollee Howes, and Deborah Phillips, *Worthy Work, Unlivable Wages: The National Child Care Staffing Study, 1988–1997* (Washington, DC: Center for the Child Care Workforce, 1998); Committee on Integrating the Science of Early Childhood Development et al., *From Neurons to Neighborhoods*; Barbara Bowman, M. Suzanne Donovan, and M. Susan Burns, *Eager to Learn: Educating Our Preschoolers* (Washington, DC: National Academy Press, 2000); Jeanne Brooks-Gunn, Wen-Jui Han, and Jane Waldfogel, "Maternal Employment and Child Cognitive Outcomes in the First Three Years of Life: The NICHD Study of Early Child Care," *Child Development* 73, no. 4 (August 2002): 1052–1072; Suzanne W. Helburn et al., "Cost, Quality and Child Outcomes in Child Care Centers: Technical Report, Public Report, and Executive Summary" (Denver, CO: Department of Economics, Center for Research in Economic and Social Policy, University of Colorado at Denver, June 1995), http://eric.ed.gov/?id=ED386297.

40 On pay, author's calculation from Bureau of Labor Statistics, "May 2014 National Occupational Employment and Wage Estimates United States" (U.S. Department of Labor, n.d.), http://www.bls.gov/oes/current/oes_nat

.htm#00–0000. On turnover, see Theresa Barry, Diane Brannon, and Vincent Mor, "Nurse Aide Empowerment Strategies and Staff Stability: Effects on Nursing Home Resident Outcomes," *Gerontologist*, June 2005, 309–317; Kristin Smith and Reagan Baughman, "Caring for America's Aging Population: A Profile of the Direct-Care Workforce," *Monthly Labor Review*, September 2007, 24; For industry breakdown by gender, see Bureau of Labor Statistics, "Labor Force Statistics from the Current Population Survey. Table 18. Employed Persons by Detailed Industry, Sex, Race, and Hispanic or Latino Ethnicity" (U.S. Department of Labor, February 12, 2015), http://www.bls.gov/cps/cpsaat18.htm.

41 Quote taken from Michael Mechanic, "Atul Gawande: 'We Have Medicalized Aging, and That Experiment Is Failing Us,' " *Mother Jones*, October 7, 2014, http://www.motherjones.com/media/2014/10/atul-gawande-being-mortal-interview-assisted-living. See also Dorie Seavey, "The Cost of Frontline Turnover in Long-Term Care," 2004, http://www.directcareclearinghouse.org/download/TOCostReport.pdf; Poo, *The Age of Dignity*, 46.

42 U.S. Chamber of Commerce and Institute for a Competitive Workforce, "Why Business Should Support Early Childhood Education," September 8, 2010, http://www.uschamberfoundation.org/publication/ready-set-go-why-business-should-support-early-childhood-education.

43 ReadyNation, "Open Letter from Business Leaders to President Obama and Members of Congress," May 29, 2013, http://www.readynation.org/about-us/signatories-business-letter/.

IX. Fair

1 President Barack Obama, "President Barack Obama's State of the Union Address," January 28, 2014, https://www.whitehouse.gov/the-press-office/2014/01/28/president-barack-obamas-state-union-address.

2 Gary S. Becker, *The Economics of Discrimination*, 2nd ed. (Chicago, IL: University of Chicago Press, 1971).

3 Kenneth Arrow, "Some Mathematical Models of Race in the Labor Market," in *Racial Discrimination in Economic Life*, ed. A. H. Pascal (Lexington, MA: Lexington Books, 1972), 192.

4 Center for WorkLife Law, "About FRD" (http://www.worklifelaw.org/About FRD.html [February 10, 2011]).

5 Some of this rise may be due to the Great Recession, which may have led either to employers specifically laying off workers with care responsibilities or to those dismissed employees suing their former employers because they were having a much harder time finding new jobs. See Cynthia Thomas Calvert, "Family Responsibilities: Discrimination: Litigation Update 2010" (San Francisco, CA: Center for WorkLife Law, University of California Hastings College of the Law, 2010), http://worklifelaw.org/pubs/FRDupdate

.pdf; Tamar Lewin, "Father Awarded $375,000 in a Parental Leave Case," *New York Times*, February 3, 1999, sec. U.S., http://www.nytimes.com /1999/02/03/us/father-awarded-375000-in-a-parental-leave-case.html.

6 See Jennifer L. Berdahl and Sue H. Moon, "Workplace Mistreatment of Middle Class Workers Based on Sex, Parenthood, and Caregiving," *Journal of Social Issues* 69, no. 2 (2013): 341–366, doi:10.1111/josi.12018; Scott Coltrane et al., "Fathers and the Flexibility Stigma," *Journal of Social Issues* 69, no. 2 (2013): 279–302, doi:10.1111/josi.12015.

7 Lisa Dodson, "Stereotyping Low-Wage Mothers Who Have Work and Family Conflicts," *Journal of Social Issues* 69, no. 2 (2013): 257–278, doi:10.1111/josi.12014; Lisa Dodson, Tiffany Manuel, and Ellen Bravo, "Keeping Jobs and Raising Families in Low-Income America: It Just Doesn't Work" (Radcliffe Institute for Advanced Study, 2002).

8 Lin left the Knicks at the end of the 2012 season. See Melinda C. Shepherd, "Jeremy Lin—American Basketball Player," *Encyclopedia Britannica*, accessed May 2, 2015, http://www.britannica.com/biography/Jeremy-Lin; Harvey Araton, "Knicks' Jeremy Lin Keeps His Cool as Heads Spin around Him," *New York Times*, February 11, 2012, sec. Sports / Pro Basketball, http://www.nytimes.com/2012/02/12/sports/basketball/the-knicks-jeremy-lin -keeps-his-cool-as-heads-spin-around-him.html; Charlie Rose, "Linsanity: Jeremy Lin's Rise to Stardom," *60 Minutes* (CBS News, April 8, 2013), http://www.cbsnews.com/news/linsanity-jeremy-lins-rise-to-stardom/; Mark Viera, "Before N.B.A. Passed on Jeremy Lin, Many Colleges Did," *New York Times*, February 12, 2012, http://www.nytimes.com/2012/02/13/sports/basketball /for-knicks-lin-erasing-a-history-of-being-overlooked.html.

9 Shelley J. Correll, Stephen Benard, and In Paik, "Getting a Job: Is There a Motherhood Penalty?," *American Journal of Sociology* 112 (2007): 1297–1338.

10 Marianne Cooper, "Being the 'Go-to Guy': Fatherhood, Masculinity, and the Organization of Work in Silicon Valley," *Qualitative Sociology* 23, no. 4 (2000): 390.

11 Ibid.; Rosabeth Moss Kanter, *Men and Women of the Corporation: New Edition*, 2nd ed. (New York: Basic Books, 1993); Julie A. Nelson and Marianne A. Ferber, *Beyond Economic Man: Feminist Theory and Economics* (Chicago, IL: University of Chicago Press, 1993).

12 Chang-Tai Hsieh et al., "The Allocation of Talent and U.S. Economic Growth," Working Paper (Cambridge, MA: National Bureau of Economic Research, January 2013), http://www.nber.org/papers/w18693; Warren Buffett, "Warren Buffett at Fortune's Most Powerful Women Summit," October 4, 2011, http://management.fortune.cnn.com/2011/10/04/warren -buffett-transcript/.

13 In a now-famous 1992 paper, three economists—Gregory Mankiw from Harvard University, David Romer from University of California-Berkeley, and David Weil from Brown University—found that the share of people

graduating from high school had a roughly equivalent or larger effect on economic growth rates than did investment in physical capital. See N. Gregory Mankiw, David Romer, and David N. Weil, "A Contribution to the Empirics of Economic Growth," *Quarterly Journal of Economics* 107, no. 2 (1992): 407–437.

14 U.S. Equal Employment Opportunities Commission, "Enforcement Guidance: Unlawful Disparate Treatment of Workers with Caregiving Responsibilities," February 8, 2011, http://www.eeoc.gov/policy/docs/caregiving.html.

15 Saranna Thorton, "Pregnancy Discrimination Act," *Sloan Network Encyclopedia*, 2005, https://workfamily.sas.upenn.edu/wfrn-repo/object /ly9ch3jv6h4w1a5q; Ann O'Leary and Karen Kornbluh, "Family Friendly for All Families," in *The Shriver Report: A Woman's Nation Changes Everything*, ed. Heather Boushey and Ann O'Leary (Washington, DC: Center for American Progress, 2009), 75–109.

16 O'Leary and Kornbluh, "Family Friendly for All Families," 89.

17 Michelle J. Budig, "The Fatherhood Bonus and the Motherhood Penalty: Parenthood and the Gender Gap in Pay" (Washington, DC: Third Way, September 2, 2014), http://www.thirdway.org/report/the-fatherhood-bonus -and-the-motherhood-penalty-parenthood-and-the-gender-gap-in-pay; Claire Cain Miller, "The Motherhood Penalty vs. the Fatherhood Bonus: A Child Helps Your Career, if You're a Man," *New York Times*, September 6, 2014, http://www.nytimes.com/2014/09/07/upshot/a-child-helps-your-career-if -youre-a-man.html; Michelle J. Budig and Paula England, "The Wage Penalty for Motherhood," *American Sociological Review* 66, no. 2 (April 2001): 204–225.

18 Ledbetter was an employee at Goodyear who found out that for nearly two decades she had been earning less than her male colleagues. Her case went all the way to the Supreme Court and she lost, so Congress passed the Lilly Ledbetter Fair Pay Act to loosen the timing restrictions on filing discrimination cases. See *Lilly Ledbetter Fair Pay Act of 2009*, 2009, http://www .govtrack.us/congress/bills/111/s181.

19 Cynthia Hess and Ariane Hegewisch, "The Status of Women in the States: 2015—Employment and Earnings" (Washington, DC: Institute for Women's Policy Research, n.d.), http://www.iwpr.org/initiatives/the-status-of-women -and-girls/#publications.

20 Joya Misra, Michelle Budig, and Irene Boeckmann, "Work-Family Policies and the Effects of Children on Women's Employment Hours and Wages," *Community, Work & Family* 14, no. 2 (May 1, 2011): 139–157, doi: 10.1080/13668803.2011.571396; Budig and England, "The Wage Penalty for Motherhood."

21 Claudia Goldin, "A Grand Gender Convergence: Its Last Chapter," *American Economic Review* 104, no. 4 (2014): 1091–1119.

22 On state and local policies, see Stephanie Bornstein and Robert J. Rathmell, "Caregivers as a Protected Class?: The Growth of State and Local Laws Prohibiting Family Responsibilities Discrimination" (University of California, Hastings College of the Law: The Center for WorkLife Law, December 2009), http://worklifelaw.org/pubs/LocalFRDLawsReport.pdf; Center for WorkLife Law, UC Hastings College of the Law, "State FRD Legislation Tracker, Last Updated: June 30, 2014," June 30, 2014, http://worklifelaw.org/wp-content/uploads/2014/07/FRD-Tracker-June-2014.pdf. Other countries provide evidence that this can work. Australia protects employees against discrimination on the basis of care responsibilities and requires employers to affirmatively provide reasonable, flexible work schedules unless doing so would cause them undue hardship. See Australian Government, "National Employment Standards (NES)," *Fair Work*, 2012, http://www.fairwork.gov.au/faqs/national-employment-standards/pages /default.aspx; Australian Government, "Flexible Working Arrangements," *Fair Work*, accessed June 15, 2015, http://www.fairwork.gov.au/employee -entitlements/flexibility-in-the-workplace/flexible-working-arrangements. The European Union's Equal Treatment Directive explicitly lays out that Member States may promote employment of and protection for workers with caregiving responsibilities. See European Parliament and the Council of the European Union, *Implementation of the Principle of Equal Opportunities and Equal Treatment of Men and Women in Matters of Employment and Occupation (recast)*, 2006, http://eur-lex.europa.eu/legal-content/EN/ALL /?uri=CELEX:32006L0054.

23 Salvador Rizzo, "Gov. Christie Rejects Minimum Wage Increase, Offers Alternative," *NJ.com*, January 28, 2013, http://www.nj.com/politics /index.ssf/2013/01/christie_rejects_minimum_wage.html; Jonathan Lemire, "Democratic Mayoral Candidates Champion Minimum Wage Increase," NY *Daily News*, March 9, 2013, http://www.nydailynews.com /new-york/democratic-mayoral-candidates-champion-minimum-wage -increase-article-1.1284055.

24 New York City Council, Christine C. Quinn, Speaker, "Council Speaker Christine C. Quinn's Prepared Remarks on Proposed Paid Sick Leave Legislation," October 14, 2010, http://council.nyc.gov/html/pr/10_15_10 _paid_sick.shtml; Jordan Weissman, "Newt Gingrich Thinks School Children Should Work as Janitors," *Atlantic*, November 21, 2011, http://www .theatlantic.com/business/archive/2011/11/newt-gingrich-thinks-school -children-should-work-as-janitors/248837/.

25 Katrin Elborgh-Woytek et al., "Women, Work, and the Economy: Macro-economic Gains from Gender Equity" (Washington, DC: International Monetary Fund, September 2013), http://www.imf.org/external/pubs/ft /sdn/2013/sdn1310.pdf.

26 For more on how U.S. parental leave (and other) policies compare with those of other countries, see Janet C. Gornick and Marcia K. Meyers, *Families That Work: Policies for Reconciling Parenthood and Employment* (New York: Russell Sage Foundation, 2003); Rebecca Ray, Janet C. Gornick, and John Schmitt, "Parental Leave Policies in 21 Countries" (Washington DC: Center for Economic and Policy Research, September 2008).

27 Arthur M. Okun, *Equality and Efficiency: The Big Tradeoff*, 2nd ed. (Brookings Institution Press, 2015), 159.

Conclusion

1 Or, as Nobel Laureate Paul Krugman put it, "a country is not a company." Paul Krugman, "A Country Is Not a Company," *Harvard Business Review*, February 1996.

2 Rachel Abrams, "Gap Says It Will Phase out on-Call Scheduling of Employees" *New York Times*, August 26, 2015, sec. Business, http://www.nytimes.com/2015/08/27/business/gap-says-it-will-phase-out-on-call-scheduling-of-employees.html?_r=0; National Partnership for Women and Families, "State and Local Action on Paid Sick Days" (Washington, DC, July 2015), http://www.nationalpartnership.org/research-library/campaigns/psd/state-and-local-action-paid-sick-days.pdf.

3 See Emily Peck, "Facebook Ups Pay, Benefits for Low-Wage Workers," *Huffington Post*, May 13, 2015, http://www.huffingtonpost.com/2015/05/13/facebook-contractor-benefits_n_7273594.html; Lydia DePillis, "Taking Aim at Tech Industry Inequality, Microsoft Extends Paid Leave to Thousands of Contractors," *Washington Post*, March 26, 2015, http://www.washingtonpost.com/blogs/wonkblog/wp/2015/03/26/taking-aim-at-tech-industry-inequality-microsoft-extends-paid-leave-to-thousands-of-contractors/; Valerie Jarrett, "Champions of Change: Advocating for Working Families," *The White House Blog*, April 17, 2015, http://www.whitehouse.gov/blog/2015/04/17/champions-change-advocating-working-families; Marlee Moseley, "Starting Now at Netflix: Unlimited Maternity and Paternity Leave," *Netflix US & Canada Blog*, http://blog.netflix.com/2015/08/starting-now-at-netflix-unlimited.html.

ACKNOWLEDGMENTS

I started this book in Cambridge, England, where I spent many weekends walking along the river Cam to Grantchester, the same path that John Maynard Keynes and his Bloomsbury friends walked years ago. I had the privilege of being a fellow at the Institute for Public Policy Research, and that time—and the many wonderful friends and colleagues there—were a daily inspiration as I conceived of this project. I telecommuted to my job in Washington, DC, and conducted all meetings—including interviewing job candidates—via video from my tiny office. That's how I hired Alexandra Mitukiewicz, better known in our office as Olenka. Every step of the way throughout this project, Olenka provided extraordinary research assistance. She's now a doctoral student in Harvard's sociology program, and I look forward to seeing how she will shape the field in the years to come. I am also very lucky that Matt Markezich and Erica Handloff stepped in to help with the final stages of the book.

Over the years, I've benefited from working alongside a community of advocates and organizers who know how to get things done. I am often humbled by the very real progress they make happen. There are far too many to name, but I want to give a special thank-you to Vicki Shabo (who also provided helpful comments on the manuscript), Judy Lichtmann, Ellen Bravo, Wendy Chun Hoon, Netsy Firestone, Jodie Levin-Epstein, Katie Corrigan, Holly Fechner, Carol Joyner, and all the members of the Work Family Strategy Council and the Caring across Generations campaign for inspired advocacy on behalf of working people around the country. I also want to thank Congresswoman Rosa DeLauro, for the (excellent) lunches that helped shaped my thinking.

When I began this project, I wanted to write something for non-economists. My friend and colleague Judith Warner helped me think through how to do this. I am grateful for her time and patience as she read (and reread) early drafts. I am also deeply grateful for the time and thoughtful comments from John Schmitt (who encouraged me to write this book and was my editor on a piece for *Dissent* magazine, where I first laid out the nascent idea), Elisabeth Jacobs, Sarah Jane Glynn, Nan Gibson, Virginia Rutter, Stephanie Coontz, Bridget Ansel, Robert Lynch, and Patrick Watson. Ian Malcolm and Christine Thorsteinsson at Harvard University Press have been wonderful to work with, and I have been very lucky to have their help with this project.

John and Sarah Jane not only read early drafts but also provided data analysis, as did Kavya Vagul, Philip Cohen, Susan Lambert, and Peter Fugiel. This was vital help, and I thank them for their analysis. Maryam Adamu and Katie Hamm kindly provided quick help on federal government expenditure data. I want to especially thank Ed Paisley, who provided valuable edits and feedback on drafts, and Dave Evans, who designed every figure in the book with creativity and lucidity. And, of course, I want to give a very big thank-you to my all-star group of fact-checkers: Jane Farrell, Julia Berley, Olga Baranoff, and Oya Aktas. Any and all errors are, of course, mine alone.

I've had the pleasure of working with many coauthors and colleagues over the years as I developed the ideas in this book. Many of the ideas that led to this book were hashed out in debates with my wonderful coauthors over the past decade, including Randy Albelda, Eileen Appelbaum, Michael Ettlinger, Ann O'Leary, and Joan Williams. My thinking has been deeply influenced by my time at the Center for American Progress and collaborations with Maria Shriver and her team, especially Laura Nichols, Karen Skelton, and Olivia Morgan. I also want to thank the center's fearless leaders past and present—John Podesta, Sarah Rosen Wartell, Winnie Stachelberg, and Neera Tanden.

I've also been lucky to have the support and friendship of a dedicated group who have funded many aspects of the research that led to this book. Helen Neuborne and Anna Wadia at the Ford Foundation, Lisa Guide at Rockefeller Family Fund, Janet Nitolli at the Rockefeller Foundation, and Michael Laracy at the Annie E. Casey

Foundation have helped me—and the community of those of us working on these issues—to frame the problem and find solutions.

I am honored to work each day with the most amazing team at the Washington Center for Equitable Growth. I am grateful to Herb Sandler, Susan Sandler, and Steve Daetz for making Equitable Growth possible. Thank you also to Nick Bunker, Korin Davis, Jessica Fulton, Casey Shoeneberger, Marshall Steinbaum, and Ben Zipperer.

This book wouldn't have seen the light of day were it not for a conversation just over a year ago. I was stuck and couldn't see how to craft the narrative. I was about to give up. Eisa Davis and her mother, Fania, provided the insights that put me on the right path; it was a fun—and fruitful—weekend.

I'm not sure why the custom is to put loved ones at the end of the thank-you list. Probably because if we didn't we'd spend our entire word count thanking them for putting up with us as we wrote. I've quoted many friends and family members—most important, my mom, dad, sister, and grandmother—and I thank each one of them for sharing their stories with me. I also want to thank my Uncle Matt, who showed me the power of mountaintop metaphors.

The biggest thank-you goes to Todd, the love of my life, who helped me hone the ideas, gave invaluable (and often funny) feedback on the manuscript, and put up with me as I spent far too many precious weekends writing.

INDEX